Action Research in Organisations

D0222900

The current orthodoxy is that 'knowledge' is the most important resource for organisational success. How then can managers develop an appropriate knowledge base to enable their organisation to grow? One possible answer is action research.

Action research is undertaken by people who are trying to understand their practice in order to improve the quality of their work with others. It is used widely to promote personal and professional awareness and development within organisational contexts. There are as yet very few texts which show how the development of personal practice can lead to management learning for organisational improvement, or which emphasise the reflective nature of improving professionalism. *Action Research in Organisations* fills the gap, and provides a seminal text which reconceptualises the knowledge base of management and organisation research. Aimed at practising managers and those studying for higher degrees, the key features of the text include:

* how managers can generate their own transformative theories of practice for sustainable organisational development
* how the principles and practices of action research may be integrated within organisational contexts
* how real people are able to claim that they have improved their workplace situations by presenting validated research-based evidence to show how they developed their own practice through action research

Jean McNiff is an independent researcher and consultant, working in international contexts. She writes extensively in the areas of professional education through action research. Her previous publications include *Action Research: Principles and Practice* (1992), and *You and Your Action Research Project* (1996, written with Pam Lomax and Jack Whitehead), both published by Routledge. She can be reached at her homepage at http://www.jeanmcniff.com.

Jack Whitehead is a lecturer in education at the University of Bath. He is a former President of the British Educational Research Association, a Distinguished Scholar in Residence at Westminster College, Utah, and Visiting Professor at Brock University, Ontario. He can be reached at http://www.actionresearch.net, which in 2000 was a Links2Go Award Winner and is now acknowledged as one of the most influential sites for worldwide developments in action research.

Routledge Studies in Human Resource Development

Edited by Monica Lee
Lancaster University, UK

This series presents a range of books which explore and debate the changing face of human resource development, offering discussion and delineation of HRD theory and, thus, the development of practice.

This series is aimed at human resource and organisation theoreticians, and is also of direct relevance to sociologists, psychologists and philosophers, as well as those working in the areas of culture and globalisation. HR practitioners and those interested in the practical aspects of HR theory will also find this series to be an important catalyst in understanding and enhancing their practice.

Action Research in Organisations

Jean McNiff, accompanied by Jack Whitehead

Action Research in Organisations

Jean McNiff
accompanied by Jack Whitehead

London and New York

First published 2000
by Routledge
11 New Fetter Lane, London EC4P 4EE

Simultaneously published in the USA and Canada
by Routledge
29 West 35th Street, New York, NY 10001

Routledge is an imprint of the Taylor & Francis Group

Typeset in Baskerville by Taylor & Francis Books Ltd
Printed and bound in Great Britain by Clays Ltd, St Ives plc

British Library Cataloguing in Publication Data
A catalogue record for this book is available from the British Library

Library of Congress Cataloging in Publication Data
McNiff, Jean.
    Action research in organisations / Jean McNiff accompanied by
    Jack Whitehead.
    (Routledge studies in human resource development)
    Includes bibliographical references and index.
    1. Organizational learning. 2. Action research. I. Whitehead, Jack. II.
    Title. III. Series.
    HD58.82 .M39 2001
    302.3'5–dc21   00-059197

ISBN 0–415–22012–2 (hbk)
ISBN 0–415–22013–0 (pbk)

Where wast thou when I laid the foundations of the earth? declare, if thou hast understanding.

Job 38.4

Contents

The contributors

Ashley Balbirnie is Managing Director of *Ireland on Sunday* Ltd. He worked with the Smurfit Group for sixteen years in a variety of roles. He was part of the team that founded *The Title*, Ireland's first sports paper, and which later evolved as *Ireland on Sunday*.

Jean Clandinin is a former classroom teacher and school counsellor. She is currently Professor and Director of the Centre for Research for Teacher Education and Development, University of Alberta. She writes extensively in the fields of narrative enquiry and teacher professional education. Her most recent book (co-authored with Michael Connelly) is *Narrative Inquiry* (Jossey-Bass, 2000).

Úna Collins was responsible for piloting national programmes in pastoral care, action research and whole school planning in Ireland. She is currently a member of staff in the Education Department, National University of Ireland, Maynooth, coordinating the postgraduate programme in School Guidance Counselling.

Jacqueline Delong is a Superintendent of Schools in the Grand Erie District School Board, Brantford, Ontario, Canada, and is currently completing her PhD thesis with Jack Whitehead at the University of Bath, UK. From her experience as a professional educator for thirty years, she advocates for improved student learning through research-based professionalism.

John H. M. Ellis was formerly a strategic appraisal manager with an international resource company and continues to work with international companies on a consultancy basis. He is currently based at the Business School, Bournemouth University, UK.

Pip Bruce Ferguson trained as a primary school teacher and for the last fifteen years has been working as a staff developer at a New Zealand polytechnic. She enjoys teaching and learning with the wide variety of educators that the polytechnic employs, and helping them to develop research skills using an action research approach.

John Garrick is a senior researcher and policy analyst at the Research Centre for Vocational Education and Training at the University of Technology, Sydney, Australia. He is widely published in the areas of informal learning, research and knowledge construction, including the popular text *Informal Learning in the Workplace: Unmasking Human Resource Development* (Routledge, 1998).

Wayne Gorman served fourteen years in the Canadian Armed Forces in NATO and the UN, and sixteen years in private industry and government. He is currently studying for his PhD at the University of Alberta, Canada, where he also has a teaching assistantship and works part-time with 'Urban' Nations and Metis people developing skills to set up an Art and Crafts Co-operative. His research interest is attempting to understand institutionalised shaming.

Derek Hobbs is senior partner in an urban National Health Service general practice, UK.

Janice Huber is at the Centre for Research for Teacher Education and Development, University of Alberta, Edmonton, Canada. She is currently engaged in post-doctoral research attending to the diverse stories of children and families as they enter into school contexts.

Chris James is Professor of Educational Management and Head of the Human Resource Management and Development Division in the Business School, University of Glamorgan, UK. His research interests cover management and leadership in educational settings.

Sharon Jamieson is Adjunct Professor, Faculty of Education, and Director, Office of the President, University of Alberta, Canada. She has extensive knowledge and experience in post-secondary education and leadership, both within the University of Alberta as well as internationally. Her research and development work attends to inter-agency collaboration with a focus on elementary and middle school teacher training from a narrative perspective. Her work as an educator and administrator has focused on creative problem-solving for facilitating collaborative planning and implementation of joint initiatives.

Julia A. Kiely is Reader in Organisational Behaviour at the Business School, Bournemouth University, UK, and is programme leader of the Doctorate in Business Administration Programme.

Carmel Lillis is Principal of St Brigid's Primary School, Dublin. She is currently working for her PhD through her self-study of her own practice as an educational leader.

Séamus Lillis has worked in public service in the Republic of Ireland and in Northern Ireland as a teacher and advisor in horticulture and a specialist in rural development. He is currently a private consultant in community development. He is studying for his PhD through action research in University College, Dublin, in association with Michigan State University.

Breda Long is a career path advisor with her local Employment Service in Cork, Republic of Ireland. She supports long-term unemployed job seekers to access opportunities in training, education and work.

Christopher Mc Cormack is a retired teacher, living with his wife Una in Kells, Republic of Ireland. He is currently studying at University College, Dublin, for his Masters Degree in Education.

Paul Murphy, a Capuchin friar, is working in the Strategic Response Group office recently set up by the Conference of Religious of Ireland (CORI) to assist religious congregations in responding to sexual abuse issues.

Liam Nagle is Vice President of World Wide Operations, Enterprise Solutions, Nortel Networks.

Oonagh O'Brien is a theologian and educator. She is a member of the team of pastoral coordinators of parish renewal in the Archdiocese of Dublin, Republic of Ireland.

Stephen O'Connor is Supervisory Teacher in the Training Unit, City of Dublin Vocational Education Committee Educational Service to Prisons, Republic of Ireland.

Carl Rhodes has worked as a manager and consultant in the fields of human resource management, organisational development and change management. He is also an Associate of the Faculty of Education at the University of Technology, Sydney, Australia. His research focuses on employing narrative and literary theory to understanding organisations. His articles have appeared in numerous journals including *Organization* and *The Journal of Organizational Change Management*, and he has recently published, with John Garrick, *Research and Knowledge at Work* (London: Routledge, 2000).

Eileen Ross has worked extensively in the United States in the fields of pastoral care in schools, and counselling and training needs in adult education contexts. She currently works as a primary school teacher in the Republic of Ireland, and also facilitates courses for personal development for adults, especially for women's groups.

Jimmy Ryan, working in the midlands of the Republic of Ireland, concentrates on general business consultancy, supporting particularly inward investment companies setting up in Ireland, the development needs of small and medium type enterprise, and team and organisation development in many sectors, including the community and voluntary sectors.

David Steeves is the Deputy Clerk of Executive Council for the Alberta Provincial Government, Canada. In 1998 he was seconded by Executive Council to the Ministry of Family and Social Services to assist with a new initiative of providing for the delivery of Children's Services in an integrated way through a regional guidance structure. In 1999 he was seconded to the

Health and Wellness Ministry to assist with a review of the delivery programmes for Persons with Developmental Disabilities.

Acknowledgements

I wish to thank the following people for studying for their Masters and Doctorate Degrees with me. Thank you for your commitment, enthusiasm and tenacity in contributing to learning and education. This book is a celebration of your good practice, as it holds promise for the future of education.

Mary Black
Catherine Buckley
Mary Buckley
Kevin Byrne
Margaret Cahill
Caroline Clarke
Moira Cluskey
Dan Condren
Suzanne Cormier Fewer
Kevin Corrigan
Denis Dodd
Mary Doherty Lally
Eamonn Dunne
Pat Fay
Martin Fitzgerald
Rita Fitzgerald
Maria FitzGibbon
Sean Fitzmaurice
Barbara Forde
Kate Gallagher
Linda Gaughran
Mary Geoghegan
Tom Gilroy
Chris Glavey
Tim Glavin
Gerry Gordon
Neil Hallinan

Margaret Healy
Clare Henderson
Deasún Hennessy
Philomena Keane
David Kearney
Anne Kenny
Teresa Leahy
Lórcan Leavy
Carmel Lillis
Séamus Lillis
Breda Long
Alec Mac Alister
Kevin McDermott
Pauline McDermott
Caitríona Mc Donagh
Fiona McDonnell
Noeleen McElroy
Sally McGinley
Miriam McGuire Shelley
Mary McTiernan
Peter Moore
Phil Moore MacMahon
Philip Mudge
Dolores Mullins
Anna Murphy
Paul Murphy
Anne Murray Donnelly

Siobhán Ní Murchú

Marian Nugent

Éamon Ó Briain

Oonagh O'Brien

Ivan O'Callaghan

Cecilia O'Flaherty

Norberta O'Gorman

Conchúr Ó Muimhneacháin

Ray O'Neill

Tony O'Neill

Thérèse O'Reardon Burke

Karen O'Shea

Órfhlaith Quigney

James Reynolds

Mary Roche

Maureen Rohan

Eileen Ross

Jimmy Ryan

Mary Slattery

Caroline Stone

Bernie Sullivan

Joe Twomey

Máire Áine Uí Aodha

Ann Whelan

Elizabeth Whoriskey

I wish to thank the following people for reading drafts of the book in part or whole, and for their helpful responses.

Noam Chomsky

Caroline Clarke

Anne Fleischmann

Lynn Raphael Reed

Eileen Ross

Jack Whitehead

Thank you also to Michelle Gallagher and Fintan Power, editors with Routledge, for their constant encouragement and faith in the project; and to David Sanders, for his painstaking work and encouragement in the copy editing stages.

Introduction

This book presents a theory of organisation as constituted by people and their relationships in organisational contexts. It is drawn from my own self-study and experience as a manager. It is written mainly for two audiences: (1) people studying on formal higher education courses, and also informal workplace-based courses, in management and organisation studies; (2) people positioned as teachers on those courses. Some will, I hope, relate to my story of how I have come to reconceptualise organisation study in terms of my own experience as I addressed the question, 'How do I improve my work?' (Whitehead, 1989). This theory is presented not as a finished product, nor in a coercive fashion. It is presented as current learning, a working theory in progress, likely to develop, a temporary best place. I hope that you as reader will take from my story whatever is appropriate to you, possibly to encourage you to theorise your own organisational experience in terms of how you give meaning to your work. Trying to understand our work is a first step to improving it.

I hope you will also share my enthusiasm for the new form of scholarship that Boyer (1990) and Schön (1995) say will enable us to rethink theory as a practical discipline oriented towards social renewal, rather than regard it as a static conceptual 'thing'. Organisation study, I believe, should provide a body of knowledge to help people deal with the living reality of their work, particularly as it refers to struggles to negotiate their identities and relationships with one another in organisational contexts. It should not stay at the level only of describing organisation structures and their possible configurations, or describing management as a set of techniques, as is the case in traditional forms. To make the change, however, requires some new thinking.

The new scholarship

Schön (1995) says that it is time to develop a new scholarship which demonstrates a new epistemology, a new way of knowing, that meets the everyday needs of people working in real-life situations.

Traditional forms of scholarship, the ones we normally live with in our institutional contexts, place a heavy emphasis on technical rationality, a form of knowledge which values facts and information, and which is generated by conventional kinds of research. This research tests knowledge against the stan-dardised criteria of hard scientific analysis and technique – 'rigorously controlled experimentation, statistical analysis of observed correlation of variables, or disin-terested speculation' (Schön, 1995: 29). The emphasis is easily recognised in traditional organisation studies and practices. It is, however, far removed from the worlds of real-life practice which are, to use Schön's language, messy, uncon-trolled and unpredictable, and which are seriously separated from the sanitised world of abstract theorising. The situation becomes one which not only poten-tially distorts the idea of knowledge, presenting it as a body of facts rather than a form of lived experience, but also potentially distorts lives as people try to live up to the standardised theory.

I visited my doctor recently with a frozen thumb. As he moved the thumb around, he paused every so often and observed how his own thumb moved. He talked through what he was doing, probably to help me understand how my own thumb works. This led to clear learning on my part; possibly also on his about teaching people how to take care of their bodies. It was a practical form of theo-rising which led us both, in this instance, to a theory of thumbs, but which has wider implications for generating theories of learning processes and the social practices in which they are embedded.

This, I think, is what Schön is referring to when he talks about the need for new theories of knowledge which are rooted in reflection-in-action, and reflection on that reflection-in-action. Like my doctor, I reflect, I watch myself as I act – is this working? is it not? – and I act in new ways as my reflection suggests. At later times, sometimes in discussion with others, sometimes as I drive home, I reflect on my reflection-in-action: could I have done things differently? How? What might have been the outcomes? This process is probably so familiar to our everyday experience that we take it for granted; yet it is possibly our most powerful way of knowing and enables us to make sense of our moment-to-moment lives.

Such practical theorising, however, is not yet highly valued by the academy. The theory–practice gap continues. Abstract theory, existing in the imagination of some people, does not fit with the real-world practical theory of others. What is needed, says Schön, is a new way of theorising which integrates theory and practice, a form of theory which is embodied in real lives and shows the process of reflecting on reflection-in-action, and which may be shared with others who are also studying their own practice.

These theories are rooted in the unarticulated tacit knowing of practitioners as they try to make sense of their lives. Much of what we do and why we do it is unknown to us. Why do I lean in the direction that my bike is going? Why do I respond to a colleague in a particular way? Our sense of what is the right thing to do is generated through a lifetime of learning from experience. Learning from experience can be reinforced through intellectual study; but the cognitive knowing is barren when separated from the life in which it is embedded. Embodied forms of knowing are rich embodied epistemologies. People come to know by trusting their deep tacit knowledge, and learning how to transform it into real experience which has use value in personal-social lives.

Action research

The new scholarship, says Schön, implies action research, a form of practical theorising in action which is appropriate to all professional contexts. 'If teaching is to be seen as a form of scholarship, then the practice must be seen as giving rise to new forms of knowledge. If community outreach is to be seen as a form of scholarship, then it is the practice of reaching out and providing service to a community that must be seen as raising important issues whose investigation may lead to generalisations of prospective relevance and actionability' (p. 31). If management is to be seen as a form of scholarship, then the practice of managing must be seen as enabling others to understand their relationships and practices as contexts of professional learning where identities may be created through discourses in which freedom of mind is valued and people are regarded as on equal footing. If organisational study is to be seen as a form of scholarship, then it is the practice of raising questions about human purpose and the development of sustainable social orders through personal and collective enquiry.

Introducing and developing these views in many organisational contexts means becoming involved in battles for ideas, which can extend not only to battles for job security and professional recognition, but, as Said says (1991), can mean life or death for some. Schön says that in many institutional contexts, this is 'a battle of snails, proceeding so slowly that you have to look very carefully in order to see it going on' (1995: 32). This may be so, but it has not been my experience over the last nine years. During these years I have been involved in quite explosive battles, sometimes conducted with restraint and professional decorum, and sometimes not; and I have learnt how to conduct myself in these battles, why I am fighting and for what purpose, and the importance of never, I hope, abdicating my own values of justice, truth and professional integrity. This book tells the stories of those battles for ideas and identity: how I have tried to realise my educational values in the face of sometimes quite stubborn and entrenched attitudes, and encouraged others to do the same; and my own stubborn resistance to forms of practice that aimed to dominate me and others as we tried to create our identities as free-minded people working together for educational goals in organisational contexts. The battles continue, and, I am coming to realise, are perhaps inevitable, for struggles are part of our daily lives, whether they are expressed in the more gentle metaphors of persuasion, or in the extreme metaphors of bloodshed. Identities are not given (though a sense of self may be developed); no one exists in a pre-political form (though I believe we exist as unique individuals whose worth is in the fact that we are human). We are all part of social contexts, which are politically constructed as people try to become the persons they wish to be, and also try to persuade others to become particular kinds of persons. The struggle is a site for the creation of identities. We come to understand who we are in relation with others through the struggle. Conflict is not the opposite of peace; it is a site for transformative struggles for peace. More of this later.

Action research generates practical theory. It is undertaken by people who want to improve their understanding of their practice in order to improve their dealings with others in social situations. Action enquiries begin by asking questions of the kind, 'How do I improve my work?' (Whitehead, 1989), with the intention first of understanding the work more thoroughly by studying it and raising awareness, and then by imagining ways in which it can be improved. The research process involves gathering data which generate evidence to show that claims to improved practice are genuine, and subjecting the evidence to the critical scrutiny of others for their validation that the practice has improved. Personal action research which asks, 'How do I improve my work?' is inevitably participative, as one researcher looks to another for validation of claims that the work has improved. It can also become collective, as people form communities of reflective practitioners, each investigating their work, and recognising that their work means work with one another. Work in organisational contexts never exists as something separate from a practitioner. It is always in relation. Relationship *is* the work. When a person investigates their work, it means that they are investigating how they are with others. When several people do this, they can collectively share their power for organisational change and social renewal.

A theory of organisation as constituted by people means that organisations are not seen as abstract entities, but as contexts in which people, whose values include independence and freedom of mind and action, come together in free association and on an equal footing with the intention of achieving common goals (Chomsky, 1996: 77). These are living processes; theories which describe and explain such processes are living theories (Whitehead, 1989). Being a person in purposeful relation with others offers a variety of experiences, some good, some not. Dewey (1916) says that examining experience is the gateway to learning; and on this view, the experience of being a person in an organisation presents powerful opportunities for learning. Indeed, the 'learning organisation' (Senge, 1990) is a place in which people can learn from their experience of being with others by reflecting on it and taking action to improve it where necessary.

The new scholarship as social renewal

I believe that Schön's commitment to developing a new scholarship is part of wider cultural and political commitments to developing ways of living in an increasingly unknowable and uncontrollable world. Significant bodies of literature covering a variety of disciplines show, for example, the need for increased awareness of our planet's fragility (Lovelock, 1991); for new forms of economy to avoid the worst excesses of globalisation and free markets (Gray, 1995); for communitarian practices that will restore social cohesion (Ornstein and Ehrlich, 1989); for the amelioration of the excesses of fundamentalist ideologies (Robertson, 1992). All emphasise how our commitment to traditional technical rational forms is getting us deeper into trouble; our technologies have already begun to technologise us. All emphasise the need, however it is expressed, to recognise and value the spiritual dimension of human living, the need for connectedness and belonging, for love and peace.

Almost a century ago John Dewey (1916) was saying similar things (as did many great educators before him). He said that social renewal lay in education. For Dewey, living and learning are intimately related: to live (pathology aside) is to learn. Organisations are contexts in which people share part of their lives together, and are rich fields for learning. They are also rich fields for education, for education is the relational process between people which fosters particular forms of learning. These ideas are explored more fully in Chapter 1.

The connections I think are clear. In social contexts, education, experience, living and learning are intertwined. Organisations – organised social contexts – are contexts with rich promise for social renewal. Realising the promise however requires a new kind of scholarship and a new kind of organisation theory that moves from a view of organisations as monolithic blocks, whose purpose is accumulation of resources by domination, to a view of organisations as sites of learning in which the quality of relationships fosters independence of mind and action. This theory sees organisations not only as learning organisations, but also as *educative* organisations. It also sees managers as educators, in the sense that they are well placed to create and nurture the conditions for learning. On this view, organisation and management theory are also educational theories.

A book of evolutions

One of the reasons I have written this book is to share ideas about forms of enquiry. I work with British and Irish universities, and teach and manage professional development programmes for educators and managers leading to higher degrees. One of the courses is research methods; research methods underpin other areas of human enquiry.

Many textbooks present information about research methods as an established fact. Research paradigms are often described as self-contained, each having a specific purpose, like tools in a toolbox. Textbooks often speak of research methods as 'tools'. While this may be so in a limited sense, it distorts the wider picture of the purpose and nature of research. Research is a social activity which serves particular human interests. It is not abstracted from, but deeply embedded in other aspects of human living. The evolutionary nature of life manifests as vast panoramas of developing historical, intellectual and cultural traditions; research is part of it all.

Among other things, I am interested in the history and philosophy of science. I am interested in how perceptions of the nature and purposes of scientific research have evolved over time, and continue to evolve (see Part II). I share these interests with participants on my courses, and they have encouraged me to write about them. In setting them out here, I am fulfilling one aim of writing a course book on research methods which, I hope, will contribute to a more holistic perception of scientific enquiry, a perception that is part of the rising participative culture (Capra, 1983; Skolimowski, 1994) and which has a long pedigree (see for example, Medawar, 1996; Midgley, 1989). Part II of the book follows through on this.

I have other aims. How we think about what we do (our mental models) influences what we do (our practices). How we think about research influences the way we do research and for what purpose. Research is usually theorised in western intellectual traditions as a free-standing abstract discipline, and this leads to a view of research practice as a set of techniques, a quite mistaken view in my opinion.

Dominant western intellectual traditions love fragmentation. Fragmentation permeates traditional organisation theory: organisations are not alive; they have no history or future. Instead, organisations are perceived as abstract entities that work in terms of discrete operations. Organisations are peopled (when they are peopled at all) by managers and others, usually designated 'workers' or, in more genteel Newspeak, 'our people', all of whom occupy separate lifeworlds.

Dominant western intellectual traditions also love binary oppositions – 'either–or', seldom 'both–and'. In popular thinking, for example, feminisms exist in opposition to masculinities – women are caring and intuitive, men are logical and good at fixing cars. Many people accept these mythologies without questioning how they came into existence or why they are perpetuated. In such intellectual traditions people are assigned to absolutist categories: black or white, insiders or outsiders, intellectual or practical. This love of absolutes emphasises confrontation, establishing zero-sum categories as facts, so that one person's well-being can be assured only at the expense of another's. I find this deeply troubling. It is also contradictory to my and others' experience of organisations as people working purposefully and harmoniously together to achieve common goals.

A possible reason for this love of fragmentation and binary oppositions is that intellectual traditions tend not to recognise the metaphorical basis of scientific enquiry and social practices, or the kinds of metaphors we use (Morgan, 1997a). I spoke above about battles and bloodshed; this reinforces an image of organisational practice as conflictual. I speak now about the oppositional basis of binary divides; this reinforces that men and women and other socially constructed categories are on opposite sides. If the metaphor of a binary divide were to disappear, however, perhaps also then its realisation would begin to disappear; if the metaphor of category were replaced with another metaphor, perhaps the reality it describes would also begin to change. Our language informs and creates our realities. Change the language and you may change the reality.

The metaphors of fragmentation and division underpin traditional forms of scholarship: analysis, correlation, contrast and comparison, variables, generalisation … They reinforce divides. Perhaps, if we embrace the new scholarship and its embodied epistemologies, new kinds of metaphors will emerge, those of integration, reconciliation and hope for harmony. Perhaps, if we commit ourselves to generating new living theories of practice we will find metaphors that more adequately represent the transformative nature of living. Living, and the metaphors we use to describe it, are evolutionary processes. Perhaps we could even move beyond metaphor, and generate theories and new forms of representation which show life as it is lived.

I am not saying that we should forget traditional analytical epistemologies. Understanding is generated within and through struggles; synthesis can be generated within and through analysis. These are not separate conditions; they are one and the same, but at lesser and more developed levels of transformation. It is a question of getting the right balance, and also of seeing phenomena as dynamic processes rather than static objects.

This could be so for all areas of experience. For example, a life can be regarded as an art form in which aesthetic values emerge as living in balance with others and the environment. McAllister (1996), in *Beauty and Revolution in Science*, for example, explains how theories which are aesthetically pleasing can generate new socially oriented forms of theory. Art forms embody, as W. B. Yeats explains through his poetry, vision and practice, both necessary and complementary. The trick is to synthesise them, to bring together, as Yeats does, the artist and the planner, and let them speak with a single voice. If our work is our art and our lives an art form, and if art is a full realisation of human potentialities, we need to develop theories which embody the theory and practice as a realisation of human potentials, to show what we might do, and how we are doing it. We also need to remember that, as houses involve planning, building and people to live in them, so the process of living involves the artist, the planner and the audience. To reach a commonwealth of understanding we need to explain our art, and give an account of our lives as we live them.[1] (See also Seamus Heaney's 'Introduction' to *Beowulf* (1999) where he speaks about creative intuition and conscious structuring.)

What, then, if we were to engage with the idea of a creative evolving scholarship which incorporates traditional 'old' scholarship within its history, that will allow the new scholarship itself one day to dissolve as an old scholarship? What if we were to regard scholarship as maintaining older traditions such as categories of analysis and definitions, as contributing towards an emergent, more refined form?

Not all western intellectual traditions follow the dominant model. Other influential texts present alternative perspectives. Popper (1962), for example, wished to show how an open society was characterised by openness to new ideas (it is questionable however whether he lived these ideas in his writing, in his attempt to eliminate contradiction from thinking). Debates on the significance of Kuhn's ideas about scientific revolutions (for example, Lakatos and Musgrave, 1970) show a deep commitment to evolutionary forms. Such texts provide ideas which others then develop. We learn from one another, and like to think that others will learn from us. Learning is an evolutionary process, as I now explain.

1   I am grateful to Christopher McCormack for bringing the points about Yeats to my attention.

Learning as an evolutionary process

Research is learning in order to gather information and to create and test new theories. Different research methods offer different ways of learning. Learning is not a static concept. It is an evolutionary process. Learning involves creating new ideas out of old ones. It does not mean entirely rejecting what went before, but making new connections and reconfiguring the networks, so that previous knowledge transforms into new knowledge that serves human purposes more adequately than older forms.

Evolutionary processes are seldom marked by sharp transitions, but involve slow, often imperceptible movement in which phenomena change into more mature versions of themselves. While it may be the case that manifestations of evolutionary processes are often quite dramatically different, as, for example, when the caterpillar metamorphoses into a butterfly, these are not sudden changes, but long, careful processes of constant transformation. Learning often has the same character. New insights which manifest as 'Aha!' experiences are often actually insights that we gradually become aware of and then wonder why it took so long to see the obvious.

The dominant western intellectual tradition is characterised by a linear order which aims for closure. This tradition is being overtaken and subsumed within a wide range of movements that emphasise the interconnectedness of mind and body (for example, Polkinghorne, 1988), and the transformative nature of reality. A lively and growing body of literature exists, some of which is informal and to be found on the 'New Age' shelves, and also much of which draws on serious scholarship to show increasing awareness of the creative and open-ended nature of human enquiry. The new scholarship requires us to revisit dominant typologies, such as those of Piaget, Maslow, Kohlberg and Habermas, which regard human processes as free-standing stages in a linear developmental process, and regard stages rather as embedded within wider transformative frameworks; and consider that perhaps stages are not stages at all but unboundaried emergent processes. It is also time to move beyond the established social scientific categories of practical, interpretive and emancipatory interests (Habermas, 1972), and regard these as elements of a transformative process whose methodology and purpose is reconciliation among humans in relation with their environment. It is time to move beyond a vision of linear progress which goes from this to this to this (see Figure 0.1), and is rooted in an ontology of being (page 42), and move towards a view of generative transformational process (Figure 0.2), which develops in an iterative way and engages with an ontology of becoming (page 43). A generative transformative order incorporates a linear order, and holds emergence within itself as an inherent feature of its form.

Figure 0.1

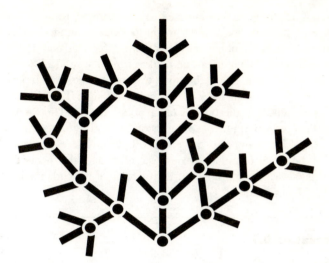

Figure 0.2

New theories of discourse

The positive nature of struggle

The practices of the old order tend to be conflictual – either–or, zero-sum. In Chapter 2 I explain that new theories of discourse (Torfing, 1999) show how human interaction is always potentially conflictual (agonistic) and politically constructed as people struggle to work out who they are in relation with one another. The emergent order, however, what Capra (1983) calls 'the rising culture', emphasises reconciliation and renewal, a toleration of conflicting views as characteristic of developing social orders. Conflict is an emergent feature of a holistic system, existing as a necessary tension for creativity. Conflict is not destabilising to the whole system so much as an opportunity which encourages the emergence of potential new forms. New theories of discourse propose that people need to find ways to co-exist peacefully while accepting the tension of recognising the legitimacy and creative potential of one another's different ideas and ways of living.

We need to find new metaphors for good social orders in which diverse forms of life can co-exist peacefully and learn from one another; and even try to go beyond metaphor. We need to turn potentialities into realities. If, at a metaphorical level, conflict represents potential tension for creative renewal, how does the transformation happen in real human situations? New methodologies, including action research, recognise how vulnerable we are and how unstable and volatile our social circumstances. People are fallible, usually at odds with one another, and frequently aiming for dominance in a variety of ways. Dominant forms of theory are not helpful here. Literature exists (for example, Rawls, 1972) to show what a perfect 'end state' social order might look like in an idealised sense, with the implication that we should all try to get there. A 'perfect' end state is however impossible to achieve. While it can be held as a regulative ideal, we need to be assured that we are not failing because we are not perfect. It is important however to try; *for it is in the trying that we create good orders*. The vision of a place called Utopia is an ideal; the process of creating our own Utopias is real. Nor should we allow our commitment to the vision to blind us to other opportunities along the way. The theory and the practice both are necessary; the theory is embodied in the practice, and an account is rendered for the theory through the practice, while always recognising that there are other new potentialities waiting to emerge (see Conversation 0.1).

Conversation 0.1

David Steeves

Back fifteen or twenty years ago when we didn't have this business orienta-tion towards the way we deal with human issues in government, there was a lot of cooperation between agencies. If the education system needed to have health-related services provided in order to get a better learning envi-ronment for children, the education system went out and acquired those resources. If the health system needed to have education resources avail-able for children who were spending an inordinate amount of time within the health environment, the health system went out and acquired the resources. You literally had schools who were operating nursing stations, and long-term rehabilitative hospitals who were operating schools, and it was all working. Then we went through the process of mandated restric-tion, so the educators were to educate, and the health people were to deliver health services. We went from these overlapping areas between the mandates to narrow mandates with service gaps between many of them. And it's the very narrow mandates with gaps between them all that really forces the area of collaborative enquiry, because you cannot allow those gaps in service delivery to exist, because people who really need those services fall through the gaps. So if you're not going back to expecting everyone to expand their mandates, then we must work in collaborative ways. Collaboration can be difficult; it's a struggle. But there is no place in the world where there isn't a struggle. If there has got to be a struggle, we have to look for the things to fight for.

Values and visions in transformation

Action research is a value-laden practice. It involves reflecting on our values, and asking ourselves whether we are living them in practice, and if not, why not.

The work of Thomas Sowell (1987) is helpful here. He links values with visions. Visions, he says, exist at a deep level of human imagining, and work as the ideals which we aim to transform into lived practice. Everything we do, says Sowell, every act of theorising, every social practice, is informed by a vision of the world and our place in it. Visions are more than dreams; they are forces which drive our lives.

Sowell says that there are, broadly speaking, two kinds of vision. He calls these constrained and unconstrained. Others with similar views have called them differently – open and closed, traditional and transformational, bounded and unbounded (for example, Mitroff and Linstone, 1993).

The two kinds of vision might appear to be diametrically opposed. A constrained vision suggests that a situation or a system is as it is, and no attempt should be made to change it into something else. Adam Smith, for example, in his *Theory of Moral Sentiments* (1976), suggested that the social challenge was to make the best use of the potentialities within the constraints of a situation. It was not, however, Smith's intention to imagine how, or even that, the system might need changing.

An unconstrained vision, on the other hand, sees beyond the stable (but possibly unsatisfactory) state and imagines ways in which it might be improved. Instead of the trade-offs of the constrained vision, the unconstrained vision sees solutions and possibilities; new ways of thinking which question established assumptions, and which go beyond descriptions of social processes to explanations for those processes in terms of their goals and intentions. Unconstrained visions see social realities as constructed by people and therefore open to deconstruction and development.

These are attractive ideas, and demonstrate the idea of how conceptual theories can transform into action theories; but to communicate the idea of the transformational nature of theory, the language needs to move beyond 'either–or'. To develop new metaphors and new forms of community living we need to start thinking 'both–and', and develop visions of how everything is part of a transformative order of emergence, including visions and values themselves. An evolutionary order contains the potential for constrained visions to transform into unconstrained visions, and in turn to transform constrained practices into unconstrained practices; for narrow human interests of accumulation and dominance to transform into more inclusive human interests of sharing and parity of esteem; for technical research methodologies to transform into narratives of reflection on experience; for old traditions of scholarship to transform into new ones; for conceptual theories to transform into action theories. Everything has the potential to be developmental and transformative, moving from closed to open forms, in the direction of expanding diversity and increasing life-enhancing degrees of tolerance – provided that human agency does not disrupt or distort the developmental order (see Chapters 2 and 3).

New theories of discourse show respect for multiple forms. They accept the conflictual nature of human living, and emphasise the need for tolerance and mutual understanding. Above all, they show that understanding is not a 'thing' that we aim for at a place removed from struggle, but a process that emerges within and through the struggle. Gray says this well: 'we will find that it is by tolerating our differences that we come to discover how much we have in common' (1995: 30); and Mary Midgley (1981: 75) also, when she notes that we have only the one planet and we all have to live on it. To do that successfully, and ensure that the planet continues to exist, we urgently need to find new ways of living peaceably with our differences of opinion. This means developing everyday attitudes of tolerance and compassion. Perhaps, when Jesus said, 'Love one another', he simply meant, 'Just try and get along together.'

The second cognitive revolution

Quite early in the twentieth century, and then increasingly in the 1950s, a new perspective emerged in the human sciences, particularly in psychology and its associated disciplines, which later came to be known as the second cognitive revolution. The main feature of this revolution was that the focus of scientific enquiry shifted from the study of people's behaviour by external observers to the study by people themselves of the reasons and purposes that inform their behaviour. Part of this revolution was the emergence of new-paradigm research, a set of research traditions, informed by humanitarian and democratic ideologies, that rejected the fundamentalism and constrained vision of empiricism, and which aimed instead to understand social practices in terms of human potential in the development of sustainable social orders. In old-paradigm (positivist) research, people are positioned as objects of study; in new-paradigm research, they are positioned as active knowers who are responsible for coming to their own insights about the nature of their lives, and acting on that knowledge.

A dramatic shift of emphasis is currently taking place in organisation studies. Pre-1960s there was a heavy reliance on control and command models; and this has carried over into a variety of prescriptive organisational practices and theories in which people are seen as dependent variables that will be affected by the independent variables of management behaviour. The proper subject matter of organisation studies was held to be the nature and internal characteristics of the organisation; this perspective was animated by a view of workers in workplaces as commodities that could be manipulated to ensure greater productivity. The method of study was rooted in 'the' scientific method, a tradition whose methods aim to predict and control behaviour and outcomes (Chapter 5). Since then fierce paradigm wars have occurred to change the focus of organisation studies and reconceptualise its purpose (for example, Burrell and Morgan, 1979). Consequently the literature now adopts different standpoints, depending on the vision of researchers, and there is currently substantial paradigm proliferation (Burrell, 1999; Donmoyer, 1996; Lather, 2000).

New kinds of questions

How organisation study is conceptualised depends on what we believe constitutes the proper subject matter of organisation studies, how it is studied, and how the study might be used. Important new kinds of questions arise. The focus of enquiry is no longer knowledge *about* the issues, but knowledge *of* them, a shift from propositional forms of theory that deal with facts and information about organisations, to dialectical forms of theory that show how people themselves can offer explanations for what they do in terms of their own values and intentions. The idea of levels of adequacy is useful here: research can operate at the levels of observation, description and explanation (Chomsky, 1965). All levels are important. We can observe and describe what is happening in terms of activities, and we can also explain what is happening in terms of reasons and intentions. Explanatory adequacy is a relative newcomer, part of new paradigms. New kinds of questions emerge. Instead of only asking constrained, analytical questions about activities such as 'What is happening? How is it happening?' there is greater focus on unconstrained, value-laden questions of the form 'Why is this happening? Should we change it? Why? How can it be improved?' These are epistemic questions, to do with the knowledge base of organisation study, and ethico-political questions, to do with the values base of human interaction; and they move organisation study from study of human activity to an enquiry of human purpose.

In discussing this issue in relation to the changing focus of linguistic enquiry, Chomsky (1986: 3) suggested that questions regarding the nature and form of enquiry need to change. He formulated three new questions:

> What is the nature of knowledge of language?
> How is knowledge of language acquired?
> How is knowledge of language put to use?

I want to adapt these questions here, because I think questions of this kind can provide helpful organising principles in the generation of theory. In asking questions such as:

> What is the nature of x?
> How is x understood?
> How is x acquired?
> How is x put to use?

when x is the unit of enquiry, we are dealing with issues of ontology, epistemology, methodology and purpose. Further, because research is a socio-political practice, and used to inform other socio-political practices, we also need to ask other questions such as:

> What is the significance of x, in terms of its implications for human living?

A new unit of enquiry

What is studied in research is called the unit of enquiry (some people use a different form of words, but the principle stays the same). In traditional forms of scholarship, the unit of enquiry was an external object of study; therefore, in traditional organisation study the unit of enquiry was an entity called an organisation. Questions appropriate to this kind of organisation study took the form:

> What is the nature of an organisation?
> How is the organisation run?
> How is the organisation put to use?

Old paradigms do not ask questions about the significance of organisations for human living.

In the new scholarship the unit of enquiry becomes people's lives and practice. In new theories of organisation, the unit of enquiry becomes the individual practitioner. Questions take the form:

> What is the nature of my practice in organisational contexts?
> How do I develop that practice?
> How do I put that practice to use?

as well as the new question:

> What is the significance of my practice for human living?

This set of questions generates all kinds of new questions:

> Am I prepared to take action?
> How do I do this?
> What does it involve?

These questions can in turn generate new action enquiries.

Living educational theories

This idea has been developed by Jack Whitehead, working at the University of Bath.

When the unit of enquiry is the 'living I' (Whitehead, 1989), 'I' study my practice as 'I' try to understand and improve it. My research generates a theory of myself. When I study my work as a manager I am potentially generating my own theory of management. When I study how I work with others in organisational settings, I am potentially generating my own theory of organisation. If I share this theory with others, and they accept it and make it theirs, it becomes our theory and so publicly legitimated; it becomes a publicly acknowledged form of organisation theory. The theory exists in the people who create it; it is a theory people live by, a theory of their lives. It is represented in the stories they tell and the words they write. The theory is embodied in people and expressed in a variety of forms. People as they live integrate their theory and practice and give a public account of it; they are their own living theories. In accounting for their own educational process, they generate their living educational theories (Whitehead, 1993).

This is, I believe, a form of new scholarship. What has until recently been seen as legitimate scholarship has been generated mainly by knowledge workers in higher education contexts. It has largely taken the form of propositional knowledge, that is, proposals about phenomena and experience. Propositional forms exclude people as knowers; knowledge is seen as an artefact, and knowledge production as the application of science. I believe we need to find newer forms of theory which may or may not incorporate propositional forms within themselves, and which are more appropriate for current needs (see Conversation 0.2). This is particularly so for how management learning is theorised and practised.

Conversation 0.2

Wayne Gorman

We are all people. We see ourselves as in the process of becoming a human being. If you look at a person who is becoming a human being, you allow for differences, you allow for changes. We are connected. Sometimes we forget that. Maybe when we are managers we forget that, because what drives a manager is the structures of an organisation, the structure of the place we manage. We are trained in specific ways, to view knowledge in particular ways, to verify it, validate it. This has to be an exact way. Knowledge on this view is hierarchical. In institutions we live in hierarchies.

I work with Native kids in setting up a co-op. We don't do anything in terms of hierarchy. We work in terms of a circle. That means I don't teach someone; I share information. They either accept it or they don't. They use it or they don't. That's OK. For us, it's more about being in relation than fitting into a hierarchy. Each person takes on a duty or a responsibility based on what they can do. But the authority rests with the group. Chiefs and leaders are western terms, imposed on other cultures. We don't work in hierarchies; we don't recognise status. There is no right or wrong. It is understood that where that person is at that time, that's their understanding. So although I am contracted to do this work, if they said they didn't need me any longer, if they feel they can walk by themselves, that's fine. I am not part of a structure. I share. They use it. That's the way it is.

Management learning

On propositional views, management appears as a unified practice which can be applied in a scientific way. This view is systematically critiqued for defining management in terms of its control functions, for confusing order with control, and for denying human agency as the creative spirit of organisations (see, for example, Wheatley, 1992: 22).

If quality of management is the key to successful organisations (Drucker, 1974) there is need for the development of a form of management theory in which managers take responsibility for their practice. The study of management practice would then ask questions of the form:

> What is the nature of my management practice?
> How do I learn it?
> How do I use my learning?
> What are the implications for me and others?

On this view, managers would regard themselves as researchers who are studying their practice in order to improve it. Because managers are situated in organisational settings as having responsibility towards others, they need to understand the nature of their responsibility. Is it their job to instruct others what to do and ensure that ensuing practices produce particular outcomes? Or is it to enable others to learn how to do things for themselves and take responsibility for the potential implications of their own practice? The first approach regards learning as a direct outcome of instruction, the input–output model that has dominated organisation theory for many years. The second approach regards learning as a creative process which is inspired and encouraged by another's interest, a model which sees organisational development as informed by the desire of all participants to equip themselves with the knowledge, skills and attitudes that will contribute towards individual and collective growth. Management is a relational process; managers need to find ways to ensure that the quality of their relationships with others will encourage individual and organisational growth, and sustain this process of organisational change through individuals' collective learning.

The responsibility of intellectuals in rethinking theory

Management learning does not happen in a vacuum. Fox (1997) describes its changing nature from management education to management learning, and identifies the locations of these different forms as the university and the workplace. Whatever the form might be, a course will probably be organised and delivered by someone with Higher Education status.

Universities are organisations. Like other organisations, they are not freestanding entities, but groups of people. To speak of university reform, therefore, is to speak of people reorganising the way they work together; and to speak of reconceptualising theory is to speak of people changing the way they think about theory.

Universities are still held as the highest legitimating bodies for what counts as valid knowledge. That means that people working at universities – intellectuals, or academics – are in the position of influencing systems of knowledge and how those systems impact on the development of a culture.

Herein lies a dilemma. The dominant technical rational epistemology encourages academics to produce abstract theory which, while useful, often has little relevance to ordinary people's lives (see p. 2; Schön, 1995). This is a comfortable state of affairs for many academics for whom the generation of abstract theory can mean avoiding the need to deal with serious world issues.

Chomsky (1966) says that the work of intellectuals is to tell the truth and expose lies. Intellectuals, he says, are a privileged elite, in a relatively secure workplace, free from thought control, and endowed with talent and reasonable amounts of time. They have the resources to enable them to uncover the truth about the world and make it publicly available.

The responsibility of intellectuals on this view is to take the lead in generating theories for social benefit. They could, for example, lend weight to new theories of organisation which see organisations as contexts for social evolution. Most contemporary organisation theory does not address issues of injustice and social disintegration (although the critical theorists have made significant inroads here – see Chapter 7). Knowledge workers need to put their best efforts into developing new theories that do. Practitioner-generated accounts constitute personal theories to show how practice can be improved (as appears throughout this book). Academics need to support the development of these theories. This however would suggest that academics need to rethink their own knowledge base, and see themselves as practitioners who want to improve their own practice.

Academics are popularly authorised as legitimate knowers. Corporations look to them for guidance in what counts as organisation knowledge. Unless corporations hear from academics that new forms of theory will serve business better, corporations will not learn to change, or, in the case of those who are changing by dint of practical circumstances, will lack confidence in the practical knowledge base that they are generating.

Universities are supposedly contexts of learning, and academics are potentially our best teachers. They set what counts as theory, and so influence organisational practices. Therefore, unless the form of organisation theory changes, organisational practices will tend to stay the same. New forms of theory are needed to account for the legitimacy of the personal practical theories of people in workplaces, in order to support personal workplace-based learning for longer-term social benefit.

A pause for thought

At this point I think it is worthwhile examining some assumptions I am making throughout, and to state that I am aware of them. I tend to assume that managers want to investigate their practice. This is not always the case. Adlam (1999), for example, tells of his spectacular failure to embed action research within a police education initiative. Police culture evidently is not entirely sympa-thetic to action research, and there was resistance to his invitation to colleagues to become self-reflective. This has sometimes been my experience too. Perhaps the reaction is common. I do not think we should accept the situation, however. Instead I think the situation itself should lead us to ask why the situation is as it is, and work towards changing it.

I am also using the idea of self-reflection (as others do in the literature) in an unproblematic way. I am assuming that there is common understanding about the term (see Chapter 2 for a further discussion). The idea however should not be treated lightly. Self-reflection, Elliott (1993) explains, is a long, complex process that often needs to be learnt and practised. It would be naive to expect people suddenly to become self-reflective when they are used to a culture of command and obedience. How do managers come to reflect on their practice and get others to do the same?

There is then the issue that many people do not want to think about how they might change their practice, when their current practice suits them very nicely. Below I tell a story of how a senior manager colleague was pleased with his current work, and would have thought me mad if I had suggested that he might need to investigate further. Even if he had seen the need, I doubt he would have wanted to do anything about it. Many people work hard to sustain practices which suit them.

There is also my consistent and perhaps naive assumption (shared by many other writers) that action research aims for personal-social improvement. We often read about 'making a difference', neglecting the fact that the difference can be for evil as well as for good. There is nothing in the methodology of action research that prevents people from asking 'How do I improve my work?' when the work is to dominate others or to refine instruments of torture. In this book, however, I am discussing ideas to do with learning organisations and professional education. It is entirely possible to learn for social disimprovement. People learn all the time how to dominate, coerce, bully, kill. Dewey is right to say that living inevitably means learning; but what is learnt is at issue. However, I think educa-tion is in some way different. Education in my opinion refers to the relationship between people such that they will grow in a life-enhancing way. Education by definition leads to personal-social improvement. This view of education would not be held by all. Whatever definition is accepted is a cultural phenomenon. Hitler's *Mein Kampf* for example offers an explicit theory of education which was accepted by his culture. This view is different from Dewey's view, which says that one cannot educate for ill. I agree with Dewey, and adopt this view throughout. This could be the reason that the Journal of the Collaborative Action Research Network took as its title *Educational Action Research*, and why many writers speak about their own work in action research as educational. These ideas are taken further in Chapter 1.

If we are serious about improving workplaces through learning, we have to endorse ideas to do with self-reflection, examining what we are doing, devel-oping educative relationships, and working out action theories to explain how learning is experienced in and through practice. If we espouse these core values, we are led to ask questions of the form, 'How do I understand my work with you as helping you to understand your work?' On this view, management inevitably becomes an educative practice. To live up to the rhetoric of 'the learning organisation' we need to remember that learning for sustainable personal-social growth best happens within educative relationships. Whenever we talk about learning organisations it always has to be within a context of educative relationships: learning organisations first have to be educative organisations. This has considerable implications for management as a new form of scholarship and how new theories of management are generated and put to use for social betterment.

Accounting for my own learning

To stay true to myself as a person and a researcher, and to avoid widening the theory–practice gap, I have to show that my work, including this book, is a living-out of everything I have said so far.

The book is a research report, a portfolio of my own professional learning as an educator. It shows how I aimed to turn my value of individual autonomy in community into a living form. It shows the development of my own living educational theory of organisational learning and my own theory of management. It is embedded in, and drawn from, my experience of moving from a position of teacher educator to an accompanying position of managing a growing organisation of professional learners comprising teachers, business managers, administrators, higher education personnel, members of religious orders, clerical staff; and negotiating with policy groups for recognition of the legitimacy of that organisation and the personal accounts of practice which its members continue to produce. It shows how people can be enabled to develop their capacity for self-direction and intellectual independence.

I never set out deliberately to create an organisation. In my work as a professional educator located mainly in Ireland, I had assumed – amazingly naively I now realise – that my own willingness to devote time and energy to creating opportunities for professionals to develop insights into their own practice would automatically meet with unilateral institutional approval and support. How wrong can you be. In some cases it *was* so, and individuals responded enthusiastically to the invitation to improve their practice through self-study. Some principals and managers immediately recognised the potential benefits to personal and organisational growth through the development of a critical perspective on practice, and embraced the opportunity wholeheartedly; many undertook their own personal enquiries; all encouraged other colleagues to engage. Research evidence exists of the benefits that such commitment brought to personal and organisational development (for example, Collins and McNiff, 1999; Condren, 2000; C. Lillis, 2000; McNiff and Collins, 1994). The stories are triumphant narratives to show how people systematically developed their practice for personal and social benefit.

MacLure comments (1996) on how often victory narratives conceal the pain and struggle behind the triumph. I agree. I do not intend to dwell on negative issues, but I think it is important to state that the ideas arose largely out of conflict and contradiction. These were often to do with maintaining my own educational practice of supporting workplace learning in the face of sometimes hostile reactions. The idea of awarding higher degrees for workplace learning is unwelcome to many traditional institutions, where the dominant stories are still those of hierarchical control. Stories of control in turn are related to stories about what counts as legitimate knowledge and who has the right to be called a legitimate knower. Stories about the validity of newer forms of practitioner-generated practice-based knowledge are often excluded from dominant discourses.

An apocryphal story illustrates this. I lunched one day with the senior manager of an institute where I worked for a time. 'I am pleased', he said, 'because I did a questionnaire in a management magazine and scored 100 per cent, so that means I am a good manager.' I had to look twice to see whether he was serious. At the time I did not have the heart to ask whether he had checked with any colleagues for their evaluation of his performance. I have had cause to regret my silence. Had I challenged his belief in the standards of judgement he used to establish his credit rating, subsequent difficulties might have been avoided – but then, a powerful action research-based organisation probably would not have come into existence in response to such thinking. So the world turns. The episode also highlighted for me how deeply ingrained into our institutional psyches is the idea that practice is a performative technique which may be judged in terms of prescribed criteria; how this view permeates debates on what constitutes effective management practice and the standards of judgement used (Management Charter Initiative, 1991); and how prescriptive propositional theory is accepted uncritically as the most appropriate form to guide practice when so often it is manifestly at odds with everyday practice. I am interested in how and why these are the dominant systems of knowledge, and I raise questions throughout about how and why they are kept in place when other systems of knowledge exist which clearly suit social purposes more adequately.

My claim to knowledge

It took time and effort to grow into an action research mentality. My doctoral work (McNiff, 1989), conducted over some eight years, records my development from propositional to dialectical thinking; and recent years have seen a maturational professional process of increasing acceptance of an unknowable future and unpredictable present. My liking for the metaphors of new science tells me that every choice about future action may be seen as what Prigogine and Stengers (1984) call a dissipative structure, a bifurcation point which offers multiple possibilities of potential, each one of which could lead to the creation of a new universe.

In a sense, life is an ongoing action research project, a constant action-reflection process which consistently aims for self-renewal with social intent. The evidence exists in terms of the reports which I produce (like this book), and also the reports that others produce to show how the quality of their life and work has been influenced through our professional relationship (see for example Gallagher, 1998; Henderson, 1998). This process has been particularly evident over recent years. I am clear about the values that guide my work: the needs of individuals for intellectual and personal-social independence; their needs and rights to live with dignity, to have their contributions valued, to create their own identities and live in a way that they consider worthwhile in company with others who are trying to do the same. My life as an educator aims to realise these values in my practice.

A primary aim of research is to create one's own knowledge and show that one has done so – to make an original claim to knowledge. The claim needs to be supported by empirical evidence to show that it is authentic. The claim I make for my action-reflection life process is that I have influenced the quality of other people's lives for good. This is not so for everyone I am in contact with; in the contested territory of what counts as the common good, and in challenging the use of authoritarian power, some people are bound to get upset. Such is the problematic terrain of educational ideas. I could say that I am helping them to think in more enlightened ways, that the tension is still a creative aspect of emergent educative order, but I have my doubts whether they would agree.

An organisation exists today in Ireland that was not there even three years ago. Over two hundred people, working in a variety of education contexts, have studied, or continue to study with me, on informal workplace initiatives, and also for their Masters and Doctoral degrees in education. The degrees are awarded by two British universities. I have nurtured and coordinated the development of this organisation without any conscious intent of developing it as an organisation, yet it has come into being and is proving to be a powerful influence in Irish education (Glavin, 2000). Because of its influence, curriculum initiatives and teacher education programmes are being developed which work towards democratic and inclusive forms (Fitzgerald, 1998). Regional initiatives are being developed (Mol an Óige, 1999). I work with Irish universities and teacher unions to develop in-service courses with a view to generating models of professional education for national dissemination (ASTI, 2000). Practitioners within the organisation are themselves developing networks and institutional opportunities for new participants (Twomey, 1997; O'Neill, 1997) and are beginning to publish accounts about their work (Condren, 1998; C. Lillis, 1998). The organisation is caught up in its own networked development, and is establishing links and partnerships at national and international levels (Farrell, 2000; Mc Wey, 1999). The development of the organisation has been timely and is, I believe, part of wider trends in Irish education towards person-centred curricula and teaching methodologies; these trends are well documented in government statements (for example, Government of Ireland, 1992, 1995, 1998, 1999a; see also Drudy, 2000; Hyland and Hanafin, 1997). The emergence of our organisation has, I think, intensified public awareness of the potential of practitioner-generated forms of research and perhaps accelerated their acceptance. It is not possible nor desirable for any individual to claim responsibility for large-scale developments. It is entirely possible however to claim that one has contributed.

I am now moving on. The organisation will develop in its own way as people take on new responsibilities. I am content that the organisation is something of worth, a real force for social and educational renewal.

Why am I writing this book, and why are you reading it?

I think the form of this book could have some significance. It is an account of the development of a personal theory of organisation and management that can be used by other people to develop their personal theories. It is a story of how my work with others has contributed to the development of an educative organisation.

How I came to these ideas was almost by accident. I have said that I had no intention of developing this organisation. However, I found myself caught up in the process, and became aware of the need to understand my management practice as well as maintain my tutorial duties. I decided to study the literature of management and organisation theory. Much of what I read took me by surprise. There was little congruence between a lot of what I read and what I was experiencing and learning in my management practice. I was already well rehearsed in the literature of educational research, and could engage critically with the ideas. Much of what I found in the literature of management and organisation study left me wondering whether what I was doing could be called management at all; and this doubt was compounded by my relationships with some others in the institutional contexts of higher education who did call themselves managers, and whose practice seemed to be geared more towards income-generation and careerism than towards education. However, 'my' organisation was flourishing, and seemed to be going from strength to strength, so whatever I was doing seemed to be working.

My action research approach enables me to theorise the purpose of organisational studies in a way that is realistic for my own practice, and to offer justification for my point of view. It also enables me to critique perspectives which present abstract theories as unproblematic givens. I am worried about why propositional forms are still accepted in an uncritical way, and why people are prepared to put up with it. Research is not a practice that exists only in the head and in reports. Research is a force in real lives, to help us find ways of making our lives worthwhile. This is my research report to show how and why I have generated my own theory of organisation, and to produce the evidence to show its validity. My story shows that dominant forms of theory and practice can be challenged, and should be challenged, and why they should be challenged.

The book, then, is a formative report in an ongoing study of organisation theory and practice. The ideas are still in process. I continue to monitor my own practice; to find ways of improving it; to involve others in the development of the organisation; to seek to influence wider systems through the now established organisational power base. Some researchers (for example, Noffke, 1997a) are sceptical of the extent to which personal enquiry can influence wider organisational systems. To them I say, Look; it is happening. It is not only possible in theory; look at the power of realised potential in practice. I and others, working together, are developing communities to improve systems through our personal commitment to improve our personal practice. In our case, we can make a very grand claim: we are helping to change the educational system of an entire country, remembering of course that Ireland is a very small country. However, size does not always matter; in education especially it is the quality of experience that counts.

Significantly, the creation of this book represents an extension of the Irish community. Colleagues in wider professional contexts around the world responded to the invitation to contribute their stories here. The family has extended, and networks have converged. The whole pattern is connected by the invisible threads of generosity and goodwill, an amazing network of care and support.

My claim is that we have created an organisation which is animated by a spirit of care and a desire to pursue educational goals. Evidence for the claim exists in this book and in a new and growing body of literature that we are producing. Our accounts provide a powerful body of evidence for establishing the legitimacy and potency of personal and collective evidence- and research-based professionalism.

The experience has been rich; it has also been difficult. Many learnings have developed; I aim to share some of them, hoping that you might want to adapt or adopt some of the insights and practices, to rejoice in the sharing of life-giving relationships, and also draw courage and strength from them to carry on when faced with significant odds that try to make you lose heart and quit. I imagine you will also come to question prejudices, both your own and others', as I have been forced to do, as you ask questions of the kind, 'How do I improve my work for the benefit of others?' (Whitehead, 1989), and produce your own account to show how you have managed your own practice such that your piece of the world is a better place because of your involvement. This is not only possible; it is essential.

Let me return to Schön's idea of the new scholarship. I believe that research communities across the professions need to find ways of sharing insights and accounts of practice that develop new ways of knowing and forms of representation. The time is right, and the need never more urgent in these days of increasing planetary fragility, increasing trends towards globalisation and the threat to social cohesion. I believe that such accounts are not only instructive, but essential in the development of good social orders that help us celebrate our common living together. We need above all to find ways to share our knowledge and humanity, and learn from one another, inspired by the vision that we can create new worlds, provided we have the energy and courage to do so.

Prologue

Contextualising the study

In this section I explain my work context and how I came to be involved in organisation study and began to appreciate its implications for practice.

Early days

In 1992 I was invited to act as consultant to a Schools Based Action Research Project (SBARP), a teacher education project developed by a small private college of education in Ireland. This was in response to a national survey whose findings indicated that, while new curriculum developments recommended a student-centred approach to classroom methodologies, these methodologies were still largely didactic and teacher-centred (Marino Institute of Education, 1992). Teachers seemed to lack confidence in turning the espoused values of participation and the development of students' intellectual independence into practice. The SBARP project identified its aim as helping teachers learn how to do this, and to evaluate whether they were having any influence on the quality of learning in schools and colleges.

The project was widely regarded as a success (Hanafin and Leonard, 1996; Hyland and Hanafin, 1997; Leonard, 1996). Research evidence exists to suggest that the quality of teachers' practice improved (McNiff and Collins, 1994), and that teachers' improved practice influenced the quality of students' learning. At this stage, however, there is no recorded evidence that the project impacted on wider education systems.

The initial intention was to support some thirty teachers, according to the staffing available. In the event, about seventy teachers took part in the first year, and this number increased over the three years of the project's life. Many participating teachers in turn influenced others in their own institutions. It is impossible to state exactly how many people were involved. The support structure was that the project team of five, as well as two members of the Vocational Education Committee's Psychological Support Service, each had a case load of up to ten teachers, and worked with them closely (the unanticipated volume in fact proved to be very stressful for the supporters). 'We walked with them,' says Úna Collins, team leader at that time. 'We never told them what to do. We listened, responded, helped them to clarify ideas and actions for themselves. We acted as critical friends and supports' (see also McNiff and Collins, 1994). I learned a great deal from observing Úna's management style, and I was to bring this learning with me into later practice. She maintains: 'Our core value is care of the individual. It is how we are with each other that matters.' Participants' accounts state that the supporters' preparedness to listen was a major factor in their own growing understanding of practice (see for example, McDermott, 1999, whose PhD work develops themes begun in these early days).

I was well familiar with how education research emphasised the need for care as the basis for educative relationships (for example, Goodlad *et al.*, 1990; Noddings, 1992; Sergiovanni, 1996). However, I had until then always equated care with mainstream education; I had not yet made the conceptual leap to link education and management, and the need for care as the foundation for successful relationships, regardless of context or profession. This came later, as I experienced how people responded to my own attempts to care for them as a manager. I began to appreciate that being a good manager is inextricably related to being a caring and trustworthy person.

The methodology for the project was an action reflection process which adopted Whitehead's (1993) plan:

- What is my concern?
- Why am I concerned?
- What solution can I imagine?
- How can I gather evidence to show the situation as it changes?
- How can I show my own influence in that situation?
- How can I ensure that any conclusions I might draw are reasonably fair and accurate?
- How will I modify practice in the light of my evaluation?

Teachers and administrators asked 'How do I improve my work?' (Whitehead, 1989) and 'How do I help you to learn?' (Russell and Korthagen, 1995). My own questions in relation to the team I was supporting became: 'How do we learn, individually and collectively, to manage educative processes with teachers and administrators?' I made my reflective reports available to the team, and encouraged them to produce their own reflective accounts of practice which they shared with one another and, to a lesser extent, with the educators they supported.

From the beginning of the SBARP project, I suggested to the college management that we should seek accreditation for the participating teachers and for the project team. For a variety of reasons we investigated accreditation routes through a British university; and eventually we negotiated to franchise a Modular Programme for Professional Development. This meant that Irish educators could receive their Masters degrees for studying their own practice, and the dissertations and reports they produced would constitute their descriptions and explanations of how they investigated and tried to improve their work.

One member of the project team formalised his studies and was later awarded his PhD for work arising from those initial beginnings (Cunningham, 1999).

A formal accreditation programme began where the SBARP project left off. For the following two years I co-ordinated the programme, acting as tutor and administrator. By 1997, thirty-one participants had graduated with their Masters degrees.

I began to realise that, although my role was expanding into management, I consistently regarded myself as a teacher; and I still do. I began to engage seriously with the literature of management and organisation studies. This led to important learnings; and it marks the starting point for thinking about this book, to address the slippage between the dominant theory and the practice of managing learning in organisations.

The subject matter of organisation study

I became caught up in the issue of what constitutes the proper subject matter of organisation studies. I knew from education research that there are important connections between what is studied and how it is studied, the unit of enquiry and the method of enquiry. I reasoned that the same had to apply to management and organisation study.

I came to realise that the mainstream organisation literature conceptualises management largely as unified and informed by a coherent set of principles which can be applied to any and all situations; these principles feature as 'what to do' and 'how to do' advice lists. Organisation is largely conceptualised as a free-standing entity of structures and processes. Within the management literature people are frequently excluded; when they do feature, different perspectives exist about their nature. I am thinking for example of Daubner's (1982) view of 'man [*sic*] depraved' or 'man deprived' (cited in Best, 1999), or McGregor's (1960) Theory X, in which people are seen as lazy and hostile and regard work simply as a means of earning money, and Theory Y, which assumes that people are positive and want to work as a means of personal fulfilment. These views inevitably colour how management practice is perceived. There are also different conceptualisations of organisation. Some theorists view organisations as abstract, mechanistic and functionalist (Chandler and Deams, 1980; Donaldson, 1995) within which people are expected to fulfil particular roles. Others view organisations as organic, power-sharing communities (Bennis, 1989a; Peters, 1992) within which people have a greater degree of self-determination to negotiate roles and responsibilities (Waterman, 1994; Handy, 1994, 1995a). Morgan (1997a) is helpful here in showing the metaphorical basis for varieties of practice.

Whichever view of management or organisation one chooses to subscribe to, the epistemological and methodological assumptions appear to be the same: practice is understood in terms of the fixed knowledge base of prescribed lists of activities or skills; to be a good manager one has to learn and internalise the script and speak it in one's own organisational context. At the time, I realised that this was the same propositional way of thinking which I had already challenged in my work as a teacher educator (McNiff, 1988, 1993) and which was far too simplistic to help me to understand how to develop a management practice that responded to the variability and unpredictability of my organisation context. I came to understand that the same kind of propositional knowledge base under-pins traditional forms both of teacher education and management education, and is equally unhelpful to everyday practice in both professions. Until quite recently teacher education has mainly been approached via a disciplines approach which assumes that if teachers understand the nature of the psychology, philosophy, history and sociology of education, they can apply those theories to their practice and become successful teachers. Interestingly manage-ment has been added to the list of disciplines: to be a good teacher you now also have to be a good manager (ironically management is narrowly defined as a set of codified practices). Similarly it appears that traditional MBA courses have focused on the disciplines of marketing, accounting, organisational behaviour, quantitative analysis, finance, operations, economics, strategy and more recently ethics. Provided managers develop a good working knowledge of these disci-plines, they will be able to apply them to practice and become good managers.

My understanding of developing an organisation (though I did not see it like this at the time) was that my work was essentially to do with people; to under-stand my work meant that I had to understand the nature of our relationships. The disciplines approach gave me knowledge about practices in general; it did not help me to understand my specific practice. This initially intuitive under-standing now crystallises into an explicit critique of much current organisation theory whose themes suggest that organisations are free-standing entities which may be analysed conceptually in terms of their working parts. For instance, contingency theory (see for example Pugh and Payne, 1977 and the work of the Aston Group) works from this premise. My understanding of organisations is that they are not abstract concepts and free-standing entities, but groups of indi-vidual people with diverse agendas who come together in community for particular purposes. To understand organisation is to understand how people try to live in a way which they consider worthwhile. Plato's questions of 'How should we be?' and 'How should we live together?' are as relevant today as ever. Asking those questions means tackling issues about how we can improve social situations by improving our understanding of them, and our understanding of ourselves as living people within them. To regard organisations and the people in them as objects of study denies the values base of social living. It requires me to stand outside the reality which I am co-creating with others and regard myself as an impartial outsider – impossible for me as a morally committed practitioner.

My work is to help people find ways of improving their lifeworld experience. This includes helping them to think in ways that are appropriate to their experi-ence, to challenge inappropriate theory, and to develop personal theories to inform ethically and politically committed practices.

My work is also concerned with developing contexts and providing supports to enable people to value their own learning. To do this I have got to grips with ideas about pluralistic democracy, and seriously rethought my own views about the nature of good societies. Until quite recently I subscribed wholeheartedly to the idealistic theories of people such as Rawls (1972), and could describe the particular prescriptive characteristics of good societies. This view informed earlier drafts of this book. Subsequent reading and reflection has brought me away from such certitude. I see that the ideas of Rawls and others are idealised scenarios which, while providing regulative ideals, do not help me to deal with the uncomfortable realities of conflict which I encounter on an everyday basis, as they manifest in the struggle for hegemony among people, the readiness with which some people (myself included) will act in direct opposition to their espoused values, and the ways I am positioned by other people that are contrary to the ways in which I position myself (see Chapters 2 and 3).

The nature of management work

In my teaching, and to encourage people to see the need for self-reflection, I sometimes ask them to draw a picture entitled 'Me and my work'. Often they draw themselves and an object, perhaps a book or a building. On this view, 'work' exists as an external thing. I used to see work like this too. From experience and study I have come to a new understanding of the nature of my management work. I have come to understand 'work' as what I do with others. 'Me and my work' means having creative conversations, reflecting and finding good ways of living.

I believe that it is the responsibility of managers to help people understand their work in order to improve the quality of their life in organisations, and by implication their wider social contexts. This aspect does not feature prominently in mainstream organisation research, a serious omission in my view.

If managers came to embrace this kind of societal mandate, one could make a case for organisations as major forces for social and ecological renewal. If management and organisation study limits its remit to offering only observations and descriptions of what is happening, however, and does not concern itself with why it is happening or how situations might be improved, the potential of organisation studies to generate theories of social evolution will be wasted. The main purpose of organisation studies should be to investigate how to develop sustainable communities which tolerate multiple agendas and nurture individual autonomy, to bring people together on terms of equality to pursue common goals.

On the view that 'me and my work' implies how one understands one's relationships with others, organisation study needs to conceptualise itself as a form of educational research. Managers need to develop their work as educators. To do this they need supports to help them theorise their practice in new ways. Managers need to see themselves as public intellectuals (Said, 1994b) to (1) tell public stories of how they challenged entrenched attitudes and systems of dominance and power; and also (2) develop discourses of reconciliation through education (see Chapter 2). They also need to position themselves as organic intellectuals (Gramsci, 1971) who are able to encourage others to tell their stories (Chapter 3) and mobilise to change systems for social benefit.

Self-study within organisational life offers important models for personal and social renewal. This should be a major focus in the professional education of managers. Management schools should make it their business to teach participants not to accept forms of theory or practice that are inappropriate for their practical everyday needs, but encourage them to question such systems in the search for appropriate forms of living and thinking (Chapter 11). Unless this happens, schools of business and management will remain stuck in old-paradigm ways of thinking that block their potential as dynamic adaptive systems, a situation that denies the very principles on which they are founded.

It does, of course, always come down to people, how willing we are to change, and the degree to which we are able to do so within wider political constraints. Stuart Crainer (1996: 53) quotes *The Financial Times*'s Christopher Lorenz as saying, 'Most managers are still stuck with an outdated view of the nature of organisations, and of their own roles within them' (Lorenz, 1994). Times are always changing; whether we want to change along with them depends on the degree of energy and commitment we are willing to spend in levering ourselves out of our carefully crafted comfort zones and catapult ourselves into instability, a sure invitation to disruption and discomfort. We all have choices about how we think the world works. I know what my choices are.

Part I

What is the nature of organisational knowledge?

This part comprises three chapters and three case stories. The stories demonstrate and explicate in action the issues that the chapters discuss.

Chapter 1 is 'Learning organisations and the responsibility of managers'. I discuss some of the assumptions that underlie the idea of 'the learning society', particularly ideas about knowledge and learning, their nature, acquisition and potential use. I also discuss some of the implications for how the concept of 'the learning society' is understood when it is problematised in the light of the multiple factors involved in the idea of learning. I talk about how it is the responsibility of managers to develop the kinds of educative relationships that will support sustainable learning for the development of socially aware organisations.

This chapter is followed by a case story by Jimmy Ryan, a management consultant in Ireland, who studied with me for his MA in Education. Jimmy is constantly enthralled by the idea of learning, and this is evident in his story. He explains how participation on our course raised his own awareness of the potential for growth as soon as he began critically to engage with his own learning. Currently Jimmy is working with managers and management consultants, and encouraging them to adopt an action research approach in their organisations.

Chapter 2 is 'Learning organisations as good societies'. I try to do two things here. First, I try to explain how important it is to problematise the idea of learning, if the 'learning' in 'the learning organisation' is to retain meaning and not become a vacuous buzzword. Part of the problematisation suggests that learning which leads to sustainable organisational growth is the same kind of learning that leads to the development of a good social order. I try to make a case for the interlinking of the ideas of learning organisations and good societies. Second, I try to show that the development of learning and good orders can best be understood by a form of theory which itself demonstrates a methodology of learning. Conceptual abstract theory is not sufficiently robust for this; newer forms of living theory are. The problem is that conceptual theory is still prized, so this often leads to differences of opinion about whose learning is valued.

The chapter is supported by Séamus Lillis's story. I work with Séamus in Ireland in an informal capacity to support his PhD studies in rural community development. Séamus's story shows the transformation in his practice and thinking, away from propositional forms towards dialectical forms. He is generating a new form of living educational theory of rural community development, which could potentially have significance for how rural community development comes to be theorised in the future, and for the development of structures at national level to support learning in local communities.

Chapter 3 is entitled 'Action research, power and control' and explains how I came to understand theories of power through first-hand experience. Power frequently carries negative connotations. It can of course also be positive, and I try to show how colleagues and I have generated our own power to combat authoritarian systems and created our own relationships of power to work towards realising our educational values for social benefit.

The case story which supports this chapter is from Pip Bruce Ferguson, who works as a staff developer at The Waikato Polytechnic. I met Pip some years ago when she was working for her doctoral studies, and was later delighted to act as external examiner for her PhD. Pip's stories are full of remarkable courage, kindness and determination to improve the quality of life for others in ways that they consider appropriate for themselves. In this story, Pip shows how she is generating powerful relationships in her organisation to transform the nature of its social practices.

I believe the stories have an internal progression to show the transformational nature of personal learning for social change. Jimmy describes a personal learning experience; Séamus shows the transformational process of thinking and practice with the potential for wider organisational change; and Pip brings the focus of learning to a systemic level. There is an iterative and generative quality to the stories: each story shows how individual learning has the potential for wider change; the progression of the stories shows how the change process begins to permeate structures at increasingly wide levels of influence. The pattern within the individual stories, and within the sequence, shows the expanding and potentially unbounded nature of influence.

The work is supported by extracts from conversations I had with colleagues who work in management capacities in a variety of contexts. Those colleagues are:

Ashley Balbirnie, Managing Director of *Ireland on Sunday* Ltd., Dublin, Ireland.

Wayne Gorman, assistant teacher at the University of Alberta, Canada, and part-time worker with 'Urban' Nations and Metis peoples, developing skills to set up an Art and Crafts Co-operative.

Sharon Jamieson, Adjunct Professor, Faculty of Education, and Director, Office of the President, University of Alberta, Canada.

Liam Nagle, Vice President of World Wide Operations, Enterprise Solutions, Nortel Networks.

Oonagh O'Brien, Coordinator of Parish Renewal, Dublin, Ireland.

Stephen O'Connor, Supervisory Teacher in the Training Unit, City of Dublin Vocational Education Committee Educational Service to Prisons, Dublin, Ireland.

While the comments are by no means representative, they helped me to focus my thinking and see issues through new lenses.

This part of the book, I hope, makes the case for a generative transformational form of organisation theory which shows its potential both for individual and social renewal. It shows the living reality of people in organisational relationships who are creating powerful connections to support their own and one another's learning.

1 Learning organisations and the responsibility of managers

As I reflect on my practice as a manager I am aware that I am always in relation with other people. My work is not a thing, separate from me. It is a personal process that I engage in. I *am* my work. Although it is my work, I do not work in isolation. My work as a manager is about how I can help people develop independence of mind and action, and help them enable others to do the same; our purpose is to achieve common organisational goals within a context of free and equal association (Dewey, 1916; Chomsky, 1996). As a manager, I try to create the conditions which will turn this purpose into reality.

I understand my work in terms of the values of individual autonomy, integrity and justice; I try to live these values in my management practice. When I evaluate my work I check whether I am living in the direction of my values, and this involves ongoing conversations with those whom I am supporting to see if they perceive me as living out these values in terms of their own lives.

Study means learning. As I study my work I am aware of my own learning. As I encourage others to study their work, I am encouraging them to be aware of their learning at an individual and collective level and use it for personal-social benefit. I am also aware of how I learn from and with them, and I ensure that they know this. This is the nature of our organisational learning.

When I first began to study organisation theory I became aware of some lack of problematisation. Terms such as 'the learning organisation', 'knowledge workers', 'knowledge creating companies' appear everywhere. Even a cursory glance reveals their lack of problematisation. What does a learning organisation learn, and why? What kind of knowledge do knowledge workers generate, and for what purpose? Do companies create knowledge as an abstract entity, and whose knowledge is it? It bothers me that terms are used willy-nilly, as if there is a universal understanding of what they mean, and their implications for real people's lives.

It is disappointing that there is not widespread serious engagement in the literature with theories of learning, teaching and education in organisational contexts, especially given that impressive bodies of literature exist on theories of learning, teaching and education, and their interrelatedness. It is disappointing that more studies do not show how theories of learning, teaching and education might influence the quality of organisational growth. The problem is exacerbated by the fact that the dominant form of theory is propositional, proposing theories about learning, teaching and education, without showing how those theories might impact on real lives. Anyone who wanted to reflect on their work would have access to quantities of abstract knowledge *about* hypothetical situations, but few real-life examples to show how theory influences practice, or how practice generates new theory. There is little support in the literature for people who might ask, 'How do I understand my work in order to improve it?', or who might have to explain to Mr Smith the reasons for his redundancy notice.

Over these recent years, therefore, I have come to see the need to go beyond traditional forms of theory. Traditional theory gives me insights and ideas, but I have to work these theories into the narrative of my life to show how, if at all, they contribute to its meaning. Sometimes existing theories are not relevant to me, so are not incorporated in my narrative. This process of weaving abstract theory into a narrative of learning from experience generates an embodied living theory of practice.

I want to explore these issues in this chapter, first by showing in a conceptual way what I think is important in existing theories of learning, teaching and education, and their relevance for organisational learning; and then to show how I think they can be woven into embodied theories which demonstrate their use value for human experience. I am adopting the same methodological approach to my enquiry as Clandinin and Connelly do when they explain the narrative inquiry approach to research: 'stories illustrate the importance of learning and thinking narratively ... . Our approach is not so much to tell you what narrative inquiry is by defining it but rather to show you what it is by creating a definition contextually by recounting what narrative inquirers do' (Clandinin and Connelly, 2000: xiii).

What follows therefore is my emergent theory of learning, teaching and education in organisational contexts, and the implications of the theory for improving the quality of organisational life.

The chapter is organised in terms of the questions:

- What is the nature of organisational knowledge: what kinds of knowledge can be generated through studying experience in organisations?
- How is organisational knowledge acquired: what kind of learning goes on in organisations?
- How is organisational learning put to use: how do we use our organisational learning to best effect?
- What are the implications for the generation of new theories of organisation in the development of learning organisations?

1 What is the nature of organisational knowledge?

It is generally agreed in contemporary organisation and management studies that knowledge is a powerful resource for organisational growth and that knowledge workers are scarce assets who need to be nurtured (Drucker, 1993; Nonaka and Takeuchi, 1995). However, the concepts of knowledge and coming to know are often treated in a quite simplistic way.

The concept of knowledge is deeply problematic. What knowledge is, how it is acquired, and how it is put to use, are contested issues.

Different views of the nature of knowledge

Knowledge exists in a variety of forms. Problems arise when some forms are seen as more valuable than, and separate from, others, as is the case in much current organisational study.

Knowledge is frequently categorised as propositional, procedural and personal (or tacit). I am presenting these for clarity as separate forms, although they are intimately interrelated, and there are many overlaps.

Propositional knowledge

Propositional knowledge is knowledge about things and facts, and is often, though not always, associated with empirical research (see Chapter 5). Ryle (1949) terms propositional knowledge 'knowledge that'. An abstract body of information exists about the world; this information is objective and value-free. It may be accessed in books, databases, and other retrieval systems. The body of knowledge exists external to and independent of a living knower. People may leave their books on the table, and the knowledge remains in the books. Knowledge exists as a static entity across time and space; it is reified (concrete and unchanging), and absolute. Propositional knowledge is often perceived as embodying eternal truths, even the Truth; this idea is often employed to justify fundamentalist regimes and orthodoxies and hierarchical forms of dominance.

Commitment to propositional knowledge (also sometimes called technical rational knowledge) dominates the organisation and management literature, both in terms of what happens in organisations (practice) and how this is studied (theory). Organisational practice is understood in terms of a fixed knowledge base of facts which may be studied and understood by observing events and behaviours, and producing descriptions of what is happening.

A view of knowledge as abstract and reified is problematic in several important ways. I shall discuss only two of them here, though there are many more. First, a view of knowledge as abstract and reified denies the idea that the existence of knowledge implies the existence of a knower. Common sense says that facts about the world are always *someone's* facts, interpreted and presented by someone somewhere, and open to negotiation with others. Factual knowledge tends to be replaced over time as newer information becomes available: for example, the heliocentric view of the universe was overtaken by a newer cosmology; Newtonian physics has been subsumed within quantum science. This does not mean that earlier ideas are rejected as useless; it does mean that people's knowledge advances with their new ideas and discoveries, and older forms need to be seen as part of wider evolutionary processes that transform existing knowledge into new knowledge. This applies to the process of knowledge generation itself. A second problematic in a view of knowledge as abstract and reified denies its socially constructed nature. Knowledge, like many human systems, is a historical and cultural phenomenon, created by and for people within their different community settings across time and space. What is so for A is not necessarily so for B; and events in one time become other events through the revisioning of history when different interpretations are offered for the same event (Boyce and O'Day, 1996). During the 1990s peace process in Northern Ireland, for example, people who were previously identified as terrorists later appeared as freedom fighters, and were then storied as enlightened political workers.

In western intellectual and cultural traditions, however, knowledge as fact is still assumed to be the main kind of valid knowledge. Even when people appreciate that this is not so, they still tend to cling, probably for comfort, to the vision of an external body of facts and information for which they have no responsibility and which offers clear and stable frameworks for social living. This fixed standpoint is more reassuring than the shifting-sands idea that knowledge is changing and unstable, a view which suggests that our thinking itself is changing and unstable, not a very secure position from which to run a company or produce public accounts of effective business management.

Procedural knowledge

Ryle (1949) refers to this as 'knowledge how'. It is a body of knowledge which refers both to procedures and also to capabilities; it is not neatly definable. Knowledge of procedures does not necessarily imply ability to do. 'I know how this works' does not automatically transfer to 'I know how to do this'. Craft knowledge employs capacities other than knowledge of procedures. Procedural knowledge as in 'I know how this works' tends towards propositional forms, whereas 'I know how to do this' implies an embodied form of knowing and leans towards personal forms of knowledge (see p. 41).

Know-that and know-how are strongly valued forms of knowledge in technologised societies, for they closely link with efficiency and productivity, getting things done on time. They underpin training and development in which know-how is transmitted as skills for jobs; and they reinforce transactional forms of communication which codify knowledge as systems to be learnt within a guild ethic of master craftsman and apprentice. They also underpin technicist forms of productivity such as just-in-time processes, where systemic slack is minimised through more efficient planning and allocation of material resources to streamline delivery.

Know-how regards knowledge as fluid, open to deconstruction and reconstruction. Know-how is often associated with the interpretive paradigm (Chapter 6), and emphasises the practical knowledge base of personal-social interaction. Social constructivists such as Glasersfeld (1995), drawing on Continental philosophical traditions, emphasise that knowledge is created within and through our practices and discourses; we are what we know and what we say, and we are constantly creating and recreating our knowledge of ourselves and others in company with others. It is not difficult to see the deep problems here for related issues such as the technologisation of work (Aronowitz and DiFazio, 1999), in which human skills are becoming anachronistic because they are easily mimicked by machines; humans are left with the knowledge but no longer have contexts for the use of their skills. The new knowledge work as developing new forms of know-how – knowing how to access and use information – has implications for the 'meaning' of work and social lives. Possibly the most important knowers in social and economic development will be those who know how to use electronic systems rather than those who know how to live successfully with others. Schooling in industrialised societies is steadily encouraging know-how forms of knowledge in the struggle for dominance through free markets and economic globalisation (see Chapter 9).

Personal knowledge

Michael Polanyi (1958, 1967) says that a vast reservoir of personal knowledge underlies our personal-social practices. We know more than we can say; our personal knowledge is unarticulatable because usually we are not aware of it – we 'just know'. Polanyi rejects a view of scientific progress as rational planning, because much scientific enquiry employs a tacit dimension which cannot be codified. 'Tacit knowledge is that vast fund of practical, local and traditional knowledge that is embodied in dispositions and forms of life and expressed in flair and intuition, which can never be formulated in rules of scientific method, say, and of which our theoretical or articulated knowledge is only the visible tip' (Gray, 1993: 70). On this view, knowledge is in the way we live our lives and is essentially embodied knowledge. Schön (1983) suggests that this kind of practical knowing-in-action is key to professional practices: professionals build up a store of experiential knowledge over time which often dispenses with knowledge of facts in decision-making. Mature management tends to employ the capacity to rely on wisdom and what feels right, and decisions to act in a certain direction can defy conscious calculation or analysis. Heron (1981, 1992) and others rightly emphasise the centrality of feelings and emotions in business and decision-making, for trust in personal knowledge involves belief and commitment to felt processes, elements that lie outside the realms of technical rationality.

Personal knowledge is knowledge in the present. Futures research (for example, Toffler, 1990) says that the most important knowledge for social progress is knowledge of the future as embodied in present practices. It is essential therefore to be present in the moment, remembering, as Polanyi says (1967), that each present moment holds its history and future eternally dynamic within itself. The values base of successful social living begins with knowledge of the self; we need to know and appreciate who we are, in order to come to know and appreciate others: 'Our real good consists in the development of our inward resources; … self-improvement is the beginning of all improvement' (Rhadha-krishnan, 1978: 12, 15). Schön, building on the work of Polanyi, talks about personal knowledge as the site for the generation of practical theories of reflec-tion-in-action (see Introduction). This is when we become aware of our values and try to turn them into reality, and we are able explicitly to articulate the process.

The changing nature of knowledge

Knowledge generation is itself an evolutionary process (Lakatos and Musgrave, 1970). Newer forms overtake older forms, and, while those older forms continue to exist and have use value, they become part of the broadening evolutionary landscape of emergent human interests. Human interests influence, and are influenced by, wider evolutionary processes; these processes are dynamic and fluid, eternally at the edge of chaos where the potential for change is at its most critical (Kauffman, 1995). Technical rational, product-orientated forms of knowledge, in a stable state of being, have the potential to transform into unboundaried forms of knowledge which are constantly in a state of becoming.

What we know, and how we come to know, are aspects of our own reality. They are not 'givens'; they are phenomena learnt from living in a particular society which has its own received worldview and assumptions about the nature of reality (MacIntyre, 1981). Traditions of knowledge are also evolutionary.

An ontology of being

The knowledge base within western intellectual traditions is shifting. Until recently it has been dominated by a view of knowledge as static and complete. Knowledge *is*, as tables and chairs and all other objects of the natural world *are*; they exist in a particular time and space, in a final, fully realised form. The nearly 400-year-old Newtonian-Cartesian legacy encourages us to see the world as a deterministic machine which, once wound up, operates efficiently and predictably in terms of its moving parts, held together by processes of cause and effect (see Chapter 5). This ontology (worldview) is essentially one of *being*: reality is apprehended as the here and now; this frozen moment of structured time *is* reality. Movement is understood as going from one boxed moment of experience to the next, like a train going from station to station. 'The state of "rest" is considered normal while movement is regarded as a straightforward transition from one stable state to another' (Chia, 1997: 74). Sitting in the carriage as the train moves along its trajectory is for some the ultimate reality. People are fixed entities with fixed interpretations of life experiences, occupying personal-social roles and physical spaces, being carried along a given, predetermined route. This is the 'science of being', which Prigogine and Stengers (1984) critique as failing adequately to account for personal-social experience as a creative, dynamic process.

The experience of 'now' as a static structure, the culmination of past experi-ence, dominates western thinking, including organisation and management study.

There is an overwhelming assumption that what is studied exists in a final form in a specific space-time; how it is studied is via an unchanging methodology which holds good for all time and is influenced by eternal assumptions.

An ontology of becoming

An alternative perspective is a 'science of becoming' (Prigogine and Stengers, 1984). Reality, including the thought processes we use to understand it, is in a state of flux, a constant process of becoming. Whatever is, is constantly transforming into newer versions of itself. Each new transformation is an entirely new creation which has evolved out of its own history. There are no final outcomes, for any experience in any moment is already in a process of change; any answer is already transforming into new questions.

This view has several genealogies, both recent and ancient. A recent genealogy is postmodernism, a perspective that believes it is impossible definitively to characterise any aspect of reality, since as soon as we try to define something it becomes something else. The very act of definition influences the nature of that which is being defined. By definition, definitions may not exist. This view stands in contrast to a view of modernism which holds that all things may be defined and understood as fixed structures and deterministic processes in a fully comprehensible, materialist world. Another contemporary genealogy is the shift from old-paradigm Newtonian science, which viewed reality as fixed and describable in terms of eternal and immutable laws, to new-paradigm quantum science, which views reality as ephemeral and transitory, with blurred boundaries between matter and energy, and which often defies rational explanation (Heisenberg, 1989).

A far older genealogy is in the Heraclitean cosmology. Heraclitus believed that reality was always changing; it was impossible to step into the same river twice, for the river was always in flow and always a different river. Heraclitus believed reality was characterised by the One and the Many, contradictions and syntheses in constant fluid interaction without dissonance. This view greatly influenced Plato, who also believed that the One and the Many peacefully co-exist throughout the natural world. It was not, however, a view held by Parmenides, a successor of Heraclitus, who subscribed to a more rational process in which One was separate from the Many; nor by Aristotle, a successor of Plato, who aimed to eradicate contradiction from rational thought, placing reason over the senses, and a view of static reality over a transitory one. The intellectual traditions of Parmenides and Aristotle found their way into western thinking, where they were further legitimised by Newton, Bacon and Descartes in the seventeenth and eighteenth centuries, and later by the empiricists Hume, Berkeley and Locke; the views of Heraclitus and Plato found a welcome home in the far older eastern intellectual traditions, in which the synthesis between body, spirit and the external world has been the animating ethos of most major faiths. 'So Plato is not the first to tell us about it,' says former President of India S. Rhadhakrishnan (1978: 16). 'We have had some ideas about this matter.'

What we know, and how we come to know, are creative processes. Existing knowledge has the potential to change into new knowledge; the process of change is both generative and transformational. Every time we strive towards a new understanding, we create knowledge anew (Polanyi, 1958); every time we engage in understanding and learning, we make a leap of faith into the unknown. We simply do not know what the next moment will bring. Old-paradigm ways of knowing assume a comfortable stable state in which new knowledge will slot into place within a predictable future; new-paradigm ways of knowing accept that the future is unknowable, and the knowledge we create now is actually influencing the future.

A process view of knowledge is increasingly evident in organisation studies. To take a few examples, William Bergquist (1998) describes the difference between old- and new-paradigm views as 'pendulum and fire'; the stable state metaphor of the pendulum shows how organisations self-correct to tried and trusted processes rather than grasp the risk of change, while the fire metaphor 'demands a focus not on the outcomes of a process but rather on the nature of the process itself' (Bergquist, 1998: 20–1). Margaret Wheatley (1992) shows how the new sciences provide more adequate metaphors for social and organisational processes, emphasising the interplay between the internal spiritual world and the external material world, and the primacy of relationships in organisational work. Robert Chia (1997) draws on the history and philosophy of science to show the embedded and often conflicting assumptions underpinning different interpretations of management learning. This emergent body of literature offers new exciting metaphors which challenge the potential ossification of human enquiry in which science itself becomes unchallengeable; and it encourages a view of science, long held by eminent scientists and philosophers of science (such as Feynman, 1992; Medawar, 1996; Stannard, 1996), as full of wonder, awe and delightful surprise.

2 How is organisational knowledge acquired?

In this section I want to show how issues of learning, teaching and education are interlinked, and their importance for organisational learning.

The acquisition of knowledge implies learning. Different theoretical perspectives produce different interpretations (theories) of how knowledge is learnt and put to use. Propositional forms focus on the learning of facts and information; procedural forms focus on learning how to do things; practical forms focus on generating personal knowledge. If we are to take the idea of 'the learning organisation' seriously, we need first to get to grips with how learning is theorised, and explain what kind of learning we hope to encourage within organisations and what its purpose might be.

Issues of learning ...

There are many theories of learning. All start from the premise that learning is part of individual subjective experience, and goes on in the individual mind-brain. Some theorists say that what goes on in the individual mind-brain can be enhanced through social interaction. Vygotsky (1978), for example, has been influential in suggesting that learning is socially constructed. Learning is a constant process of transforming existing knowledge into new knowledge through personal-social interaction. Children and adults learn from one another: constructivist classrooms (Brooks and Brooks, 1993) and constructivist workplaces (Hodgson, 1997) are sites for socially constructed learning. The fact remains, however, that what is learnt and how it is learnt are matters of individual interpretations of experience.

The idea of varieties of learning experience permeates the literature, with an impressive pedigree in the philosophy, psychology, sociology and history of education, yet it is consistently ignored in the design of programmes of management learning. MBA courses assume that learning is all of a type (Cunningham and Dawes, 1997), that learners are a homogeneous group who all learn in the same way, with an emphasis on logical-linguistic capacity. There is also a naive assumption that everything to be learnt can be taught, a faith in propositional knowledge and its 'delivery' via transactional methodologies which ignores the affective nature of experience and the emotional side of learning (Fineman, 1999). This is highly restrictive for potential management learning.

Consider, for example, some of these influential ideas about varieties of learning experience (there are many others).

Gregory Bateson (1972, 1979) suggests that different forms of learning should be understood as developmental processes. His daughter, Mary Catherine Bateson (1994) explains how learning is often acquired peripherally, without conscious attention.

David Kolb (1984) demonstrates that individuals have preferred learning styles. He adapts Dewey's ideas (1916) that we learn when we reflect on experience. Kolb's action–reflection learning cycle was a precursor to much of the action research literature.

Chris Argyris (1999; Argyris and Schön, 1974) proposes the existence of single-loop and double-loop learning. Single-loop learning focuses on a particular content or subject matter which engages the cognitive capacities. Double-loop learning involves reflecting on the learning process, and is a self-reflective practice that engages meta-cognitive capacities. Learning contexts usually involve both single and double-loop learning, but dominant forms of management education organise curricula mainly in terms of single-loop learning and deny learners valuable opportunities for expanding their mental range and taking responsibility for their own learning (see Ellis and Kiely, Chapter 11).

Donald Schön (1983, 1995) writes of the high ground, where theorists develop abstract theories in sanitised conditions, and the swampy lowlands, where people negotiate the everyday muddle of life, working things out for themselves and developing their own practical theories of work. It is important, says Schön, that we get our feet wet and embody the theory in our practice as much as locate it in the head.

Multiple intelligences as individual ways of knowing

The theory of multiple intelligences shows the need for awareness of differentiated ways of learning. Gardner (1983) challenges conventional ideas that there is a single 'intelligence'; or indeed that there is a 'thing' called intelligence. Instead, he suggests, we should think more in terms of intelligences, multiple ways of making sense of the world. In 1983 Gardner identified at least seven intelligences: logical, numerical, visual-spatial, musical, bodily-kinaesthetic, interpersonal and intrapersonal. In later work he expanded the list to include spiritual intelligence. Goleman has extended the theory to include emotional intelligence (Goleman, 1996). These ideas have had impact in education and community development (for example, the Project Zero at Harvard University: see Chen *et al.*, 1998; Veenema *et al.*, 1997), and are now making their way into business and management. Handy (1990, 1997) draws directly on Gardner's original hypotheses, and Postle (1989) creates four new categories of intelligence – emotional intelligence, intuitive intelligence, physical intelligence, intellectual intelligence. Whitaker (1997) also introduces the idea of managerial intelligence, which he says 'is an intelligence needed to work with and through other people' (p. 16). He suggests a classification of managerial abilities as creating, planning, organising, communicating, explaining, motivating, evaluating.

Whichever way matrices and models are drawn up, the theme remains that people think and come to know in a multiplicity of different ways. Gardner's original reconceptualisation of the idea of intelligence emphasises the epistemological basis of practice: when we come to know, and use our knowledge, each one of us is developing a personal epistemology of practice. Our lives are not simply a series of activities, but practice founded in a personal knowledge base. Hayek puts it well:

> The growth of knowledge and the growth of civilization are the same only if we interpret knowledge to include all the human adaptations to environment in which past experience has been incorporated. Not all knowledge in this sense is part of our intellect, nor is our intellect the whole of our knowledge. Our habits and skills, our emotional attitudes, our tools, and our institutions – all are in this sense adaptations to past experience which have grown up by selective elimination of less suitable conduct. They are as much an indispensable foundation of successful action as is our conscious knowledge.
>
> (Hayek, 1960: 26, cited in Sowell, 1987: 41).

Feelings and emotions

Nord and Fox (1999) are concerned that the individual is ignored in organisation studies, and Fineman (1999) and Gagliardi (1999) lament that the affective, the aesthetic and the spiritual elements of human living simply are not entertained as serious issues. Very little attention is paid in organisation studies to how the individual feels, either in workplaces or on professional development courses. Yet feelings and emotions are absolutely central to learning processes (Heron, 1992).

Take, for example, the need for motivation in workplaces. Abundant research evidence exists to show that favourable conditions foster optimal learning. An excellent example is *How Children Fail* (Holt, 1982); the lessons from childhood travel well to adult life. Holt says that children often learn to be 'stupid' in school as a result of boredom or resistance. Children occupied in mundane repetitive tasks are not motivated to be creative, imaginative or enthusiastic. The same principle applies to all organisational contexts, particularly workplaces. Hassard (1999) talks about how workers fill their time purposefully to alleviate the worst symptoms of boredom and alienation. Learning is still going on, but what is learnt is at issue.

These are selected examples from a vast literature on experiential, affective, personal-social, emotional and kinaesthetic forms of learning. There is a significant literature to suggest that cognitive learning should always be placed within experiential and affective learning. Given this volume of research, it is difficult to understand why the dominant literature of management education remains propositional, deliberately ignoring affective elements, adopting transactional forms of teaching, and insisting on the primacy of abstract conceptual knowledge. Cunningham and Dawes (1997: 119) comment on the irony that management qualifications indicate knowledge about management, but do not mean that the person is able to manage; in the same way that Whitehead (1998) remarks how it is possible to gain a Masters or Doctoral degree in education without showing that one has influenced the quality of education for anybody anywhere.

Pathology or coercion aside, we can never stop learning; it is part of the process of growth. The issue becomes what is learnt, how effectively it is learnt, why it is learnt, and the purposes to which learning is put. These then become issues to do with the nature and purposes of teaching.

... and teaching ...

Managing is seldom seen as teaching, though teaching is increasingly seen as managing, particularly in the current economic and political climate that regards education as a for-profit business. The practices of management and teaching occupy similar social and institutional spaces, espouse similar values, and have the same purposes of encouraging people to learn how to acquire, refine and modify knowledge for social benefit (that is, provided management is conceptualised as a social practice and not as a technique to be applied).

Teaching presupposes the existence of a learner apart from the teacher, and is always undertaken in contexts of learning. Teaching is always understood as teaching for learning; it does not stand by itself. The quality of learning in a teaching-for-learning relationship is influenced by the quality of teaching. It is the responsibility of teachers to teach for learning, not for their own self-interest, and to serve the best interests of the learners in their care (see Conversation 1.1).

One sometimes hears comments such as 'I've taught it; if they haven't learnt it that's their problem.' Not so; it is the teacher's problem. Similarly, it is the manager's problem if people in workplaces do not know what they are supposed to know or do, or how they can acquire new knowledge.

Conversation 1.1

Sharon Jamieson

Although I work as a senior manager in the University, I come to work every day as an educator. 'Manager' is almost a foreign term to me. Sometimes I and the people I work with need to reinvent ourselves as a team, and that means people accepting the responsibility of making decisions about their own lives and work. You don't seek permission, if it makes sense to you; you take action and if you make a mistake we'll talk about it later and learn from it. If you are accountable you have to have the courage to make decisions, because that is where people learn. I don't learn if everything is going perfectly for me, or if I don't know that things aren't going well. I learn when there is a dilemma. It's my job to help people come to those kinds of realisations.

Curriculum

A core debate in the education literature is around how teaching/managing methodologies reflect curriculum content, and by implication curriculum *intent* in that curriculum content is supposed to reflect the needs of learners rather than the needs of those who design the curricula. The debate is equally applicable in contexts of management learning, and how that then influences the quality of organisational learning.

A curriculum, it is supposed, represents and caters for the needs of learners. Stenhouse (1975) proposed that curricula can be organised in terms of an objectives model, which sees curriculum as a 'thing', possibly a timetable; or a process model, which sees curriculum as a relational process between people; or a combination of both. Elliott (1998) developed these ideas. He suggests that an objectives model is rooted in a commitment to socially engineered change and serves the interests of policy-makers; while a process model aims to foster personal autonomy and serves the interests of participants. An objectives model encourages didactic methodologies which aim for closure and avoid problematising issues; a process model encourages participative methodologies which resist closure and encourage the questioning of the assumptions underlying accepted practices.

These different commitments have a long genealogy across a wide variety of disciplines, one of which is political science, in which questions are raised about the forms and purposes of education. For example, Carr and Hartnett (1996) show how, in the struggle for educational ideas, different versions of democracy are trotted out to justify a particular practice. An elitist version suggests that 'ordinary' people are incapable of speaking for themselves, and elect others to speak on their behalf; another version says that all people are able to speak directly for themselves (but are often prevented from doing so) (Held, 1987). Curricula that operate from the first version assume that more powerful voices may speak on behalf of the less powerful, and are organised in the interests of the more powerful; curricula that operate from the second version assume that all are able to speak for themselves, and are organised to meet the individual needs of all participants. How a curriculum is organised represents the interests of the group felt to stand most to benefit. These are ethico-political issues, and, because organisational curricula are usually drawn up by curriculum designers rather than negotiated by participants, political issues tend to be foregrounded at the expense of educational ones.

How curriculum is theorised, and how constructed, influences whether it can be seen as a realisation of particular values. Elliott (1998) says that curriculum should be regarded as something we do in company with others, a teaching-for-learning process. It is, he says, a creative conversation in which people address issues of personal-social living, and how knowledge in all its forms can help them to live together successfully.

Radical methodologies

Some contemporary work focuses on which kind of teaching methodologies encourage learners to reframe questions in a way that will make what is learnt meaningful and relevant to their own experience. This work focuses on radical or critical pedagogies (Apple, 1993; McLaren, 1995), and in adult education the development of critical thinking (Brookfield, 1987; Mezirow, 1991). Some researchers (for example, Hutchinson, 1996) show the potential impact of these methodologies for social renewal and less violent futures (see also Chapter 7).

While the rhetoric around these issues can be very impressive, there are significant dilemmas in their implementation in organisational contexts. Teaching for critical understanding raises issues of democracy, social justice, entitlement and rational thinking (Giroux and Shannon, 1997). Radical management practices do the same (Garrick, 1998). Practitioners are urged to find ways to help others to challenge givens, and to find better ways of doing things. Difficulties tend to arise, however, when they do. The rhetoric of school-based teaching encourages students to exercise their right to rational thinking. When students do this and, for example, take Friday afternoons off, they are quickly brought to book. In schools we teach children to question, but we do not expect them to question us, their teachers. Similarly, managers might teach employees to exercise their critical thinking within and on behalf of the organisation but not against the organisation, and particularly not against themselves. It takes real courage on the part of teachers and managers to invite critique of their own practice. This is however an ideological assumption and practical requirement of action research, and is what it takes to enable organisations to realise their potential as forces for social renewal.

... and education

Dewey (1916) says that life is a process of continuing growth, and education is to do with growing. Education is not something that goes on only in formal class-rooms; it happens everywhere, in bus queues, garden centres and homes. The nature of the relationship between people determines whether or not the encounter might be termed educative, in the sense that it could lead to further education and growth for the participants. Nor is education only for polite society: 'A clique, a club, a gang, a Fagin's household of thieves, the prisoners in a jail, provide educative environments for those who enter into their collectives or conjoint activities, as truly as a church, a labour union, a business partnership, or a political party' (Dewey, 1916: 21). The potential for education is everywhere. Education, says Dewey, has not a functional purpose. It is not to get a job, or create a particular kind of person; education 'has no end beyond itself' (p. 53), no end other than more education. A relationship has no end beyond itself other than the ongoing relationship.

Conversation 1.2

Stephen O'Connor

We are in this business to help individuals. We sometimes hear the debate about whether prison education is supposed to be a means of rehabilitation. To assume that means that people were habilitated in the first place. Many of our people never felt part of society, so what we try to do is make connections with them. To talk about rehabilitation is far beyond us. I can only think in terms of helping the individual. What goes on beyond that is largely out of my control, and is not part of my area of expertise anyway, and there are so many other influences at work. We can't do anything about that. While we are quite flexible and broad we are not so broad as to think that we are character solvers or welfare people. We are educators. We learn as much from our students as they do from us. I suppose we can give them certain life skills to enable them to make their lives better, and they can choose or not whether to use them, but if we set out with an aim of making a better society, we are almost saying that we know what is better for other people in their situations. We can't do that. All we can say is, 'We will help you identify what you think is good for yourself, and we'll show you what our perspective is on this, and we'll engage in a dialogue about it. After that it's up to you.' Nothing is compulsory. It's always an open ended transaction between equals.

Education is a concept like love – its meaning lies in the relationship between people. When John loves Mary, John acts in a way that is towards Mary's good. John's actions are Mary-directed; Mary is the beneficiary (although John is probably also a beneficiary because caring for Mary probably makes John feel good as well). John takes care that everything he does is best practice, so he concentrates first on checking that he is acting in a way that is going to be in Mary's best interest; he monitors and reflects on his own practice so that it is as he feels is best for Mary. His enquiry is at one and the same time self-centred and other-centred. Mary is doing the same. She is also checking to see that she is acting for John's benefit. Love, like many other personal and interpersonal practices, is a mutually caring practice enacted reciprocally.

The same is so of education. Education is not a 'thing'. It is a relational process. The issue is what happens between people to enable them to engage with creativity and commitment in their own learning.

The things people do in relationships are a surface manifestation of the deep-level values they hold. Much of what informs practices is tacit. In order to understand how we might improve our actions we need to tap our deep tacit knowledge and raise it to explicit levels of awareness (see Figure 1.1). We need to become aware of our educational values and potentials in order to develop educative relationships. We need to be aware of the nature of our transformative practices as we aim to turn our values into practice. What we do in the process, moving from the tacit to the explicit, is the practice that matters.

Figure 1.1

3 How is organisational knowledge put to use?

How, then, are theories of learning, teaching and education lived out in organisations? Where do they appear in organisation theory?

Learning through action

I have heard that, before they can get their taxi cab licence, London taxi drivers have to acquire and demonstrate 'the knowledge'. This is an in-depth knowledge of the streets of London, the best routes to get to destinations, and current road situations. This factual knowledge is acquired not only by studying maps, but also by driving around London, developing mind-maps and bodily-kinaesthetic awareness of locations. Being a good taxi driver also involves dealing with people, anticipating their needs, and getting them to where they want to be.

On these principles there are few differences between being a taxi driver and being any other kind of practitioner. 'The knowledge', the practice, is a synthesis of different kinds of knowledge and different ways of knowing. No one kind is free-standing or more important; they are interdependent and complementary. Together they provide personal theories of practice.

There is a dilemma here. The embodied knowledge of taxi drivers would probably not be recognised by universities as valid knowledge. Taxi drivers would not get credits towards an MBA for getting an examiner to the station on time. The university expects excellence in abstract knowledge, not practical capacity. However, the reality of practice is the reverse: workplaces depend on practical capacity more than abstract knowledge (Fox, 1997). How to resolve the dilemma? At present, practitioners are expected to conform to university expectations. It is high time that the university accommodated practitioners' needs more. This point is developed further in Chapter 7.

Personal theories of organisation

Dominant forms of management theory are propositional (Cunningham and Dawes, 1997). This kind of theory gives pointers towards good practice, but does not help anyone to theorise their work in a practical way. Abstract theories do not often help managers find ways to improve their practice. Personal practical theories do. Through developing their own personal practical theories of how they, like taxi drivers, can find their way through organisational territory, develop mind-maps and a sense of what is the right thing to do in any particular situation, and help people to get to where they want to be, managers develop personal theories for organisational growth.

Dominant propositional theories regard organisation as an object 'out there'. Organisations are not real; they are virtual. This view does not respect the experience of real people in organisations, nor their values. Understanding organisation is understanding people; theories of organisation are theories of people. Researchers are people, not Martians, so when we speak about people we are speaking about ourselves. This is important for action research. As well as a moral commitment arising out of the values of sharing our humanity, it is also a methodological necessity. Trying to understand people from an outsider perspective is not helpful in trying to understand how we can work together to improve organisations. It takes energy, though, and the commitment to care, for practitioner researchers to see themselves as participants rather than external observers. Staying outside the situation does not lead to theories of human enquiry, only theories about it.

Implications for management learning

Managers are consistently persuaded to believe that to understand what is happening in organisations and make appropriate decisions they need to consult case history or invite an external expert to identify problems and propose solutions. The answer is assumed to lie 'out there'. This faith in technical rationality has led to a series of innovations over recent times which supposedly solve organisational issues – downsizing, outsourcing, re-engineering, excellence, total quality management. Crainer (1996: xv–xvi) suggests that these are fads which give status (and income) to their creators, but do little to help managers get to the heart of their matters. Corporate faith in external expert knowledge often leads to the adoption of elaborate defensive routines that Argyris (1990) says managers sometimes construct to shield themselves from the uncomfortable reality that they and others need to identify their own problems and work out for themselves how to solve them.

The dominant knowledge base of management translates into training and development, the delivery of specific knowledge and skills. While there is a good deal of rhetoric about individual and organisational learning, expectations are still fixed on information transmission models. This applies to all participants. Knowledge remains abstract and packaged; it is transmitted hierarchically. The expectation remains that managers will deliver knowledge and foster skills. 'As soon as the need for learning is identified, programmes, workshops and seminars are designed to deliver a message considered most appropriate from the corporate culture or management perspective' (Ryan, 1999: 10). This has little to do with individual and organisational learning, and everything to do with reinforcing the idea of managers as those-who-know. The responsibility of managers on this view is to keep up to date with important current information, to have well refined presentation skills, and above all to convey the image of an expert who has answers. As well as creating a dependency culture, this view can be threatening to managers, and can lead to intense feelings of inadequacy and failure if they actually don't know the answers but need to look as if they do (see Conversation 1.3).

Conversation 1.3

Ashley Balbirnie

I was first put in as MD at the age of twenty-three or four and I have been running companies ever since. Now, over sixteen years later, I still think it is great on the job experience, and you get much better at dealing with people. But it never totally resolves that question of where you can learn better or where you turn to learn or express doubts or anxieties. When you are put into running a company, especially at an early age but I suppose at any age, the last thing you want to do is appear that you are unsure about what you are doing, about what decision you ought to make. Then it can go the other way. You want to present the image that you are in control and you know what you are doing, so yes, promote me to the next job. That doesn't resolve anything. All you are doing is camouflaging things and covering over the cracks.

I would with no statistical research bet solid money that if you could get true answers, the majority of managers would feel that they are over-promoted and they are going to get caught out. A chunk of their consequent behaviour is ensuring that they don't get caught out, and that quite often shows in their treatment of the people who are working for them and their consequent inability to get the best out of those people. It all goes back to what I was talking about before, the lack of security, the lack of confidence, the fear of being caught out because they don't really believe they deserve to be where they are.

Management implies learning. Organisations, like all realities, are always changing. They are subject to external social and cultural influences, and also to internal changes, as the members within the organisation learn and grow from everyday experience. Everything is in a constant state of flux. Managing this process means learning how to respond and adapt creatively. Managers need to be open to this process and not to be defensive; being open about learning in practice is essential for organisational development. Learning to manage personal development comes before supporting other people's development. It can however initially seem threatening, because it means accepting the inevitability of making mistakes and appearing vulnerable. A new management culture needs to develop, which moves from a model of instruction to a model of learning. This view is often resisted, given also the volatile and transitory nature of work; many people still want stable conditions and fixed answers. The stability, however, is one's own confidence and ability to learn how to deal with change. Management is always about learning to change oneself, how to change practice to adapt to, or influence the direction of, other external changes.

The idea of being a better manager in ten easy steps is a myth. Being a better manager is not an objective you achieve; it is a process you engage in. To be a better manager, you have to find ways of improving what you do; this is some-thing you learn for yourself, often in company with others, not something you are taught. All too often we look outside for our answers; we learn to be helpless. 'Instant management' books are appealing with their quick-fix answers and seductive reassurances. Managing change means we have to do our own learning. This also means accepting that practice might need improving and we might make mistakes, which is difficult, because dominant management cultures generally forbid managerial vulnerability. So managers not only have to accept the risk of exposing their humanity to others; they also have to battle against the flood of prejudice that refuses to acknowledge the humanity of managers in the first place.

As long as propositional knowledge remains the dominant knowledge base of management theory, the knowledge base will perpetuate itself by requiring managers to fit their practice into normative expectations. This does not help to prioritise personal-social development in organisations.

4 What are the implications for the development of learning organisations?

The following issues arise.

The need for new kinds of theory

Organisation study needs to develop new kinds of theory to inform organisational practices. By organisations I do not mean only businesses; I mean contexts in which people come together for a variety of reasons to achieve commonly agreed goals. When people come together purposefully they can generate significant collective power for personal-social renewal. This view needs to be embedded in organisation study. While there are signs that organisation study is shifting focus, both in terms of what is studied and how it is studied (see the Introduction in Clegg and Hardy, 1999), the subject matter of organisation studies still remains the organisation itself as an object, rather than people within organisational contexts.

The dominant view of studying organisation as an object is sustained by the kind of theory used. The dominant form of theory is propositional. Organisation appears as an abstract thing, no flesh and blood people, although there are functionaries called managers and workers. The thing is a unified entity 'out there', and can be analysed in terms of formal structures and processes. Management also appears as a 'thing', a coherent practice; its relationship with the rest of the organisation is frequently presented as unambiguous. The outcome is propositions *about* organisation. This approach assumes that reality and experience may be analysed in terms of fixed categories, and these categories are universally applicable and comprehensible, and timeless, beyond change. It also assumes that there is a common discourse to describe reality and experience, and the discourse is fixed, like the realities and experiences it describes.

The virtual reality of abstract theory is often far removed from people's own experienced realities. Reality for many people is incoherent, disjointed, constantly shifting; it is often not possible to make sense of experience in a coherent way. How is it possible to make sense of joy and pain in abstract terms? Joy and pain are matters of personal subjective experience. We might relate to one another, but we can never directly experience the joy and pain of another person, nor they ours. Research that tries to explain real-life experience in terms of fixed categories often distorts the reality it is trying to represent. For example, the widely accepted work on *The Seasons of a Man's Life* (Levinson *et al.*, 1978) took as its research population a small number of men in a special context. This sample was then taken as the definitive working model for the whole of humanity. It is often a case of forcing a story into a particular framework, regardless of fit or appropriateness, a question of square pegs and round holes.

In the creation of propositional theory, the researcher stands outside the situation and describes it from their own point of view, much as an artist would paint a picture according to their own perception of reality. There is speculation about whether L. S. Lowry painted elongated figures because he suffered from a vision idiosyncrasy that made him perceive figures in an elongated way. How we construe reality is influenced by how we perceive reality. Descriptive picture theories are one person's view of reality, which may or may not be held by the people who are being described. It is unlikely that the figures who appeared in Lowry's paintings perceived themselves in as elongated a form as Lowry depicted them. However, in that situation, Lowry was in charge; he was the painter. His version of reality was his truth.

This is what most researchers do; it is what I am doing here. We write about phenomena from a personal perspective and claim that as our truth. We might be mistaken. Things might not be as we think they are. We always need to remember that our own thinking is a practice conditioned by our own culturally and historically situated process. All of us are in a constant state of transformation, so what we think and how we think are also always changing. Many people forget this, and sometimes are not even aware of it.

The need for generative transformational theories

Propositional forms of theory are inadequate for understanding organisation as a living developmental process. Propositional theories are fit for the job if we conceptualise organisation as a fixed abstract concept, and if we believe that it is sufficient to observe and analyse activities and make proposals about how these might be made more effective or efficient. The narrow technicist focus of the theory parallels what is perceived as a narrow technicist practice, and one reinforces the other. If practice is regarded as technique, propositional theories are adequate.

While the word 'organisation' might be an agreed linguistic item, the nature of experience of organisation cannot be linguistically defined: the 'meaning' of organisation can be understood only in terms of how real people make sense of their experience in organisations. For this we need a more robust kind of theory. Building on previous work (McNiff, 1995, 1996), I continue to make the case for generative transformational theories which explain the generative transformational processes of real life. Organisation practices are always changing. Organisation theory needs to develop a form that embodies change. Knowers and their knowledge are changing phenomena in a changing world; people change their practice as they try to develop their lives. This means studying their own changing work, and telling the stories of their own learning processes as they tried to make a difference for good.

Self-study is now an established form of practical theorising in teacher professional education (see, for example, Hamilton, 1998; Loughran, 1996). The approach is already evident in management and organisation study (Marshall, 1995; Ryan, 1999); it needs now to be firmly embedded. Managers and the people they support need to produce their own theories of practice, and collectively compile bodies of case study evidence that in turn constitutes a legitimate managerial and organisational literature (see Conversation 1.4)

Conversation 1.4

Sharon Jamieson

The point about action research is the common pursuit of adding to knowledge and knowing that in the sense of our understanding or humanity, in our way of being in our work, we are constantly growing in everything. If we are to approach our work that way, or our life in that way, there is in a sense a framework that has to be developed to add to that store of knowledge. It can't be in an objective sense of 'That works for that.' There needs to be a larger understanding. An action research approach helps me to define myself in a narrative way, to be aware of my own motives and understandings.

The responsibility of managers

These views imply that our personal-social practices are inherently temporary and transitional. Nothing is static; everything is in a constant state of coming into being. Managing change is not primarily about managing change for other people. It is about learning for ourselves how to do things differently.

The word 'change' in English exists in transitive and intransitive form: I change something, and I also change. Change can certainly be an external force. I can hit someone on the head, and probably change the shape of the head. This kind of approach however (explained in Chapter 3 as behavioural approaches to power) is not educational and is unlikely to engender long-term personal and social renewal. Oonagh O'Brien (see Conversation 1.5) talks about social change as 'one heart at a time'. The kind of change that leads to sustainable personal and social renewal is a property of an organic system itself: the system changes from within, and moves in the direction of its potential to be life-giving and creative. Managers need to encourage and support this developmental process, in themselves and in others. The focus of management research is for managers to develop their own learning about how best to support others in doing the same. Management on this view becomes praxis, morally committed action in the service of others.

Conversation 1.5

Oonagh O'Brien

My work is to do with generating community, and in a sense you can't talk about community without talking about leadership. I think the issue is to understand the nature of leadership. In the context of my present work in the Church, many ordained clergy would say that they were trained as 'lone rangers'. Seriously. I get the sense that their training told them that leaders didn't need people, didn't need support systems and that they were given by ordination some special gift of service to the community but not an expectation of personal support from that community. We talk about mission and mission statements, but I think mission has got very confused with service. In organisations that can often happen. In terms of capturing one heart at a time, it is very easy to get drawn into the language of structures, and these would be well established hierarchical structures in the Church, so it requires effort to be collaborative. In terms of how to influence change, it's down to the values people hold, both of themselves and of other people, and about relationship. In my work, it's not about saying 'Look, this is what the Church says.' It won't have any influence on you unless it can tap in in some way to your values. It is at a spiritual level, that you actually believe that it's a better thing to do. Within a community people are taking equal responsibility for their own action and for the group action, so it's about having information, making sure that you have information, it's about reflecting on issues rather than taking the word of one person. As a leader it's my job to ensure that people know what they need to know in order to make informed choices.

The potential of action research for management learning

Action research is now well established on professional development initiatives. Professionals are assumed to be the best judges of their own practice. If they wish this view to be taken seriously, they need to produce research-based evidence to show how and why their professional judgements may be respected. The kind of evidence they produce is embedded within the accounts they offer to show how and why they feel they have improved the quality of personal and social experience for others.

Action research means that practitioners systematically reflect on and evaluate what they are doing. They identify any elements they think need attention, and try to change them for the better. Improvement is an aim of action research. 'Improvement' does not necessarily imply that something is deficient; it does imply a process of constant up-grading. The first step for practitioners is to improve their understanding of their work, and then use this understanding to improve social situations. The answers are not 'out there'; they are in ourselves, but accepting this requires honesty, energy and commitment. Action research regards practice as a creative, adaptive process of responding in a thoughtful way to personal-social situations. The focus of the research is the practitioner, the 'living "I"' (Whitehead, 1993), who continually asks, 'How do I improve my work in order to help you to learn?' (Whitehead, 1989; Russell and Korthagen, 1995).

Action research should generate a dialogue of equals, in which all parties hold themselves accountable for their practice. Teachers, managers and external researchers should not invite others to investigate their practice without being prepared to do so themselves. We should aim to live our espoused values in our practice, and not give out contradictory messages.

All organisations potentially provide informal and/or formal contexts for learning. The nature of the learning, what is learnt and how it is learnt, remain contested territory. Organisations should take on the responsibility for the ongoing education of their members, by helping participants to learn how to learn, to work towards autonomy, and to challenge structures and processes that aim to close down opportunities for learning and growth. This has implications for the allocation of resources and corporate commitment to support the professional development of managers, to help them take on a special responsibility as champions of education. To fulfil this potential, and to act as agents of sustainable change in their organisations and the wider social environment, managers need support to develop confidence in the appropriate knowledge base that will enable them to live in this direction.

Learning about learning

Jimmy Ryan

I am a course participant on the MA in Education course. Our group is based in Thurles, in the midlands of Ireland. The course has provided me with an opportunity to re-assess my own understanding of learning, and has enabled me to get to grips with ideas to do with education and how learning is encouraged in organisations.

Background

This contribution is an account of my own professional learning as a management consultant in relation to my developing understanding of the nature of intelligence and personal learning styles and their implications for workplace learning. As part of the MA course, we studied a module entitled 'Teaching for Learning'. For this module, Jean, our tutor, asked us to undertake our personal research into a chosen area around issues of intelligence and styles of learning, and then to present our findings to the rest of the group. When we made our presentations, Jean became part of the audience, whose task it was to provide critical feedback to the presenter, in a supportive way, both to validate the findings and also to provide further ideas to develop the work. How we presented the research was for us to decide. I had chosen to study the theories of multiple intelligences, preferred learning styles and accelerated learning, believing that my increased understanding of these areas would enrich my own management practice in the workplace. I chose to present my ideas using an interactive style where I invited the audience to participate in the presentation by responding to how my ideas might impact on their own learning and whether they saw potential implications for the learning of others.

Before I undertook my research I felt that my first task was to try to understand my own current thinking about how people learn. This, I quickly realised, involved thinking first about how I learned.

My earlier thinking

Learning has always been a passion for me. I have been in various education environments since the age of four – national school, secondary school, various third level institutions, management schools. None, I now realised as I reflected, had helped me to become aware of the issue of how I learn or whether I could learn more effectively.

I reflected that perhaps one of the most important influences on my attitude to learning was my first job as an apprentice with the Electricity Supply Board, a public utility company. The environment there was one where tradesmen, proud of their craft, were committed to the point of being passionate about how well we 'learned our trades'. Management was equally determined that we should learn the underlying theories during our sandwich courses in the local Institute of Technology.

Success in both areas was valued by the organisation, by providing opportunities for advancement within the organisation as a skilled tradesperson or, for those more academically inclined, to become technicians or engineers. Either way, learning was valued, and this was an exciting place for a young person who was eager to exercise his learning potential. This experience also helped me develop an enquiring attitude to work. I have never viewed a job as an end in itself but rather as a learning or development opportunity. One of the family jokes is, 'Don't worry; Dad still hasn't decided what he wants to be when he grows up.'

Possibly the most significant impact of this compulsion for learning has been on my evolving management style and philosophy. The key aspect of my concept of a manager's work is to understand the knowledge and skills necessary for the success both of the organisation and its members, and then to create the environment necessary to encourage learning to happen. This influences my present work as business consultant. I am conscious of my own responsibility to help managers understand the importance of being open to learning themselves, and being prepared publicly to acknowledge their own personal growth and development as a means of encouraging a learning culture in their organisation.

Prior to my involvement in my MA studies I had not thought too much about how people learn, about the nature of intelligence, or the significance of learning styles for motivation or learning readiness. When I did think about these issues, it would have been very much in the traditional terms of understanding Binet's Intelligence Quotient (IQ) tests as a viable measure of intelligence and consequently of a person's intellectual capacity and potential. I would also have assumed that this is somehow a fixed value for each individual, with the implication that this is a factor over which individuals have little or no control. I would not have considered issues regarding personal learning styles or readiness for learning. I know that I have always had a deep sense of frustration when I could not help individuals to see the power of learning, an issue so obvious to me, yet possibly, I now realise, quite alien to others because it was not appropriate to their own interests or learning readiness.

This looks frightening to me now. I see serious contradictions in my own practice. It is particularly worrying, given that I have spent so much time in the business context in areas of influence as a middle and senior manager developing my own knowledge, understanding and skills in areas such as organisation behaviour, people development, and people empowerment. I have also worked on the premise that if people could be helped to understand themselves and their reasons for learning, and how they respond to given types of stimuli, then they would also understand how and why they behaved in particular ways. I anticipated that the outcomes of these improved understandings in organisational terms would be a better and more effective working environment and that people would have the opportunity to grow and participate more fully in the workplace.

My concerns now led to some serious reflection. In retrospect I believe that my thinking could be seen as informed by traditional empirical management philosophies and behaviourist organisation epistemologies. This is not surprising when I consider that in common with most of my generation of managers, my understanding and thinking in relation to people has moved through a variety of traditions: from the motivational categories proposed by Maslow (1954), Alderfer (1972), Hertzberg (1966), McClelland (1961) and McClelland and Burnham (1976); through the concepts of the 'psychological contract' as explained by Argyris (1960) and Levinson (1962), and further developed by Kotter (1973) and Wrightman (1964, 1974, 1977); and, in more recent times, by Peter Senge's work (1990).

However, the dilemma remained for me. In spite of my commitment to learning, I still had not engaged with the ideas of what learning means, nor how it manifests in my own or other people's professional lives. The idea of individual learning has featured very little in the formative literature of my own practice, and I wonder whether it features significantly in the wider literature of organisation studies. Certainly theories of individual learning are not evident in organisation theory, or how theory influences organisational practices; even in organisations that aspire to perceive themselves as learning environments or learning organisations, it has been my experience that theories about people and their learning reflect managerial commitment to traditional theories of organisational behaviour which are strongly behaviourist in orientation. Seldom if ever is there practical evidence of commitment to individual epistemologies of learning.

Some reflections on my understanding of the nature of work

With my usual passion for learning, this time in relation to my proposed presentation, I got to grips with the ideas of multiple intelligences (Gardner, 1983), learning modalities (de Porter, 1993), and accelerated learning (Smith, 1996). This learning led to some profound and unanticipated insights.

When I reflected on my current practice I came to appreciate that while I and other colleagues who work in progressive companies that espouse the philosophies of the learning organisation recognised the need for learning throughout the organisation, we still aimed to train and develop people using the old tried and trusted delivery methodologies. We still aimed to train groups.

It is a chastening thought that many of what we consider our greatest successes as managers may have come about more by luck than good management. I am led to think that perhaps the more progressive companies in which managers and supervisors develop individual relationships with employees through support structures such as appraisal systems are more successful in moving away from an ethos of training and developing cultures of learning. Received wisdom had led me and like-minded manager colleagues to believe that if we used state of the art technology when 'training' employees, then all good and loyal employees would quickly and easily absorb what we had to tell them and respond accordingly. Indeed, such has been our faith in our presentation skills and the excellence of our technology that anyone who expressed difficulty in learning was put down simply to being awkward.

My thinking and that of most of my colleagues in the business community would have been directed at identifying the new skills required by employees and then determining the most acceptable or effective means for introducing the skills to the people, in other words, retraining people. In the business world I think 'training' might be synonymous with 'instruction' in the educational world. In both contexts there is an assumption that trainers/teachers will do something to people so that they receive skills. Issues such as job enrichment or redesign seem to be addressed in terms of organisational needs, quite isolated from questions of individual learning potential or readiness.

Managers are not foolish enough not to consider the impact of the individual on the job, but this always seems to be from the perspective of a capability to do work or complete new or more complex tasks. We trawl the organisation database to select those individuals whose IQs indicate that they are capable of achieving designated tasks. During times of reorganisation this can be critical in terms of how we view the potential of our human resources. An implication is that we are not fulfilling the potential of all our people because of our very narrow view of intelligence. This could also be a significant factor in terms of gender issues in the workplace, and whether women are appointed to senior management positions within a male-dominated hierarchical management system. In people terms, at the very least, it is a serious issue of social justice.

These ideas reflect my own view of work which I have long seen in terms of skills, not jobs. On this view, when we talk about redundancies, it is the skills, not the people, that should become redundant. The realities of work are sadly often different. I see an ongoing dynamic: as the nature of work changes there is a need for new learning, and new learning generates work of a different nature. This dynamic characterises the learning organisation. However, we managers seem to have lost sight of what is the most creative and natural way of getting work done, by insisting on turning work into a grouping of tasks that we call jobs and then compounding this by taking the concept of a job and turning it into something sacrosanct and supposedly for life. By aiming to theorise work as fixed categories rather than as a changing phenomenon which demands a flexible response, we risk alienating workers from work which would normally be well within their capacity.

I believe that learning is focused at the level of the individual, which is also very much in keeping with the principles of action research. Perhaps the cumulative effect of individual learning is what makes a learning organisation. We managers must be prepared to value learning as a real business asset and be prepared to invest in it particularly when resources are limited or scarce. Investment in learning must be understood as part of the solution, never a problem.

A personal learning experience

My new insights were thrown into sharp relief by a significant learning episode.

I had undertaken my preparatory research for the module and proceeded to present the work to my peers. As part of my presentation I put up an overhead projector transparency showing a model of Smith's (1996) accelerated learning cycle. I explained to the group that this was a model of an accelerated learning cycle and paused for a while to allow them to look at the model and absorb the content before I went on to describe the seven stages in the model as outlined by Smith.

A colleague in the group suddenly said in some frustration that she wanted me actually to talk to the model as I presented it, rather than stand silent while she tried to work it out for herself. So I talked it through, and she then thanked me and expressed a sense of relief that I had done so. Other colleagues in the group confirmed that they too had experienced similar feelings. I was somewhat taken by surprise by the episode, but even in my rapid effort to alleviate her anxieties, I was aware that I was theorising the episode in terms of my sudden insights about the multiple influences that impact on how people learn, and how important it is for presenters to be aware of the full spectrum of people's learning modalities.

This was an awesome piece of learning for me. My work as a business consultant varies from a formal presentation style in seminars to being a participant in workshops and seminars. My preferred personal style tends to be interactive, where I involve people but also use overheads and flip chart material for explaining models and concepts as they arise, as well as share anecdotes based on personal experience. The reaction of my colleagues during my presentation caused me not only to stop and think in order better to understand their needs in relation to their learning styles, but more importantly I was forced to reflect on why I had acted as I had.

This was an absolute revelation. I realised that my style of presentation changes when I am unsure or uncertain of the material that I am presenting. In moments of insecurity I tend to rely on the overheads, and I depend more on the group understanding of what is presented. I also tend not to say too much for fear of getting myself more deeply into areas I don't fully understand. This complies with the Denis Healey theory of holes: when you are in one, stop digging. I can recall presentations (embarrassingly so) when I have moved from a topic on which I was very comfortable to one on which I was less sure, and back again, and felt that I had 'gotten away' with it quite well; but I could never understand why the responses of participants always changed so much with the change of activity.

I later came to reflect that the episode marked the beginning of a change in professional practice, in which I began to move away from a technical orientation in presentations, to being aware of the individual needs of participants. I also reflected that presenters must also have a preferred learning modality and very likely a preferred style of presentation which may be incongruent with participants' needs. I am working on these issues now as part of my raised awareness to my own professional learning.

Summary

In summary I can say that managers need to be open to their own process of learning as much as the people whose learning they are supporting. There is need for constant reflection on experience, and a sharing of learning to see does it in fact meet people's needs for growth. I would never have achieved such insights unless I had been prepared to try to understand the reasons for my colleagues' frustrations during my presentation; and a rich opportunity would then have been denied for me to reflect on my practice more comprehensively with a view to understanding and improving it. I became aware of the participative nature of learning, as well as the imperative to be sensitive to the needs of others, as they were sensitive to mine.

Business needs to move away from a narrow technicist focus of getting the job done. The major resource for getting the job done is people; and this implies that business managers need to take into consideration the well-being of their people, particularly as it relates to their continuing need for learning. The learning society is made up of learners, not people who need to be trained in skills, but people who need to be encouraged to explore for themselves their own learning styles and potential. The way to improving business effectiveness is by first improving the quality of experiential learning in the workplace.

Reflecting on my learning experience

I have come to understand my learning as a developmental process. It has been encouraged and nurtured by my colleagues on the course. I am aware of how our group is a learning community, and I am also aware of the part each one of us plays in relation to the others. We listen carefully to what each person has to say, we encourage, we critique. We respond in a thoughtful way, treading gently so that we do not damage sensitive egos, but always mindful that we also need to challenge and encourage growth. I have learnt much about my own capacity to support others in the group. I listen and intervene when I feel others are stuck, or someone needs support in developing an idea. I have come to see what I do in our seminars as a form of teaching; we teach and learn from one another.

This is encouraged systematically by Jean, who acts as a catalyst for learning in the group. She has the capacity to recognise individual and collective needs within the group and to range effortlessly across a spectrum of roles that includes, but is by no means limited to, tutor, mentor, facilitator, friend and even counsellor, transcending the diverse personal and work experiences of colleagues. In fact, for me it was her openness and her enthusiasm for engaging with learning environments familiar to some but occasionally outside the experience of others, and enabling us to find areas of mutual interest and learning, that initially sustained me when I joined the programme, and that encouraged me to explore new epistemologies of learning. This I feel has also engendered within what for me, at the beginning of our course, was very much a disparate group of individuals, a sense of camaraderie, self and mutual worth, and individual and collective growth that must be central to a learning community. We have all come a long way together, each in our own way, and helping one another. In turn, I hope that we will continue to help others to learn.

2 Learning organisations as good societies

The issue is still what kind of theory is most appropriate to understand organisation as a context in which people come together on an equal footing to achieve mutually agreed goals.

I have come to understand organisation theory as a form of educational theory. Trying to understand the nature of organisation as people in purposeful relation has led me also to think about the nature of education. If I accept Dewey's ideas that education is not a 'thing' but what happens between people in caring relationships; and if I hold educational values that recognise the specialness of every individual and every moment; then I have to theorise organisation as a site for the nurturing of human potential for good through considerate listening and thoughtful response. I try to live this theory throughout my management work. I do not regard my work as separate from me; my work has its being in my relationships with others.

I have not encountered this kind of explicit, evidence-based link in the literature, and this troubles me, for how is it possible to speak meaningfully about 'a learning organisation' without seriously considering the questions, What happens when an organisation learns? What does it learn? How does it use its learning? What needs to happen for an organisation to become a learning organisation?

Learning does not always imply teaching. We quickly learn not to put a hand on a hot stove a second time; we hum tunes without consciously having learnt them. Learning happens continually, often at an unconscious level. Learning can be deliberately nurtured and accelerated, however, perhaps most obviously through the provision of the right kind of conditions – a sympathetic teacher or an environment of encouraging relationships. To speak about a learning organisation, therefore, an idea which implies the conscious nurturing of individual and collective learning, is deliberately to engage with ideas about education and how the quality of relationships can support or diminish learning experience.

The language of teaching, learning and education is traditionally the language of schools and colleges, not yet the language of organisations, especially when those organisations are for-profit businesses. Business cultures have taken on the rhetoric of 'the learning organisation', but so far teaching and education have not noticeably entered the lexicon. Neither has the practice of organisational learning caught up with its own rhetoric. There is often an assumption that employees should learn, while those positioned as superiors are somehow exempt. The power relationships arising from such asymmetrical practices would militate against any attempt to institutionalise learning for personal-social growth.

The language of the learning organisation needs to develop new terms and concepts, new attitudes which regard managers as teachers and educators, people who encourage relationships to nurture learning. For this to happen, however, new institutional cultures need to develop to demonstrate corporate learning as the basis of good organisational practice. Managers need to regard managing as teaching; for some this will mean new learning. Managers should not only use the rhetoric of the learning organisation, but also position themselves as teachers who are developing their practice within their own organisations, to generate their own theories of management-as-teaching.

1 What is the nature of a learning organisation?

I am learning what kind of learning needs to go on for an organisation to claim status as a learning organisation. Learning clearly goes on all the time. Hassard (1999) presents different theories for how workers learn to kill time and while away the hours (Ditton, 1979; Roy, 1960). Such instances however do not capture the spirit of 'the learning organisation'.

I believe entirely in the idea of the learning organisation. I manage one. When I evaluate my work to check that participants find their experience worth-while, I receive the following kinds of feedback:

> All our meetings are learning occasions. ... I am aware of my own practice, the importance of being an educator as well as manager ... I am more in touch with myself, and am no longer dependent on others' judgements ... I no longer say and do the things that I thought were expected of me.

> I have learnt to make changes to my practice which have benefited my students in my class and myself. They speak of the benefit in their reflective diaries.

> I now realise that I can speak for myself. I can generate my own living theory of knowledge equally as valuable as that composed by experts who write about educational knowledge. Being involved in this action research approach has helped me to realise that there are no absolutes. This has been difficult for me, as I am one who speaks out of certainty.

> (These comments and others in the book are from evaluation documents from course participants in Ireland, 1999.)

A major learning for me has been that the idea of a learning organisation is inextricably linked with the idea of a good society. The same values underpin both. These values are to do with freedom of mind and action, care of others, equality and mutual entitlement; they are informed by ideologies which hold all people as of equal worth, valuable by the fact that they are human. Realising these values in practice is a matter of becoming aware of one's values and finding ways to live them in practice, sometimes in spite of political influences which do not wish this to happen. The realisation of such values constitutes what many would regard as a good society. Being a member of a learning organisation should be life-enhancing and worthwhile. What is learnt among other things is a sense of self in relationship with others, and the potential for continuing growth.

I am not here advancing a theory of organisations as free-for-alls in which people fulfil personal ambitions and their own agendas. Clearly organisations exist for a functional purpose (people can come together for a purpose, such as having a cup of coffee, without constituting an organisation). I am however saying that organisations serve wider purposes than the fulfilment of pragmatic goals. Regardless of the degree of their commitment to organisational goals, people should enjoy their organisational experience as life-enhancing, worthwhile and an opportunity for personal-social growth. Time spent anywhere can amount to experience. Whether people's organisational experience presents opportunities for growth is a corporate responsibility. I am saying that organisations should have as a main purpose the provision of conditions for learning; that managers should have a main purpose of developing their practice as morally committed praxis; and that all participants should have a main purpose of encouraging personal and collective morally committed practices. These are the humanitarian organisational purposes of producing self-aware responsible citizens within which the technical rational purposes of material production are embedded.

I have also learnt not to adopt a romantic view of the nature of social interactions. Organisations are pluralistic societies in which there are multiple agendas; they are sites for struggle in which people can hold seriously conflicting views arising out of opposing values systems, and strive to persuade others to adopt their views. The success of an organisation lies in whether people can learn to coexist peacefully while holding conflicting views, whether they can learn to regard others' needs as equal to their own and work together towards other pragmatic organisational goals. An unsuccessful organisation is one in which such learning does not take place, and struggles for hegemony manifest in relationships of dominance, control and subservience.

This is my theory of organisation. It is somewhat at odds with much of the dominant research, which regards organisations as abstract structures, and regards the study of those structures as a main purpose. I believe that the main purpose of organisation study should be to help people find ways to create life-enhancing practices, taking as a litmus test whether or not the most vulnerable member of the organisation feels it is a good place to be. The mindset I adopt is also quite different from the one adopted by many social scientists for whom it is sufficient to generate only abstract theory. The problem is, if we continue to work only with abstract theory, and generate theories *about* organisation, we will not make progress in understanding how to renew organisations or wider society.

The theories give us pictures of where we are going; they do not give practical guidance how to get there. In this sense, abstract theory acts as a force to prevent the development of good orders, for we stick with the vision and do nothing to turn it into reality. It is enough that the idea is in the head; it is not necessary to find ways of putting it into practice.

I want therefore to consider how abstract theory can be potentially disabling in creating organisations as good societies, and how we might overcome the problem.

The limitations of abstract theory

I have come to these learnings both from my own experience, and also from studying some very interesting contemporary work in discourse theory. Žižek, for example, also regrets that most social scientific theorists produce abstract theory, presenting it as established fact. He calls this an 'ideological fantasy'.

> They [theorists] know very well how things really are, but still they are doing it as if they did not know. The illusion is therefore double: it consists in over-looking the illusion which is structuring our real-effective relationship to reality. And this overlooked, unconscious illusion may be called the *ideological fantasy*.
>
> (Žižek, 1989: 32–3; emphasis in original; in Torfing, 1999: 116)

And Torfing (1999) says that presenting abstract theory as fact is misleading and potentially dangerous, because people are persuaded to believe that what is imagined is what should be, and they become disillusioned and give up when they fail to live up to the theory. In this sense, abstract theories operate as 'totalizing ideological representations' (p. 116).

I touched on this issue in Chapter 1. Human enquiry is often presented as picture theories, pictures of how things should be rather than how things actually are. A problem arises however when we agree with the theory but fail to live it in practice. We find ourselves positioned, in Whitehead's (1989) words, as 'living contradictions' in which we say one thing and do another. For example, a primary school teacher in Cork recounts:

> For my action research project I wanted to communicate to the children the importance of listening, so I conducted informal interviews with them to see what they thought. I found myself telling some children to be quiet because I was trying to listen to what someone else was saying. I suddenly became aware of the amazing contradiction: silencing children in order to establish the importance of listening.

The theory is one thing: putting it into practice is another.

Slippage between theory and practice is everywhere (see Conversations 2.1 and 2.2). No one denies the importance of abstract theories of learning organisations and good societies, or the importance of vision for art and living, but we also need practical action theories. 'We need to know both what sort of society we would like to create and the concrete means of moving towards it' (Giddens, 1998: 2). Theories that do not go beyond the imagination do not tell the whole story. Žižek spells this out in relation to the work of Habermas, part of whose theories hinge on the concept of the ideal speech situation and the conditions needed to achieve intersubjective agreement: 'Habermas's theory of communicative action provides a clear example of the role of ideological fantasy at the level of science: even though Habermas admits that the ideal of an unbroken communication will never be realised, the whole theory presupposes that the ideal speech situation has already been realised [when clearly it hasn't]' (Žižek, 1990: 259, cited in Torfing, 1999: 116). In this sense, abstract theory contains in-built failure, for 'We act as if the totalizing and reductive forms of ideology are true and serious, although we know they are not' (Torfing, 1999: 117). The danger here is that, because we know that the theory exists only as an ideal, we might be led to believe that it is unachievable. Provided we pay lip service to the ideal, we don't need to do anything else.

Conversation 2.1

Liam Nagle

One of the problems with management education as it is currently practised is that it is too theoretical. To be successful in organisations, people have to know what to do at a practical level, and how to do it. You cannot learn this from a book. To some degree it is in your genes, or you learn it from experience, but it involves figuring out what the important thing is and then doing it at speed. Managers need to learn how to do this, and the only way is through practice. Thinking that you can learn these things at a theoretical level without developing them first through practice is to fantasise about how to run a business successfully. You have to learn it on the job. Theory helps, but practice is where learning is located.

Conversation 2.2

Stephen O'Connor

In our context the only way we can operate is through informal learning, to help people identify what they want to learn, and then to provide the resources for them to do that. This has emerged out of praxis. It is just totally pragmatic. We didn't come at it from a philosophical angle. We had all read our John Dewey, and we knew the principles on an intellectual level. But something different happens when you actually go into a teaching–learning situation and try to do that. In a formal education situation when you have got twenty kids who all want to be somewhere else, John Dewey will help you out, but unless you actually make the connection with those kids it just becomes empty theory. The same is so here in prison education. We could not survive by doing a standard curriculum. The curriculum is so varied, people wander about, and there seems to be total confusion to any outsider coming in, but there is order in the chaos. People are learning primarily through the relationships which we work hard to develop. We are all very aware of learning going on, but our practice is not primarily informed by formal theory.

Developing theories of action

Let me show this process in action. I want to use the writing of this book as an example of how a person's understanding can develop so that they overtake abstract theory and generate action theories.

I have been writing drafts of this book for the past year. In earlier drafts I was careful to show that I enjoyed and benefited from the work of, among others, John Rawls, whose ideas about the nature of good societies is highly influential. I wanted to show how the work I was doing lived up to Rawls's ideas of justice as fairness and deliberative democracy (see p. 73). To do so however would not tell the full story. It would not tell of the struggles involved in trying to realise those visions in practice, nor of the frustrations when things went wrong. Was I failing the theory? Was the theory failing me?

I work in two main contexts: in higher education institutional contexts with Irish and British accrediting universities, and with groups of participants who are studying in Ireland for higher degrees awarded by those universities. Anyone who works with institutions and with groups of people knows how problematic the work can sometimes be. I have tried hard to live up to Rawls's criteria of fairness and equal speech, but in many cases this has not worked. This is particularly so of institutional contexts of higher education, but it is also so with course participants. No matter how well-disposed, people in groups can still get cross and impatient, myself included. If the good society demands justice as fairness and deliberative democracy, it has clearly been out of our reach. Does Rawls expect perfection? I am more inclined to think in terms of ongoing development, rather than perfection. I relate to Iris Murdoch's idea (1985: 62) that it might be well to interpret Jesus's 'Be ye therefore perfect' as 'Be ye therefore slightly improved'. I can see slight improvement on an ongoing basis through my efforts; perfection, no.

Let me give an outline of the ideas of Rawls which I try to live in practice, and explain how, although I have often failed in grand style (and still do), trying to get to grips with why I fail in some respects has led to insights of how I might be succeeding in others.

Rawls (1972) says that good societies have the features of justice as fairness (everyone has equal entitlement), and distributive or deliberative democracy (everyone has an equal chance to speak). Justice, says Rawls, does not guarantee fairness. The tortoise and the hare might begin the race together, but they are at different vantage points because of their makeup. The fact that minority groups might have equal rights, and these are even protected by legislation, does not ensure that minorities get to exercise those rights in an equal way. Justice as fairness would ensure not only entitlement to equality of access but also equality of outcome. If less fortunate members of society have not the goods potentially to achieve equality of outcome, the collective needs to ensure that those goods are supplied, such as provision of care facilities in the workplace for children of working parents, and privileged access to housing for people on low income. The idea of deliberative democracy is related to Habermas's ideal speech situation, and suggests that all people have equal entitlement to speak and be heard; it is the responsibility of the strong collective to ensure that they have full participation in the democratic process. I want all this to be a feature of my work contexts.

As well as reading Rawls's ideas, I also enjoy his critics, particularly the work of John Gray, whose insights give me heart. Gray (1995) points out that we are not all born equal, nor are free to choose life paths. Life is not fair. We are born into circumstances over which we have no choice – we do not choose our parents; we have no say in how we look. If we really took the idea of justice as fairness seriously, we would address issues of whether the rich should part with some of their money to support the poor, or whether we should all compulsorily donate healthy organs to save lives.

Justice as fairness and deliberative democracy, says Gray, are ideals to strive for. We need to remember however that we live in agonistic (conflictual) societies. 'The term "agonistic" comes from the Greek word *agon*, which has the meaning both of a contest, competition or rivalrous encounter, and of the conflict of characters in tragic drama' (Gray, 1995: 68). This means that people have conflicting and often incommensurable claims, all of which should be regarded as potentially legitimate. In the Salman Rushdie affair, for example, the outrage felt by Islamic groups was fully justified on the grounds that Rushdie's work presented an affront to their beliefs, while Rushdie could claim the right to freedom of expression as a creative writer (Appignanesi and Maitland, 1989). The resulting impasse grew through lack of commitment to reaching a mutually agreeable compromise.

I relate strongly to the critique. I recognise that all the contexts of my life are potentially agonistic. Many encounters have appeared as consistent attempts to talk with people who do not want to listen. This has applied particularly in relation to people in institutional university settings. On the one hand I have tried over the years to persuade colleagues in Irish universities to develop initiatives to enable practitioners to study their own practice and generate their personal theories. These colleagues know about the courses I offer through British universities, and I have suggested that they should consider developing similar initiatives so that Irish educators would not need to go across the water for accreditation. Such overtures have been met, at best, with a sympathetic hearing but no hope of action; at worst, with hostility. At the same time I have tried to persuade British universities to let me develop practitioner research programmes further than their current state. These overtures have been met with resistance because of accountability trends in British educational administration – increasing financial awareness, increasing quality control, increasing bureaucratisation of education.

My teaching scenarios, while usually successful, have also often been conflictual. However, here I feel I can take strategic action to reduce potential dislocation, since I am in a leadership position. While recognising that we are all subject to the usual off-moments, I have tried to set guidelines for group conduct which accommodate Rawls's ideas, and I have worked hard to model them. From my observations and records, I can trace a growing awareness and improvement of practice in the groups and, by implication, throughout the whole organisation. People seem to be benefiting from their new-found autonomy, and are able to express their pleasure in learning:

You allow me freedom to develop my own theories.

You have helped me to determine my own worth.

I believe I am a better administrator since embarking on action research projects.

In my leadership position I am able to negotiate rules and models with partici-pants for successful group practices. I have not been able to do this however for the higher education institutional locations where I am not in a position to nego-tiate rules. I am really interested in why this should be so.

I am thinking of Searle's (1995) ideas of how organisations are constituted and regulated (see also Chapter 3). Searle says that organisations are maintained by people agreeing to and obeying public rules. This has not been my experi-ence. I can see that provided everyone agrees to the rules and obeys them, society runs smoothly. But the deeper issues still exist as to who sets the rules, who decides to obey which rules, and how they are persuaded to do so. While I seem to have fostered rule-guided societies in the groups I teach, why have not the same principles applied to my dealings with people in higher education insti-tutional settings? Are the rules different? Why do I not have a hand in setting the rules for personal-social conduct?

Class antagonisms and popular-democratic antagonisms

Theories of discourse have again been helpful. In *Politics and Ideology in Marxist Theory* (1977), Laclau examines the nature of ideological interpellations, that is, the way that people are discursively constructed as roles and identities. He says that there are two main forms of interpellation: class antagonisms and popular-democratic antagonisms. I can relate these ideas to my context. The class antagonisms I have experienced are mainly in relation to those people in university and other third-level or government agency settings, who place themselves 'above' practitioners in workplaces, and who value technical rational forms of knowledge, and hold practical forms of knowledge in lower regard. (This does not apply to all people in those settings. Many colleagues working in institutional settings who hold values around the social benefits of practitioner-based learning experience the same difficulties.) Established hierarchical power relationships suggest that the university and its agencies have control over what counts as legitimate knowledge and who should be regarded as a knower. The work I have been doing with practitioners has challenged the dominance of technical rational forms, so strategies have been exercised to keep me and my course members under control. While I have met and challenged the dominance of technical rational forms, I have not overcome them. I live with them, and adapt to them. Fortunately, because I work at a distance and also maintain my independent status as an unsalaried researcher, I enjoy relative autonomy. I am able to interpret course content and course management in my own way, provided I demonstrate to the university that the educational experience of course participants is high. This has meant that course participants can research their own practice (which they want to do) while at the same time fully meeting assignment assessment criteria. Course participants' results lists at university examinations boards display a rich sprinkling of distinctions. The quality of work is not in doubt. The courses have a 100 per cent pass rate. Validated evidence exists that course members are benefiting from their study. I deliberately use the resources available to me to change institutional cultures. The legitimacy of personal claims to professional knowledge is rigorously validated and constitutes a powerful body of scholarship. The body of work contributes to wider bodies of evidence which are systematically reconceptualising the knowledge base of institutional knowledge.

I believe that the quality of work is a direct result of overcoming the popular-democratic antagonisms that Laclau speaks of, and which can manifest as ideological disagreements among course members. I have overcome this by deliberately nurturing a quality of care throughout my practice, and indicating my firm expectation that others would do the same. I shall return to this theme shortly, but two comments perhaps indicate the general ethos that we have created:

I feel safe and secure in this study group. I feel valued and encouraged to participate.

You laid down the ground rules in the first instance, and made it clear that you expected them to be respected.

Over the year that I have been writing this book, I have struggled long and hard with the problem of how to integrate theory and practice. Intuitively I relate strongly to the abstract theories of Habermas, Rawls, Searle and many others, who give us insights into what might be, and these gave me hope and determination. At the same time I know that these visions are presented as perfect 'end states' which I will never achieve. No matter how well course participants relate to one another, they still disagree on substantive issues, often in a challenging way; and I encourage this disagreement because I believe that divergence of opinion is healthy and avoids group-think and conformity. I try to encourage disagreement in an atmosphere of tolerance, telling truth with kindness. Because people do come to tolerate diversity, so that the ideals of justice as fairness and deliberative democracy are then lived in practice, it has dawned on me that negotiating the process of disagreement actually *is* the good order. We find our way through the struggle, sometimes in a haphazard way, but we do find our way provided we go on faith and care. The good order, I have come to realise, does not exist 'out there' as an unachievable ideal; it is here, with us all the time as we work through our disagreements. Jesus said that the kingdom of heaven is here on earth. We create our heaven through our effort, not as an end product but as present experience. A good society is not unattainable perfection; it exists already here, in the way we are and how we live together.

Abstract theories then are only part of the equation, not the whole. To move on and develop theories of good societies we need theories of action, theories which confirm that even if we do live in agonistic societies, we can still learn how to overcome our differences. This learning has consolidated into my own theory of the nature of a learning organisation, an organisation that learns how to nurture and value the personal-social development of all participants. I believe I have also learnt not to be oppressed by failing to live up to received theory, but to be liberated by generating a theory of living with adversity and growing in understanding.

2 How are learning organisations created?

Fukuyama (1995) argues that successful organisations are built on social capital, energetic goodwill and commitment by individuals who have decided to work together for a particular purpose. I agree. Such groups can constitute powerful bodies for social change. 'Never underestimate the power of groups of committed citizens to change the world. In fact, it is the only thing that ever has' (Mead, 1973, cited in Henderson, 1996: 123). The basis of social capital, says Fukuyama, is trust, and 'is formed through education in a variety of ways' (p.

113). He goes on to explain the benefits for organisations and societies that are high in trust, and the disadvantages for low-trust organisations.

Generating trust however is not straightforward. Living together as groups requires considerable energy and compromise – 'hard political work' (Gray, 1997: 139). Living together usually involves trade-offs between the values of different individuals and between individual and group values. The conditions of life are always contested when constraints and obligations jostle with desire for attachment and the need to be valued. The tensions that are an inevitable part of social living also constitute the richness and variety of its experience.

Fukuyama's theories are propositional, abstract. He assumes that there is unified understanding around concepts such as trust and trusting practices. He also assumes that trust exists as an abstract entity 'out there', somehow divorced from the realities of life. These assumptions operate on the same principle as Searle's rule-based societies: provided we all understand what trust means, and we can get people to trust one another and agree to the rules, things are fine; getting people to agree to try in the first place, and then building up trust, is not so easy.

I have said that human societies are always and inevitably agonistic. If human societies are agonistic, how can trust be established?

Laclau and Mouffe say that relationships are potentially inherently conflictual or adversarial, not in the sense of enmity, but in the sense that people are always potentially in a political relationship with one another, trying to work out who they are and how they should be. The decisions they come to are matters of discourse, what they say and do to one another. Decisions about identities and relationships are discursively constructed. Discourses are not 'given' by any external agency as scripts, but are created as living meanings. Because the meanings we give to our lives help us to understand who we are, and also to reflect on the values that we live by, discourses always embody an inherent struggle for hegemony (power), as we try to live in one direction rather than another. This is also potentially a site for conflict, as one set of values is prioritised over another. Discourses seldom run smoothly. They are always subject to other events, circumstances and insights. There is no given structure to social living; all social structures are negotiated and agreed (or not), and therefore susceptible to dislocation, which, because of its unfixed nature, 'contains the very possibilities of temporality, possibility and freedom' (Laclau, 1990: 41–3; in Torfing, 1999: 149).

These views might appear at first glance as negative, emphasising the seeming impossibility of ever reaching peaceful states. On the other hand, they might be seen as offering a methodology of hope. By emphasising the ambiguous and volatile nature of human relationships, as well as the primacy of politics, Laclau and Mouffe help us to see the importance of working out solutions to social problems in spite of the obstacles to peace which we create for ourselves and others; and of the potential positioning of real people as 'strategically thinking actors' (Torfing, 1999: 147) who find ways of creating new social scenarios for better living. There is room for everyone, faults and all: 'For not only do Laclau and Mouffe insist upon grounding pluralist democracy in a political community;

they also insist that this community makes room for individuality' (Torfing, 1999: 6) (see also Conversation 2.3).

Conversation 2.3

Stephen O'Connor

In our context, and probably within other contexts, it is vital to establish a good personal relationship with students. Many of our people come from situations where because of the rigid formality of their learning elsewhere they have found it difficult to express themselves. So they give out to us, and we try to reply in an equally frank, honest but at the same time appropriate manner, so there is an openness to letting honest emotions show at times, within limits, always accepting that at the end of the day we have to have resolution, we have to have closure on whatever conflicts arise. It's an unwritten thing that it's OK to explode in front of the teacher, as long as afterwards you come along and put it right. And there are so many extraneous things going on here. You're going to do a class on history, and someone may have just come off a bad visit and they want to talk to the teacher about that, and it seems absolutely unreasonable that they shouldn't, and very often everything would stop while they talk about the issues that concern themselves. We would see that as part of the learning process. It's not counselling in any way. It's relating to our students. Any educator worth their salt would want to get involved in the wider context of their students' lives without being intrusive.

I take comfort from these ideas. They say that I do not have to live up to abstract expectations in order to be valued. I bring this learning to my work, and in trying to create a context for everyone to learn, I try not to be judgemental and to meet people where they are. I try to listen and encourage others to do the same. The quality of my listening *is* my response. I try to bring consistent values of respect and acceptance of the person to every encounter, in an effort to live out my vision of a learning organisation as one in which all participants feel confident and safe enough to explore their own potentialities of learning (Macdonald, 1995). Rawls cites Sidgwick (1907) in saying that everyone needs to feel that they are living in a safe society. Jean Clandinin has developed this theme in the 'Safe and Caring Schools' initiative she and others are developing in Alberta (available on http://www.education.ualberta.ca/educ/research/trifac/Safe_and_Caring/introu.html).

How could I theorise this aspect of my practice?

Danger theory

I saw a TV programme once on the work of Polly Matzinger and her idea of danger theory, and it seemed to present a useful metaphor for understanding how pluralist forms of life can be accommodated. When used in the development of a living theory of organisation, danger theory can show how organisations can be safe and caring places, danger-free zones in which people can experience their lives as creative, worthwhile processes of personal-social renewal.

Here are the main ideas.

Polly Matzinger, working in immunology, has developed an innovative and radical view of how the body protects itself from danger.

> Since the 1950s immunologists have believed that the immune system learns early in its development to tolerate tissues that surround it. These tissues are viewed as 'self', and the immune system refrains from harming them. Any other tissues are viewed as 'non-self' and cause the body's immune system to suddenly spring into action and launch armies of white blood cells against these foreign 'non-self' viruses, bacteria or organs transplanted from another person.
>
> (*The PHOENIX CORErespondent*, 1996)

Matzinger has challenged this view (1994), showing its inconsistencies: why does the mother's body not reject the foetus, for example, while still rejecting harmful bacteria? She proposes the idea of danger as a triggering mechanism for action. The immune system lies quietly on guard, waiting for signals that dangerous elements are at work in the organism. As soon as the immune system receives signals that tissues are dying unnatural deaths, it mobilises the white blood cells to attack the source of danger. The immune system does not discriminate between 'self' and 'non-self' but between danger and harmlessness (*The PHOENIX COREspondent*, 1996).

The metaphor is helpful I think to imagine how a system can tolerate 'deviance' or 'non-self' provided the deviance presents no danger to the system. When extended to social systems, it suggests that all participants within the system can peacefully co-exist, even when one element brings the system into temporary disequilibrium. A dynamic adaptive system can maintain its own internal order by accommodating innovation without distortion; the order itself is already one of constant internal transformation and adaptation. If a novel phenomenon presents danger, however, by damaging other participants, the system needs to exercise disciplinary measures. Dealing with novel phenomena can sometimes bring a system to the 'edge of chaos' (see Lewin, 1993; Waldrop, 1992), where the system is in a transition period between maintaining its own form and accommodating novelty, or relinquishing that form to become a new pattern altogether.

Danger theory is suggestive of how radically new ideas and forms can be tolerated within existing systems, and how pluralistic viewpoints and modes of existence can co-exist peacefully. If an intrusive element becomes life-threatening for another, in that it sets up an antagonism, the system swings into action to contain the disequilibrium, preferably through negotiated means, but, if this is not possible, through exclusion. In the case of the body, one set of cells kills off another. In the case of social interaction, views in conflict may be resolved, or result in a parting of the ways, sometimes through violent means. The metaphor also suggests that destabilising innovative forms are essential for the survival of existing systems. Tension provides the incentive to the system to exercise its own creativity in order to develop in new ways. A system that remains stuck in rigid structures is open to the onslaught of newer, possibly more cogent and energetic forms of life. Rigidity nurtures fragility. This reinforces the need for generative learning which is not only necessary for the social development of organisations, but essential to give them the necessary edge to ensure their survival.

There are serious implications in this analogy for issues of personal and collective living. While divergence in opinion might be essential for organisational well-being, how the disagreement is resolved influences the extent to which social capital and the nurturing of a good society may be encouraged. Bernstein (1991) talks about how we respond to conflict (p. 337). The usual ploys of the 'adversarial' or 'confrontational' style are to find points of dispute and expose weaknesses in an effort to strengthen one's own espoused position. In pluralistic and politically constructed societies, however, 'the question becomes how we are to respond to this pluralism', and he suggests that what is needed is 'dialogical encounters, where we reasonably explore our differences and conflicts', and, in particular, 'to nurture the type of community and solidarity where there is an engaged fallibilistic pluralism – one that is based upon mutual respect, where we are willing to risk our own prejudgements, are open to listening and learning from others, and we respond to others with responsiveness and responsibility' (pp. 338–9).

Do I do this in my work? I hope so, and I try to encourage others to do the same:

> Your management of our group is so pleasantly done (trust, regard for different personalities and different needs, lack of pressure to contribute, an interest in all opinions, sincere listening and comment) that I feel it safe to express an opinion and know that it will not be ridiculed. I feel I am making a worthwhile contribution and that my opinion will be incorporated into the group work.

Do I do this with colleagues in higher education institutional settings? I don't know. That has to be a future action enquiry.

Social capital and education

To return to the idea of social capital, Fukuyama says that the way to build it is through education. I agree. I also think we need to remember that learning and education, though interlinked, are different.

Learning organisations, educative organisations

Senge (1990) developed the idea of the learning organisation. 'The organizations that will truly excel in the future will be the organizations that discover how to tap people's commitment and capacity to learn at *all* levels in an organization' (p. 4, emphasis in original). Perhaps in emphasising the 'all' Senge was echoing Schön's ideas that the new scholarship implies corporate learning, not only learning how to use the rhetoric but actually learning how to change one's practice. Senge speaks of organisational learning as cooperative and constant; people share ideas and create meanings through creative, educative conversations.

Education, I have said, is to do with the quality of interactions among people. If the interactions encourage people to learn, the relationship can be called educative. For organisations to be learning organisations, they first have to develop an educative culture. Relationships within an organisation define its culture; the relationships *are* the culture. An educative culture is one in which relationships foster learning. A key condition for organisations to become learning organisations is that the culture is educative; it is difficult to see how learning for sustainable organisational growth can become part of the institutional culture if educative relationships are not prioritised.

The basis of education is care. When people care about one another they act in ways that are other-directed. In caring organisational cultures, people feel valued and important, and are inspired to learn, to become enquiring and critical, to extend care to others. Care is not sentimental; in its strongest form it implies respect, recognition and acceptance; in its weaker form it implies cooperation as a form of mutually agreed efforts for survival (Axelrod, 1990).

> There's a trust and a bond in our entire group that I feel is unique. We respect and like each other and we can laugh with one another without anyone ever taking offence. Unlike the rather unhappy experiences a lot of employees seem to have in workplaces, and teachers seem to have in schools, where collegiality is often sadly lacking, our group has a lovely sense of caring and mutual support. We all learn an enormous amount from each other. This is partly due to the individual members of the group being nice people, but that's not the whole reason. Jean's firm guidance, her high moral and ethical standards and her equally high expectations of academic rigour have made a huge impression on all of us. I believe I am a better practitioner since embarking on action research projects. I love being involved with this work. I have learnt so much already and I'm excited by the thought of all I've still got to learn. I feel enthusiastic about my work and less inclined to ponder on early retirement or pension plans!

This view however is often alien to dominant corporate cultures which are defined more by hierarchical patronage than educative relation. Grundy (1996) for example speaks of the 'thin, straight-line' management 'which is often valued within modern management theory and practice because of its promise of efficiency and effectiveness both in relation to decision-making and accountability' (p. 106). She laments the lack of collaborative practices within dominant cultures: 'I have heard it argued on university committees (usually by those who hold leadership positions) that the vast majority of people within the organisation are demanding: "Let the leaders lead. Don't ask us what to think – you are paid to do the thinking, just tell us what to do"' (p. 108).

Shifting such attitudes is a daunting prospect, yet this is what needs to be done if the learning organisation is to become a reality. The problem, as I see it, lies in the need for Senge's '*all*' to be accepted by '*all*'.

Back to the new scholarship

How then to overcome dependence on abstract theory and take the plunge into action theories? To do so means breaking with tradition, because most organisation theory and organisational cultures still value abstract forms. Most theories of change are technical rational theories which advocate some kind of theory of action linked with a theory of organisational change (see for example Zuber-Skerritt, 1996).

The new scholarship means a new epistemological focus, a new social focus and a new moral focus. The new epistemological focus is on the development of personal theories to show practical learning; the new social focus is on the participative nature of personal action enquiries; the new moral focus is on a living out of ideologies of democracy and equality. New organisational scholarship requires everyone to take part, on an equal footing, to find ways of creating autonomous selves working collaboratively to achieve common goals. I would call this educational.

The new scholarship requires managers publicly to position themselves as learners, not an easy task but feasible. Case studies exist to show the process, and also to show the benefit for organisational learning (see Lomax, 1996; Whitehead, 1994). By positioning themselves as learners, managers also make public statements that they care sufficiently about what they are doing and the people they are supporting to become insider researchers, not outsider spectators. Education never happened because one person told another what to do. Education always happens because people are intentionally present to each other.

Conversation 2.4

Sharon Jamieson

My work is based on values. If I view my work with staff from an administrative perspective, that puts a narrow construction on my job. If I regard people as employees, that is wrong. I take my work as an opportunity to do something worthwhile. I see myself as a coach or a mentor to contribute to people's learning and career. I am always prepared to talk to people and help them grow and see and do things in different ways. It is quite difficult to do that in my job, but that is what it is all about. I take my work as an opportunity to do something worthwhile in relation with others.

3 How are learning organisations put to use?

For some people, the organisations they are in are part of wider society; for some, an organisation is their main experience of society. Organisations have potential for their own renewal and also for wider social renewal. What happens at local level has the potential for wider influence (see Figure 2.1) The potential lies in people who are willing to learn and use their understanding for social benefit.

There was probably never greater need than now for social change, with state institutions systematically being undermined by private industry and social welfare being eroded by selfish forms of state capitalist autocracy. The choice is still whether to be a democrat or an aristocrat (Chomsky, 1996: 93). The choice, in educational terms, is whether to opt for the freedom to think for oneself and be in control of and exercise one's own choices for action, in negotiation with others, or whether to succumb to the comfortable slavery of traditional abstract

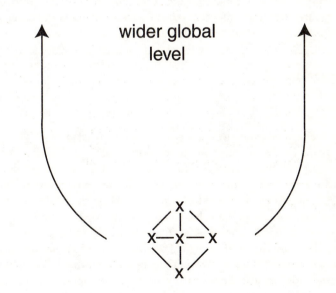

Figure 2.1

technical rational forms. Trying to develop sustainable futures with the promise of universal social justice does imply struggle.

I once read a story about two spacemen who were captured by aliens on planet X. The aliens, thinking that the spacemen were primitive creatures, imprisoned them in a cage. A small mouse-like creature crossed the floor of the cage, whereupon the spacemen caught it and placed it within a small makeshift cage of their own. The following day, to their surprise, they were set free. When they enquired the reason for their sudden release, the aliens informed them that they realised the spacemen must be intelligent; only intelligent beings would imprison another being.

This is a nice example, I think, of Popper's idea of closed societies, based on slavery (1962). An open society, in Popper's terms, is one in which 'individuals are confronted with personal decisions' (p. 173) and accept the responsibility of making them. In these terms, intelligent beings would strive to free themselves and one another. They would learn to find ways towards personal autonomy through collective negotiation. The major aim of learning organisations on this view is to develop free-minded people within pluralistic contexts of divergent opinion. The major social aim of learning organisations is to encourage individuals to think about their wider social contexts, and challenge unjust practices in the interests of social justice.

For businesses this would be very difficult, since the dominant world economic order is one of selfish accumulation of wealth, a rolling back of social programmes and systematic oppression of the poor and needy. A glance at most newspapers will show the contradiction between espoused theories of democracy and the theories-in-use of autocratic capitalism. The front page slogans of democracy and care are counterbalanced by the back page accounts of increasing incidences of rape, murder, and children living below the poverty line. Books on action research are unfortunately not available to the world's illiterate.

Conversation 2.5

David Steeves

In government, you have to work everyone to effect social change. The one that I've not been able to have any success with at all is the business end. I can work well with the volunteer sector, I can work well within the political side, I can work well within a bureaucracy. I can't crack the business mindset. It's almost too focused. I can get good business people to volunteer. But actually to get business leaders to say, Yes, we have an emerging societal responsibility, I don't think we're there. It's like they seem to have what they do pretty well in their sights, but they can't entertain something on the social side of the equation without jeopardising what it is they do. I don't know if you can join the two.

It is the responsibility of managers to decide whether they are prepared to stand up for what they say they believe in if they claim to be managing a learning organisation. 'The learning organisation' becomes just another fancy slogan if it does not take seriously issues of how to improve social orders, whether on a local scale or at world level. Anything will do. Any improvement is still improvement, no matter how small (remember Iris Murdoch).

So the challenge for learning organisations is not to learn how to produce more goods, but how to produce, as Dewey says (1916), free human beings who come together on terms of equality with wider social intent. The challenge for learning organisations is to decide what is worth learning, what counts as valuable knowledge, who needs to know, and who decides.

4 What are the implications for organisation theory as a form of educational theory?

The shift towards learning in organisations means that organisation theory needs to regard itself as a form of educational theory. Managers need to position themselves as teachers, and work towards providing contexts that encourage education. Management education should concern itself with nurturing personal-social education in organisational contexts, and business education should shift from a purely commercial focus to a focus on social responsibility.

If the focus of organisation study is to offer descriptions and explanations for how people come to live in particular ways, then a main purpose of organisation practice should be to encourage practitioners at *all* levels of an organisation to offer accounts for their own professionalism. The values base of management needs to be explicit: what is it we manage, and for what purpose? This places management within a context of moral-political enquiry, as managers are encouraged to give reasons for individual practice and demonstrate their accountability to those whom they support.

Organisations need to support organisational learning for personal-social growth. Lifelong careers may be a thing of the past, but corporate responsibility for lifetime education is not. Informal learning in the workplace needs to be encouraged and planned and provided for, not as part of the hidden curriculum towards socialisation (Garrick, 1998: 71) but as an emancipatory process that places people in control of their own environments (Welton, 1991, cited in Garrick, 1998). Further, informal learning in the workplace needs official conduits through which it can transform into formal learning for higher education accreditation.

This is already happening, but processes and opportunities for access need to be strengthened and given higher profile. Business and teacher professional education through in-house programmes for university accreditation is now firmly established in many countries. Partnerships between universities and workplaces are developing everywhere. In New Zealand (see Pip Bruce Ferguson's story, p. 115) this has even been extended to invite private practitioners to accredit work, part of the neoliberal moves towards free markets and entrepreneurialism.

If, however, informal practitioner workplace learning is to have the opportunity to transform into formally accredited learning, both universities and businesses need to develop appropriate processes within already existing structures, and develop new structures; and also develop new attitudes that recognise the legitimacy of these processes. There are two major issues here: (1) the recognition of the legitimacy of practitioner research as a form of professional learning; (2) recognition of its legitimacy within traditional university and business institutional cultures.

Legitimising and institutionalising practitioner action research

Legitimising practitioner action research

Practitioner action research has created its own knowledge base and established itself as a legitimate research tradition. Workers in this tradition are systematically building up a body of knowledge to establish credibility, not only in terms of the quantity of research accounts, but also in the refining of the criteria and standards of judgement that are used to legitimise the research process itself. This process is now well under way in teacher professional education. It is not so advanced in management professional education. Effort needs to be expended in management professional education to develop appropriate criteria and standards of judgement by which to assess the quality of managers' personal accounts of practice which claim to show improvement in the quality of learning in workplaces.

Institutionalising practitioner action research

Legitimising the processes of action research in terms of its internal validity and the public demonstration of its potential for personal-social renewal is one thing, a relatively easy first step in light of the second step of embedding it within university and business institutional cultures, both of which tend to take a hardline stand within technical rational traditions.

Many universities still survive as deeply conservative contexts which value technical rational forms. While universities can no longer ignore practitioner research as a real force in professional education and its accreditation, there is continued reluctance to accept it as 'real' research, and persistent efforts are made to retain research as an exclusive category for the kind of research knowledge generated by higher education workers (see Anderson and Herr, 1999). The mainstreaming of professional education as a context for bona fide practical theorising presents a crisis for a university tradition which now finds itself in an economic and moral bind. Decisions need to be made about whether to maintain an elitist form of technical rational knowledge (and possibly miss out on the huge market that practitioner-based forms of professional education represents), or whether to accept practical knowledge as a central epistemological plank and possibly change elitist traditions of knowledge for ever. How universities tend to cope with the dilemma at present is to domesticate action research accounts, so that they fit in with dominant technical rational knowledge traditions. Middlewood, Coleman and Lumby (1999) present a good example of how dominant knowledge traditions succeed in gentling the masses: research is undertaken by academics on practitioners who undertake their research on others in workplaces. Yet such accounts carry their own indictment. In this case, while school-based research should 'keep pupil learning at the centre' (p. 134) the editors report a course participant's comments on her own research that 'the research ... cannot produce clear evidence of pupil learning remaining at the centre'; and a second report that 'We changed that system following the investigation, but it hasn't made any difference to what goes on in the classrooms with the students' (p. 135). Why should anyone be surprised, when the reports are reports *about* people, rather than the reports *of* people *for* people. The work that some other action researchers are doing in encouraging practitioners to produce their own living accounts of practice, generated through their own self-study, is a different matter altogether, and sets a tradition of radical knowing through self-critique (see, for example, Hamilton, 1998), quite outside the bounds of technical rationality, a form that requires new criteria and standards of judgement from within the enquiry process itself (see Whitehead, 2000).

Businesses also still survive as deeply conservative contexts for the production of technical rational forms of knowledge. In discourses about learning organisations the tendency is still to commit to objectified knowledge, the criteria of performativity which legitimise it, and the rationalist standards of judgement used to assess its worth. Some businesses however know no other way. I hear continually from participants on management education courses, as well as managers on my courses, that firms will readily commit to the principle of workplace learning and its potential transformation into accredited learning; and firms will also financially support initiatives towards human resource development to raise awareness of personal potential. As soon as the budget is threatened, however, these are the first aspects of corporate spending to disappear. Sophisticated rhetoric fizzles out in the hard light of fiscal necessity.

There are real issues here for institutional learning, a matter as much of real world necessity as of moral philosophising. The visions of Newman (1915) and MacIntyre (1990) of universities as contexts in which people can work out ideas which shape identities, providing safe and caring places in which constrained disagreement may flourish (MacIntyre, ibid.), need to become a reality if universities are not to risk being overtaken by newer legislated agencies who will better do the job of legitimising forms of knowledge which demonstrate their use value for social living. The vision of businesses as recognised sites for the development (and possible accreditation) of human potential could well be realised, and businesses may soon come to see themselves as special kinds of universities, offering their own awards and developing a new knowledge base. Liam Nagle (Chapter 11) comments that newer forms of technology could already dispense with many institutionally based education programmes. Whether institutions want to retain their status quo, or change their remit to meet the demands of contemporary living, the managers of those institutions themselves need to do some serious thinking about where they want to be in the future and how they want to get there. The *laissez-faire* policies of market forces need to be abandoned in favour of corporate planning for a sustainable future through education. This is so for universities and businesses who may shortly find themselves in direct competition for a new body of knowledge workers comprising practitioner action researchers in organisational contexts.

For me, the future in this regard is very bright, though I must admit, like Chomsky (1996), to a conflict between long-term visions and short-term goals. I am all for the democratisation of educational knowledge. I believe that universities are in people, not buildings. If the university will not come to the people, the people must make their own university. Movements in this direction are already under way, in franchised courses, in-house professional development schemes, the delegation of responsibility for accredited programmes to freelance workers, the development of distance-learning programmes through ICT. These are the contexts where I am located. It is possibly just a matter of time before organisations take on the responsibility for accreditation themselves. The neoliberal trend suggests that governments will soon give degree-awarding status to businesses. While my vision for a highly educated and socially aware citizenry would have reservations about this trend (because I am at heart quite conservative in my love of traditional liberal university life and what it stands for), my short-term goals would be to support these developments if they promised greater access to education and the valuing of personal contributions to social living. If this is the direction of the new emphasis on workplace learning, and is part of the potential of learning organisations, those organisations need to mobilise to create their own legitimation processes for themselves as sites for professional education, a long-term investment process that would have significant return for real lives. Given these entrepreneurial times, who dares wins.

Journeyman

Séamus Lillis

Introduction

I am a community development consultant. My work involves me in assisting communities improve their practice. For some time I have specialised in assisting practitioners strengthen their approach to community development. Among other initiatives, I have been responsible for bringing together practitioners from the Republic of Ireland and from both traditions in Northern Ireland (Mc Wey, 1999). Through conversational learning we review our practice of community development. I am in the process of establishing a foundation in Ireland with assistance from Michigan State University, which will be geared to promote best practice in community development across the island of Ireland.

Over two years ago I was awarded a research scholarship jointly funded by the Irish Department of Agriculture and Rural Development and the United States Department of Agriculture. I hope to be awarded a PhD by University College Dublin in the year 2001. My research is about practitioners enriching their practice of developing communities in a rural setting.

Early training

Originally I trained for a career in agriculture. I worked in the public service sector in the Republic of Ireland as a horticultural advisor, then as a teacher of the certificate in horticulture and finally as a specialist in rural development. My training was a traditional one where I learned the methods of empirical science, which I applied to my practice as an advisor and teacher in the production of crops. I brought to my work the understanding that processes of development could be understood using universal categories of analysis; variables could be manipulated to effect change. This process would apply to whatever might be the unit of enquiry (whether humans or plants). Essentially I was a strategist whose aim was to bring about desirable change in crop production practices. A basic assumption was that my recommendations rested on research findings that were predictable and replicable.

Contemporary theories of rural development in Ireland are informed by the theory and practice of agricultural production. The relatively recent popularity of rural development arises from the reform of the Common Agricultural Policy initiated by Commissioner Mc Sharry in *The Future of Rural Society* (Commission of the European Communities, 1988). This initiative eventually put rural development centre stage, particularly as an attractive and reliable channel of European funding. The Department of Agriculture and Rural Development, whose professional staff had similar training to mine, administer rural development in Ireland. This training and background gives rise to an expectation that progress in rural development is deliverable in much the same way as for crop or animal production, that is, on a blueprint basis.

Developing insights

At the early stages of my research I became aware of the limitations of traditional quantitative approaches. My main insight was that rural development cannot be understood using quantitative approaches because it is an ongoing, developmental process. The process of rural development is generally transformational. By this I mean that participants' expertise develops and changes qualitatively over the years. Unlike agriculture it is not influenced by external forces, nor can its progress be predicted in definitive ways, as the scientific paradigm would suggest. Rural development differs from agriculture too in that its end products are not foreseeable and certainly not quantifiable. Its ways are not reliably replicable.

I came to two closely related insights: rural community development is context grounded and it is practice driven. By 'context grounded' I mean that each community is unique. By 'practice driven' I mean that a theory of rural community development that has no practical significance is meaningless to the community whose living it is aiming to describe and explain. My early training in empirical research methodology could not cope with these features.

Looking back

It took me a long time to take the methodology of action research on board. My ingrained way of thinking and my hankering after certainties meant that, early on, I expected to end up with the same kind of definite end product to which I had always been accustomed, that is, an external, independent body of knowledge. I thought this type of knowledge should be dependably replicable and should apply universally.

Advantages of action research

When I first undertook my doctoral studies I met with Jean, and we agreed, in consultation with the university, that she would act as an informal advisor to my work. Our early conversations led me to understand that everyday practical knowledge was the most appropriate epistemology in rural community development. The answers to such questions as, 'How do I improve my understanding of rural community development?' and/or 'How do I improve my practice as a practitioner in rural community development?' are reliable starting points for any theory of rural community development which I might generate. These findings would probably also be appropriate for other practitioners. I believe that, by generating my own theory of community development, and sharing that with others, I can help them to produce their theory for their particular context and practice. With Jean's encouragement, I discovered for myself that the theory I was formulating from the examination of my own practice – my own theory – could be demonstrated to be effective in developing both the theory and practice of rural community development. I became aware that I had always had these ideas but, because I had been caught in the constraining traditions of empirical paradigms, I had not surfaced the ideas for myself. It was a liberating experience to feel that I could access my latent knowledge and that mine was a legitimate and valuable way of thinking.

I had previously assumed that, when the work with communities had come to an end, I could continue to be prescriptive in my conclusions and recommendations, as I had been before, in keeping with the traditional role of researchers (of whom I was one). The old paradigm held that researchers had expert and exceptional mastery, and that their research was valid and pertinent. They held the right to tell the community, perceived as being inexpert, what was best to do in their long-term interests. This might be described as strategic benevolence with a dollop of the nanny state. It was also undemocratic and sat uncomfortably with what I considered to be best practices of community development.

My thinking had now moved on. The original basis on which I had operated as an advisor and teacher relied on my being a specialist resource, somebody with particular knowledge that set me apart. I had been licensed to advise. That now changed, and I began to see myself not as an external expert but as someone who was involved in the research process and was therefore a participant.

Meeting new challenges

In rural development, I risked being ineffective. My perception of myself, possibly born of other people's expectations of me, was that I was the 'expert'. However, communities do not need someone else's 'expertise'. The developmental process is more complex than that. Previously, when I launched a community development process, I would speak about what was feasible, about the community's capacity and its state of readiness. In other words, efficacy was being determined by the community's particular context. This I came to understand was an inadequate basis for helping communities to accept the responsibility for their own developmental process. Traditionally, rural community development looks to a response from the practitioner, who facilitates the community in finding what is within its capacity. In reality, communities do not look to some external and centrally prescribed blueprint or universal antidote. Communities are already self-directive. Their developmental process must be practice-driven to have any significance to the community.

For me, as an agent of change, making the journey from strategist advisor to rural community practitioner involved the interplay of new kinds of principles and practices and coming to grips with and owning my values publicly and for the first time. Values had never been discussed in my public service career. The journey was an experience in growth and in development, in challenges and in self-assertion. It was the beginning of a journey of discovery and of vulnerability, of discomfort and breakthrough, of occasional regression and frustration. It is still ongoing, and will probably never end.

The focus of my research has shifted. I felt that when I was in the traditional role of an advisor, I worked *for* farmers, and that as a novice rural community development practitioner I worked *with* rural people. I have come to understand that I work *on* my own practice, and that implies acting (in the sense of doing and trying out), monitoring, thinking about, learning and transforming. Since I started this research, there has been a shift of focus from trying to bring about an integration of miscellaneous abstract information, to focusing on how I improve my practice through research, that is, the creation of new knowledge about what I am doing in company with those whom I am supporting.

The new focus

I have become the focus of my research. I am studying my learning, my practice and me. I have become a practitioner-researcher.

My thinking around rural community development has progressed to the point where I have significantly revised my notions of the role of practitioners, traditionally understood as those who bring understanding about the processes of community development to members of the communities. I see my work now as helping people find their own answers.

In the past I would have adopted the assumptions of the traditional model, and seen the practitioner as the 'professional', as the source of expertise, who principally initiated rural community development in the countryside and was responsible for training participants and the maintenance of standards. This was a straight continuation of my roles as teacher and advisor. However, if the aim of the practitioner in authentic rural community development is to foster independent rural communities, I could see serious flaws in that approach. Independent, unfettered communities, if they were to become a reality, would have to reject dependency on their practitioner-professionals, a view which was inherent in the model of practitioners as experts.

My thinking moved on now to one of practitioners ensuring that they collaboratively build up competence within communities to the point where communities become independent and practitioners can largely withdraw from regular contact. But does that still leave practitioners in charge of formative training? It seems to me to be wrong – or at least lacking in consistency – that communities could be systematically deprived of the opportunity of determining their own training needs. In a recent conversation with Jean we talked through the idea of how practitioners are different from school-based teachers. In schools it is the students who move on; in effective community development it is the practitioner who must move on. Any thoughtful practitioner who holds values around the need of groups to claim their own independence is conscious of the long-term disadvantage of depriving participants of their right to conduct their business independently and competently. It is the practitioners who must make themselves redundant, by helping communities to become aware of their own potential for learning and self-direction, and then who leave so that communities can get on with their lives in the way they see fit.

Towards unfettered development

I think therefore that practitioners act with good authority when they encourage the independence of participants and invite them to work actively towards that goal. I feel directive strategies fail, either on the grounds of inherent shortcomings and inadequacies or because they tend to smother initiative. When practitioners model an action research approach for participants, they are encouraging participants' long-term survival and autonomy. Where they create a legacy through which participants themselves have learned to turn automatically to discovering their own capacity to review past activities and assess further opportunities, practitioners' work will have been well done.

It follows that over time the distinction between how practitioners go about their work and how participants do so will become blurred. This is because all share the goal of making the 'expertise' element of practitioners' contributions superfluous. I mean 'superfluous' in the sense that the community has itself assimilated much of that expertise and, more significantly, discovered its own potential for growth in directions which it has identified as desirable for its own ends. While participants can learn from practitioners, their most valuable learning, I believe, is how to develop their own expertise for their own community and grow in their ability to conduct their own affairs. Indeed, this could be seen as the main work of practitioners, to encourage members of communities to come to know their own capacity for self-knowledge and self-direction. So in a sense there will be no practitioners, only participants in community development. I think Donovan (1978: vii) says it well.

> In working with ... people do not try to call them back to where they were, and do not try to call them to where you are, as beautiful as that place might seem to you. You must have the courage to go with them to a place that neither you nor they have ever been before.

Surprise! Surprise!

I recall Jean alerting me to the prospect of the unforeseen in my findings. The unexpected prize of this undertaking is likely to be the modelling of and the dissemination of action research itself as a serious resource in fostering rural community development. This is because action research is essentially democratic. It involves people in managing their own concerns. It relies on their input for authentic evaluation. It encourages locally based research on local concerns and it promotes enhanced and dependable practice. Action research in itself would become a new way of advancing the practice of rural community development. So a methodology that I initially saw as an almost incidental instrument which would deliver my research findings was itself to become the significant outcome of the work.

The inner response

The impact of my research on me as an individual is leading me to question (and probably abandon) my earlier public service role as a 'strategic' advisor and teacher, whose aim was to generate certainties (see for example S. Lillis, 1984). My preoccupation was to create and rely on plans, to be in fact a benevolent strategist with an attendant temptation to manipulate and prescribe how others might behave. This involved spending considerable 'quality' time trying to match up, control and sanction a lifestyle, values and aspirations set and preserved by employer institutions.

Jean was my principal guide on this excursion of discovery. She refused to give me immediate applicable 'answers' that would allow me to get on with the work. She challenged me to state what my concerns were. Once I had identified them, she wanted to know what I was prepared to do about them. The reflective thinking that came out of this process persuaded me to examine my own values and to realise that, in hoping to influence others, I could only be effective if I concentrated first on improving my own practice. Having been allowed to discover this for myself, I came to own the process and to move on resolutely and with a surer step. What Jean had modelled for me was a transformative learning experience. What she modelled, by permitting me to take responsibility for my own discovery, is itself a form of emancipation, which I now model for others. This I believe captures the idea of transformational learning, where we learn from one another, and bring our learning for the consideration of others, whether or not they might use it to help them to learn.

Conclusion

This is a liberating way. It involves being open to serendipity, to the realisation that no matter how hard I may try, I do not get to control developments. Unpredictability has the effect of paralysing the 'expert'. It also makes us acknowledge the human conditions of vulnerability and failure, which are themselves occasions of greatest challenge in life. These are the challenges found in communities. I would describe my journey as moving from being a strategist (albeit high-minded), dependent on external knowledge, to being a journeyman like everyone else and capable of sharing inner wisdom. I am glad to take my place in community, unambiguously. In leaving strategic planning behind, I know I can become more authentic, more in tune with humanity and with my own personal values.

3 Action research, power and control

During recent years I have been struck by the variety of responses to action research by different communities. Workplace-based practitioners welcome it. They frequently comment, 'This is what I do in any case, only now there is a theoretical framework to it.' The easy way in which practitioners relate to the methodologies is borne out I think in the ready take-up for courses, and the ways in which people rapidly transfer their learning into strategies to improve workplace experience on a range of fronts. Quite the opposite happens in many encounters in higher education institutional contexts, particularly the more conservative ones. Reactions vary from interest to hostility. This has made me think carefully about what action research stands for to provoke such a variety of reactions, some of which can be quite emotionally charged.

I have come to appreciate, as Schön says (1983, 1995), that all organisations live by their own epistemology, their own way of knowing; and that any one way of knowing uses its own legitimation criteria and standards of judgement. The dominant epistemology at the university is technical rationality, knowledge of facts and information, which is validated by testing for academic rigour through normative ways such as controlled experimentation and statistical analysis of manipulated variables.

Schön describes the topology of professional practice as a high ground where people work on clean abstract ideas, and a swampy lowland where people try to work out problems of real living. Universities are located mainly on the high ground. Research carried out there, says Schön – 'real' research in conventional terms – often has little relevance to the real-life needs of people. However, because the high ground has come to be revered over the centuries, what happens there is deemed proper, both by its occupants and also by those in the swamps below. Studies conducted in the swamps are not quite legitimate: at best, problem-solving; at worst, what we do in any case.

With the growing popularity of action research the situation has changed dramatically. Those working in the swamps claim legitimacy for their work as real research; this claim is vigorously contested by the holders of the high ground, because (they say) methodologies such as action research are invalid since they rely on forms of knowledge, such as tacit knowing and intuition, which cannot be subjected to the rigorous tests of conventional analysis. Action researchers respond that their research needs to be judged by its own criteria, such as relatability and authenticity (Bassey, 1999), and standards of judgement which are the living values people bring to their own lives (Whitehead, 2000). So the shouts echo up and down the slopes.

I am aware, when I go from workplace to university contexts, how the language changes to match the prevailing epistemology. I am aware of the power play in the different contexts, and of the power relationship between them. I am aware of how I am positioned by people within those contexts. When I am working with course participants I tend to be treated as a close friend and ally, but not an insider, because I am their supervisor; and when I challenge an opinion or ask them to rewrite an assignment they sometimes place me squarely as an outsider, in an opposite camp: 'It's all right for you university people', they say. This is probably a defence strategy to legitimise projecting their anxieties onto me, and it is my job to accept those anxieties and work with them. When I visit universities the same principle works in reverse. I sometimes encounter high-ground occupants who speak slightingly of practitioner research and question its value. These people let me know that I am an outsider, not a 'real' member of staff. While they respect my work, I am kept in my place. I have to say that this is not my experience with most people in the faculties I work with, who are progressive and democratic, and I know they sometimes encounter the same difficulties in wider organisational contexts of negotiating the territory and using the right language. Indeed, I have much cause to be grateful to colleagues in the two British universities I work with for their support to bring the work forward to such an extent. They have fought battles on my behalf. But I do remember an occasion when I was told by a senior manager whose judgement I questioned, 'Remember you are only a part-time lecturer.'

The epistemologies we use reflect our social commitments. Traditional forms of scholarship value abstract issues, often far removed from the real world, from which crisp, well-formed conclusions can be drawn. New forms of scholarship value problems of real living for which there are no clear-cut solutions but a terrain of possible options. It is up to the researcher to make a responsible best guess which one to choose. This is often not a rational decision so much as inspired guesswork and trust in experience and intuition. Inevitably differences of opinion arise between groups working from different epistemologies about the legitimacy and use value of those epistemologies. These debates about epistemologies and methodologies are actually debates about social purpose and what right one person has to explore an issue from within one set of values rather than another. They are issues to do with identity and worth, and the right to pursue a chosen form of life; as well as the way one group feels it can dictate to another what they should do and why. In issues to do with identity and worth, power and politics are always present.

I believe the emotional reactions to action research arise because of its perceived threat to the dominant epistemology. Action research became prominent during the 1980s and 1990s, particularly in the literature of teacher professional education; it is seen as possibly the most significant development of recent times (see the Foreword by Douglas Barnes in Hamilton, 1998; see also Zeichner, 1999). Its profile is rising in management learning (see for example the special edition of *Management Learning*, summer, 1999). A validated theoretical basis of action research is now well established. Anxious reactions probably relate to the fact that practitioners claim the right to be regarded as the best judges of their own work, supporting their claims with rigorously validated evidence; and this claim for epistemological and professional equality poses a challenge for conventional forms of professional education, where traditionally practitioners have been seen as the consumers of research knowledge, generated, usually in higher education contexts, by expert consultants and academic theorists.

The new scholarship can be threatening to the dominant paradigm. As long as innovative practices remain low key they might be tolerated by an establishment that wishes to appear broad-minded. When they become publicly acclaimed, and the locus of power appears to be shifting, this represents a challenge to the establishment, which then needs to take action.

Learning about power

I have learned about these issues through first-hand experience. I constantly find myself negotiating contexts which demonstrate different relationships of power. I have become aware of how I am engaged in power struggles; how I can generate my own power; how I can continue to encourage groups of practitioners to become aware of the incredible potential of their own sense of community and use it strategically for social renewal. I decided to study theories of power in order to understand my situation, what I should encourage and challenge, and how and why.

Contexts of power are many and varied. Here I want to identify three which have been particularly relevant for my situation.

1   The continuing theory–practice gap

The first context is in the literature of organisation studies.

Many writers espouse the rhetoric of educational values while demonstrating self-contradictory practices. On the one hand inspirational literature exists: companies should 'tap the intellectual capital of their workers to create and expand knowledge' (Nonaka and Takeuchi, 1995: back cover); managers should become researchers to guide an organisation's learning process (Senge, 1990); practitioners in all work contexts should shape their own answers, invent them and reinvent them (Handy, 1995b); managers should develop themselves and others (Drucker, 1974). I was initially delighted when I first encountered this literature. Action research is capable of delivering on it all. People are encouraged to reflect on their practice (Schön, 1983, 1995); to imagine future scenarios and take appropriate action (Mintzberg, 1989); to evaluate and modify their practice (Juran, 1988); to take stock of available resources and adjust actions (Champy and Hammer, 1993), all within an inspirational ethic (Peters and

Waterman, 1982; Kanter, 1989) for sustainable social change (Drucker, 1974; Bennis, 1989b).

As I developed my reading I began to wonder where action research was. Some forms of action learning were there (see Pedler, 1997), but this appeared to be marginal; besides there are differences between action learning and action research (though they tend to be blurred these days). The dilemma was compounded for me when I began to make invitational presentations at business schools in the UK, and found that action research was virtually unknown to some, this as recently as 1998.

Where too were the people in the mainstream literature? The individual seemed to have disappeared, or have been deliberately excluded (Nord and Fox, 1999). It is difficult to see how high-sounding educational principles can become a reality without people.

I became increasingly aware of this theory–practice gap, familiar in mainstream education research. The rhetoric trumpets for democratising practice and empowering practitioners (Hargreaves, 1996), but is quite low key about putting the rhetoric into practice. This was reminiscent of my doctoral studies in Personal and Social Education in schools curricula (McNiff, 1989), when I discovered that PSE was often dragooned into the service of social engineering: let them be educated, provided they are educated as we wish them to be (Pring, 1984). Mainstream organisation research appeared to generate conceptual theories about how organisations should be, without stepping into domains of action theories about how to accomplish this.

There is little doubt that the situation is changing as I write in 2000, yet the nature of the change is interesting. Anderson and Herr (1999) explain how corporate cultures are often hostile to action research, regarding it as a potential threat to the establishment, and communicate to all staffs what are acceptable institutional norms and expectations. Therefore in many institutions, action research becomes normalised: practitioners recognise that in undertaking their action enquiries they might be challenging institutionalised norms, and so go for a gentled version of action research that will not upset senior personnel. However, if action research is to be taken seriously as living out the values of social justice and democracy, then *all* participants need to be seen as experts who are knowledgeable about their own lifeworld and needs, not only managers and teachers, but also students (Steinberg and Kincheloe, 1998) and parents (C. Lillis *et al.*, 2000; Smyth, 2000). So, by extension, should *all* participants in *all* organisations (see p. 81; Senge, 1990). The question arises who is prepared to be regarded as a participant and who decides whose story should be heard.

2 *The closing of institutional minds*

The second context is in relation to working with managers in professional institutional settings.

I recounted how the suggestion to develop accredited programmes of teacher education was initially welcomed by the institute that I was working with. After eighteen months of successful implementation (possibly sufficient time for the potential – and challenge? – of the initiative to be perceived by the wider community?), considerable pressure was brought to bear from a variety of sources to close the programmes. By now practitioners were clearly benefiting from their studies: this claim is supported by the production of successful course work of 31 participants and their Masters dissertations, a 100 per cent success rate. People's learning was beginning to influence their workplace practices (for example, Cluskey, 1997; Gaughran, 1998; Whelan, 1997 – I could cite 31 names here). This was congruent with policy recommendations (Government of Ireland, 1992, 1995) and the more progressive educational research literature (for example, Burke, 1992) that practitioners should take responsibility for evaluating their own practice and producing research-based evidence for its effectiveness. Today in 2000 this has become the animating spirit for nation-wide professional education courses for teachers (Government of Ireland, 1995) and also professional education courses for in-service providers (Government of Ireland, 1999b). In a few short years the early efforts to establish action research for higher degree accreditation on a small scale have filtered into national programmes. At the time however, there was concerted effort by particular interest groups to stop the work, and in 1995 my courses were officially to be 'reconfigured' and my involvement terminated. My response was to challenge the decisions in a variety of ways, including through the law, and later successfully to negotiate direct with the accrediting university to continue the work with practitioners without local institutional mediation. Course participants responded to the threatened shut-down by mobilising, challenging decisions, insisting on my reinstatement, and bringing their studies to successful closure.

This was a powerful learning experience about the exercise of authoritarian power and how it can be resisted. I also better understood aspects of chaos theory that suggest how resistance at one point of a system encourages emergence of new forms at another. These were lessons for life, difficult but necessary for future growth.

My situation taught me also to be aware of the potentially unethical use of leadership (Conger, 1998). I could have manipulated course members to act on my behalf. In the event I deliberately distanced myself from the activities of course members, choosing to fight my own issues separate from theirs. I think this action reinforced the character of the group as a chosen community (Chapter 9) who share collective commitments without a nominated leader; and it has significant implications for the discussion below of the nature of the power of educative communities.

3 Dealing with the power of institutional control

The third context is in relation to working with some managers in higher education institutional settings.

In 1997 I was appointed as a part-time lecturer with the accrediting university, a short contract position which did not jeopardise my independence. This enabled the current courses to complete successfully that year.

When the courses ended, I was anxious to maintain the momentum, and worked hard to persuade the university to authorise me to develop new Masters programmes. A reluctance to commit on the university's part led me to investigate alternative routes via a second British university, whereupon the first university expressed renewed interest and allowed me to go ahead. I did however begin courses leading to MPhil/PhD awards with the second university. This meant that I could offer escalator routes to higher degree accreditation for workplace practice. The outcome, five years on, is that an island-wide network exists of self-study groups, all of whose study impacts directly on the workplace, which in turn has attracted the attention of national agencies.

The model is that I support four groups for Masters degrees in various locations around the island and one group in Dublin for MPhil/PhD degrees. Resources are arranged by the universities in the form of library access in Ireland and at the home UK universities, as well as provision of resource banks locally; and the quality of learning experience of course members is high. Colleagues from the universities visit their respective groups regularly to ensure that course members' needs are met, and also to provide occasional teaching input. Quality control measures are stringent, to meet the designated standards of the Quality Assurance Agency. Being a member of the network appears to be a valuable experience in which people can learn from one another. I regularly monitor my own practice to ensure its quality, and make my evaluative documents available to the respective universities.

At a personal level, I have been fascinated by the attempt by some university-based people to control my practices and the practices of those I support. There were always different perceptions of my identity, and whose work it was. Was I a part-time employee, or a bona fide researcher with whom the university was in a collaborative partnership, or both? There were also different opinions about the identity of course participants. Were they students in an outreach centre of a British university, or practitioners working to improve the quality of their own work contexts or both? Increasingly exchanges between me and these colleagues took on the form of a hegemonic discourse which, as Laclau (1977) says, is characterised by the struggle for identity (see Chapter 9; see also Conversation 3.1). It took time to realise that my identity was not in an institution and to have confidence in creating myself as the person I wished to be. I consistently resisted domination on all fronts. Today I maintain my own chosen identity, and this is respected, I believe, though not without question.

Conversation 3.1

Wayne Gorman

I've been institutionalised all my life, in orphanages, in the army, in government. What many institutions do is shame people. Take for example the company I work for part-time. They want to employ Aboriginal youth on a part-time basis, and when their services are no longer needed, they are dismissed. That's hiring cheap labour, not honouring the person. The money is the driver. People speak about the fact that we're going to give these poor kids an opportunity to work for six months. They are not. They are doing the same thing that society has done for ever – marginalising, hurting them. That's what they are doing but they can't see that. They can't see beyond. Why are they so slow to see that? I am not sure whether they want to see it.

Sometimes institutions understand very clearly what they are doing in this shaming process, but sometimes they do it unintentionally, too. When a teacher puts a mark on a piece of work it often becomes a mark of shame. That wasn't the intent, but it happens, because then a person shares the mark with someone else, and they compare, and someone wins and someone loses. Marks do not honour where all people are. We need to think about these things.

The work has had significant impact in Ireland, and I now also work by invitation with several Irish universities in developing action research approaches, and with national agencies (see Introduction). This is entirely in keeping with my original intention in 1992 to try to embed action research within Irish education systems, not as a further form of colonisation, but as trying to reconceptualise the knowledge base of professional education. I can claim that, working with others, we have changed organisational structures and practices. This might have appeared initially as irritating to some, but at the end of the day the challenge that I and my action researcher colleagues have posed has been accommodated within existing systems and is recognised as holding promise for new directions in Irish education.

My encounters with institutional power have led me to study it seriously. I have come to understand that power does not exist as a 'thing' that can be acquired, developed or devolved, as much of the traditional organisation research literature suggests, mistakenly I think. Concepts such as subsidiarity, power sharing, empowerment, are all concepts that derive from the idea of power as a thing. Power is not a thing. Power exists in who people are and what they do in relation with one another. Relationships can be life-enhancing and they can also be destructive; people can encourage and they can also diminish.

How we are with one another constitutes the nature of our power; people in destructive relationships can collectively close down one another's opportunities for growth; people in life-enhancing relationships can collectively generate their own power to support themselves and one another. These insights have developed directly from relating my academic study to my own experience.

1 What is the nature of power?

The concept of power is crucial and widely used, yet until recently not well theorised (Dyrberg, 1997). Dyrberg explains how power has come to be understood in terms of two traditions. These are

1   behaviourist traditions that found their apogee in Lukes's (1974) 'three faces of power';
2   a newer 'turn' beginning with the work of Foucault, who saw power as 'presuppositionless', that is, not as a given entity but as a feature of relationships between people. Foucault's work has directly influenced newer theories which see power as constituted in and through interpersonal relationships.

What follows is a brief and inevitably incomplete explication of these ideas, sufficient I hope to show how action research might be construed as power-constituted relationships among communities of people, with educative potential, an important idea in any new theory of organisation that locates itself in real lives and interests.

The three faces of power

Power is traditionally understood as 'the ability to make a difference' (Dyrberg, 1997: 11). Behaviourist approaches place it as an objective force, a thing which people have and use. The 'first face of power' (Dahl, 1986) is 'power over' and is found perhaps most strikingly in the work of Weber. An external relationship exists between power and the person over whom power is exercised. Its implementation is sequential and causal: A gets B to do something that A wants B to do, but that B would not normally have done. The exercise of power can be seen by empirical proof: the way that B acts is caused by A's possession and use of power. Power is seen in discrete events and is possessed by individuals. It is acquired by attribution: some people such as leaders are agreed to have power, though the issue of how they may use it remains problematic. Power is used to make a difference in the sense of 'bringing about change'; change is seen as a cause-and-effect relationship between events which is instigated by a powerful agent.

The 'second face of power', as described in the work of Bachrach and Baratz (1962) places power within social contexts. Power is still studied in relation to behaviour, especially as those behaviours represent conflicts of interests. However, the idea of power expands from 'power over' to 'power to': the one-directional power that A has over B results in decisions and actions as events; but

B also has power to decide or act, or not to decide or act. Power now works two ways. Power is socially constructed and negotiated, because people as individual agents have a say in how they choose to act. Power may also be used to prevent conflict occurring; on this view, power still exists as a reified thing which is external to human agency.

The 'third face of power' is Lukes's critical response to the inadequacies of the first two. He criticises them, 'both for being behaviourist and subjectivist, because exercises of power in each are perceived solely in relation to decisions taken by agents' (Dyrberg, 1997: 63). The third face is characterised by 'no-decision', that is, power does not necessarily stem from decisions, but from patterns of social relationships. Lukes speaks about 'systemic power', the influences in the patterns which often become 'systemic bias', because people sometimes are not aware of how their relationships influence them to use power or to be objects of power. This bias can become institutionalised: 'the bias of the system is not sustained simply by a series of individually chosen acts, but also, most importantly, by the socially structured and culturally patterned behaviour of groups, and practices of institutions, which may indeed be manifested by individuals' inaction' (Lukes, 1974, in Dyrberg, 1997: 64). Lukes shows how the origination of power is in the real interests of people. However, power is still theorised (negatively) as the power of domination, a thing used by people in their relationships. Power is a feature of a given social order: the order is inevitably understood as hierarchical, and the exercise of power further strengthens this.

It is possible to draw a loose comparison between the three faces of power and Habermas's theory of human interests and show how this theory translates into a three-paradigm view of social scientific research (Chapter 4); and to show the relevance of the comparison for organisational theory. The first face compares with Habermas's technical interest, and the instrumental focus of empirical research, in which the aim is to control and predict behaviours. This is consistent with a view of organisations as objective structures, and of management as keeping things, including people, under control. The purpose of organisation research is to maintain hierarchical systems: it is informed by an ethic of domination and subjugation (see Chapter 5). The second face compares with Habermas's practical interest, and the social orientation of interpretive research, in which the aim is to understand behaviours and assign meanings to them. Organisations are complexes of social relationships, and managers learn to maximise these to ensure efficient productivity. The purpose of organisation research is to understand the nature of social relationships in order to ensure smooth operations; its ethic is social amelioration (see Chapter 6). The third face compares with Habermas's emancipatory interest, and the liberating focus of critical theoretic research, in which the aim is to help people become aware of the visible and invisible influences that potentially distort their understandings of their own lifeworlds. The purpose of organisation research is to raise people's awareness to the influences that disempower them, and try to free themselves (see Chapter 7).

Foucault's power analytics

Foucault rejects the idea of power as an object. Power, he says (1980), is not derivative; it does not exist in agencies or structures. Power is in the relationships among people as they try to understand who they are (their identities), and as they construct their identities with others. Individuals do not live in isolation; they are, pathology or coercion aside, social beings whose identities are always negotiated with others. Who people become is a matter of politics. An individual is not 'given' in a pre-political sense; people will often try to force others to become the kinds of persons they wish them to be. Power is not an object to be used in the construction of identity; power *is* identity. We do not encounter power as such; we encounter practices which are discursively and politically enacted. We live in and through these practices, and people become the identities whose identities are being formed. Power, says Dyrberg (1997: 93), is not a game to be played; it is the nature of the game itself.

This view has considerable implications for organisation theory and how it is used for organisation practices. Power is people, how they are individually and how they are together. People's identities are always in process of becoming; organisations are sites in which people struggle to negotiate which identity they will become. Power is not located in any one part of the system: it exists everywhere. Moreover, 'the power relations existing through [a system, or an organisation] do not necessarily conform to those which find expression at the level of the regime ... The point is, then, that the very conceptualisation of power constitutes an inseparable part of power struggles: discourses *on* power are also discourses *of* power' (Dyrberg, ibid.: 86). Organisational theories which speak *about* power are discourses *of* power: they influence organisation practices as practices of power. What I am writing here is a discourse about power, and also a discourse of power: and I am aware of what I am doing and why – see (3), p. 109.

2 How is power acquired?

If power is seen as an object, it can be acquired, devolved and shared. It becomes a negotiable commodity. If power is seen as relationships among people, its character reflects the quality of the relationships. When people care about one another they create identities that are committed to autonomy in life-enhancing practices. Discourses *about* care are discourses *of* care. When people do not care about one another they aim to control the creation of other people's identities, and turn them into the kind of person they want them to be.

Most organisation theory understands power as an object, derived from agency or structure (see Conversation 3.2). This body of theory also regards organisations as objects. Most organisation research addresses issues of how power is sustained and used in organisations for particular purposes. An example is in *The Construction of Social Reality* (Searle, 1995). Searle argues that social reality exists largely because of the agreement of the people who create it. In organisations, for example, people maintain designated positions as long as public opinion allows them to. If they fall from grace, they will use their already established power base to restore favour. Searle says that there are two kinds of facts: brute facts and institutional facts. Brute facts are about realities that exist outside human agency – Everest exists and birds sing. These are givens. Institutional facts are so because people agree to them: Clinton is President. Institutional facts are held in place by rules, and there are two kinds of rules: regulative rules and constitutive rules. Regulative rules regulate social practices: cars drive on the left in the UK and on the right in the USA. Constitutive rules are the kind of rules needed for a system to operate in the first place: when driving cars we aim to avoid other cars. Provided everyone sticks to the rules, the social system operates smoothly.

Conversation 3.2

Stephen O'Connor

The stereotypical view of someone who goes to prison is that they are somehow stupid or educationally subnormal; I've heard those terms used. That is not our experience. Even people who have literacy problems are often very intelligent. We have people who do very well within the formal provison that we offer once they get a foothold. But sometimes they are put down by other so-called educated people who can often be quite rude. Possibly it's an issue of control. Here we try to enable people to find their voice.

I'll give you a striking example of that. Once a year we have a public speaking event, and our students get help in the art of public speaking. The topics that people choose from the outside are often witty but they can be quite superficial. The topics our chaps choose, and it has been remarked from people outside as well as from ourselves, are topics that they choose from their own life experiences. They will talk about the problems of social deprivation in the first person. They bring their learning, their life experience, to their situations. It is quite moving to hear people in a public way having their experiences validated by the expression of them. I know there is an element of catharsis for the invidual involved, but that's not the point. They are saying, 'What I learned about social deprivation I learned from being there. What I learn about abuse is not what I read in the papers; I learned it from experience. I know about it.' It's very powerful and liberating for those who listen. The formal educators sit there and get it straight between the eyes. All the formal education system did not do for these people.

No, there is no way that our people are less than others; it's just that the others like to think they are and they try to make sure things stay that way.

The problem is (see Chapter 2), such theories do not explain the necessary conditions for people to agree to the rules in the first place, or what happens when they do or do not. There is an assumption that the rules are fixed entities, resistant to challenge or change. Practice however does not comply with the theory. In real world social and organisational practice, change is inevitable and probably desirable in all aspects of a system, even in the categories of analysis used. Not only are the rules liable to change, but also the very concept of rules. Machiavelli knew this.

Which form of theory?

Current forms of organisation theory which conceptualise power as an object are still dominant. What they say about power is still held as true: discourses *about* power are discourses *of* power. Ironically, those who espouse the value of power as an object use the power of relationships to maintain their own theory. These usually manifest as strategies of control. The issue also arises about how power is legitimated. Academics and others who work with abstract theory constitute groups of knowers who generate their own power to keep those whom they regard as non-legitimate knowers under control.

How comes it that power is vested in some, and they are agreed to be 'in power'?

Strategies of social control

Strategies of social control, and strategies to maintain that control, are intimately related. Here are some examples.

Allocation of blame

Many strategies exist to control people. Which strategies are used depends on the degree and anticipated strength of opposition. The task is to get B to do what A wants B to do, even though B might not want to do it. In totalitarian societies, says Chomsky (1996), the task is straightforward and achieved through brute force and terror. In democratic societies, however, where overt terrorism (at least by ordinary citizens) is disallowed, more subtle forms of control have to be used. This usually amounts to constructing a propaganda system to communicate messages through the culture so that norms are unconsciously internalised. Workplaces are used to maintain the status quo through social engineering and the reproduction of social norms (Bourdieu and Passeron, 1977). A favoured strategy is allocation of blame: in schools students are taught to expect failure by teachers who are taught this too. In workplace contexts employees are rendered impotent by disempowering practices; Morgan (1997a) speaks of some organisation contexts as psychic prisons.

The locus of control exists both internally and externally: internally within individual personal beliefs and collective norms and values; externally as vested in an outside authority. The most powerful chains are the ones we forge ourselves, so the most effective strategies, as Gramsci (1971) shows, is to impose a set of beliefs and practices in such a way that people come to internalise them, thinking that it was their idea in the first place. The aim is not only to control practice but also to control thinking itself. This is evident everywhere; there are jobs called 'just a secretary' and 'only a dishwasher'. Encouragement to be a good team member often carries a veiled message to conform (Schrage, 1989).

Allocation of blame is known as attribution theory. Dispositional attribution is to put the blame on people and their 'disposition'; situational attribution is to put the blame on a situation. So when the local drunk falls on the pavement, the tendency is to pass her by. It is her own fault and there is little sympathy with her. When someone slips on the slippery floor, however, there is a rush to help. Similarly there is a tendency to blame the situation when one is personally involved in a mishap – 'The cup broke because the handle was loose' – or to blame someone else when one is not personally involved – 'The cup broke because she is clumsy.' Compensatory measures involve the same principles: children are slow, or less intelligent, or, in more generous talk, disadvantaged by their home or social circumstances. Outside agencies can be conveniently scapegoated when it is too obvious to place blame directly. In workplaces workers are recalcitrant and difficult, as in McGregor's (1960) Theory X, and should not be mollycoddled but be forced to toe the line. Unemployment is self-inflicted; people should get on their bikes and find a job, as Sir Norman Tebbitt memorably put it. People are expected to fail; they are persuaded to collude in their own failure by acknowledging their deficits. This is so endemic in technologised cultures, and so entrenched in the corporate psyche, that questions are seldom raised about how the underlying structure might give rise to inequitable practices and be directly responsible for failure. Even less are questions raised about how the structure came to be in place, or whether the concept of structure is legitimate. As Fanon observed (1967), it is difficult to see whether the sky is blue with a boot on your neck.

Manufacturing consent

Such strategies are commonplace in organisational practices. Voices raised in resistance, whether the contexts are board rooms or church bazaars, are suppressed. The most common tactics are the manufacturing of consent (Herman and Chomsky, 1988) and the creation of necessary illusions (Chomsky, 1989):

> Harold Lasswell explained in the *Encyclopaedia of the Social Sciences* that we should not succumb to 'democratic dogmatisms about men being the best judges of their own interests'. They are not; the best judges are the elites, who must, therefore, be ensured the means to impose their will, for the common good. When social arrangements deny them the requisite force to compel obedience, it is necessary to find 'a whole new technique of control, largely through propaganda' because of the 'ignorance and superstition [of]

... the masses'. In the same years, Reinhold Niebuhr argued that 'rationality belongs to the cool observers', while 'the proletarian' follows not reason but faith, based upon a crucial element of 'necessary illusion'. Without such illusion, the ordinary person will descend to 'inertia'.

(p. 17)

It appears that some people are capable of thinking for themselves, while others are not.

The crisis of legitimation (Habermas, 1973) extends to making judgements about who is qualified to say who is entitled to be regarded as a fully fledged human being, and to be in control of the criteria for those judgements. This is illustrated by Carol Tavris (1993), who recounts how two new disorders became prevalent among slaves in colonial America. The first was *drapetomania* and

> was diagnosable by a single symptom: the uncontrollable urge to escape from slavery. Slaves who 'suffered' from the other disorder, *dysathesia aethiopica*, revealed many symptoms of their 'sickness' – destroying property on the plantation, being disobedient, talking back, fighting with their masters, or refusing to work. ... Thus, doctors were able to assure slave-owners (and themselves) that a mental illness, not the intolerable condition of slavery, made slaves seek freedom. This explanation conveniently turned the desire for liberty into a 'sickness' that was the problem of the slave, not the slaveowner.
>
> (pp. 176–7)

This kind of reasoning might seem laughable today, yet it is used systematically in workplaces, homes, schools and other organisations. Interest groups deliberately fabricate mythologies and implement systems of terror which range from the coming of the bogey man to the coming of the end of the world.

So why do perfectly normal, decent people believe them? Some psychologists believe that certain personality types are prone to indoctrination. Adorno, for example (Adorno *et al.*, 1950), suggested that some people are particularly susceptible to autocratic forms of authority; while other psychologists such as Milgram (1973) and Zimbardo (1969) demonstrate that perfectly normal, decent people are capable of amazing feats of inhumanity under conditions of duress or when allocated to a role, even to the extent of killing someone because they were told to do so.

Foucault shows how people in institutional settings are led to think and act in particular ways; some of his most important work draws on studies of people in prisons and asylums. In *Discipline and Punish* (1977), Foucault uses the analogy of a panopticon, a special prison in which all prisoners are kept in cells such that they cannot see each other, but can be seen by a central jailer, who is himself invisible to the prisoners. The jailer is able to see everyone at any time without being seen himself. This constitutes continual surveillance; the jailer's 'gaze' is the major controlling force. The most effective surveillance is to get the prisoners to internalise the 'gaze' and monitor themselves. The metaphor can be extended to multiple social contexts. One wonders whether management by walking about might sometimes be construed as surveillance.

Chomsky says that people are systematically persuaded to believe information presented through the culture, and that cultural development is itself controlled by elites for their own interests (see Chomsky, 1996; see also Chapter 9). I have to agree. I also agree with Chomsky that people can be helped to see what is happening to them by individuals and groups who have the courage to speak out against the dominant culture. In the case of developing a form of organisation theory that will support efforts towards social progress, those people would include academics who have the courage to depart from dominant (sometimes imposed) institutional epistemologies, and work towards generating newer theories that act in the interests of people in everyday workplaces.

3 How is power put to use?

Mary Midgley (1992: 158–9) quotes a passage from Paul Davies's book *Superforce*:

> Letting imagination have free rein, it is possible to envisage mankind [*sic*] one day gaining control over the superforce. To achieve this would enable us to manipulate the greatest power in the universe … We might even be able to manipulate the dimensions of space itself, creating bizarre artificial worlds with unimaginable properties. Truly, we should be lords of the universe.
>
> (Davies, 1984: 167–8)

But why should we want to be, even if it were possible? 'What is all this power *for*?' asks Midgley (1992: 159; emphasis in original). There are shades here of Francis Bacon's exhortations to learn to dominate nature, to torture her secrets out of her. Perhaps people who want to conquer outer space should first check that all is well in their own inner space. It is a matter of common sense, if not moral intent, that we should aim for power, not to escape to other worlds, but to improve our own.

I said above that discourses *about* power are discourses *of* power. I said that I am deliberately engaging in a discourse of power. I am quite clear about how my power is generated, how I use it, and how I hope to continue using it.

The nature of my power

My image of power is that it is somehow a latent potential in us all that waits for an appropriate trigger to come to realisation. The generation of power is an emergent property of systems, including humans. A powerful stimulus for the realisation of deep-level potential is human interaction. When people come together they tap into their latent potentialities and transform them into real power which can then be used according to their goals. These goals, as noted before, can be for good or ill.

The source of my power

I am aware of the generative nature of my own power. I am aware of the values I hold for education, and how those values become reality through trying to live in a way that is congruent with them. This is essentially a personal exercise, because I have to believe in my own personal knowledge, and trust in my own sense of creativity and right living. It cannot be solitary, however, in the sense that my living is always in relation with others. Whatever power I have is generated through my relationship with others, because my living is other-directed. I find that I need long periods of time alone, to think and enjoy my space, but when the time becomes too long the colours of my life begin to fade, and I need to connect with community. I also need to commit energy to activating the power. When I become lazy or selfish, the power goes. Power, like the bodies in which it is located, needs always to be used to stay bright.

Using my power

I use my power to encourage others to discover and use theirs. I also use it to challenge autocratic practices which try to close down opportunities for others' growth. I do both these things in the next section.

This book as a discourse of power

If this book constitutes a discourse of power, then I want to use it to develop theories of how people can enjoy worthwhile organisational lives. People should not be subjected to bullying or persuasion to become the kind of person others want them to be. People need to feel valued, and they have a right to create their own identity in negotiation with others. I am therefore challenging the dominant theory that requires people to take on the identities others create for them, and adopting instead a theory that says we are allowed to create our own identities.

Role theory

We are who we come to believe we are. By internalising externally imposed norms we can dangerously come to convince ourselves that we are the person other people want us to be.

It is important to remember that no one is ever unencumbered. No person can ever be free of their history or culture, of their gender, or their upbringing. We are conditioned from birth to become a particular kind of socialised and normalised person. We internalise the gaze and control ourselves very well. It is also important to be aware of the postmodern issue of whether the 'self' exists, or whether each one of us is a social construction. Perhaps common-sense reassures us that each one of us is a living human, with feelings and ideas and our right to a place in the world. This person is unique in time and space.

The first step to reducing the unfreedom, says Freire (1970), is to become aware of our own situatedness and to recognise it for what it is. This is a root exercise of power knowledge (Foucault, 1980). When we come to know, we activate our power; we need first to become aware of conditioning forces and work to resist them. Freire's work, and that of his colleagues Peter McLaren, Henry Giroux and other critical pedagogues, laid the groundwork for radical pedagogies and a systematic politics of dissent within a framework of socialism: 'Critical pedagogy ... remains committed to the practical realisation of self-determination and creativity on a collective social scale ... critical educators need to wage nothing less than war in the interest of the sacredness of human life, collective dignity for the wretched of the earth, and the right to live in peace and harmony' (McLaren, 1997: 13).

Social scientific theories can be related to role theory. Role theory uses a drama model which says that life is a play in which we are actors and directors; people-as-objects are allocated to particular roles as directed by others-as-subjects. This represents a deep power relationship in which one person decides who another person is, and the other person fits into that slot. The approach is authoritarian; people come to feel that they should comply, or be labelled as deviant and awkward.

Role theory is disrespectful of individual autonomy. 'In the dramaturgical model people are construed as actors with lines already written and their roles determined by the particular play they find themselves in. Nor do they have much choice as to how to play those roles in any particular setting. They learned how to take up a particular role through observation of others in that role' (Harré and van Langenhove, 1999). Some individuals are refused parity of esteem; powerful others make decisions for them. This requires some to learn helplessness, to abdicate choice and responsibility in making decisions, and to become docile – 'Just a housewife'. In extreme contexts, people kill one another because they are expected to regard one another as enemies; they are not able to question who is writing their script or for what purpose (Fanon, 1967).

Positioning theory

On the other hand, we can reject the theory that says we should occupy roles others have created for us, and regard ourselves as agents. Positioning theory says that people-as-subjects have the right to determine their own positions – a proactive agency stance in which we decide the kind of person we wish to be, and we work consistently to recreate ourselves. 'We are not only responsible for our own lives but there are multiple choices in relation not only to the possible lines that we can produce but to the form of the play itself' (Harré and van Langenhove, 1999: 42).

Positioning theory is located within the wider paradigm of social constructionism, and is a core principle of action research. It holds that people create their own realities. To the extent that we can be free of our own cultural and historical situatedness, we have the freedom to construct the reality we wish to have, in principle at least. Positioning theory says that we live our lives through conversational processes which take place in relation to various levels of interaction: intrapersonal, interpersonal, institutional and cultural. We create our selves and other selves through our discourses; our situations become narratives. The office therefore is not a physical structure but a fluid process of relations; not a place we are in but a context we create (see Conversation 3.3). When we position ourselves as particular persons, we are acting out of our own sense of agency.

Conversation 3.3

Ashley Balbirnie

It would be one of my greatest passions to run this office in a different way, different from what I and a lot of other people are used to. I want to make it democratic. We created this organisation from the ground up, so we did not inherit attitudes, but to this day there is still a debate about whether or not I should have an office. I choose not to because, at a corporate level, I want it to be seen that it isn't a closed door or a locked office. Many colleagues however want me in an office. They say, 'You're the MD; you should have an office.' It's possibly something we've inherited from the British newspaper culture, the hierarchical set-up, and so it's what people expect, but it's not what I want. I am honestly staggered. Three years we have been here and they are still trying to get me in an office and I am still trying to get across that I don't want that. Changing attitudes takes years, and we probably don't even see the outcomes of our efforts until we have gone.

This has implications for how people think of themselves and the spaces they occupy in organisations. It also has implications for the kind of theory we endorse. In role theory, the organisation is a structure, fixed and unchanging, in which there is a place for everyone and everyone knows their place. This view draws on machine metaphors, deterministic and reductionist: people are spokes in a wheel. An organisation is successful in terms of how well its parts function; the aim of the organisation is instrumental productivity; learning relates to efficiency. On the other hand, positioning theory urges people to see themselves as active choosers, participants in a creative conversation about who we are and how we can live together successfully. The organisation becomes a context for multiple conversations that reflect the constantly changing perceptions of participants and the constantly evolving future scenarios they imaginatively create together.

This is all, of course, supposing that people work in contexts where they are able to do this, and are not subjected to the exercise of authoritarian power that prevents them from doing so in the first place.

4 What are the implications for organisation theory as a discourse of power?

Schön says (1995: 31) that the new categories of scholarly activity 'must take the form of action research. What else could they be? They will not consist in laboratory experimentation or statistical analysis of variance, nor will they consist only or primarily in the reflective criticism and speculation familiar to the humanities.' They must relate to our knowing-in-action, and, in terms of this chapter, how that knowing-in-action generates power.

Action research encourages people to be active knowers. They find their own solutions to workplace issues. Individually and collectively people have the responsibility for deciding how they should act. This means negotiating with others; the basis of negotiation is confidence in one's own personal knowledge. There are implications here for the new worlds of work and employment, where work stability has disappeared and personal gain is rapidly becoming the basis of the work ethic. As a methodology for individual and social renewal, action research holds promise as a resource for people to imagine and implement plans for their individual well-being, and also to authorise the collective to negotiate their own interpretation of a common good.

Organisation studies emphasises the importance of the new knowledge work. On an action research reading, knowledge work implies knowledge of self as well as knowledge of facts and procedures: the development of personal awareness, the capacity to learn and adapt, the ability to work with others. Terms such as 'development', 'capacity' and 'ability' are terms of influence, aspects of discourses about power. I said at the beginning of this chapter that power was generally understood as the ability to make a difference (Dyrberg, 1997). When the action research proceeds from educational values, the difference must be for social good.

Action research is a participatory practice, both as a methodological necessity and as a social impulse. Individual practitioners validate their claims to improved practice by seeking validation for those claims from other practitioners. The seemingly essentialist individualistic question, 'How do I improve my work?' aims both for personal improvement and social benefit, because work is a relational practice whose values include improvement of the quality of human living in a sustainable environment. Contrary to some trivial critiques, action research is not self-indulgent nor narcissistic. It is a rigorous discipline, an ethico-political commitment to care and to pluralistic forms of practice.

Participatory action research has the capacity to generate significant power for social renewal. Power is the nature of relationships. Communities of action researchers are committed to education, the reciprocal practice of mutual teaching-for-learning as manifestations of qualities which enable people to grow in danger-free contexts.

Educative organisations

It is not enough for organisations only to be learning organisations. Learning can lead to 'making a difference'. To ensure that the difference is a difference for good, organisations need to conceptualise themselves as educative organisations, whose relationships very clearly demonstrate the educative potential for making a difference for good. Educative relationships are very powerful.

I believe that the stories in this book show the amazing potential of action research as a discourse of power. People working individually and collectively have shown how studying their own practice has brought benefit to others in the workplace. They also show how they are influencing wider organisational and social systems for good. They show how being in community enables them to be aware of their own potential for influence (see also Chapter 9).

For my part, the positive relationships I enjoy with members of this now island-wide (and extending) community act as a continuing source of strength and inspiration. The positive power generated in and through our relationships helps me to keep the negative experiences in perspective, and concentrate on the serious business of celebrating good practice.

I am moving on, and this has given me reason again to think carefully about power. We are responsible, says Antoine de Saint-Exupéry in *The Little Prince* (1991), for that which we grow to love. Je suis résponsable de ma rose. Am I responsible for my colleagues? I think not. I hope I have enabled people to become aware of their own power in community. I hope I have done this without encouraging dependence. As yet I don't know where I am bound; as my colleague Caroline Clarke on the doctoral programme says, we are brought to places where we have something to do. It is time for me to begin to withdraw. I am also aware that in a developmental process such as that which is happening in our organisation, leaders have to get out of the way so that other people can shine in their own way. We shall see.

I know that I have come to appreciate how action research generates an organisational knowledge base whose patterns reflect the transformation of individual knowing into cooperative practices. To what extent this may become a reality is largely down to managers and organisational leaders, whether they wish to recognise how power is constituted in relationships and so work with people to understand the nature and potential of their own relational practices, or whether to maintain status power as expert knowers and control others' practices. The first option requires managers to see themselves as in relationship; the second option allows them to keep their distance. These are matters of personal commitment. I believe that these ideas raise questions about how we theorise our practices in terms of our motives, and accept responsibility for the consequences.

Collaboration for co-liberation

A story of intentional intervention

Pip Bruce Ferguson

> People know what they do; they frequently know why they do what they do; but what they don't know is what what they do does.
>
> (Foucault, quoted in Dreyfus and Rabinow, 1983: 187)

Introduction

How does one find out 'what what we do does'? Why is it important to know? How can we intervene in our own practices, in order to change and improve them? These are the kinds of questions that have dominated my thoughts over the 1990s.

I work as a staff developer in a New Zealand polytechnic, a position I have held since 1985. It's an interesting job. I'm responsible, with a team of colleagues, for assisting with the development of teaching skills in new staff at the poly-technic. New Zealand polytechnics have developed along technical/vocational lines and only comparatively recently have acquired some of the practices and trappings of academia. So our staff have tended to be appointed largely on the basis of practical work experience. My unit helps tree surgeons, motor mechanics, cooks, accountants, nurses and the like to develop the teaching skills they need in order to help their students' learning. It's always stimulating, frequently exhausting and a continual learning experience for us all.

New Zealand has been afflicted by the New Right ideology of user-pays, market forces dominance throughout our economy. It has had serious implica-tions for people's access to equitable health, education and social services provision. This ideology was introduced through the fourth Labour government from 1984 to 1990, when Labour lost to National (a conservative party). The National government has continued New Right policies and thinking with a vengeance. In education, such thinking has resulted in the introduction in some schools of bulk funding of teacher salaries, and the suggestion that parents should be issued with vouchers allowing them to 'purchase' education from 'desir-able providers'. Fortunately this scheme has not yet been introduced, and with the recent (November 1999) ascent to power of a Labour government, supported by Alliance and Green Party members as coalition partners, it is unlikely to be promoted further at present.

However in 1990 an Education Amendment Act was passed through Parliament which sought to promote the competitiveness that New Right ideology sees as ideal. Where, traditionally, only universities in New Zealand have offered degrees, the Act made it possible for polytechnics, wananga (Maori tertiary education institutions) and private providers to be able to offer degrees also. This has had far-reaching implications for practice within polytechnics. Whereas the Education Amendment Act (1990: 33) described how in universities 'research and teaching are closely interdependent and most of their teaching is done by people who are active in advancing knowledge', this situation has never been typical of technical education institutions. Their role has traditionally been a pragmatic one of equipping individuals for the workforce. Codling (1997: 84), for example, describing a 'typical New Zealand polytechnic', claimed 'an institutional history dominated by teaching to the virtual exclusion of research'.

Our polytechnic opted to offer degrees in 1991, taking up the government's encouragement, and seeking to 'maintain market share' in an increasingly competitive environment. How that decision came about, and the intricacies of its implications for staff, formed part of the content of my doctoral thesis (Bruce Ferguson, 1999). However, the introduction of degrees had a huge impact on the polytechnic and required staff who had never previously seen themselves as researchers, to engage in research if they taught on degree programmes. I could see, back in 1991, that our decision to offer degrees would change the face of polytechnic education, and have major implications for the culture of the polytechnic in which I work, The Waikato Polytechnic (TWP). Accordingly, I decided to play an active part in the ongoing development of the polytechnic. I sought to ensure that the teaching practice that Codling identified as dominant in polytechnics, and that is so valued by our staff, was valued and promoted as our research culture emerged.

Developing a teacher-friendly research culture

My intervention was based on my own experience of action research. As part of my own teacher training as a new staff member at TWP, in the late 1980s I took a course in action research with Professor Tony Morrison, lately of the University of Auckland. I could immediately see how appropriate the approach was in helping teaching staff to engage in meaningful research. So I successfully introduced an action research course into the teacher training programme that my unit offers. The action research course is optional, and the numbers taking it have not exceeded nine per year – frequently fewer. But my hope was that action research would act as a catalyst to help develop, at TWP, a research culture in which teachers' experiences were valued. To help me systematically to investigate 'what what I do does', I enrolled in doctoral study at the University of Waikato, with my course and its effect on staff here as the focus. The doctorate was completed during 1999.

It is easy for staff in large organisations such as ours, the third largest polytechnic in New Zealand, to feel powerless in the face of change. I sought to ensure that the values that I and other teaching staff here hold dear were maintained and strengthened in our changing culture. The New Zealand Qualifications Authority, a qualifications setting and controlling body formalised under the 1990 Act, decrees that

3. The teaching staff involved in [degree courses]:
   ...
   b. demonstrate significant and verifiable involvement in research
   (NZQA, 1993: 12)

I was aware, through my involvement with staff across the polytechnic, that this requirement was striking fear into many hearts. For some of our staff, their only experience of research has been the 'men in white coats in laboratories' type of research. Many saw research and teaching as quite separate activities. One of the foundation staff whom I interviewed for my thesis claimed that

If you've got a project that you want to research, well then you should divorce yourself from [your] job for twelve months, two years, to do that research.

I wanted to help staff see that research is not something to be feared, something which would require them to 'divorce' themselves from the teaching that they love in order to pursue – to show them how, using action research, they can continue to develop their teaching skills as a form of research, thus meeting the requirements while continuing the practice which they value. I wanted to break down any sense of dichotomy between teaching and research.

In what other ways did I seek to help our research culture develop in ways that valued teaching practice? I joined the newly constituted Research Committee as an elected staff representative (1992–94) and was active in helping to develop teacher-friendly definitions of research (Bruce Ferguson, 1999); in encouraging staff to attend the yearly New Zealand Action Research Network conferences, organising one here in Hamilton in 1996. I actively promoted the work I was doing for my thesis in a series of papers and workshops both on site and at conferences elsewhere; counselled, supported and mentored new researchers within the organisation. Having investigated, in my Masters thesis (Ferguson, 1991), some of the ways in which Maori, the indigenous people of New Zealand, have been disadvantaged in the education system, I wanted to ensure that our developing research culture also recognised and valued Maori ways of researching. I participated in two working parties that looked at ways of valuing Maori practice, one in the use of the Maori language in assessment, and one that developed a very innovative set of protocols for conducting research with implications for Maori (White *et al.*, 1998).

The theorist whose work I used most extensively in my thesis is Michel Foucault. Foucault's contention is that power should be researched

less from the top-down point of view of policymakers, and more from the

bottom-up perspective of everyday life within the architectural spaces of institutions such as prisons, hospitals, asylums, and schools.

(Middleton, 1998: xvi)

Foucault saw power as being not held by dominant groups, but exercised via
'micropractices' that operate in everyday life to control and shape individual
bodies towards conformity and subjectivity. Power, according to Foucault, is not a
possession or a capacity (Foucault, 1980); it does not emanate from a king or
from the state. Rather, it

> must be analysed as something which circulates, or rather as something
> which only functions in the form of a chain. It is never localised here or there,
> never in anybody's hands, never appropriated as a commodity or a piece of
> wealth. Power is employed and exercised through a net-like organisation ...
> in other words, individuals are the vehicles of power, not its points of applica-
> tion.

(p. 98)

This view of power is heartening for individuals working at grass roots in large
institutions. It holds up the possibility of intervening actively in one's own environment; of analysing the 'micropractices' through which power operates, and
challenging or working to change these where they breach one's own value
system. Where our staff were now required by political prescription to engage in
research if they taught on degrees, I believed that they could use this requirement to promote the values that they believed in. As Middleton (1998: 3) says,
'Political orthodoxies, although powerful, are never monolithic. There are always
oppositions, alternatives, resistances, and creativities.' If they had to do research,
why not research the teaching that they felt was central to their jobs, rather than
feel they had to 'divide their energies' by engaging in forms of research that were
strange, possibly difficult to learn, and potentially irrelevant to their practice?

How did it work in practice?

So far, I have held up my hopes for the benefits of the action research approach
in helping staff having to engage in research. I have claimed that it would help
them to overcome fear of research, and to take a creative approach to meeting
the changed political and educational requirements of their jobs. I have
suggested that my intervention was designed also to value and promote Maori
ways of researching. So how did the intervention work in practice? I would like to
claim that my course was an unmitigated success, that it had resulted in communities of researching teachers within TWP. However, I have to make more modest
claims. I have entitled this contribution, 'Collaboration for co-liberation'. Part of the
co-liberation I have experienced was not only my attempt to 'liberate' staff from
perceptions of research as something foreign and fearful that would interfere
with, rather than develop and support, their practice. It was also my own 'libera-

tion' from faulty perceptions about how action research may best work in an institution such as ours, and how my own practice can inadvertently be oppressive
despite my best intentions.

Staff liberation

First, then, I shall look at the effectiveness of action research in helping staff to
overcome concerns about the unfamiliar nature of research, and how it has
helped them to research their teaching. Then I shall investigate how action
research works best in our context. Finally I shall look at ways in which my practice has been revealed to be oppressive of Maori ways of operating despite my
attempt to support these ways.

In the action research course, staff learned how to refine and improve their
teaching practice. One commented that her work had helped her to cut down her
marking. 'Yes, markedly. That was what I was after and it certainly worked, and I
don't think the students felt cheated at all.' One had been teaching keyboarding
skills using a package that she despised. To her surprise, her students valued it.
'The results received clearly indicate a positive response to the X programme,
and that students on the whole feel it is a valid and useful means of learning the
keyboard.' This discovery helped her to overcome the negativity that she had
previously felt towards the package. An engineering teacher tried a problem-
solving approach to his practical classes, rather than the previous structured
approach that was common in his department. 'In repeating [the labs] this year, I
went into it a lot more confident in the way I was going to do it ... I know that the
students last year, 50 per cent of them, preferred it [the new way] over the traditional way and this year, I just went into it with a lot more confidence.'

Many of the teachers found that their interest in researching their practice (and
the research requirement that they disseminate the results in some form) had
boosted their confidence. 'It's given me the confidence, I think, to take work done
by the students to the international arena, whereas I wouldn't have done that
before.' 'It has increased my confidence, it has made me realise that some of the
reflecting and so on that I do within my work can be developed and can become
a form of research.' 'It enabled me to take a chance of applying for some money
from the [research] fund and it made me feel that I would really like to do more.
Yes, it is very empowering in fact and I have said that to many people.'

I based my identification of action research as a familiar approach for our staff
on my observation of the reflective practice that good teachers here (and elsewhere) used intuitively (Woodhouse, 1997). But reflective practice tends to be an
internal process; action research stresses collaboration and the dissemination of
results. The confidence mentioned above that the action researchers developed
gave them courage to present their results to peers, even when they felt trepida-
tion about this.

> I think it has had very positive effects. Just for instance at the end of last year
> when they were wanting papers for [an in-house conference], I could stick

my hand up and say 'I'll do it!' I wouldn't say it was totally easy, it required a bit of guts to do that. When you stand in front of your peers, you think … they are just going to sit there and think what's she doing, standing up there? What's she got to say? So it wasn't exactly easy, but it enabled me to do that and then other people in the department who came to that were aware that I was doing it, and were able to say, Oh, that's a good idea; I might do some videoing.

This quotation shows the catalytic (similar to what McNiff calls in this book 'generative transformational') effects that I hoped action research might bring about in departments. Through the dissemination of this teacher's work, others became aware of the benefits of videotaping teaching practice in order to critique and improve it.

How easy did these practising teachers find the action research approach to learn? As I had hoped, many identified the reflective practice approach that they had already used as compatible with action research, and were delighted to realise that this was a familiar process which could also be counted as research. One said she appreciated 'the recognition that a lot of techniques of enquiry and development I use could actually be called research, with a little brushing up'. Another commented on her surprise in 'recognising that I do do research without ever having put a handle on it before; that was quite an eye opener'. A third commented that 'I've got a better understanding of concepts. I think the course probably brought together many skills that were lying there, but I think it actually brought them together.' Finally, a Maori researcher identified her sense of familiarity with the approach: 'There were lots of processes that came out of the particular action research project that I was doing that I had always been doing. For me, the process of action research is an everyday thing.' These feelings of familiarity are well summed up by McNiff's comment: '… far from being ad hoc and woolly, action research raises to a conscious level much of what is already being done by good teachers on an intuitive level' (McNiff, 1988: 7).

Her words were supported by one of the action researchers, commenting on the value of the course for her.

I think it was very valuable, one of the most valuable things I have done. A lot of things you learn and you put them in the filing cabinet and you may bring them out later, whereas you can always remember this, regardless of what you are doing you can see that and it's there, you don't forget it.

I have spent quite some time concentrating on the benefits of the course for staff, as this was the main practical focus of my work. I also believe that their words show ways in which we as educators have collaborated to improve our practice as teachers – me sharing my action research theoretical knowledge with them, and they sharing their practice and increasing knowledge with me.

Personal liberation

Now I want to look at some of the ways in which the work liberated me from distorted perceptions and incorrect assumptions in my context. One's situatedness can distort one's perspectives of how one's environment operates.

The most significant discovery I made was that I had inadvertently subverted the catalytic possibilities of action research by the way I had located the process within an assessed course. Participants on our courses are frequently the only members of their department who can be spared at one time. Therefore, when action researchers were required, at the end of the first three-day block, to designate a research question and decide how they would proceed to research that, they came up with questions that mattered to them but that were not necessarily attractive to colleagues within their departments. Accordingly, they had difficulty gaining collaborators for their work when they returned to their department, and most had to carry out their work as solitary action research. I discussed the difficulties of this – both theoretically and practically – in the thesis (Bruce Ferguson, 1999). I had chosen to introduce the action research process via an assessed and certificated course quite deliberately. Staff are required, as part of their employment contract, to undertake teacher training. Given the resistance many expressed to research, it seemed appropriate and strategic to introduce action research skills through courses that fulfil employment contract requirements, rather than just to offer action research courses and hope there will be some 'takers'. Unfortunately this perspective was faulty.

It is not that action research cannot operate catalytically at TWP; more that questions to be researched need to be developed by the collaborative group, not by an individual who then tries to co-opt others into the project. Partly because of my enthusiasm for the action research approach – an enthusiasm that was supported by their Head of Department – a TWP section, the teachers of English to Speakers of Other Languages (ESOL) group, decided to carry out action research into ways of improving ESOL teaching at TWP (Musgrave, 1997; Musgrave *et al.*, 1996). The project continues to the present. There are eight ESOL teachers involved; one other ESOL group is now doing action research into the functioning of a language Self-Access Centre here, and another staff member is doing an action research PhD. Within that department, therefore, action research has acted catalytically. But all eight in the original project worked together on the question and methods of operating. The caution that emerges from this learning, then, is to be very careful about deciding how to introduce action research in an organisation, and to choose ways that will maximise the potential for changed practice, if possible.

Another area where I achieved some degree of 'liberation' was to do with Maori cultural practices. Traditionally, Maori processes are verbal rather than written. One of my action researchers, a Maori educator, carries out all her teaching in Maori. Most of her department's social interaction and much of their academic interchange also occurs in the Maori language. The polytechnic, however, currently requires all their documentation in English, despite Maori being an official language of New Zealand. This Maori action researcher brought home to me the oppressive nature of my own course assessment requirements for her. I try, in the course, to give staff an insight into some generic research skills (proposal and report writing) which are not necessarily required in other action research approaches. This is so that they will understand the research requirements that impinge on colleagues using other approaches. One staff member commented that 'I have more empathy now for colleagues who are undertaking research', so the course has achieved its purpose in this respect.

But the Maori action researcher brought home to me that the written report was a double burden for her.

> The language thing was difficult because on one hand a lot of my data was being collected and delivered in Maori, thinking and the discussions with staff and people involved in it were in Maori, and then having to bring it together in English ... I was actually doing it in Maori and then translating and thinking, Oh, no, I'm going to have to do it in English and when you are reading data in Maori and then having to write it up in English, there's just that jumping around and also the meaning was lost sometimes or distorted.

This is a constraint that should have occurred to me (it's possible for Maori students to submit assessment work in the Maori language, but I hadn't thought to emphasise that to this staff member). Now that I have been given this insight into the oppressive nature of my assessment requirements, I am more aware of the need to ensure that Maori students in my courses are aware of their rights.

Constraints and accommodations

I mentioned above a constraint that I had inadvertently placed on one of the Maori action researchers. My environment, in turn, placed constraints on me. In general, I found the situation of operating as an 'insider researcher' (Gorinski and Ferguson, 1997) beneficial. However, there were times when my positioning made me feel vulnerable. As Douglas expressed it, those holding an ambiguous role are 'perceived as dangerous because they do not neatly conform to accepted boundaries' (Douglas, 1966: 102; see also Schein, 1995). My decision to engage in activity to develop our research culture before this activity was common gave me an ambiguous role, similar to that experienced by new researchers within predominantly teaching departments. I had to struggle throughout the years of study to gain any financial or time support for my work, above what is normally received by staff as part of their normal professional development. Most of the work was done in my own time, over weekends and during leave periods.

Partly these constraints arose because policy around research, and research funding, emerged little by little, as a result of test cases such as mine. So the first person to present with an atypical situation suffered from being the 'guinea pig' as policy was developed. I was aware that this was likely to occur at the outset, but underestimated the emotional impact on me of this marginal status. The struggle I faced is indicated in the following excerpt from my research log:

> 12/11/93: [Team discussing workloads:] I had research listed down with areas for development, but Chris [my boss] shifted it back under teaching in general. The upshot is that it still doesn't attract a time allocation and I honestly don't think she still, after all my work, sees it as a significant area for development. It is such a drag having to convince her of something that seems so self-evident to me.

I could fill an entire chapter with the communications problems that exacerbated my situation as a new researcher! (see Bruce Ferguson, 1999: ch. 6). I tried to turn these constraints to positive ends by working to ensure that the barriers I faced are not encountered by subsequent staff. I tried, as Bell, Gaventa and Peters (1990) entitled their book on the work of Paulo Freire and Miles Horton, to 'make the road by walking'. I believe the road for subsequent researchers is just that little bit smoother and clearer because my action researchers and I have done our work.

Conclusion

It is impossible to summarise the results of over five years of study into one chapter. I have attempted in this chapter to give you some insight into how I, as a committed action researcher, have attempted to work collaboratively in order to achieve liberation for myself and my colleagues from potentially constraining political and educational requirements. I believe that the work has been worthwhile. It has given me insight into ways that my environment operates. It has contributed to research definitions being accepted here that strongly emphasise teacher-based research. In one of our formal documents, it is stated that

> Research at the Institution is expected to:
> - assist staff employed by the Institution to maintain currency in their field of knowledge, or
> - contribute, either directly or indirectly, to the identification and improvement of best practice in teaching and learning at the Institutions; or
> - be applied to stakeholder activity (student, staff and the wider community).
>
> (*The Development of Research at the Institutions*, The Report of the Research Working Party to the Board of Deans, 1 April 1999)

I hope that this brief description of the intentional intervention of an action researcher has helped you to see how you might seek to intervene in your own context. I'd like to close the chapter with these words from two of my action research colleagues. Their words support the claims I have made throughout the chapter.

> To find that you can manage to do [research] on the hoof is quite a breakthrough.

It has made me think, yes, I can do research. That it is not such a thing reserved for the very high and mighty, but the little common tutor can hop in there and dabble their feet ... It wouldn't be so daunting the next time.

Part II

How is organisational knowledge acquired?

This part provides an overview of the three main social scientific and educational research paradigms – the empirical, interpretive and critical theoretic research paradigms. It shows how the paradigms are informed by, and inform, the technical, practical and emancipatory interests as identified by Habermas (1972).

The relationship is explained in Chapter 4. Here also a case is made for research now to go beyond these established interests and recognise a new spiritual interest which develops out of the other three, and embeds them within itself. Chapter 4 also shows how the nature and focus of research is changing, from traditional categories and functional purposes, to new categories and communitarian purposes.

Chapter 8 explains the aims and purposes of action research, and gives an overview of how it can be carried out. The chapter later adopts a narrative form to show how action research may generate a theory of living which is informed by communitarian and spiritual values.

At a surface level, this part of the book may be seen as a free-standing research methods text. In this I hope I am meeting the wishes of course participants, as explained in the Introduction, to produce a text that shows how research is embedded within emerging cultural traditions, and also reflects the changing nature of scientific enquiry.

At a deep level, and as contextualised within the book, it shows the evolutionary nature of forms of enquiry towards good social orders. I am trying to show how, as the purpose of research evolves in the direction of an interest of social amelioration and sustainability, so its methodologies also demonstrate increasing inclusiveness and awareness of issues of social justice.

In presenting the discussion I have also tried to show how newer research methodologies move increasingly towards open forms, and how attitudes of tolerance and compassion for human welfare overtake and subsume functional interests. Within this part of the text I hope it is possible, both in content and form, to see the development of research methodologies and research interests towards social cohesion and good social orders, and the evolutionary potential of research processes to realise themselves as such. Research is done by researchers, and is a social practice. The practice of doing research can be socially pleasant or conflictual, depending on how researchers see themselves in relation with one another. How we are with one another constitutes a research process; we need to find ways of doing research to encourage thoughtful conversation, not confrontation. In this section I am hoping to show that, if we use the research process as an opportunity to reach deeper understanding of how we can live together more peacefully, we actually transform the process of doing research from a functional activity to a good social order. We undertake action research for the purpose of understanding who we are and how we can live successfully with one another.

Case stories follow Chapters 5, 6 and 7 which reflect the themes discussed in the chapters. They are written by Paul Murphy, Breda Long and Eileen Ross, all participants on the Masters courses in Ireland, and all in different geographical locations. Paul is a counsellor who facilitates religious congregations in coping with sexual abuse issues; Breda is an employment counsellor for long-term unemployed people; Eileen has recently left convent life and taken up work as a teacher. All stories show how the authors critically reflected on and came to rethink their own practice, how they became aware of what they were doing in the light of their greater understanding, and how this understanding then informed their work. They also show how their understanding has enabled them to move towards a more open way of being, and how they have developed new personal epistemologies of practice through the process of reflection on action.

In setting out the stories of Paul, Breda and Eileen, I am trying to show how my own understanding of the importance of teaching research methods deepened through my teaching. Concurrently, Paul and Breda and Eileen and I were all developing our separate, but interlinked, epistemologies of practice. In this way I believe the stories are part of the development of a community of enquirers, which respects the originality of mind and critical judgement of each participant and at the same time enables me, as tutor/educator, to understand my educative influence with the individuals and the community.

4 Doing research

An aim of this book is to rethink the knowledge base of organisation theory. I agree with Schön (1995) that we need to move from traditional forms of scholarship and develop new ones. This move will take some effort. It involves serious debates about the legitimacy of the research paradigm one chooses to work in and its epistemology. In revolutions, it is important to be as familiar as possible with the situation one is attempting to change, in order to show how the current situation has potential to transform into a more improved version of itself, and why the new version might hold greater promise for social betterment.

In order therefore to show the potential for the emergence of a new scholarship out of current traditional forms it is important to engage with the traditional categories, and show how action researchers are able to generate newer categories which suit human purposes better than previous ones. This is especially important in light of the revolution also taking place in contemporary thinking about the purposes of human existence, in which there is significant emphasis on the need for attachment and connectedness, for a rejection of conflict, and a search for new paths to peace and reconciliation. To meet the challenge we need to recognise the integrated nature of mind, body and spirit within the individual, and also find ways to integrate communities, a particularly difficult task if we remain stuck in old ways of thinking which emphasise fragmentation and domination. We need to find new integrated forms of enquiry that move beyond traditional categories in an effort to understand how participatory practices can lead to new integrated social traditions.

Edwards (1998) rightly speaks of this vision as a 'compassionate revolution'. I agree, but we also have to be clear about what needs to be done to help the revolution along. The first task, in my view, is to change our ways of thinking (see also Ornstein and Ehrlich, 1989), move beyond old-paradigm scholarship, and engage critically with emergent holistic paradigms. To do this we need to go back to our roots, carefully consider where we have come from and where we might be going, and what needs to change in order to get there. In developing new ways of thinking, therefore, we need first to understand what is involved in traditional ways of thinking, and how these ways are maintained and safeguarded, in order to change them.

I want to use this chapter to investigate the traditional scholarship and its categories, and then to suggest how we might move on to newer ways of thinking in the new scholarship. Traditional epistemologies favour technical rationality and analytical categories. The chapter explains first what these categories are and how they are used. It explains how these traditional forms serve currently identifiable human interests. Newer human interests are emerging, however, and these require new forms of research and newer categories. The chapter goes on to discuss these. It is organised as two parts to show the different emphases.

The chapter discusses how knowledge is acquired through the process of doing research and its potential uses. Knowledge is a complex and problematic concept (Chapter 1); the idea of research knowledge, the kind of knowledge generated by research, is even more complex and problematic, especially now that we are considering that there are different ways of doing research, with different purposes, which generate different kinds of knowledge.

I want to stay with the organising questions, but now frame them so that the first two concentrate on understanding traditional research categories while the second two show the potential for transformation to newer categories. The chapter is therefore organised as:

Part one:

   What is the nature of research knowledge?
   How is research knowledge acquired?

Part two:

   How is research knowledge put to use?
   What are the implications for social living?

PART ONE

In this part I discuss the nature of traditional research categories, and show how they are applied within existing typologies of human interests.

1 What is the nature of research knowledge?

The idea of traditional research is reasonably straightforward and well documented. It is about investigating a particular issue in order to find out more about it and then sharing the findings. As with many organised activities, it involves special features and procedures. The process of doing research however is seldom simple. It is always a social practice, and questions arise about what should be done, by whom, and for what purpose. Research is always done by a living someone; it is not an abstract phenomenon that just happens.

Doing research is more than just activity. Research involves special features such as monitoring practice and gathering data, reflecting on the process, and making the findings public. The special features of traditional research appear below at (2).

Doing research, doing knowledge

In Ireland you would hear people say, 'I do be here'. 'Be' in Irish Gaelic (Gaeilge) is an active verb: 'bím' = I do be. The same idea travels to knowledge. Knowledge is an active process, something we do rather than something we acquire.

Popular opinion holds that research is conducted only in academia and other formal contexts. This is not so. It is conducted everywhere, in formal and informal settings, and can be done by anyone. Many people do research without naming it as a process. Growing fuchsias, watching how they grow, keeping notes of their progress, exhibiting them at a flower show, and talking about how you grew them is as valid a research process as formally testing drugs under laboratory conditions. There is nothing mysterious about doing research.

Knowing and coming to know (epistemologies) are part of research processes. There are different ways of doing this (methodologies), and researchers have different reasons and intentions for doing research, depending on how they perceive their own realities (ontologies). Some believe knowledge to be objective and value-free, stripped of ethical considerations; others believe knowledge to be subjective and value-laden, conducted with social intent. The values and purposes a researcher holds influence their choice of research methodologies.

For example, you might want to know how many shoppers bring their young children to your supermarket on Saturday mornings, so that you can provide sufficient purpose-built trolleys. You would probably first monitor numbers of shoppers over a period of time. This is an objective form of research, aiming to gather statistics and turn them into marketable knowledge. Or you might want to find out people's opinion of a facility such as baby-with-adult car parking, or how a service such as bag-packing can improve the quality of shopping experience; turning this kind of information into marketable knowledge needs a more interpretive approach. Or you might want to find out whether the quality of shoppers' experience in your store could be improved if you invited your employees to become actively involved in promoting the firm's quality of service in return for some profit-sharing; in this case you would find ways of creating marketable knowledge out of shared ideas. You have used different research approaches for the purpose of finding ways to promote supermarket profitability. You have selected particular research methods for specific purposes.

Components of research

Traditionally it is held that research processes have three main components:

ontology	a theory of being, a view of things 'as they are';
epistemology	a theory of knowledge, including a theory of how knowledge is acquired;
methodology	a theory of how research is conducted.

Doing research is also a political process. The way that people investigate issues, and their reasons and intentions, are often influenced by considerations outside their control. Doing research is never neutral. It is done by someone with specific aims and intentions. There are often many behind-the-scenes decision-makers: policy-makers decide that an issue needs investigating; a researcher is appointed to do the job; accountants allocate research funds. Human factors are primary: the researcher does not leave one set of values at the door and take up another for the research. Similarly the knowledge that is generated is not abstract; it is part of the processes of people asking purposeful questions. These processes are also socially constructed: people jockey for position power according to the values and intentions that inform the research.

Potential dangers of linguistic definitions

Giving definitions for ontology, epistemology and methodology is a useful starting point, but there are potential dangers. The definitions refer to what the words 'mean' as items of language. In one sense, all words have meaning in terms of their linguistic definitions; we can look them up in a dictionary. In another sense, this idea of 'meaning' is limited because it is open to (mis)interpretation. One person's idea of a table might not be the same as another's. How we interpret linguistic definitions is a matter of personal subjective opinion. Another problematic is that meaning, as Wittgenstein says, is not only in the words we use, but in the way we live. The word 'love' may be defined in a dictionary, but when the action does not fit the definition, confusion sets in.

Although definitions of research processes exist, it is through doing research that the meanings become clear. The same principle applies throughout. It is possible to 'know' the theory of doing research in an abstract sense, but we can be said to know – critically engage with – the theory only when we demonstrate our knowledge in a practical way by doing research. In this way, research transforms from a conceptual discipline to a real-world practice, and the knowledge base moves from propositional descriptions to embodied explanations.

Research and human interests

Habermas, a major theorist in social science, rejected the traditional positivist view that knowledge is a neutral activity done by an external 'mind' somewhere, resulting in the generation of pure knowledge (1972, 1974). He claimed that knowledge is always a product of a knowing subject who is driven by particular desires and interests. Human practices could be understood in terms of their underpinning values and intentions.

Habermas developed a theory of 'knowledge constitutive interests'. Personal-social practices may be broadly categorised in terms of three major sets of interests: the technical, the practical and the emancipatory.

Technical interest

The main concern is control of the environment through the production of technical knowledge. This kind of knowledge is prominent in empirical research (Chapter 5), and has been central to much scientific and technological progress. It remains essential for processes of material production, particularly as they relate to industry and manufacturing. The problem, as Habermas and others see it, is that technical knowledge is held by some as the only kind of valid knowledge. In organisations, technical interest might be seen as control of work and its processes. A narrow instrumental view results in understanding organisation as a deterministic process and management practice as technique.

Practical interest

Practical interest focuses on understanding, meaning-making and interpretation, and has become prominent in interpretive approaches to research (Chapter 6). Organisations on this view are communities of reflective practitioners in rational interaction; management practice aims to support dialogue. Communicative action, Habermas maintains, goes beyond the narrowness of technical knowledge and involves understanding others and their lifeworlds. Communicative action aims to generate intersubjective agreement, shared interpretations and meanings. Habermas points out that this process itself can lead to distorted understandings, because we are all conditioned by our own cultural and historical circumstances; what we do and think is subject to forces of which we may or may not be aware. We need to understand those forces and how to deal with them in order to understand the wider social systems in which our decision-making and communicative actions are embedded.

Emancipatory interest

Emancipatory interest helps us to free ourselves from dominating forces which control our knowledge and actions. By revealing and breaking free of external forces of control we enable ourselves to get on with creating lives that we consider worthwhile. Organisations become communities of self-reflective practitioners, aiming to improve their own understanding of and engagement with their work practices. This view has been enthusiastically adopted by social scientists who want to find ways in which work and social conditions can be improved, and it features prominently in critical theoretic forms of research (Chapter 7). Action research stems from critical theory and shares the same ideologies of social freedoms, and the rights of practitioners to be regarded as the best judges of their own work and therefore accountable for its quality.

The special place of organisation research

Organisation research has a special contribution to make towards global sustainability. It crosses philosophical and geographical boundaries, and integrates insights and practices from different paradigms, disciplines and cultures. The potential exists for developing theories of lifelong learning as a transformative process. Study of organisation has an established tradition of drawing on other progressive disciplines, such as systems theory, which also provide useful metaphors for research processes.

There is a tendency in the literature to equate 'organisation' with 'business organisation'. This can be confusing. Governments and local communities, for-profit or not-for-profit, are organisations in the same way that corporations are. I stated before that I do not equate organisation with business. Other writers who share this view maintain that people in all organisations constitute forces for social change: 'Expression of special interests and the working through of collective actions require the agency of organizations … We live in an organizational world in which organizations are the means through which interests are realized' (Egri and Pinfield, 1999: 225).

Other writers do equate organisations with business; for them, too, business organisations have special potential for social change, possibly unachievable by other kinds of organisation such as governments and action groups. 'Organizations may be in the most advantageous position to facilitate unprecedented awareness for society and resolve highly complex problems based on their capacity to mobilize resources and often to transcend political entities' (Robinson Hickman, 1998: 496). Corporations have the power and potential to implement social change by taking on for example the responsibilities of local and national governments for social change, sometimes through privatisation (Drucker, 1989); or to involve themselves in community and environmental issues (Brown, 1992, cited in Parker, 1999). Business provides opportunities for coherent lifelong learning opportunities, and also for an amelioration of many existing social problems.

Regardless of their functional purpose, organisations, as groups of people in community, have significant potential to reconceptualise what counts as prime human interests, and to find ways to realise those interests through organisation study. The time was never so right for for-profit and not-for-profit organisations to establish their positions as agencies for social renewal, beginning with their own internal renewal through appropriate kinds of person-centred research; and then to work closely with academia to legitimate this potential for generating new theories for social renewal.

These ideas are already evident in the literature. Organisation research is strongly related to open systems theory and its ontology of becoming, and draws consistently on the work of learning theorists such as Argyris, Bawden, Schein, Schön and others. Metaphors and models of the new sciences are a strong influence. Interdisciplinary methodological links exist (Burrell and Morgan, 1979). Burrell (1999) especially shows how human enquiry draws on metaphors, discourses and genealogies of analysis that are common to many fields of experience, and how findings in one area may influence others. Some writers foreground the ethico-political dimension of organisation research as a 'sacred science' (Marsden and Townley, 1999; see also Marshall and Reason, 1997). Business organisations are urged to move beyond a narrow technicist focus and reconceptualise themselves as agencies for social change, particularly in the 'new era organisations' (Robinson Hickman, 1998). Increasingly there is recognition in new-paradigm research that people constitute organisations, and there is increasing need for a variety of approaches within organisation study to account for how people work together for personal and social development. I continue this discussion below in section 3.

2 How is research knowledge acquired?

This section outlines some of the main practical features of research. Many texts are available on conventional research; the following are pointers of some of the most common aspects.

Significant features of research

Research processes tend to share significant features that qualify them as research rather than, say, expression of personal opinion. Key aspects are:

- Research aims to generate new knowledge and make a claim to knowledge. The claim is contained within the findings of the research, either as a summative conclusion, or as part of the formative process of doing the research. The researcher aims to show an improvement of understanding of the external situation 'out there', or of what is going on in the mind, 'in here'.
- Research is usually planned in advance, based on a design, or plan, which outlines intentions, objectives and procedures, and which shows an identifiable starting point and subsequent progression. The original design can act as a check that the research has achieved what it set out to do. Action research recognises that the research is a developmental process in which aims and research questions may change as the research develops.
- Research aims to gather, interpret and present data, to show the reality of the situation it is investigating. The data is sorted and presented in a publicly available form, and is presented as evidence to support the claim to knowledge. Data is not the same as evidence. Evidence is produced by analysis of the data in terms of criteria that show how the research aims might have been fulfilled (see p. 135).
- Research aims for validity, to show that the evidence is not fabricated, and why the claim to knowledge is legitimate, not a matter of personal opinion. In some contemporary work, newer terms such as 'authenticity' and 'trustworthiness' are substituted for 'validity'.

- Research involves reflection on the process; the researcher monitors actions and provisional findings, documents these systematically, and makes accounts available for others, although dissemination might be limited and depends on the research remit.
- Research has use value; other people may learn from it. In empirical research, this is stated as generalisability; new-paradigm research talks about learning and sharing.
- Research aims to be comprehensible and authentic. Others can understand what it was about and see the real-world process. In empirical research this involves issues of replicability; in new-paradigm research others can learn from the research report and apply the lessons to themselves.

Making an original claim to knowledge

Research aims to make an original claim to knowledge in the sense that the researcher knows something that was not known before. The claim can be around a substantive issue, such as making a specific contribution to an area of enquiry: Alexander Fleming discovered penicillin, for example. The claim can also be a personal knowledge claim that one understands something which one did not understand before. Polanyi (1967) says that every time we prefix a sentence with 'I now know that ...' we are adding to a personal and public store of knowledge. The fact that a piece of knowledge existed before as the property of person A does not deny the fact that it can become new knowledge for person B.

Formulating a research question

Different kinds of research have different purposes. Empirical research aims to test a hypothesis by demonstrating a cause-and-effect relationship between events. Interpretive research aims to produce descriptions of what is happening in a particular set of circumstances. Critical theoretic approaches aim to explore issues of freedom and power and find ways towards emancipation. Action research aims to find ways of improving social situations by improving personal understanding in order to take appropriate action.

Heuristic questions are helpful – What? Who? When? Which? Where? How? Why? The first five aim to offer descriptions. How? and Why? type questions aim to give explanations. Different research approaches ask different kinds of questions.

Bassey (1999) says that the purposes of research can be loosely defined in terms of these different kinds of starting points. He categorises them as:

a research question, which defines the research purpose in terms of specific information: for example, How many shoppers bring young children to your store on Saturday mornings?

a research hypothesis, a statement that something is so, and you have to check it out:

for example, Shoppers who bring young children to the store will inevitably look for a purpose-built trolley to transport their children.

a research problem, which sets out a difficulty which the researcher then aims to resolve: for example, How can we continue to attract shoppers with children by providing them with special trolleys, while discouraging them from taking the trolleys off-site?

a research issue, a loosely defined area of enquiry which the researcher aims to focus on: for example, What other kinds of service can we provide to attract more shoppers with young children to the store?

It is important to try to identify the kind of question or issue to be asked. This helps clarify the research purpose and design. Sometimes however the question does not emerge until the research is under way, and is part of the process of 'progressive illumination' (Parlett and Hamilton, 1977) which is a particular characteristic of practitioner action research.

Data, criteria and evidence

A claim to knowledge needs to be supported by evidence to show that the claim is authentic and trustworthy. Evidence is drawn from the data.

Data refers to information about what happens during the research process. It can be gathered using a variety of techniques, from statistics-based surveys and questionnaires to qualitative interpretations of narratives. During the research, a researcher would probably gather quantities of data, only some of which would be relevant. They need to identify, probably at the beginning of the research but also possibly as it progresses, which criteria they feel will indicate whether or not the research is achieving its aims and fulfilling its purpose. The data is sifted and analysed in terms of these criteria. In empirical research, which aims to test a hypothesis, the criteria are fixed from the start. In action research the criteria tend to change as the research progresses, and new forms of evidence emerge. It is very important not to throw data away too soon, if at all.

Issues of validity

Traditional standards for good research practice focus on issues of validity and reliability, that is, does the research do what it claims to do, and are the findings to be trusted? In empirical research, validity and reliability translate into replicability and generalisability: if the research is repeated, will the same findings present, and can the research process be generalised to other like processes? This has long been a problem for new-paradigm research, because traditional criteria tend to be used to judge new forms of research which actually require different kinds of criteria altogether (see Chapter 10). Traditional forms of research, rooted in Newtonian mechanistic forms of science, aim to produce generalisations: what is true for one is true for all. Newer forms of research tend to focus on singularities, one particular case. The aim is to understand what is happening in one particular situation, rather than apply the same process to all situations.

Ethics

Research is a human practice that aims to generate knowledge which will have use value in the lives of others. It is therefore an ethico-political process, because knowledge and its use are contested issues. Texts exist which set out the ethical criteria for doing research in general (for example, the American Psychological Association, 1987, and the British Psychological Society, 1991) and specific aspects such as use of language (for example the British Sociological Association, 1989; see also Robson, 1993). Professional associations draw up their own codes of ethics. The main issues addressed in ethical considerations are the avoidance of harm, respect for participants' rights to confidentiality, participants' full access to data which concerns them, their right to withdraw from the research, their right to honesty and protection from deception (see McNiff *et al.*, 1996). Researchers also need to show respect for the research process: to work within the law, to report findings honestly, not to fabricate data, to avoid plagiarism in research reports, to respect copyright laws (Bassey, 1999). It is also important not to suggest that the research reached a 'successful' closure which it did not. This is particularly important in action research, when a main concern is to show the development of understanding which often happens because things did not go according to plan (see Ó Muimhneacháin, 2000).

Charles Kingsley's 'Mrs Douasyouwouldbedoneby' in *The Water Babies* (1995) is a good role model for ethical conduct.

Research paradigms

Different ways of doing research are often called paradigms, following the work of Thomas Kuhn (1970). Kuhn shows how scientific ideas emerge over long periods of time. There are long stretches in which broad agreement exists among members of research communities about what constitutes 'normal science'. However, other ideas exist, and over time they become evident, possibly in a small way to begin with, and then the momentum increases, until they break through the barrier of 'normal' practices and launch a challenge to the status quo. Not unsurprisingly the new form is often resisted by the establishment, who will use the power at their disposal to quell the uprising. This gives rise to a period of extreme turbulence in which one set of ideas, which is often incommensurable with another, battles for acceptance and/or supremacy. Although critiqued, Kuhn's idea of paradigm shifts has been used widely as an analogue to explain how rival versions of truth compete for legitimacy, and debates amounting to paradigm wars (Casti, 1990; Woodhouse, 1996) proliferate in the literature (for example, Donmoyer, 1996; Lakatos and Musgrave, 1970; Lather, 2000).

Following Habermas's typology of human interests, a three-paradigm view of research has emerged in recent years in social scientific and education research.

Burrell and Morgan (1979) have developed a similar typology. The multi-paradigm approach has been well developed by Carr and Kemmis (1986) and features in other educational research (for example, Bassey, 1999; Hitchcock and Hughes, 1995). The three paradigms are the empirical, the interpretive and the critical theoretic, all of which hold different purposes and commitments as forms of enquiry, and which are the focus of Chapters 5–7.

PART TWO

In this part of the chapter I want to show how traditional categories of scholarship need to be reconceptualised in order to develop an integrated form of theory that is capable of explaining the emergent integrated form of human interests. Traditional categories of human interest – the technical, practical and emancipatory described above – now need to become embedded within a newer inclusive interest that aims for the development of community. Organisation study can play a significant part here, in the generation of new forms of theory to show how the vision might become reality.

3 How is research knowledge put to use?

Above I explained how Habermas's typology of human interests provides a framework for how and why research is undertaken. A particular research approach would be used, depending on which interest is prioritised. This quite recent view of the pluralistic nature of research extends across the range of scientific enquiry. Influenced by the destabilising work of Kuhn and Feyerabend in the 1960s (Dieks, 1994), it has become accepted today that a broad range of approaches is necessary for different purposes.

I want to suggest that these different ways of doing research, which appear to be separate in terms of serving specific interests, are actually aspects of a wider transformational process which moves towards synthesis (but not closure). The synthesis of interests is achieved through recognising an inclusive interest that holds other interests within itself as part of its own emergent order. The synthesis is achieved through methodologies of care and reconciliation. I also want to suggest that organisation study could be the field within which the synthesis becomes most evident and has greatest impact.

A new transformational human interest

Habermas's typology can be seen as an evolutionary process that widens from an instrumental focus on technicality; to participatory forms in the practical; and then to forms of freedom in the emancipatory – transformative movement from being to becoming. The development now continues to an interest of human relationship, an interest which contains the other interests as part of its evolutionary unfolding, and now recognises also the aesthetic, the compassionate, the spiritual, the sacred. Technical knowledge makes our computers work and keeps planes in the air. Practical knowledge helps us communicate effectively, to understand one another's point of view. Emancipatory knowledge helps us understand potentially oppressive forces and how to overcome them, and not to give in to the temptation to become oppressors ourselves. Relational knowledge helps us to understand the nature of our humanity and our interconnectedness with others across a network of dimensions.

Forms of knowledge do not emerge as a linear process; they are transformational. Knowledge emerges and transforms, constantly pushing human limits and capacities to know. Earlier forms are embedded within more complex forms. The more we strive to know, the more complex our forms of knowledge become. We develop new epistemologies to help us understand our own widening experience. All forms of knowledge are necessary within the broadening commitment to know ourselves and one another. As knowledge transforms, so does the knower. Knowing at a more developed level enables knowers to live in ways which transcend (and incorporate) technical, practical and emancipatory forms. They are necessary aspects of the learning process which help us to progress.

Recall however the discussion in Chapter 2. I said there that new theories of discourse show how understanding can be distorted if conceptual categories are regarded as fixed. The same principle applies here. Human interests and ways of knowing are not fixed conceptual categories, although they are presented here as such: metaphors to illustrate real-life processes. Human interests and ways of knowing are lived processes. They are sites of human struggle in which real people work out solutions to dilemmas. We try to make sense of our complexities of living in multiple ways, concentrating here on technical issues, there on practical ones, there on emancipatory ones. As we struggle to make sense we develop deeper insights into how we should be and how we should be with others. It is in the struggle that we realise our capacities as humans, how we are compassionate, tolerant, forgiving. We come to realise through the struggle how we wear our differences as commonalities, how we belong together within and through the struggle.

Ó Murchú (1997a) speaks of the nature of spirituality as an innate quality of human experience that manifests as a form of belonging. We are all part of the same reality; a greater reality is contained within us. He cites the beautiful words of Teilhard de Chardin: 'The Body is the very universality of things … My matter is not a part of the universe that I possess totally. It is the totality of the universe that I possess partially' (p. 52). Capra *et al.* (1992) explain that belonging is a reciprocal act of faith and trust; living beings belong to one another, to the earth, and ultimately to the universe. These ideas are at the heart of new scientific theories, where relation is both ontological experience, and also the way to understanding. What we come to understand, and how we come to understand it, are inextricably linked, as are experience of the inner spiritual world and the outer material world. The micro and the macro contain the same order; whatever is going on 'out there' is already 'in here'. The person and the environment, and the way that they co-exist meaningfully, are parts of the same reality, linked by ties (Bateson, 1972) in ways that no one fully understands, but evidence of which is there if we care to look.

4 What are the implications for social living?

The question arises: What are the potential implications for organisation theory as serving a human interest of relationship?

I said that organisation study could be a major location for the development of a new theory of human interests. This can be achieved under certain conditions. First, organisations and academia have to work together to generate such a theory; the only kind of theory that would make sense would be a theory that describes and explains lived processes which transform into living theories. Second, organisations need to move beyond the narrowly defined interests of profit and corporate expansion, and reconceptualise their main purpose in terms of human well-being. Third, there has to be a concerted effort to promote the legitimacy of practitioner-generated knowledge. This in itself generates a fourth condition, related to a human interest of relationship: the need for *all* participants to regard themselves as practitioners on an equal footing who *all* account for their own practice in relation with one another. There are doubtless other conditions which would emerge through the struggle of trying to realise these values.

In the meantime, an obvious starting point is in management education.

Management learning as a new professionalism

Management is generally regarded as a professional practice. Professionalism tends to be understood in terms of whichever human interest theorists commit themselves to. At a technical level, professionalism is equated with efficient performativity, the capacity to get things done and on time. At a practical level, it emerges as the capacity to work with others and effectively to manage processes. At an emancipatory level it manifests as helping others to become aware of personal choices, and to exercise those choices responsibly. Within a new interest of shared humanity, it means developing personal accountability in order to encourage others to do the same. Organisation theory has the potential to become a theory of social integration.

Professionalism on this view is an emergent phenomenon. It parts company with a traditional stage developmental view of attaining a specific level at which one may be termed a 'Stage 1' or a 'Stage 2' professional. This is how stage developmental theorists such as Piaget, Kohlberg, Maslow, Riegel and others explain the development of learning and moral responsibility. Professionalism is a transformatory process in which we intensify our understandings of what professionalism means and how we can live it more meaningfully in our lives with others.

Schön (1995) explains how institutional knowledge comes to exist. In universities the theory–practice gap is maintained by a focus on technical rationality.

Practitioners are taught the theory which they then apply to practice. This is the basis of conventional forms of professional education across the professions. The reality of practice is however beyond applied theory; common sense shows, as Schön points out, that people learn the job on the job, a kind of intelligence-in-action that includes 'not only the exercise of physical skills but acts of recognition and judgment' (p. 29). The instrumental view that practice can be predicted, controlled and catered for by strategic planning is overtaken by a view of practice as unpredictable, surprising and creative. An epistemology that assumes a fixed knowledge base of disciplines – what to do and how to do it – is inadequate to account for acts of recognition and judgement which call into question issues of value and purpose. It needs rather an epistemology of practice that provides justification for reasons and intentions, and a living out of those values and purposes as a conscious practice.

Generative transformational methodologies

The new forms of scholarship also call for new institutional methodologies, generative transformational methodologies which promote an ontology of becoming.

The work of David Bohm (1983, 1987) provides helpful metaphors for what those methodologies might be. Bohm suggests that people see the world in two different ways. The first way is to see reality as fragmented, existing as objects and things in separate compartments. The way it all works is linear and sequential: $A \rightarrow B \rightarrow C \rightarrow n$. It is one-directional, an inherently fixed structure. Another way of seeing reality and the way it works is as a whole which is in a constant process of becoming. Whatever is, is constantly evolving. Things unfold into different versions of themselves, in a seamless flow of transformation, and each new transformation is unique. On this view, reality itself is a transformational process, and everything in the universe is interrelated, and anything that happens in one context influences what happens in another. For Bohm, underpinning the whole idea of reality as an evolutionary process is an implicate, generative order, of which the linear order is a part, but only a part and not the whole.

This is the same issue that appeared in Chapter 1. Related to issues of professionalism, it shows that methodologies, epistemologies and ontologies are not only conceptual categories, but are developmental processes which have their meaning in the way that people live. Professionalism is not an abstract category. It is a way of living with others and providing public accounts to show that one's practice has use value in the lives of others. The legitimation of professionalism is not an abstract phenomenon, achieved by ticking boxes in a competencies checklist. It is the commitment of people positioned in universities and those positioned in workplaces to agree that accounts of practitioner-generated research constitute a legitimate body of knowledge to show the nature of 'knowing in action' and its potential value for personal-social renewal. The accounts themselves are not artefacts. They are representations, living stories people tell of how they are together; and they exist in a variety of forms – as written documents, as stories told in staff rooms and seminars, as doodles on notebooks.

Moreover, this has to be a collectively agreed participatory undertaking. No one is a spectator. All are participants. Each person aims to show how they worked with others to generate personal accounts of practice. These ideas are evident in the stories in this book.

Bohm's idea of a holographic universe shows the fractal quality of human experience; what is experienced in one part of the system is experienced throughout all parts in greater or lesser degrees of intensity. Personal accounts of practice have potential influence at collective levels. One person's experience informs another's.

I shall leave the discussion here for the time being and take it up again in Chapter 10, in relation to new theories of organisation. To summarise, an image of transformational process helps to develop the idea of a methodology that shows both the transformative and synthesising elements of human enquiry. We aim to understand varieties of experience in our effort to understand what binds us in our humanity. By understanding the different interests in human experience, and by appreciating the need for a diversity of approaches to enable us to explore and share our common humanity, we engage in a more transcendental way with the experience of what it means to be 'a living I' (Whitehead, 1993) in a community of other 'living I's', each of whom is concerned to ensure a quality experience of living for all. I believe we really are making progress in addressing Plato's questions of how we come to understand what it means to be human, and how we might live successfully together.

5 Empirical research

Background

The long mediaeval era transformed into a time of great intellectual and cultural upheaval. During the fifteenth and sixteenth centuries, three major cultural epochs occurred: the Renaissance, the Reformation and the Scientific Revolution. These heralded the onset of the Enlightenment, a shift from faith to reason as the basis of beliefs about the world. The Scientific Revolution, associated particularly with Newton and his contemporaries, marked a radical shift in what was held to be the proper subject matter of human enquiry, away from how an understanding of the world reflected the glory of God to an exploration of how man (women were invisible) might become more like God, especially in terms of how a better understanding of nature might lead to its more effective control. This cognitive revolution was also inspired by the development of sophisticated technology: the compass, gunpowder, the printing press, and, particularly, the mechanical clock (Tarnas, 1991: 225). The new identification of knowledge with science led to a view that science was the enduring source by which all human practice could be judged; this had significant implications for the later development of the Enlightenment project (see Chapter 9).

Two major figures stand out at this time: Isaac Newton and René Descartes. Newton, building on the work of Copernicus, Galileo and Kepler, taught that the world might be seen as a giant clockwork mechanism, and the work of God was to act as a master clockmaker who wound it up and then maintained a watching brief. This shift to a mechanistic cosmology was paralleled by a shift in the philosophical worldview. Descartes claimed that truth could stand outside humans. This generated a dichotomy between processes of thought (how we think) and objects of thought (what we think about), between the rational thinker and the material world. Because people's bodies were part of the material world, the mind and body were separated. 'In Descartes's vision, science, progress, reason, epistemological certainty, and human identity were all inextricably connected with each other and with the conception of an objective, mechanistic universe; and upon this synthesis was founded the paradigmatic character of the modern mind' (Tarnas, 1991: 280). As it appeared in the modern worldview, a knower was separate from the object of knowledge, and science was a value-free process of discovering facts about the world.

The legacy of Francis Bacon in the seventeenth century is also enduring and has particular relevance for new theories of organisation. Bacon saw the natural world as an object of domination by humans who, in the Christian tradition, were a species of special worth and whose inalienable right it was to exploit the natural resources at their command. This view, combined with the Enlightenment emphasis on rationality rather than faith, and the increasing instrumentalisation of science, led to the creation of technologies of exploitation which have virtually exhausted the living world such that, according to the Gaia hypothesis (Lovelock, 1991), it is now poised to shrug off the species that is destroying it in an effort at self-renewal.

The Newtonian view of science gave rise to what has become known as the scientific paradigm. This holds that human enquiry is best undertaken using the 'scientific method', a term rightly criticised by Medawar (1996), who claims that there is no 'one' scientific method. Scientific method may be understood in a variety of ways: science 'is not only a method of discovery and verification, it is a pattern of sharing knowledge' (Bateson, 1994: 189). The Newtonian–Cartesian legacy, however, holds that 'the' scientific method helps us to understand the world so that we can predict what will happen and, ultimately, control it. The system of control lies in assumptions of cause and effect: if x then y. Reality is fragmented, existing as separate structures, and experience is linear. It is possible to manipulate both reality and experience as variables, so that particular outcomes will be assured; these outcomes constitute data which may be validated through analysis, usually statistical, and then applied to other like events. The validity of the research lies in its capacity for replicability and generalisability; what works in one system will work in another; there is one set of cognitive prin-ciples and models appropriate to understanding all realities.

The implications are far-reaching. Modern applications of the 'scientific method' are particularly visible in the botanical-agricultural paradigm. A plant food administered to a control group of tomato plants will, it is supposed, result in better outcomes. 'Better' may be understood in quantitative terms, such as number and size of tomatoes. The emphasis is on productivity: quantity is the indicator of quality. The criterion for judging quality is statistical measurement, and the functional standards of judgement involve to what extent all tomatoes come up to expectations.

When applied to human enquiry the metaphor breaks down. There is an assumption that humans will behave in the same way as tomatoes – passive, unaware, controllable. The ethical tone shifts from empirical (an interest in generating objective knowledge) to empiricist (an interest in controlling behaviour). Researchers holding empiricist commitments often regard humans as objects of enquiry, to be researched on. The researchers themselves consider the research process to be value free, and see themselves external to the research process; in fact, they must stay external so as not to contaminate results by their presence. This kind of attitude legitimates experiments like those carried out by Milgram (1973) and Zimbardo (1969). These experiments would probably be outlawed today, but it is only a hop to experiments conducted in the global theatre of a much more sinister and wide-ranging scale in which human behaviour is engineered by one powerful group sometimes to exterminate entire populations (see also Martin and Frost, 1999).

1 What is the nature of empirical research knowledge?

Gibson writes (1986: 7):

> Instrumental rationality represents the preoccupation with means in preference to ends. It is concerned with method and efficiency rather than purposes. ... It is the divorce of fact from value, and the preference, in that divorce, for fact. It is the obsession with calculation and measurement: the drive to classify, to label, to assess and number, all that is human. As such, it is the desire to control and dominate, to exercise surveillance and power over others and nature.
>
> (in Scott and Usher, 1996: 85)

Empirical approaches continue to be the dominant propositional paradigm both for organisational practices and for their study. 'The normal science of organisation needs little introduction. It builds on the belief that organisations are hard, empirical things capable of being studied using scientific techniques' (Marsden and Townley, 1999: 406). Clegg and Hardy (1999) note that until the 1960s there was an 'orthodox consensus' (Atkinson, 1971) that organisations were unified and orderly entities whose goal was increased productivity and whose operations were determined through rational decision-making. The task of management was to control processes of production for maximum efficiency of output. Prized knowledge was knowledge of the means of production. Organisation study involved the collection of objective data to show the functional process of the structures of an organisation.

Times are however changing. Previous views have been dislodged and seriously challenged by a plethora of alternative approaches, 'contra' approaches according to Marsden and Townley (1999), which critique and replace the assumptions of the dominant view. It can also be argued that the stereotypes of neo-classical views are essentially modernist, regarding social structures as given, unproblematic and resistant to deconstruction. The fact remains however that empiricist approaches are still regarded as 'normal' science in Kuhnian terms, relying on, for example, objective data-gathering techniques which assume that people may be manipulated as variables and standardised criteria that aim for replicability and generalisability of results for research validity. These approaches are vigorously defended by powerful individuals such as Donaldson (1985) and powerful theoretic approaches such as structural contingency theory (Donaldson, 1999) and organisational ecology (Baum, 1999).

Morgan (1997b) explains how the nature of bureaucratic organisations is changing. 'They used to be places. They used to be things' (p. 8). Now they are ephemeral, 'continually creating and re-creating themselves through changing networks of communication based on "real time" communication' (p. 8). However, while newer forms might be a more frequent reality, traditional bureaucratic forms are still the norm for many people in organisations. Organisational practices are experienced as hierarchical structures of dominance; corporate life as fragmented and task oriented. Emotions are not visible, and, if they are, are quickly ruled out or eradicated (Fineman 1999: 293). Aesthetic values are ignored (Gagliardi, 1999). Technical rational forms are the legitimate way of knowing. Practices tend to be compartmentalised and functional: people are isolated within their responsibilities. Traditional bureaucratic forms are characterised by Weber's (1978) views of centralisation, hierarchy, authority, discipline, rules, career, division of labour, tenure (see the Introduction to Clegg and Hardy, 1999: 8). In for-profit organisations, the emphasis is placed on ritualistic and competitive performativity for income generation; little attention is given to the personal well-being of people, as for example in the mechanistic production lines of Ford and Taylor, themselves products of the strict orthodox attitudes of the time, who institutionalised mechanistic ways of working which potentially reduced people to robots. Everywhere there is alienation and hostility among the workforce.

The basis of this caricature is the Newtonian–Cartesian paradigm which presents knowledge as a commodity, abstract and neutral and underpinned by a cause-and-effect form of logic. Knowledge generated through empirical research constitutes a reified truth, a view that is itself a caricature of real-world living, where truth is negotiated among people as they struggle to be valued in their chosen ways of life. Perhaps the idea of packaged truth is appealing; it somehow absolves people from the responsibility of making their own decisions. Whatever the reasons, faith in reified truth is evident within many descriptions and explanations of organisational practices, although it might not reflect real-world experience of organisational practices. Theory and practice occupy different realms and are separated by a gulf of uncritical thinking. A perception of knowledge as abstract and value free encourages a view of a perfect reality. This is well illustrated by a story told by Foucault (1977) about Grand Duke Mikhail's expectations of people: ' "Very good," Grand Duke Mikhail once observed of a regiment after having kept it for one hour presenting arms, "only *they breathe*" ' (p. 200; emphasis in original). The idealised vision of a perfect reality is not too far removed from the scientific management vision of Taylor (1911), who imagined business as a perfect system of production; the best way to achieve a particular job was to match a worker to a task and reward or punish them according to their performance (Crainer, 1996: 4). The same principle is still in operation today, for example in the theory of re-engineering, in which organisational processes are broken down and analysed in terms of their constituent parts, in order to predict and control maximum production efficiency through restructuring (Champy and Hammer, 1993). There is debate around the extent to which these practices actually are implemented in organisations and the kind of effect they might have. Smooth running and technical efficiency may be an aim of technical rational theory; it is not always the practice.

Alienation in the workplace

Marcuse (1964) notes that for institutions to be successful they must make unthinkable the possibility of alternatives. Traditional organisations aim to be self-perpetuating, and protect themselves from unwelcome change in stringent ways that defy challenge. Marcuse explains the process of alienation through institutional forces and reveals the one-directionality of hierarchical control.

In his introduction to David Bohm's work, Lee Nichol (1996) shows how Bohm explains that alienation is part of a view of fragmented reality which has serious implications for human living.

> To illustrate the significance of fragmentation, Bohm often used the example of a watch that had been smashed into random pieces. These pieces are quite different from the parts that have gone into the making of the watch. The parts have an integral relationship to one another, resulting in a functional whole. The fragments, on the other hand, have no essential relationship. Similarly, the generic thought processes of humanity incline toward perceiving the world in a fragmentary way, 'breaking things up which are not really separate'. Such perception, says Bohm, necessarily results in a world of nations, economies, religions, value systems, and 'selves' that are fundamentally at odds with one another.
>
> (Nichol, in Bohm, 1996: viii)

We are not very much advanced today from Cartesian times, according to some theorists. Alvesson and Deetz (1999: 186) for example, comment that alienation is very much part of contemporary modernist discourses and 'works on the basis of control, the progressive ritualization of nature and people, whether workers, potential customers, or society as a whole'. Modernist views might have been challenged by postmodernist ones that problematise work contexts and the idea of fixed structures, but there are still plenty of modernist practices around. Control is still a major agenda and traditional behaviourist notions of power as making people do things against their will are still highly visible. While the shift from manufacturing to service industries might have forced a refocusing on what is controlled, control is still the objective (Alvesson and Deetz, ibid.). Things are perhaps not changing as rapidly as anticipated.

Stories of alienation are everywhere, in how people cope with work which is tedious and frustrating (Hochschild, 1983); how they challenge imposed forms of conduct (Garrick, 1998). The stories reach their zenith in portrayals of management as a reified force, the 'them' in reductionist 'them and us' caricatures. Perhaps one can appreciate how discourses of alienation became part of organisational culture in the 1920s and 1930s, when Fayol's principles of management prioritised the division of work, discipline, the chain of command; and Ford's vision of standardisation, both for people and cars, was maintained by efficient managers who kept everything in its place. It is however surprising when those same discourses appear in contemporary work. Noon and Blyton (1997) are an example. They write: 'it is important to recognise that management and workers can be characterised as two groups engaged in a structural conflict; ... management's key concern ... lies with labour's performance' (p. 7), and they explain how the distinctiveness of 'two sets of rationalities' is a co-existence of 'management rationalities and workers' counter-rationalities' (ibid.). Organisations, according to Noon and Blyton, are run by omnipotent managers: 'the rules as defined by management are the ones strictly adhered to by the workforce' (p. 206).

Morgan (1997a) laments this still dominant empiricist view: 'The whole thrust of classical management theory and its modern applications is to suggest that organisations can or should be rational systems that operate in as efficient a manner as possible' (p. 21). He also points to the potentially dehumanising and dispiriting effects of this approach:

> Much of the apathy, carelessness, and lack of pride so often encountered in the modern workplace is thus not coincidental: it is fostered by the mechanistic approach. Mechanistic organisation discourages initiative, encouraging people to obey orders and keep their place rather than to take an interest in, and question, what they are doing. People in a bureaucracy who question the wisdom of conventional practice are viewed more often than not as troublemakers. Therefore, apathy often reigns as people learn to feel powerless about problems that collectively they understand and ultimately have the power to solve.
>
> (p. 30)

2 How is empirical research knowledge acquired?

The methods of the natural sciences are rooted in the manipulation of variables to support a hypothesis. It is assumed that the validity of a claim to knowledge can be demonstrated by the effects that manipulation of independent variables can have on a dependent variable. Whizzo plant food is tested with beneficial results on an experimental group of tomatoes which are then compared with a control group. It is assumed that Whizzo will have the same beneficial effect on any and all groups of tomatoes. The growth of the tomatoes (the dependent variable, DV) is controlled by use of a resource (the independent variable, IV). Similarly organisational practices (the DVs) can be influenced and adjusted by management practices (IVs), supporting a hypothesis that organisational practices will be improved by a particular management style. If the management style is of the right kind, organisational practices will be influenced accordingly. The practice can then be extended to all contexts, with predictably identical results. McDonald's is a good example that shows how standardised practices are maintained throughout the whole organisation. There are well-prescribed codes and routines that sell a commodity which never varies. The same is so for many franchised operations which will often go to great lengths to ensure that the image and practices remain uncontaminated. Routinised practices embody the normative criteria of replicability and generalisability of the scientific method (see Morgan, 1997a: 24, on the 'McDonaldisation' of work).

Organisation research has operated traditionally within this paradigm, and still does to a large extent. Perhaps its most striking manifestation is in free markets, a practice which assumes that one model may be applied universally with standardised results. On this view, cultural traditions become so many variables to be manipulated to achieve the desired effects (see Chapter 9). Empirical research aims to generate theory of a propositional nature, theory about organisations, which helps organisations to find ways to operate more efficiently by controlling and directing behaviours for optimum effect. Relationships become commodities which may be manipulated. People are seen as variables, and outcomes are predicted and controlled in terms of how management action, the IV, will impact on people as DVs. An example of this view is structural contingency theory, which aims to produce a scientific body of knowledge about how organisational structures influence organisational behaviours (see for example Pfeffer, 1982). The research focuses on constructing theoretical models to explain how organisations best operate in terms of contingency factors such as size, strategy and technology.

The scientific method is alive and well in contemporary practices. Some recent initiatives adopt the same principles of the scientific method while dressing them up in the discourses of humanitarian and liberal-democratic philosophies. Initiatives such as downsizing, outsourcing and re-engineering perhaps appear as honest rogues, thinly disguised ruses to reduce corporate slack in light of economic efficiency; but ideas of total quality management and excellence, the more enlightened ways forward, also adopt the same methodological basis of understanding how organisational systems work best if carefully adjusted and manipulated. A consistent message is that 'If x then y: if you do this, that will happen.' The principle extends from the caricature of managers controlling workers to the more derisory contexts of consultants and theorists controlling corporations. Every time a firm calls in a consultant there is an expectation that the consultant knows better, has an answer, and can guide the firm in the best direction. The agricultural-botanical paradigm is equally at home in world-class corporations as in a garden greenhouse.

Management learning

The idea of 'if x then y' extends to traditional forms of management education. It is assumed that there is an abstract body of knowledge which, if learnt and then applied, will improve practice. Theory and practice remain separate. The dominant kind of theory is propositional, knowledge about facts. In traditional MBA courses this appears as separate disciplines about organisation and management practice. When translated into practice these can appear as technical skills, and are judged in terms of performance indicators and objectivised criteria. I am reminded of my colleague on page 20 who scored 100 per cent on his questionnaire. This kind of technical rational approach denies the values base of management as a human practice and reduces it to technique.

The form in which knowledge is transmitted is via a transaction between teacher and taught, a master–apprentice model in which a knower passes prescribed knowledge to a trainee. Freire (1970) called this a 'banking model'. The new business-speak of education and training is 'to deliver a curriculum', part of the metaphor of bringing a set of packaged principles and practices to trainees who will then use them at the right time and in the right way. The teaching–learning model is one of training and development rather than education. Newer perspectives (Easterby-Smith and Thorpe, 1997) suggest that institutions need to move away from a delivery model and see management learning in the wider light of helping managers understand how they can help people help themselves. Critiques show the barrenness of traditional courses (Cunningham and Dawes, 1997; Hodgson, 1997). Yet reports also indicate that policy requires training rather than learning, and technical excellence which meets specified abstract criteria rather than creative and appropriate responses in workplaces as a context for and a form of practical learning in action (Easterby-Smith and Thorpe, 1997).

Contra methodologies have loosened the stranglehold of traditional forms in recent years. Research evidence now exists to show a move away from technical rational forms to more person-centred strategies, with implications for how this might influence the quality of personal-social practices (for example, Lomax, 1996; Marshall and Reason, 1997; Whitehead, 1994). This could possibly indicate a coming together of high-ground and low-ground practices in an attempt by each to recognise the need for the integration of theory and practice.

3 How is empirical research knowledge put to use?

The industrial world continues turning because of empirical research knowledge. Technological and scientific development is rooted in technical rational knowledge. It is widely acknowledged in the literature that the most powerful workers are knowledge workers, in the sense of people who know what to do, how and when to do it, and how best to predict and control future outcomes from their present knowledge base. Las Vegas thrives on empirical research knowledge. Management on this view concerns itself with how best to harness and direct that knowledge for maximum efficiency.

The brave new worlds of the future however need to be more than a dream of technical excellence. While media reports suggest it might be possible in a very short while to replace most aspects of a human body, questions begin to arise around whose body it is and what is the quality of experience of the mind-brain within that body. It might be a dream of the future that organisations become self-replicating technologies, in the same way that computers can programme themselves; and to a certain extent this is current reality with automation replacing people at an accelerating pace. What happens to people when they have been replaced by their own technology? Issues of the changing nature of work and a potential jobless society are high currency (Rifkin, 1995). Increasing competition, technologisation, globalisation, all features of the scientific paradigm, give rise to concerns that most people will find themselves with the whole of their futures before them and nothing to do.

I know this feeling well. I took early retirement through poor health at the age of 46 from my work as a deputy head of a large comprehensive school. Overnight I went from somebody to nobody. In school I had a highly visible institutional role, a clear identity, a set of responsibilities. Suddenly I did not have to answer to anyone. I lost my identity. This experience taught me the importance of work as a context for self-fulfilment, for achieving a sense of personal and professional worth, for developing attachments in a community setting. As time went on I learned that I was capable of creating a new identity, but I think my personal and spiritual awareness was strengthened by the intellectual awareness that was being developed through my own action research studies. In recent years, as I have recounted, my professional situation has been one of insecurity and risk. I have opted to gamble on whether I can realise my vision of chosen communities of self-reflective practitioners by working with groups of practitioners, and enabling them to see and put into practice their own potentials for personal and social growth, and also to persuade the academy publicly to legitimate this process and so shift the knowledge base of professional learning.

I firmly believe that the future is not predetermined nor predictable, but exists in the moment. What we do with this moment influences all the future moments of our lives. We cannot, and probably would not wish to reverse most technological achievement, but we need seriously to address issues of 'What price people?' in our new organisational contexts. We rush around in an effort to save time; we drive ourselves to distraction in order to create new technologies to make our lives easier. We technologise ourselves in our commitment to clocks and pocket organisers. Technical knowledge and technical achievement have use value in people's lives only when they are perceived as phenomena within a wider process of human living, functional aspects that serve people, rather than monster creations that take over both their own means of production and the people who create them in the first place.

Clear affinities exist between this view and Habermas's ideas of the relationship between theory and practice, between people and the systems they create (Habermas, 1974). In efforts to realise technical excellence, and thus ensure market competitiveness and territorial dominance, we concentrate our efforts on technical rational ways of knowing which eradicate from the process the people who are meant to be beneficiaries and the knowers themselves.

Technical knowledge can be used quite ruthlessly by powerful groups whose interests are served by perpetuating the status quo, generating norms of fear and defensiveness, feelings of isolation, for managers as well as for other practitioners. Technical rational forms of knowledge reinforce relationships of dominance that ensure that some people work at becoming the kind of person that powerful others want them to be. McDonald's 'Hamburger University' instructs its members how to demonstrate 'all-American' virtues of warmth, sincerity and enthusiasm (Boas and Chain, 1976); service industries require employees to smile at all costs (Hochschild, 1983), particularly in current situations where the quality of a company is judged in terms of the value-added of how customers are treated. Research that generates technical rational theory goes a long way to reproducing existing systems that subscribe to inequality and oppression; to ideologies that privilege one person above another, and which legitimise practices to maintain existing power relationships. It goes a long way to endorsing a view of people and their environment as objective units that are open to exploitation.

Technical rationality remains the dominant form of workplace knowledge, and the main way of studying organisations. In light of the special position of organisations to constitute, reproduce and change social and cultural norms, and how organisational practice might provide a model for wider social practices (Robinson Hickman, 1998: Introduction), a vast resource is being marginalised and often ignored in terms of how practitioners in workplaces can come to realise that they actively have the power to shape and influence their own future.

4 What are the implications for organisation theory as a theory of social renewal?

I want to go back to the legacy of Francis Bacon, who maintained that nature existed to be dominated by humans. By extension, nature includes humans, which become objects for domination and exploitation.

In Chapter 9 I explain how the Enlightenment generated its own project of imagining a universal civilisation which would be judged in terms of 'genuinely universal, tradition independent norms' (MacIntyre, 1988: 335), which exist in a transcendental sense, independent of cultural diversity. The Enlightenment project is western in origin, and takes western society as the model for the universal civilization; in most of the literature this is assumed to be the United States. Fukuyama (1999) for example unquestioningly sees the US as the major civilising force whose cultural traditions should be replicated and generalised on a global scale, a claim as arrogant as it is short-sighted.

Many nation states have resisted the influence of the Enlightenment project by maintaining their own cultures and traditions. I share my time between Ireland and England. Both countries subscribe to similar political and economic policies, yet their cultures and traditions are totally different, and I learn to adjust my ways accordingly. Japan also and other manufacturing countries have maintained their own cultural traditions while adapting western marketing strategies to a high degree of sophistication. However, although cultural diversity remains, much of the industrialised world has bought in to the philosophy of the free market, a philosophy that aims to secure maximum productivity for the lowest cost. The free market and its trends towards globalisation causes untold social disruption and human suffering, as people move to jobs away from local communities, parents work different shifts, portfolio and contract work result in loss of job stability, an increase in crime and incarceration become evident in societies who subscribe to the free market ethic, and the earth's resources continue to be exploited at a rate that cannot be sustained.

At the core of the increasing global disruption is the prioritisation of technical rational knowledge, which in turn fuels greediness and the will to power on the part of wealthy minorities. The earth is assumed to have limitless resources which do not need replenishing. People are assumed to be pieces whose movements are controlled by market forces, and who are dispensable when no longer needed. Forecasts vary as to how long the earth will continue. A substantial literature indicates that unless urgent action is taken the earth has a just short while left. Reports from the Worldwatch Institute (as cited in Henderson 1996 among others) warn of the over-rapid consumption of earth resources; the work of scientists such as James Lovelock (for example, 1991) and Stephen Jay Gould (for example, 1990) say that humans are one species among many who the earth will reject in its efforts at self-regeneration. The special edition of *Time* (April/May 2000) on *How to Save the Earth* gives a State of the Planet report which makes alarming reading. Ó Murchú (1997b: 177) cites Lord Rees-Mogg of the WorldWatch Institute as saying in 1992,

> If we are lucky, mankind [*sic*] as it is, has about fifty years left. Most of the graphs on human development, population, ecology, nuclear proliferation and the spread of disease are on an explosive curve. The lines shoot off the graph somewhere in the middle of the next century.

The next century is here.

The soldier in Oliver Stone's production of *Born on the Fourth of July* said, 'If you ain't part of the solution, you're part of the problem.' We urgently need to take action, not against the planet or against one another, but against ourselves, our own complacency that things will turn out right without our personal intervention. Each one of us has the potential to make a difference for good, and the moral responsibility to do so. We need to change our attitudes, our ways of thinking, to see people and the planet not as separate from ourselves, but as sharing a common heritage and a common future (if we are lucky). Taking action was never a part of the empirical research paradigm, which aimed to generate static propositional knowledge of facts and information. We already have the most important information we need – a few more years. We need to move on, find ways of generating more important kinds of knowledge – wisdom – to help us understand what we have to do to survive and secure a quality experience of life; and concentrate more on developing and legitimising other kinds of knowledge which see humans as self-aware, critical knowers whose lives are fashioned as much by understanding and the desire to change as by accumulating facts and information.

The potential for social renewal through organisation studies is significant. The potential will not be realised until we begin regarding organisations as groups of people in dynamic relation, not variables. We urgently need new theories of organisation, and a strong body of case study evidence to show the justification of the theory in terms of social renewal at a local and global level.

I have presented ideas in Chapter 5 about empirical research, suggesting that this approach is not appropriate for many aspects of human enquiry. Regarding people as objects to be manipulated does not move us on in understanding how to improve personal practice. I have presented the ideas in a conceptual way. For the ideas to take on meaning and show their potential implications for real life, they now need to be contextualised in a story of real life.

This happens in Paul Murphy's story. Paul shows how his practice was initially informed by the empirical paradigm, how he came to see its limitations in helping him make sense of his work, and how he moved to more person-centred approaches that suited his purposes better. He shows the development of his personal epistemology of practice that moves from a view of persons on whom solutions can be imposed to a view of persons who are ultimately responsible for their own lives in relation with others.

Rehabilitating sexual offenders in religious communities

Paul Murphy

My work is to do with the rehabilitation of sexual offenders in religious communities. A member of a religious community myself, I work in a counselling role both with offenders and also with the members of the communities into which they will become reintegrated. My work is educational in its broadest sense, in that I am trying to help all members of the community to find tolerant and compassionate ways of living with one another in the face of personal and collective distress. I have to help all members of the community learn how to cope with new, traumatic circumstances, and there is as yet no set of guidelines to help people in my position to know how to do this. To help me draw up some provisional guidelines, as was my brief when I was first appointed to do this work, I decided to enrol on the MA in Education course, in the hope that I would have the opportunity to investigate my practice to help me understand better the nature of what I was doing.

It was here that I came to study research methods. I studied empirical, interpretive and critical theoretic methodologies; and I decided to investigate my practice using an action research methodology. This, I felt, would enable me to research my own practice and generate my own theory of how I could help offenders and their communities. The attractions of the action research approach were that it required me to study my own work, that it did not expect answers but invited further questions, and acknowledged what Schön (1983) refers to as the 'messiness' of real life. I related strongly to all these qualities in what I was doing, and was glad to have found a methodology that paralleled and legitimated the complex and developmental form of my work.

Throughout my studies I have tried to understand how religious communities can be helped to rehabilitate a sexual offender who is one of their members. This has involved me in analysing the ways of learning that communities adopt, and also the assumptions within different approaches to rehabilitation. I have come to see how these approaches themselves manifest the assumptions of different research methodologies. I want briefly to explore these two issues here.

Analysing approaches to rehabilitation

When the Church in Ireland recently became aware of the instance of sexual abuse among members of the clergy and religious Orders, it turned to psychotherapists, among others, for assistance. The psychotherapists advised that sexual offenders be sent for intensive personal change programmes in residential centres established for that purpose. The usual form these programmes took is as follows:

- the uncovering and acknowledgement of the pattern of abuse perpetrated;
- the identification of the factors which create the conditions under which the perpetrator abuses and continues to abuse;
- the development of some understanding of the impact on the victim of the abuse and a fundamental change in attitude to a feeling for those abused;
- the commitment to a process whereby the perpetrator can avoid situations which may increase the risk of re-offending.

(Walsh, 1999: 44)

On the return of an offender from such a programme to his community, the task of that community is two-fold:

1   to assist the member in question to live an offence-free lifestyle;
2   to reincorporate him into the community.

While a religious community is not a therapeutic community as such, it is, nevertheless, a place where healing is meant to take place. In this respect, it takes up where the therapeutic centre leaves off, assisting the offender to maintain the behavioural changes brought about in the course of his treatment. How the community then acts is dictated to them by the form of the therapeutic approach employed in the residential programme.

I discovered that there were broadly two approaches which communities adopted, which I here call the 'old' and the 'new' approach.

The 'old' approach

On his return from the therapeutic centre, the offender comes armed with what is known as a Relapse Prevention Plan, a 'self-control programme designed to teach individuals who are trying to change their behaviour how to anticipate and cope with the problem of relapse' (George and Marlatt, 1989: 2). The offender's adherence to this plan would be monitored by the community, through the person of the superior, by means of a contract drawn up by the therapeutic centre. The superior and the community are required to keep the offender under close surveillance. Not surprisingly, this often leads to a 'him and us' situation, which, to my mind, is at variance with the second part of the community's task which is to put in place a healing and constructive atmosphere for all concerned. Furthermore, it is often the case that the community inherits much more from the therapeutic centre in terms of attitudes, which can be quite hostile to the spirit of community living. The offender is distrusted, a clear off-spring from the therapy.

The most common form of this approach is Cognitive Behavioural Therapy (CBT), a behaviourist approach, based mainly on the work of Skinner (1954) and

Beck (1989). It assumes that the human being is eminently programmable, and no contact of a personal nature is required. While the therapist is supposed to seek a collaborative relationship with the offender which is characterised by warmth, authenticity and empathy, they see the offender's behaviours as the subject matter for therapy. The CBT approach encourages lack of engagement with the offender as a person, and this rubs off on the religious community who tend to distance themselves from him, thereby

a   going against one of the basic tenets of their way of life;
b   doing a certain violence to themselves.

The 'new' approach

The 'new' approach is indebted to humanistic psychology. The assumptions are that, despite their propensity to terrible actions in certain circumstances, all people are inherently good, and can find ways themselves, particularly when supported by loving communities, to overcome their worst inclinations. On this view, according to Rogers (1967), 'the only learning which significantly influences behaviour is self-discovered, self-appropriated learning' (p. 276). This is learning which cannot be taught, although it can be nurtured. For the offender, the implication is that it is only when he discovers for himself why he should stop behaving in an abusive way and adopts a non-abusive lifestyle, out of conviction, that real progress can be made. This is the path to long-term, sustainable, offence-free living.

If the perpetrator is unable to move from relying exclusively on external factors to control his abusive behaviour and does not undergo a transformation of the heart as well as the mind, the conditions that were implicated in his abuse may well reappear and overwhelm his resolve (Walsh, 1998a: 53–4).

From my studies, I came to see the clear links between research paradigms and approaches to rehabilitation. The 'old' approach is influenced by the empiricist assumptions that people can be controlled and directed, that a change of attitude is a matter of manipulating variables; while the 'new' approach is influenced by the new-paradigm assumptions of people as free agents who make decisions about their own personal-social purposes and intents as influenced by their values and understanding of their relationships with one another.

Working with communities

I have brought these understandings to my work with communities. I believe I have come to understand that the learning the community must engage in is always in relation to their fellow member who is an offender. Since sexual abuse is primarily about a failure to engage in respectful and authentic relationship, the remedy for it lies in trying to help the offender to experience respectful and authentic relationship. According to Walsh (1998b: 54), the offender needs to 'move from a place of disconnection to connection with society and learn to build up community … he needs opportunities to relate constructively with others.'

I believe that the religious community of which the offender is a member is obliged first, in justice to all his potential victims, and then in justice to itself, to provide him with such opportunities. The failure, for whatever reason, to make these connections on the part both of the offender and of the community is a sure recipe for relapse.

One of the services the community can offer to the offender is the opportunity to give an account of himself, a practice which embraces the same values as action research of personal accountability to others, and the desire to find ways to improve.

I would say in summary that the 'new' approach represents a shift in emphasis away from an almost exclusive reliance on an external controls regime to one which, while acknowledging the role played by cognitive-behavioural techniques, places the therapist–offender relationship centre stage. This has implications for the religious community, requiring a shift from a purely supervisory role to one which tries to cultivate relationship-building and personal accountability as key elements in the rehabilitation of the offender. It has also had considerable implications for my practice, for I have come to see that my main work is to support the communities, as much as the offender, in terms of whose needs are at stake in discussions of rehabilitation. In fact, I have come to see the non-offending members of the community as the neediest party in this situation.

Implications for practice

I would suggest, from study and experience, that communities need to take care in choosing a therapy which is compatible with the community's religious ethos. In order to avoid confusion, the community must also clarify the parameters of their pastoral role in relation to that of the therapists.

I think the change to a relationship-centred approach can best be facilitated by adopting those conditions which Rogers would insist are necessary to bring about that significant learning which is a prerequisite for continuing behavioural change – namely, genuineness, acceptance and empathy.

Genuineness

If the community is to be genuine in their relationships with the offender they need to have grown in self-awareness and come to terms with their own issues concerning sexual abuse. If, for example, they have not acknowledged their anger at what the offender has done to his victims, and the fear that they can experience in relation to the repercussions on their reputations of the disclosure of his misdeeds, they can easily, consciously or unconsciously, direct such negative emotion at the offender. The community needs to acknowledge its sense of loss, and grieve appropriately. They need to renew themselves in their tradition of respect for the individual and care for those in most need of healing.

Acceptance

Because of what the offender has done to his victims and to the community the full acceptance of the offender can pose a very real problem. The community needs to learn how to separate the offender from his offences, and see him as a person in need. It would be hypocritical of the community to demand that the offender refrain from abusing if they failed to address abusive practices of whatever kind in themselves.

Empathy

To empathise with the offender the community must become acquainted with his world. They must educate themselves about the condition that is sexual abuse and also the therapeutic experience he has been through. They must understand that for sex offenders there is no cure: 'there is only the hope of better self-control and behaviour management' (Blanchard, 1995: 49). The offender has to live with this fact every day. To realise that others appreciate his situation can increase his sense of being accepted.

The community therefore has much work to do on themselves before they can even begin to help the offender. However, the arena in which they can work both on themselves and with the offender is already in place – the regular community meeting attended by all the community. It is here that the offender will have the opportunity to perceive that the community is genuine in their relationships with him, accept him and empathise with him. This 'local chapter', as it is called, while often taken up with day-to-day business matters, is also a place to address the real psychological needs of the community. The complex process can be enabled by an external facilitator, experienced in the fields of sexual abuse and group work, and this is where I find myself increasingly, in a position of helping all to negotiate their way through a distressing but hopeful process.

Influences on my own work

The key influence has been the realisation that the 'new' approach is more compatible with the ethos of religious community life than the 'old' approach. It also fits very well with the process of ongoing education which is meant to be a feature of community living. Because of this compatibility and the support flowing from it, it seems to me that the 'new' approach is more likely to result in non-offending behaviour than the 'old'. Also in this connection the changes proposed are in keeping with the spirit of the mandate I received to pursue this line of work. A very serious concern for me is the need to do justice, not only to the victims and potential victims of sexual abuse, but also to the offender himself – treating him in a non-abusive way – and to the non-offending community themselves.

I believe that thinking and acting are interdependent, so I would like to make more explicit the link between the 'old' and 'new' approaches to rehabilitation and the mindsets which inform them.

The 'old' approach to rehabilitation betrays a positivist mindset. It is assumed that if the offender is made to conform to definite, imposed behavioural rules, then the desired outcome of non-offending will be achieved. The participation of the offender is limited to his obedience. There is then no need for personal engagement between the offender and his community. The mark of success here is calculated on how the offender fares in respect to the predetermined rate of recidivism.

The 'new' approach demands the participation of the offender as a *sine qua non* of his improvement, and, not only that, seeks to achieve the desired outcomes of non-offending and re-incorporation in the community, by means of a dialectical process between offender and community. Both are thus required to change as they learn to cope on an ongoing basis through their shared responses to the tasks confronting them. Justice and respect for all concerned is the desired outcome.

While sexual abuse is an unmitigated evil, nevertheless I hope I have shown how the rehabilitation of a sexual offender can, paradoxically, act as a catalyst in the furtherance of the community's own growth and development.

I have come to a deeper understanding of my own work through studying my practice, and I can make informed choices about how to work with all members of the community in their attempts to reclaim their lives in the context of their chosen way of life. This study will also help me in my present work which is that of assisting religious communities in similar circumstances on a country-wide basis.

6 Interpretive research

Background

A changing view of scientific enquiry

From the late nineteenth century onwards, science itself underwent a profound transformation. The natural and physical sciences abandoned Newtonian physics and its view of a deterministic universe in favour of a quantum view of science which saw reality as unpredictable and often incomprehensible (Heisenberg, 1989). The new physics began to replace the normative mechanistic model as a metaphor to understand human interaction. A view of social activity as a dynamic system began to emerge, as well as the idea of systems as emergent processes rather than planned structures. Early general systems theory (for example, Pareto, 1935) developed and came to prominence from the 1940s (for example, Bertanlanffy, 1950, 1968), providing new organising metaphors for human enquiry.

Massive technological change accompanied the social and political turmoil of the nineteenth and twentieth centuries, particularly as reflected in the new potentials for domination afforded by quantum science and its products, mainly weapons of destruction. The social disruption of world wars and economic and political instability generated a greater demand than ever for integration and community to maintain social order in a chaotic and increasingly threatening world. It was becoming clear to many that technical rationality was inadequate to address issues of longer-term social survival.

The work of Freud and his contemporaries in psychological enquiry also contributed to dislodging the worldview of human action as deterministic. The individual came to be seen as a not entirely rational entity in a trade-off situation with wider social processes. The study of society was no longer a simplistic overview of planned activities; instead, new methods had to be developed to explain social processes as dynamic interactions among people who are often driven by forces outside their own awareness and control.

Here was the onset of the second cognitive revolution, a period of extreme turbulence as the dominant paradigm began to shift from the prediction and control of behaviour to an understanding of the reasons for behaviour. A new paradigm, an interpretive approach, began to emerge. This rode side by side with the dominant scientistic approach, which, as Kuhn says is the way of paradigm shifts, are characterised not by a smooth transition from one approach to another, with a clear break-off point, but by periods of sometimes uneasy co-existence of approaches; so at the same time it was (and still is) possible to discern for example the rampant behaviourism of psychometrics along with an increasing focus on individual understanding as the basis of human practice.

The emergent interpretive paradigm

The interpretive paradigm grew out of the hermeneutic tradition. Hermeneutics was the name originally given to the practice of interpreting religious texts by Protestant theologians in the seventeenth century (Carr and Kemmis, 1986: 86). Later the term came to be associated with the interpretive understanding of literature and the arts. In the early twentieth century German social scientists such as Dilthey and Weber developed interpretive approaches as alternatives to positivist views of knowledge.

Another major influence in interpretive approaches was the emergent interest in anthropology. From the nineteenth century onwards, more efficient travel and communications began to open up the world, and social scientists became interested in naturalistic research, the study of people and phenomena in their natural settings. Linguists undertook elaborate studies of esoteric languages (Lyons, 1970) and anthropologists followed the tradition of the great explorers by studying people in their native habitats (Benedict, 1934; Mead, 1970). These studies offered descriptions of social interaction but not necessarily explanations for why they happened or what their purposes were.

Several research traditions emerged, all with different opinions about the proper focus of enquiry. Phenomenology, whose key theorists were Edmund Husserl and Alfred Schutz, argued that social scientific enquiry needs to start from where people are. Individuals' interpretations of their own lifeworlds are their truth. Ethnomethodology also developed, an approach that argues that social phenomena should be studied in terms of the accounts that people give of their own experiences: the focus is people's everyday practical reasoning. Reality, it is suggested, should be interpreted in terms of participants' understandings. Human enquiry came to be seen as the study of people in terms of interpretations of their own lifeworld experiences. No consensus appeared, however, around issues of who should be a researcher – an external observer or people themselves – or whose research it was – the external researcher's or the people's.

While interpretive approaches have now gained universal acceptance as methods for describing social practices, the form of theory has not changed and remains propositional. The method of enquiry has always involved observing individual processes from an external perspective. While systems theory continues to be used widely as an analogue to describe and explain social processes, it is also still used from a descriptive perspective which seldom takes into consideration actors' accounts of their practice, or the values base, reasons and intentions for their actions. The situation remains as the objective study of people by external observers. This constitutes a potential power relationship between external researchers and those whom they are researching, in terms of who has the right to make judgements about whose practice, and who decides.

1   What is the nature of interpretive research knowledge?

The still dominant positivist approaches of the scientific paradigm hold that ways of knowing are fixed and all of a type, as is the kind of knowledge generated. There is one reality and one form of knowledge which is external to a knower, reified and good for all time. Interpretive researchers challenge this view. For them, knowledge cannot exist without a knower. It is always and inevitably the property of an active agent, a thinking mind. Because people are social beings and influence one another, knowledge also must be socially constructed; and it changes as the lifeworlds of people change. Knowledge is not 'objective', external to people and imposed by a neutral observer, but created by people from their own understanding of experience. Because people are all different, and have their own perceptions and interpretations, there are also multiple truths; knowledge is subjectively created and intersubjectively negotiated. The aim of interpretive practice, according to its major theorists, is to achieve intersubjective understanding of a particular situation (Habermas, 1979; Gadamer, 1975).

With the emergence of the interpretive paradigm, the emphasis of social scientific enquiry shifted from the empirical observation and description of a supposedly external and static reality to an effort to understand the meanings that people give to their lives. Humans, unlike the notionally 'lifeless' matter that the natural sciences study, not only react, but also act purposefully; their experiences and interpretations are meaningful (Haralambos and Holborn, 1991: 707). The method of *verstehen*, the German word for 'understanding', came to be applied to the study and interpretation of social situations. Generally speaking, one could say that whereas the scientific paradigm focused on issues of prediction and control in human enquiry, interpretive approaches were concerned more with descriptions that showed understanding and meaning.

Especially from the 1960s onwards interpretive research appeared on a range of fronts in the human sciences: for example, Weber (1961) and Outhwaite (1975) in sociological enquiry; Young (1971) in the sociology of education; Silverman (1970), Weick (1979) and Burrell and Morgan (1979) in organisation research. Burrell and Morgan's multi-paradigm approach proposed different frameworks for knowledge generation which, they held, were alternative and incommensurable forms (see also Burrell, 1999).

The emergence of these more person-centred and qualitative forms in organisation study presented a significant challenge to the dominant scientific paradigm, both in terms of how organisations are understood and also how they are studied. Previously they were understood as static empirical objects which were studied in terms of their functional structures by the gathering of quantifiable data, which could then be analysed and presented in order to forecast trends and control behaviour through the implementation of strategy. New interpretive paradigms showed organisations as groups of people engaged in making meaning of their social lives within organisations; they observed their own social interactions, and by studying and pooling their interpretations of the qualitative data they generated, could reach intersubjective agreement about the nature of their social lives. Their findings were then interpreted by an external researcher. This relationship between the researcher and the researchees persistently led to the problematic of ownership and legitimacy. Whose research? Whose data? Whose interpretations? Who says? These are issues which have less to do with methodological appropriateness, and more to do with the politics of dominance and control.

The mediated nature of interpretive research knowledge

Interpretive research is always an act of mediation, and is therefore caught in the double bind that (1) whatever is presented is mediated information, which is then (2) presented via a propositional form that itself is a mediating device.

Mediated knowledge

At its most authentic, interpretive research knowledge continues to provide insights into multiple contexts of human living. Travel and natural history TV programmes give access to new worlds; news broadcasts and newspapers keep us up to date. Mediated knowledge however is always someone else's more direct knowledge of a situation; what is filtered and how it is filtered are hidden processes, known to the interpreter who makes decisions about whether to share them with the audience.

Researchers such as Brookfield (1987), McLaren (1995) and Giroux (1988), working from a critical perspective, show how mediated knowledge can lead to misinformation and distorted communication. Umpteen examples exist of how stories are misrepresented by the media. Stories of genetic engineering and biological weaponry for example are sometimes deliberately suppressed in the interests of corporate profit. Years before events in East Timor became critical in the 1990s, Chomsky (1982, 1985) had noted how reports of abuse of human rights were marginalised in the press. Interpreted knowledge is valuable for keeping us informed about what is going on in the world, but we need to remember that the messages we receive are always someone else's messages, mediated in terms of what they consider should be publicly available knowledge or what is privileged information.

Awareness of the complex nature of interpretive research needs to be high in management learning, particularly in light of the fact (see below) that interpretive approaches are now a fully recognised methodology in organisation studies. Managers need to be aware of how the existing language of a sacred story (also see below) masks the power relationships endemic to interpretive approaches. An action research perspective would then enable people to challenge those relationships and change their situations.

Theory as mediated reality

Kant and Schopenhauer explained that we could never have direct access to reality, if it exists at all. Whatever might exist is accessed through our senses. We can have first-hand experience of our senses; reality mediated through our perceptions is always second-hand.

The same is so of interpretive research. Theories generated are propositional, and contain second-hand information about other people's experience, seldom the first-hand experience of the external researcher, although the researcher presents the account. The world that interpretive research represents is virtual; it is not 'our' world but a world that exists as representation. Interpretive research tells stories of experience, but it is other people's experience. To tell one's own experience moves the account into another paradigm: autobiographical research, for example, or narrative enquiry, or action research. Interpretive research has as a main focus the researcher's interpretation of other people's experience. Stories that tell of others' experience run the risk of diminishing the status of people whose experience they are reporting. Erica Holley (1995: 16) for example writes about her experience of being included and excluded as an 'object' of other people's research in teacher education: 'included because teachers were described; excluded because a teacher's voice didn't speak to me except through the interpreter, the researcher'. She recounts her reactions to reading Jane Miller's (1990) *Seductions: Studies from Reading and Culture*:

> [Jane Miller] uses seduction as a metaphor to show how women are excluded from literary theory. For 'women' read 'teachers' as the metaphor fits. Thus teachers are seduced by academics who simultaneously include and exclude us in their writing and teaching. Our presence is taken for granted and yet denied and we are enticed into narratives which reduce us by exalting us.

The same might be said for organisation and management literature that simultaneously includes and excludes people in all contexts from their own narratives of life.

Interpretive accounts in organisation studies therefore always have a Janus-like quality. They describe others' practices; these descriptions are presented as a concrete and final account which is not open to deconstruction by those whose stories are being told. The propositional form of theory lends an aura of authority to the accounts, particularly when presented by prestigious figures such as academic tutors or well-respected consultants. The voting public however always needs to remember that the accounts are other people's accounts, and the other people, no matter what their clothes, are people like the rest of us.

2 How is interpretive research knowledge acquired?

As the paradigm developed, so did arguments about the right to ownership. While there was agreement that actions need to be interpreted in terms of their meanings, questions emerged that were to raise ongoing problematics from within and without. How are meanings agreed? whose interpretations are valid? Ownership of the data and their interpretation, and who is entitled to own and interpret, became key issues. Should participants be seen as actors generating and interpreting their own meanings, or should their practices be studied and interpreted by external researchers, either with or without participants' involvement or consent? The situation becomes more complex in light of whether the researcher is an outsider researcher, standing outside a social situation and suggesting interpretations to be negotiated with participants; or whether the researcher becomes an insider researcher, and a participant within the research situation.

Whose knowledge?

Phenomenological and ethnomethodological perspectives held that people's own interpretations must be respected and taken as 'truth'. Garfinkel (1967), for example, believed that it was inappropriate for external researchers to make judgements about other people's actions: only the people concerned knew and could comment on their own circumstances. In cultural anthropology, Clifford Geertz (1973) argued that 'thick descriptions' ought to be the unit of analysis – 'the detailed ethnographic explication of an individual cultural system that sought to understand its complexity but without fitting it into a theoretical framework' (Fukuyama, 1999: 157). Claude Lévi-Strauss (1963) also insisted that actors' accounts were valid interpretations of data – an emic approach rather than etic, personal accounts by actors rather than distanced accounts by observers.

A sociological perspective, however, including that of Weber, held that only outsider observers' perspectives were legitimate. 'If action stems from subjective meanings, it follows that the sociologist must discover those meanings in order to understand action. Sociologists cannot simply observe action from the outside and impose an external logic onto it. They must interpret the internal logic which directs the actions of the actor' (Haralambos and Holborn, 1991: 19). It would appear on this view that an external observer's accounts are more valid than those of the persons involved in the active situation. A Weberian perspective said that when case studies are produced they should be presented as data to support the researcher's interpretations and claims to knowledge. This approach is however not so far removed from empiricist methodologies which do research *on* people without their cooperation, often without their consent. The practice remains today for example in some higher education contexts where salaried researchers use the efforts of research assistants to boost their own work. It is also the practice of some consultancy firms to enter organisation contexts to work with participants in terms of making sense of their practice, and then impose their own solutions for identified problems.

At the heart of the debate is whether or not people can think for themselves. In research contexts this appears as questions about who is qualified to do research and what is the proper subject matter of research, about who the work process belongs to and who should be in control of the means of production. If all people are assumed capable of being responsible for their own work, then they should make judgements about their practice as responsible, reflective practitioners. If they are not assumed capable of doing this, authority to make judgements about their work comes to be vested in external observers – in institutional practice contexts this would be supervisors, managers, external consultants, and the like. The power play is never far away. Established interest groups maintain their gatekeeping position in terms of what counts as knowledge and who should know.

Whose theory?

The interpretive tradition is now as respected a form of organisational theory as the scientific tradition (Clegg and Hardy, 1999). Although the paradigm wars are still evident (for example, Donaldson, 1985), they are perhaps less prominent than before. New cases are made for the acceptance of paradigm proliferation (Burrell and Morgan, 1979; Donmoyer, 1996), with significant variation, and more tolerance (Bernstein, 1991). Organisation is increasingly understood as systems of human processes in which certainties about roles and structures are seriously destabilised; new emphases are appearing that show organisations as constructed in terms of gender (Calás and Smircich, 1991), ethnicity (Ferguson, 1994), and individual 'difference' (for example, Rose, 1990). Organisations are increasingly theorised in terms of narratives, not the grand narratives of totalising concepts and structures, but local narratives of personal experience and interpersonal attachment (Gilligan, 1982).

As well as shifts in the way that organisations are understood, parallel shifts have taken place in the way they are studied. There is today for example interest in the metaphorical basis of organisational study; organisations are seen as narratives of experience (for example, Morgan, 1997a; Grant and Oswick, 1996); and case study is used extensively as data to show organisational processes, using a variety of forms of representation. Increasingly also aspects of narrative enquiry are being used in interpretive approaches, although narrative enquiry and autobiographical research have developed their own traditions, which tend to be more at ease with critical theoretic and action research philosophies (see for example, Connelly and Clandinin, 1990). There are considerable cross-overs; no one paradigm is 'pure' in the sense that it operates within clear demarcation lines, and many approaches dip in and out of others. There is much methodological borrowing and sharing, and what Giroux (1992) calls border crossings.

The question remains, however, whose theory it is, and how the theory is put to use.

The idea that an external observer may make decisions about other people's practices constitutes a theory–practice gap. The external observer offers a theory about another person's practice. Schön refers to this as 'the hierarchical separation of research and practice' (1983: 27), a situation in which an authorised 'knower' makes judgements about others' work from a distanced perspective, and uses their authorised power to consolidate their own power base – a closed-circle, closed-shop mentality in which the truth of power dominates over the power of truth (Foucault, 1980).

The issue goes beyond questions of methodology and becomes one of ethics and social justice. It raises questions about the right of one person to judge another, and the legitimacy of their interpretations. It also raises issues of power: how more powerful narratives potentially block and exclude weaker voices (Said, 1994a: xiii), and how less powerful people are prevented by the more powerful from questioning autocratic decisions. In terms of issues of knowledge, it is assumed that external researchers have a privileged right to 'know' which they may use without negotiation if necessary. Clandinin and Connelly (1995) speak about Crites's (1971) idea of the 'sacred stories' of personal and public life: 'Crites makes the point that sacred stories are so pervasive they remain mostly unnoticed and when named are hard to define' (p. 8). The sacred stories of organisation studies are that theory is applied to practice; know-that and know-how are prioritised over personal forms of knowledge – a 'rhetoric of conclusions' (Schwab, 1970, in Clandinin and Connelly, 1995); and recognised 'knowers', particularly those located in higher education settings, should be regarded as knowledge producers more readily than people in 'ordinary' work-places. These sacred stories do not accept a view that higher education is itself a workplace context; nor do they accept that those positioned as generators of academic knowledge are 'workers', practitioners in the same sense as those whom they view as consumers of the knowledge they generate. Alternative stories are presented to contest these stories (for example, Winter, 1999); but they are hard to dislodge. They are embedded within cultural psyches, often with significant implications for wider social practices. The idea of the right to episte-mological dominance for example extends readily to other areas of colonisation and territoriality; and it is not difficult to see the same attitudes and practices in many historical and current arenas of conflict where ownership of land is an extension of the right to ownership of knowledge (for example, Kearney, 1997).

This for me is one of the most significant inherent contradictions within the interpretive paradigm as a theoretical framework. While it claims to be rooted in moral considerations of entitlement to equal recognition by all participants, and a dialogue of equals, it often manifests as a perpetuation of dialogues of asym-metrical voices, in which dialogue becomes the prerogative of those on the winning side, used to control the colonised; and it turns into the familiar mono-logue of domination. The form of theory is safeguarded by protectionist methods; external researchers often go to extraordinary lengths to prevent those whose practice they are studying from thinking for themselves, and they wheel in stories of expert knowledge to intimidate and control their clients. Nowhere is this more evident than in traditional professional education courses where partic-ipants are required to undertake a piece of research on a workplace situation while the supervisor maintains the role of academic consultant to the research, disregarding the fact that supervisors also ought to practise what they preach and monitor their own work to ensure that they are supporting course participants' needs rather than their own.

3 How is interpretive research knowledge put to use?

The products of interpretive research, that is, accounts about other people's practices, are used to add to a body of propositional knowledge about organisations. It is assumed that practitioners will use this information to guide their own practice. People will learn from the accounts of others, and will use this vicarious experience as exemplars. So one person's practice is seen as a near-approximation to another's, if not a direct copy. It is anticipated that what worked well in one situation will work in another. This situation is reminiscent of the empirical research paradigm, in which replicability and generalisability are criteria of validity.

If it is possible for one person to base their practice on another's, there would be an assumption that practice is unified and can be understood as a standard set of principles and techniques. This is seldom the case. In commenting on the work of Deming (whose approach eventually became known as Total Quality Management) Crainer tells the following story: 'A manager once told Deming: "I need to know the minimum level of quality necessary to satisfy a customer." Deming commented: "So much misunderstanding was conveyed in a few words."' (Crainer, 1996: 145). The assumptions of the hapless manager are however evident throughout the literature of corporate improvement: if they can do it, so can we; all we need to do is find the formula and apply the techniques.

While learning from others' experience can be a powerful form of learning, it generates something akin to what Laurillard (1993) calls 'second-order knowledge', that is, knowledge of descriptions about experience rather than knowledge gained directly from experience. Learning about one's practice by adapting the lessons from another's offers an entrée into a virtual world, not a world in which one is positioned as a knowing agent in an active change process. Learning how to model one's practice on someone else's does not make one a better practitioner. It encourages a continuation of the theory–practice gap, where practice is seen as separate from the practitioner, and what is needed is knowledge about practice as a set of techniques, rather than engagement with practice as lived experience.

Interpretive research knowledge is used consistently by many researchers (consciously or unconsciously) to maintain the dominance of propositional theory and their own privileged position in making judgements about other people. Interpretive researchers decide who speaks, whose voice is heard, what is edited out from the discourses and what slant is given to an interpretation. Interpretive researchers speak about and on behalf of others, privileging their own voice, telling stories of other people's experience.

'Speaking about' is common practice in management education. Interpretive approaches do not encourage practitioners to give an account of their own process of developing knowledge. Practitioners are not encouraged to show how they generated their own knowledge or tested its validity against existing knowledge. Practice is still regarded as an abstract phenomenon, voided of the values base of real-life work.

These ideas are critical in discussions about professional competence. How do professionals demonstrate their professionalism and have their claims to good practice validated? In workplaces, practice is affirmed when the job gets done and people feel good about outcomes. The kind of knowledge base that under-pins such events tends to be personal practical knowledge (Chapter 2), the kind of wisdom that is gained through experience and considered practice, Laurillard's (1993) 'first-order knowledge'. This kind of knowledge is not however valued by the academy, which still operates within an empiricist culture (see p. 2 above, Schön, 1995). The academy prefers to value second-order conceptual knowledge *about*, rather than knowledge *of*. This is validated by conceptual forms of assessment such as written examinations and competencies-based profiles. Fox (1997) comments on the contradiction: in both the USA and the UK, technical rationality is favoured in university syllabuses, rather than crit-ical examination of practice.

> Paradoxically, it is the technical and functional orientation to management education, with its reductionist approach, which is most criticised by prac-tising managers in both the USA and the UK for being least relevant to their problems. It would appear that managers want management schools to offer more than technical trouble-shooting; rather, they want them to offer theories and ideas which address wider problems.
>
> (p. 23)

Appraisal in workplaces

The issue is critical in contexts of work appraisal. Performance appraisal is part of contemporary discourses of accountability and markets; it is often understood as the capacity to attain specified objectives. In normative training models, managers are assumed to set targets for employees to reach – Management-by-Objectives, and Management-by-Results. This view is critiqued by Keep and Mayhew (1999), among others, in terms of the assumptions that underlie training policy. Citing James (1991: 4), they say, 'This situation reflects a contin-uing belief on the part of many managers that their staff are "incapable of thought" '. They go on to say that reasons for this are various, including

> the legacy of low-trust industrial relations, where passive consent rather than active commitment was the norm, and where knowledge and skills were the contested terrain over which managers and workers (particularly craft workers) fought for control of the work process. The overall effect has been to encourage a reliance by many UK firms on a narrow managerial elite leading a mass of ill-trained workers.
>
> (Keep and Mayhew, 1999: 128)

Esland *et al.* (1999) explain how these assumptions carry over into appraisal prac-tices: 'The employee is supposed to identify weaknesses or gaps in their skill or knowledge bases which can, with the aid of appropriate training or develop-ment programmes, be overcome. In this way, what is essentially a management device is presented as a means of employee empowerment: the employee takes responsibility for his or her own training needs and means of occupational advancement' (pp. 171–2) – essentially a competencies approach to professionalism, in which a competence is identified as 'an underlying characteristic of a person that is causally related to effective or superior performance' (Esland *et al.*, 1999: 172, citing the definition of competence offered by Boyatzis, 1982).

A competencies approach has come in for sustained critique, mainly for its functionalist approach and the assumptions of overarching organisational goals within which specified skills and behaviours may be identified (Burgoyne, 1993). Drawing on the analysis of Foucault (1991), Esland *et al.* (1999: 173) cite two categories of knowledge: *connaissance*, an acquisition of knowledge which does not change the knower, which is akin to Schön's (1995) view of technical rational epistemologies; and *savoir*, the development of knowledge which transforms the knower, similar to Schön's idea of personal practical epistemologies. Technical rational epistemologies are favoured by institutions but are often far removed from the realities and needs of practice; while practical personal epistemologies are immediate and necessary, but are not valued institutionally (see Fox's comments above p. 169).

This whole view of appraisal and evaluation as an aspect of managerial practice is a direct outcome of a commitment to technical rational epistemologies and a reliance on mediated knowledge. It is assumed that managers are superior to other practitioners; that they can identify what counts as best practice; that they can judge the quality of other people's work in terms of normative categories of skills and behaviours. People count in so far as they come up to expectations, otherwise they need to be re-educated; hardly a context for the development of organisations as learning communities in Macmurray's (1950) terms: 'The ideal community is a universal one in which all personal relationships [are] positively motivated, all its members free and equal in relation' (p. 85).

I shall have more to say on these issues in Chapter 10.

4 What are the potential implications for organisation theory as a form of reflective practice?

First-order personal engagement with experience means reflecting on experience, and learning how to do things differently. This however relegates propositional knowledge to a subordinate position; and it is unlikely that interest groups within the dominant culture would lightly give up their favourite positions and commitments to conceptual knowledge. 'Social change does not occur by wishing it,' says Chomsky (1997: vii). 'As Frederick Douglas once observed, Power concedes nothing without a demand. It never did and it never will.'

The power of interpretive approaches lies in the promise of ready-made answers and a successful closure. If x then y; if you listen to the accounts and apply the lessons to your own practice you can be sure of a satisfactory outcome. Unfortunately, practice belies the theory. Contexts of practice are different; people and their learning are different. We can listen to one another's stories and empathise; but what we do with that learning within our own situation-specific contexts is always a matter of personal reflection and judgement. Interpretive research is rich but limited: no one ever changed a situation by telling stories of others' experience, although the stories themselves might be the inspiration that people come to act on and live by.

Social change, however, requires new methodologies and new philosophies; and this moves us into new paradigms in which change is a central focus and people become active agents in their own lives. Social cohesion arises from a cultural milieu in which people tell their own stories of experience. The modern campfires of office coffee tables and conference rooms are locations in which we share our stories and learn from one another. We listen respectfully and recognise the victories and setbacks as part of a personal process of coming to know, in order to use the new knowledge for a better world. We listen and learn, from the stories themselves and from the experience of listening and empathising. We grow as we help one another to grow.

New theories of organisation move from a situation of one person's mediating another's meaning to encouraging individuals to work out their own meaning in company with others. All parties learn in the telling of stories. The teller is able to frame and reframe the story, to reflect on the questions that inspired the story and assess in hindsight whether the question was appropriate or needs to be rethought. They are able to reflect on the process of thinking in action, and show how they were able to live in a way that was congruent with their values such that they feel they influenced other lives for good. The listener can encourage the process, not as a confessional, but in helping the teller to develop insights of practice to bring a new light on particular aspects. Listeners learn a great deal for their own practice when they really listen. Managers have to listen, and share in the conversations by telling their own stories, and arrange for people to meet and talk on company time.

Sharing stories and learning from them however is not part of interpretive philosophies, and does not inspire people to take responsibility for their own work. In new theories of organisation we use approaches that do. These stories show the situatedness of the individual and how they worked to improve their understanding in order to try to improve their social situations. They emphasise the individual accountability of practitioners, and the collective responsibility for nurturing learning from experience, and in this way contribute to a new view of professionalism that lies in the way that people live their lives. The lessons learnt from the telling and sharing of stories travel far beyond the workplace, and have significant implications for social renewal.

In this conceptual presentation of the main ideas of interpretive research, I have pointed out the potential injustice involved when one party speaks on behalf of another. This is shown now in contextualised form in Breda Long's story. Breda comments on how she articulated for herself the values of justice and democracy that underpin her work, and became aware of how she was denying these values in her practice by tending to speak on behalf of others. Through reflecting on her work she became aware of how she could change her practice and encourage others to speak for themselves and so live her values in practice. She came to reconceptualise her leadership as a form of practice in which she enabled others to take responsibility for their own ideas and develop their capacity to speak and claim ownership of their own knowledge.

Understanding my work as a group leader in employment counselling

Breda Long

For my MA studies I undertook an action research project into my work as an employment counsellor. The project was based on developing a job search skills programme designed for long-term unemployed people. Initially I had intended to research and evaluate the delivery of the programme, but as the research progressed I came to see that I needed first to understand what I was doing as a group leader. To do that, I also had to find out more about the nature of groups and how they functioned. My research focus therefore came to be myself and how I interacted with others in a group situation.

The original idea for the job search skills programme developed because I wanted to create a programme that was specifically designed for unemployed people. Most programmes I have encountered have been geared towards school leavers, graduates, employed people, all of whom had the confidence or desire to job search effectively. The job search skills programme I designed, I hoped, would reflect the needs of an unemployed person. It would help build self-esteem and confidence, identify the benefits of working or not working, and help people to derive support from the group which would strengthen their learning.

My values

Some of the beliefs I already held were reinforced by the study. One belief was influenced by my values of social justice, that leaders should encourage democratic participation within groups. Another was the belief that people should be given the opportunity to realise their career potential, and the opportunity to reflect critically on their career decisions (Maslow's (1954) idea of self-realisation). Based on these beliefs, any groups I worked with were participative, and informed by an 'education of equals' model (Ballyantyne and Teale, 1990). Here the emphasis is placed on the individual's ability to reach his or her potential, and outcomes are the responsibility of the learner. Mezirow *et al.* (1990) describe this as critical-emancipatory learning, in which new knowledge frees us from delusions about ourselves; we reflect on what we have learnt, and act on those reflections.

My experience in groups was to do with practical application based loosely on the five categories of leadership function as suggested by Gibb and Gibb (1955: 22–3). Here leaders are concerned with group task and maintenance functions of

initiating   group actions, steps, procedures;
regulating   summarising, pointing out time limits, restating goals;
informing   bringing information or opinion to the group;
supporting   emotional climate that holds groups together, voicing group
                      feelings, encouraging;
evaluating   helping groups to evaluate decisions, goals, procedures,
                      testing for consensus.

I especially took to heart the advice of Corey and Corey (1997: 7):

> If you operate in a theoretical vacuum or cannot draw on theory to support
> your interventions, your group will not reach a productive stage. It is like
> flying a plane without a flight plan.

I believed strongly that the role of the group leader was important. My perceptions of the leader's work, however, changed in interesting ways during the
course of my study. I always believed that the leader should facilitate a group;
significant learning happened when I discovered the extent to which a leader can
influence a group. This growth in my own perception that I was influencing, and
not only facilitating, had a profound impact on my actions as a group leader.

My initial thinking

When I began my study, therefore, I believed that I was a group facilitator, not a
leader. Because the groups were participatory, my role was the task and maintenance role identified by Gibb and Gibb (see above). I also believed that by
designing the job search skills programme with the needs of unemployed people
uppermost, in that we were examining the reasons for their taking up employment, I was being responsive to their needs. I believed that people working in
groups were more receptive to new ideas if they had peer support. To achieve
this I felt that group leader style should be participatory rather than adopt a
lecture mode, so I set out to make the groups participative.

I spent some time studying the literature of group dynamics, the skills of group
leaders, and the role of the group leader. As the study progressed I became
increasingly aware of my values of social justice, as they applied to the rights of
all parties to express their opinions. Studying the literature gave me the ability to
imagine strategies whereby I might realise these values.

My research methodology required me to monitor my practice. I was studying my
work as a group leader, so I monitored my actions, and reflected on them systematically. My data-gathering methods were a personal reflective journal, in which I
recorded actions on a regular basis, and wrote comments on the learning arising
from reflection on those actions; and I also conducted informal conversations with
participants, which I tape recorded and transcribed, always ensuring that participants edited the transcript to their satisfaction before I undertook any kind of analysis. Initially I analysed the transcripts in terms of my own categories of analysis.

As the research progressed, I slowly became aware that perhaps I was not living my values of social justice in my practice. For example, I said at the beginning that I had designed the job skills programme to meet the needs of the unemployed person. Now I began to question whether I could be sure that the need really was being met. I came to the ironic conclusion that perhaps I was interpreting what course participants' needs were, rather than inviting them to speak for themselves. In this way my practice could have been oppressive rather than emancipatory. Similarly, when I analysed the transcripts I began to see that I was imposing my own interpretations, and not inviting the participants to make informed judgements about their own contributions.

This process of enlightenment took several months, and was aided by the critical response of research group colleagues to my accounts of my research during our study sessions. They pointed out to me that if I was to be in a position of influence as a leader, I needed to live out my values so that people saw that I was authentic. I began to wonder how I might make my practice more democratic and so live out my ideals of the 'education of equals' model.

I came to the decision that the only way I could be sure that I was living out these values was to include participants in the whole process, and invite their ongoing evaluation of my research. This would involve full disclosure on my part of what I was trying to achieve. It would also involve asking them for their support. This appeared quite risky, but because I tend to be open and welcoming to new ideas I was quite happy to go ahead with the plan.

My actions

I identified one group of ten people as my research participants and invited them to work with me. They were happy to agree to do so. The job search skills programme was quite short, only thirteen sessions of two hours' duration each, so we decided to work intensively.

I wanted to investigate how I was influencing the group, particularly in terms of whether they were developing independence of mind and confidence to make their own decisions about future plans. To encourage them, I deliberately ensured that my own practice was inclusive. I listened carefully to what people said, I responded in an encouraging manner. I encouraged all members of the group to do the same. I set up group exercises to ensure that people knew one another and felt at ease. If conflict arose, I dealt with it openly, rather than ignore it which I would have done previously. I invited people to challenge me, and when they did so, responded truthfully without any attempt to avoid the issue. In general, I became more open about my work, and found that my own self-confidence built in the process.

I continued to monitor my work, but now I invited critical evaluation from participants about what I was doing, and the progress I was making in relation to themselves. This was not easy. The way I evaluated progress was in terms of whether they felt they had developed increased autonomy and capacity to become independent of me. I made the transcripts of conversations available, and asked participants to give me feedback on what they thought had happened. I wrote up accounts of our interactions, and invited commentary by participants on my reports. Participants produced their own reports in return, and this I took to be evidence that they had improved their capacity for taking responsibility for their own learning, and to reflect critically on their work.

Reflections on the process

This was a period of great learning for us all. Many things were learnt. I learned that I was in a position of leadership, and how to use my influence for social benefit. I also learned about my own ability to work with groups in a supportive way in order to encourage their independence of mind and action, and take responsibility for their own lives. I believe participants learned about working together, and also about their own capacity for learning. I think we lived out the 'education of equals' model, in that we shifted from an originally split group in which a clear power relationship was evident, where I was leader and they were followers, to a model in which I began to follow their lead and we regarded one another as participants intent on achieving a particular goal. We came to understand how we shared our power to achieve these goals.

At the end of the course, while not everyone had found a job, at least they knew what they had to do to find a job, and had the confidence to do so. I believe that they left the course better able to take responsibility for finding work than when they arrived.

My learning

From my study I have learnt that as a group leader I am in a position of some influence, but in order to use that influence for the benefit of the people I am working with, I need to understand first how I am with the group, and encourage them to understand their interrelationships with one another. The responsibility for setting up interactions to enable them to do so is mine as group leader. I lead them in the sense of encouraging them to find out how they can help themselves and one another. I do not direct. All I can do is set up conditions for their learning, and encourage them to learn. If they do not wish to partake, that is their choice and I respect it; but I also understand people's vulnerability, encourage them in a variety of ways, and provide appropriate supports along the way.

I have learnt much about myself, and the way I work. I understand my values base better, and I consciously try to live out my values. I guard against attempts to speak on behalf of other people. I consider people able to speak for themselves, and I encourage them to do so.

I continue to monitor my practice, even though I am no longer part of a formal course of study. When you undertake an action research approach the process is never-ending, and there are always new areas to be explored in the development of practice.

7 Critical theoretic research

Background

At the same time as interpretive approaches were challenging positivism, another view was developing that challenged both positivism and interpretivism. Both methodologies, suggested an emerging group of critical theorists who came to be known as the Frankfurt School (Horkheimer, Adorno and Marcuse, and later Habermas), were inappropriate for social scientific study, in that they ignored the power-constituted basis of human relationships and the hegemonising influences of some over others. While interpretive approaches might like to think that they were encouraging the emergence of people's voices in the interests of emancipatory social practices, those voices were always and inevitably conditioned by their own historical and cultural legacy. People could not be free until they realised that they were unfree.

A new approach was needed that enabled people to recognise their own situatedness within politically constructed social situations, see what was happening to them and how that situation had arisen, and challenge the historical and political bases of those influences. If workers were subjugated, why was this so? If some people were assumed to have control over others, why were the assumptions left unchallenged, and what did subjugated groups do to change both their current situations and also the thinking and cultural traditions that allowed the thinking to continue? This view constituted an ideology critique, a process in which people become aware of how they have been conditioned through cultural and historical forces to adopt ways of thinking which will lead to the perpetuation of false perceptions of themselves.

Initially these views were informed directly by those of Marx:

> We do not anticipate the world dogmatically, but rather wish to find the new world through criticism of the old; ... even though the construction of the future and its completion for all time is not our task, what we have to accomplish at this time is all the more clear: relentless criticism of all existing conditions, relentless in the sense that the criticism is not afraid of its findings and just as little afraid of conflict with the powers that be.
>
> (Marx, 1967, cited in Carr and Kemmis, 1986: 137–8)

Probably the most influential member of the Frankfurt School was Jürgen Habermas, who systematised these ideas into a theory of critical social science. This refers to the critiquing of the historical, cultural and political processes that persuade people to think and act in ways which are not necessarily of their choosing. A critical theory is an outcome of this process. The contributions of Habermas are probably unparalleled in critical social science, particularly in the relationship between theory and practice (Habermas, 1974). He challenged the positivist view that abstract theory drives practice as a linear process, and insisted that theory and practice had to be integrated so that the theory could be part of practitioners' lives: the theory was embodied in, and enacted through, the practice. This would then move from the idea of rationality as technique, and instead nurture a view of reasoned action as praxis, guided by Aristotle's idea of *phronesis*, an idea of the right way of living. To promote the development of praxis there had to be an 'organisation of enlightenment', where some people help others to understand what they are experiencing – an essentially teaching-learning process in which guidance was offered by an 'organiser' (manager) in an educative way:

> The vindicating superiority of those who do the enlightening over those who are to be enlightened is theoretically unavoidable, but at the same time it is fictive and requires self-correction: in a process of enlightenment there can only be participants.
>
>   (Habermas, 1970: 372, cited in Carr and Kemmis, 1986: 149)

The whole thrust of this approach is towards emancipation and democratic practice, and constitutes Habermas's theory of an emancipatory social science. However, the theory still stayed at the level of theory; Habermas identified the need for, but never engaged with, a theory of social action, for which of course he has been criticised, but which does not diminish the power and organising potential of his ideas.

1 What is the nature of critical research knowledge?

Critical thinking is not necessarily critical theory, but critical thinking is at the heart of critical theory. Critical theory is the formal term given to a system of thinking that begins by understanding that nothing in human relations is given. Everything people do and say is conditioned by other influences, both from the external social world and also from the inner mental world. Personal-social situations are not given; they are created by people in situations.

A positivist view of knowledge is inadequate to recognise the socially and culturally constructed nature of knowledge. Critical theorists hold that knowledge is never a fixed absolute entity, existing in a transcendental sense separate from people. Any investigation into the nature and acquisition of knowledge must always regard knowledge as what is produced in and through the social relations of practice. Knowledge is created through discourses, the way that people speak and act.

Foucault (1980) and others maintain that what we say and do influences who we and others become. Knowledge resides in language: language is the main way in which people make sense of the world, and knowledge not only is acquired through language but also comes to reside in language. Language is a major symbolic way of creating meaning. People express what they believe through language: they use language to show how they create meaning through the way they live their lives. Meaning is not only in words: most importantly, it is in the things we do.

Two examples illustrate this. The first is drawn from the work of Edward Said (1994a), who shows how colonising attitudes permeate the literatures of imperialism. Books represent the cultural attitudes of their times, and these attitudes themselves constitute a 'grand narrative', which usually goes unquestioned and unheard, similar to Crites's idea of sacred stories (see p. 167). Said comments on the lack of critical awareness even among those who ought to be focally aware of such issues: 'One of the difficult truths I discovered [in working on *Culture and Imperialism*] is how very few of the British or French artists whom I admire took issue with the notion of "subject" or "inferior" races so prevalent among officials who practised these ideas as a matter of course in ruling India or Algeria' (1994a; xiv). Similar critical blindness is a feature of many people in institutional life who find their identity in their institutional role. Categorising oneself as a senior manager or 'just a worker' can often afford a place of safety and personal ontological security, in which one does not need to give justification for action; behaviours and attitudes are normalised and become part of workplace routines. Grand narratives, whichever category they spring from, clearly have the power to suppress others; workers oppress managers as easily as managers oppress workers: 'The power to narrate, or to block other narratives from emerging, is very important to culture and imperialism, and constitutes one of the main connections between them' (Said, 1994a: xiii). What are the grand narratives of an organisation; and are there other grand narratives of emancipation and liberation that confront established knowledges? How are the conflicts managed? How do some narratives become accepted, and what are the forces of control that decide which narratives are spoken and which are silenced?

A second delightful example of how knowledge resides in language is in the story of *The Paper Bag Princess* (used in a research project reported in Munsch, 1980: cited in Harré and van Langenhove, 1999: 50–1), in which a princess called Elizabeth and a prince called Ronald are planning to get married. Unfortunately a fiery dragon appears, burns Elizabeth's castle, leaving her dirty and dishevelled, and carries Ronald off by the seat of his pants, but still holding on to his tennis racquet. Elizabeth is very angry, finds a paper bag to wear, follows the dragon and sets about rescuing Ronald. He however does not want to be rescued by a princess who is sooty and has nothing but an old paper bag to wear, and he tells Elizabeth to go and tidy herself up and come back when she looks like a real princess. 'Elizabeth is quite taken aback by this turn of events, and she says "Ronald, your clothes are really pretty and your hair is very neat. You look like a real prince, but you are a bum." The last page shows her skipping off into the sunset alone and the story ends with the words: "They didn't get married after all".'

There is cause for reflection, however, from the responses from children who read the story as part of the research: many children perceived Elizabeth as a bad princess, because the dragon had set about her; some boys were fascinated by her nakedness; other boys perceived Ronald as a hero because he held onto his tennis racquet in spite of great odds. Hegemonising discourses that communicate cultural norms block critical thinking which is informed by understanding that, even though things appear to be institutionalised by divine consent, it ain't necessarily so.

Critical theory and postmodernism

While these two ideas are not the same, there are strong affinities. Critical theory challenges the idea of givens and stereotypes, on the assumption that whatever exists in the social world is an outcome of systems which are always created by people, often for purposes of domination and control. The ideas of gender and race for example are often used to perpetuate work and economic practices that marginalise women and some ethnic groups and justify paying them low wages (see for example, Mitchell and Reid-Walsh, 1997).

Postmodernism challenges the view that there are fixed structures and categories in the first place. Nothing can be categorised. Nothing is definable because nothing can be taken at face value. A book may be construed variously as a collection of ideas, the derivative of a tree, a source of inspiration. There is no fixed 'meaning', nor does a book have 'meaning' except in relation to its user. The idea of 'meaning' itself is redundant. Definitions are not helpful because the act of definition has a potentially distorting influence. As soon as we try to pin something down it is somewhere else. Gender and race are socially constructed categories. There are biological sexes and skin colours, but the ideas of gender and race are categories of analysis which have been created in order to identify and therefore control people. Billington *et al.* (1998) make the point that social categorisation leads to control. Postmodernism challenges the view that anything may be categorised: by definition (though definitions are out) the idea of 'postmodernism' should not exist since it is a fixed category.

While critical theory and postmodernism are not the same, their affinities place them in the same political plane of challenging prejudice, unearthing hidden systems of control, giving voice to the silent oppressed, and deliberately making the familiar strange.

2 How is critical research knowledge acquired?

Stephen Brookfield (1987), and other adult education researchers show how contexts of adult education provide opportunities for people to question received wisdoms and imagine alternative future scenarios; and how reflective practice contributes to the development of rational societies. Critical theory embodies a critique of inequitable social relationships, and of uncovering the underlying prejudices that sustain them. In that sense, critical theory is an organising principle for the deconstruction and reconstruction of social norms and organisational practices. Critical thinking, if not critical theory, needs to feature everywhere, to enable people to decide whether their lives are worth living, and what might need to improve.

Critical thinking involves self-reflection. The term 'reflective practice' was popularised initially by Donald Schön (1983), and serious scholarship exists to try to explain the process of self-reflection (for example, Ghaye and Ghaye, 1998; Lomax, 1996; the journal *Reflective Practice*). The phrase unfortunately has also entered the literature in an unproblematic sense, and is often used simplistically to denote 'thinking about things', a not very helpful conceptualisation. Self-reflection is complex and involves understanding one's own process of coming to know, an appreciation of what happens when tacit knowledge becomes explicit, and the transformation that takes place in the individual during the process. Self-reflection does not come easily. It is a developmental process and, like meditation and other personal-social practices, improves with practice.

Thinking critically constitutes a rigorous methodology, in which practitioners confront a particular phenomenon, and deliberately become aware of, and carefully examine, their own response to it. I remember my first visit to India, my first encounter with lizards on the ceiling and ants across the walls. Within a day of being on campus I found myself longing to move to a European hotel, and was prevented from doing so only by an awareness that moving out would have been the grossest discourtesy to my Indian hosts, people of remarkable kindness who had denied themselves in order that I should enjoy good conditions. Through not moving (though I didn't rationalise it at the time), I became aware of my own prejudices, my own expectations that life everywhere was what I had until then experienced – instant running water and lizard-free rooms. That episode was a real turning point in my own awareness of my learning: my complacency had to be dislodged to make way for more open awarenesses. Now I try never to take anything for granted. I try to live with an attitude of gratitude that I do live in a society that has water on tap, and I work towards supporting those who don't.

Thinking critically is about learning: we learn how to see through new eyes, and this is a conscious process deliberately undertaken. Polanyi says it well: 'My eyes have become different; I have made myself into a person seeing and thinking differently' (1958: 43).

It is much more comfortable to stay in the comfort zone of not asking questions, either of self or others; but inertia and reluctance to engage never made a difference for good.

Critical approaches to organisation theory

The literature grows on critical approaches to organisation theory and practice, most, but not all, of which focuses on showing the socially constructed nature of relationships and the hegemonising influences that maintain asymmetrical power relations. A main goal 'has been to create societies and workplaces which are free from domination, where all members have an equal opportunity to contribute to the production of systems which meet human needs and lead to the progressive development of all' (Alvesson and Deetz, 1999: 192). To achieve this goal, much of the literature concentrates on exposing processes and attitudes which systematically marginalise and dominate some groups: see for example, the work of Marshall (1984) on the deliberate exclusion of women in management; or Casey's (1996) work on how the 'manifest' curriculum of work is accompanied by a hidden curriculum that socialises workers; similar to Lynch's work (1993) in mainstream education on the hidden curriculum that aims at the socialisation and intellectual domination of young people at school. The values base of Dewey's views (Chapter 2) on education appear in direct contrast to those which regard schooling and workplace learning as leading to the production of a more skilled and competitive workforce in the interests of market domination (see Halsey *et al.*, 1997). This is also illustrated in the work of Winter (1999), who shows how higher education has been reinvented as an industry, how higher education, and knowledge itself, have been commodified to ignore the values base of meeting human needs and instead concentrate on commanding a profit. Critical theory in organisation research aims to expose the processes of gentling the masses that lead to the objectivisation of knowledge and work, and their co-option as weapons of oppression. It shows how the socially oriented values base of organisations is systematically trivialised, and replaced by a focus on knowledge as information, work as technique, and the existence of organisations as effective means of securing profitable ends through social engineering.

The ideas of challenging the authoritarian use of power and making visible the hidden forces of persuasion have a long and respected history. Socrates died for these ideas; Jesus was a powerful revolutionary who 'caused an authority crisis' (Steindl-Rast, in Capra *et al.*, 1992: 184) by articulating the methodological and epistemological basis of a new care-inspired paradigm which was in direct conflict with dominant philosophies of coercive power. Socrates and Jesus, and countless others who have challenged autocratic practices, were silenced by the interest groups whose orthodoxies they challenged. The twentieth century with its massive cultural and political upheavals has provided clear contexts for revolutionary ideas to become systematised and codified in a public language of resistance, a language which also offers alternative visions of how the world might be.

A public language of resistance and change within social scientific contexts began quite recently in the 1970s and 1980s. Work by, for example, Burrell and Morgan (1979), Frost (1980), Deetz and Kersten (1983) and Willmott (1987) in organisation studies, and by Carr and Kemmis (1986) and Reason and Rowan (1981) in educational research, provided seminal texts that raised questions about taken-for-granted normative scenarios which embedded epistemological and methodological issues in an unproblematic way. They aimed to expose the cultural and historical processes that endorsed the development of normalising processes and the anaesthetisation of critical reflection. A strong ideology critique exists today that initially drew on the ideas of Marx and focused on processes of domination by owners and later managers in the subjugation of the workforce (Braverman, 1974; Clegg and Dunkerley, 1977), and has since shifted its focus to examine why these forces of oppression continued as seemingly unchallengeable (Burawoy, 1979; Alvesson and Willmott, 1996). Similar shifts are evident on a range of fronts; for example, cultural studies (Giroux and McLaren, 1989); feminist and gender studies (Raphael Reed, 1998, 1999); liberation and feminist theology (Boff, 1985; Schüssler Fiorenza, 1983). The shift is embedded within the wider shift in the focus of scientific enquiry: from descriptive to explanatory adequacy, from the production of descriptions of social phenomena and processes to an explanation for their institutionalisation and resistance to change.

Organisation studies provides a particularly fertile ground to investigate this turn in human enquiry. Issues such as the increasingly transitory and fragmented nature of work, trends towards the globalisation of market economies, reductions in the workforce, the dissolution of social cohesion, all emphasise the need for research that explores reasons and intentions with regard to deep-level human values and goals. As yet this is not major in organisation research, but questions are being raised. Garrick for example comments (1998: 79): 'Contemporary work-based learning strategies rarely deal in self-criticism, paradox, irony or doubt, yet it is precisely these qualities that give substance to learning ... more research and theoretical development is needed on the dialectical interaction between oneself and social formations.' In my view, unless theory and practice are integrated in clearly recognisable ways to show how theory arises from and is embedded within practice, the gulf will widen between those who think and those who do. Critical theory can realise its emancipatory potential by providing the intellectual means to work towards the development of practical methodologies that are rooted in real-world practices. There is urgent need for the production of research accounts such as the case studies in this book, that break with the reification of conceptual analysis, and produce real-world stories of how critical practice led to improved social situations.

Critical approaches to management

Traditional approaches regard management as a technical activity and ignore the social relationships in which it is embedded and from which it draws its meaning. Theory is separate from practice; management is a discrete discipline occupying a separate space in the organisational lifeworld. On this view, management is represented as a 'neutral technology of goal achievement that carries with it no implicit moral commitments and consequences' (Alvesson and Willmott, 1996: 17).

Management however always exists in terms of the wider organisation and its purposes and is always a social practice. Management is work, and managers are human beings. Managers are not 'them', although they are often represented as such (for example, Noon and Blyton, 1997); and indeed this functionalist view can lead to feelings of alienation on the part of managers. Management has to be linked with organisational development and the personal development of its members (Covey, 1990; Covey *et al.*, 1994; Mintzberg, 1973).

Depending on which literature you read, therefore, managers can be angels or devils. Theories in the literature however do not necessarily represent the way that managers perceive themselves. Managers are part of workforces, and subject to exactly the same pressures as those whom they manage. The very idea of managers as 'managing people' is a constructed discourse: even when managing people is presented as a humanistic enterprise (as per Peters and Waterman, 1982, for example), the discourse is still embedded within an ideology of corporate culture in which management is a function which aims to encourage the internalisation of a particular set of values. Critical theorists raise questions about how management is theorised, not only in terms of what good management practice should look like, but also in terms of how managers think about their work and produce their own theories of management. The responsibility of management and business schools, on this view, is to help managers raise their own awareness of how grand narratives persuade them to distort their own understanding of practice into a particular conceptual framework and adopt practices that are contradictory to their own values. When I was first appointed as deputy headteacher in a secondary school, there was an expectation from some colleagues that I would follow the example of my predecessor in punishing pupils severely; and today in my practice as teacher educator there is an expectation by some higher education colleagues that I adopt an authoritarian stance towards my 'students'. I consistently resist such pressures. It is important to follow one's own values of respect for educative relationships: while people have different sets of responsibilities in work processes, all participants are entitled to the same degree of respect. I think it is important to try to live out one's values and resist subtle and sometimes not so subtle attempts by others to control one's thinking. Sometimes it can feel very lonely and threatening; but in my view educative management involves a lot of faith in your own personal commitment to the power of speaking your truth quietly and not being false to your own sense of right living.

3 How is critical research knowledge put to use?

This book has been the hardest writing project I have ever undertaken. It has demanded quantities of reading, and writing and rewriting. It has called into question my confidence and sense of rightness in what I am doing. I am not sure what reactions will come; but the text now seems right for me in its content and form, and I have learnt to have faith in my own and others' tacit understanding of writing that tries to be authentic and unselfconscious.

The dilemmas of writing have been mainly to do with what form the book should take. Early drafts were written in a propositional form. I aimed to present factual information about issues. This was not what I wanted to do, but it seemed to be the acceptable form for books on organisation theory. When my friend and best critic Jack Whitehead read the drafts he commented, 'Yes, a book full of interesting ideas, but nothing unusual in terms of moving us on.' I was disappointed; we all like to think we have something useful to say. 'I had thought ages ago of telling my own story,' I said, 'and showing how the ideas came out of the experiences.' 'Why don't you then?' said Jack.

The present form of the book arose out of that conversation. 'Why don't you then?' acted as my spur to critical thinking and action. Why wasn't I writing the book as I wanted? Why was I sticking to conventional forms? 'If you stay with conceptual forms you will have allowed yourself to be colonised by traditional forms of scholarship,' Jack had said. So why was I colluding in my own colonisation? I think my answers would be around issues of confidence, and the anxiety not only of writing about critical ideas but also of writing in a form that seemed to challenge established norms.

To remind you, my background is in school-based teaching and teacher education. I know the educational research literature reasonably well. I have moved into formal management practice only in the last few years and am still finding my way through the literature. Although I have already read quite widely, I still lack confidence in my own knowledge base. I am reluctant to challenge theories in the literature because this would seem presumptuous for a newcomer; yet for me there is no other way if I am to remain true to my values of truth and honesty. I tell it as I find it.

Critical theory is highly visible in the literatures of education and organisation theory. The rhetoric is awesome. There seems to be an assumption however that if writers can inspire others to see the value of the theory and its implications for practice, the practice will somehow look after itself. This is not how things work. To make things happen, we have to live up to our own theory, and challenge and change that which we perceive as contradictory to our values of social justice.

My dilemmas have arisen from a variety of contexts: (1) substantive issues to do with how (a) management, (b) management learning and (c) management teaching are theorised; and (2) methodological and ethical issues to do with the failure of critical theorists to live up to their own rhetoric.

1 Substantive issues

(a) How is management theorised?

The nature of theories of management are changing. Technicist approaches are being challenged and replaced by humanitarian and socially aware approaches. Critique has been a significant factor in generating new rhetorics about democratic and enlightened management. The rhetoric however does not always get turned into practice. Keep and Mayhew (1999), for example, examine the assumptions that underlie current training policy in the UK. They say (p. 127):

> The creation of TECs, Industry Lead Bodies, NCVQ, and the National Training Task Force all reflect beliefs that managers, particularly private sector managers, have access to a set of techniques, knowledge and skills that are not available to other sections of the population, and that possession of these attributes makes them uniquely qualified to 'solve' a series of deep-seated structural problems in the country's education and training system.

Statements like this lead one to wonder just how much slippage there is between theory and practice, between the rhetoric in the literature and the implementation of official policy positions.

(b) How is management learning theorised?

Traditional approaches rely on the conceptual base of management theory. Managers learn abstract theories and apply them to practice, mainly with the intent of controlling human and material resources. This approach has been challenged by critical theorists of management (Willmott, 1997) and by advocates of action learning and action science (Revans, 1982; McLaughlin and Thorpe, 1993; Pedler, 1996). These theorists address issues of the need to learn from experience and to develop the capacity to deal with immediate problems of practice. This approach foregrounds the social and educational responsibilities of managers. Both approaches however still operate from within a conceptual form. Note for example this sentence from Willmott (1997: 171):

> When applied to management education, critical action learning combines the pedagogic philosophy of action learning with critical traditions in an effort to better understand and transform contradictory forces that play upon organizational work.

There is still apparently an assumption that critique is applied to a context, rather than demonstrated within a context. I admire the work of critical theorists, but I would also like to know how they have critiqued and challenged practices in their own workplaces, and their own practice, and the consequences for their own learning.

(c) How is management teaching theorised?

Not much comment appears about the processes of teaching in management education. What exists is drawn mainly from the literature of adult education contexts, and is often quite traditional in orientation (for example, Knowles, 1984; Jarvis, 1987). New work on radical pedagogy is appearing, drawing on the ideas of Paulo Freire (for example, McLaren, 1997) and which encourages participants to develop confidence in their own capacity to question. Few writers actually do this however; Stephen Brookfield (1987) is an exception. Mezirow in particular has raised awareness of self-reflection and a critical response to normative discourse (1991; Mezirow *et al.*, 1990).

My concern throughout is that many writers consider it sufficient to engage in the language of critique without demonstrating their commitments in their practice. Even those who articulate the same concerns as I do here still do not show their own process of critique from within their own experience (for example, Lynch, 1999). We are still dealing with ideological fantasies (Chapter 2), which assume that once an idea enters the head it automatically transfers to practice, an erroneous idea which has led to wars. It is one thing to talk about the need for critique; showing the process is something else.

2 *Methodological and ethical issues*

I have become aware, since my conversation with Jack, of how I have been intimidated by traditional forms of scholarship, and so felt constrained to stay within them. I have become aware from experience how forms of scholarship are themselves politically constructed. Alvesson and Willmott (1996: 34) explain the need for critical awareness in management research: 'Both established and "progressive" ways of making sense of management exclude sustained consideration of how, historically, subjectivities and functions of management are defined, refined and pursued through processes of moral and political struggle.' I am now aware how these same words apply to the process of generating theory: theories are also ways of making sense that are defined, refined and pursued through processes of moral and political struggle. Commentaries on critical theory may be challenged in some cases for demonstrating a certainty without producing concrete evidence for its existence, an attitude that is at odds with the basic principles of critical theory.

From these insights, as well as from my experience of working with people in higher education contexts, I have refined my own understanding of the political processes involved in developing an appropriate form of theory, how systems of knowledge are held in place and why. I have discovered that organisation theory in its dominant form is actually far removed from studying organisation and is more to do with maintaining the status of theorists.

The task of a critical social science is to critique. That is self-evident. The task of critical social theorists is to discover the truth about the world (as Chomsky (1966) says is the task of intellectuals – see Introduction) and make it publicly available. The current situation in the critical theory movement seems to be that critical theorists challenge other people; they do not challenge themselves. This applies to movements other than critical theory. Most intellectuals do the same. This is hardly surprising, for it is normal for privileged minorities in institutional and business life to speak with authority from within their own protected contexts about what ought to be done, but they seldom take the lead and do it themselves.

The favourite place for many intellectuals is in the mental and emotional territory that they have colonised. This territory is located on Schön's high ground. They produce abstract theories about how the rest of the world should operate. The system of knowledge they promote is held together and disseminated via a sophisticated propaganda system that permeates the culture; indeed, a system of knowledge creates and controls a culture. The system of knowledge is held together by appeal to the status and prestige of its creators. It is popularly believed that academics work consistently to promote the truth, that their major concerns are educational, and that their project is towards social betterment. Because they enjoy significant prestige as a social grouping their work is held in high regard and their words believed. What they say comes to be held as a compelling story, and the citizenry is willing to believe it unquestioningly. From my experience, it is not the case that all academics work for social betterment and hold educational values. While some do, others seem to be more concerned with careerism, personal kudos and financial security.

The way in which elites protect themselves is by communicating messages that what they say is the truth. If people question these messages they are quickly brought into line, or controlled so that their voices are made inaudible or factored out altogether. It can be dangerous to challenge sacred stories.

The system of knowledge in which most intellectuals' identity is vested is technical rationality. Identities in university and corporation circles means jobs and their accompanying benefits of wealth and prestige, so no one is going to let go in a hurry of a system that serves them well. The purpose of organisation theory, on this view, is to maintain the privileged position of a privileged minority; indeed, this could be seen as the purpose of theory generation across a range of disciplines. While it appears that theorists are producing theories about particular subject matters, they are in fact producing theory, words on paper, that does little in a practical sense except support their own status as generators of theory. Regardless of content, the form of theory remains the same – conceptual, abstract, reified, oppressive. The form of theory is deliberately maintained and safeguarded – a conscious policy which is implemented ruthlessly.

I have no doubt that hands will rise in the air at this. Many sincere intellectuals believe they are doing a worthwhile job by producing abstract theory which, while very interesting, does little to give insights into how to improve practices or save lives. Perhaps a litmus test for the use value of any particular theory is to invite the creator to live it out and see if it works.

4 What are the implications for organisation theory as a critical social science?

Of course we need critique. Said explains (1991) that once criticism goes, solidified prejudice and atrophy set in. 'I take criticism so seriously as to believe that, even in the very midst of a battle in which one is unmistakably on one side against another, there should be criticism, because there must be critical consciousness if there are to be issues, problems, values, even lives to be fought for' (p. 28). Criticism is essential to the evolution of good orders: 'criticism must think of itself as life-enhancing and constitutively opposed to every form of tyranny, domination, and abuse; its social goals are noncoercive knowledge produced in the interest of human freedom' (p. 29).

Any new theory of organisation knowledge should have this characteristic: noncoercive knowledge produced in the interest of human freedom. I wonder to what extent current forms of critical theory do this. While the rhetoric espouses the value, the practice often belies it. Critical theory cannot remain as an abstract discipline; to fulfil its own agenda it needs to show in what way it is noncoercive and to what extent it promotes human freedom. The production of abstract theory is both coercive, in the sense that it contributes to and reinforces the already dominant epistemology of technical rationality; and oppressive of human freedom in that it prohibits experimentation with new forms of expressing the critique. If you find yourself bristling while reading any of this, the dominant epistemology is doing its job well – maintaining its own privileged status as a legitimate form of knowing that blocks other stories from being told in their own way.

If critical approaches to organisation theory are to fulfil their potential of improving understanding and practice in organisations, first theorists need to engage seriously with these issues. Are they living their values in their practice? Are they showing the reality of critique for real lives? Or are they producing picture theories in which they describe the processes and then leave it to others to imagine how the theory might become practice?

Organisations as sites of freedom

For organisations to help people to understand and develop their capacities for responsible living, there must first be an institutional commitment to personal autonomy and intellectual freedom. This can happen only within a system in which constraints and threats are lifted and people encouraged to challenge not only the ideas and opinions of others but also their own. This is surely very difficult. It is important for institutions to provide supports as they encourage critical thinking. Critical theory encourages people not to accept the status quo but to challenge self-serving practices and oppressive regimes. People who choose to challenge however run the risk of encountering a hostile backlash (Brookfield, 1987). While encouraging the development of critical thinking, educators and managers also need to help people to build up their own personal, intellectual and social resources to withstand unjustified retaliatory critique.

My first work in Northern Ireland was a teacher education project in the curriculum area Education for Mutual Understanding. I found that teachers tended to see education for mutual understanding as something which they taught children, not something which they needed to do themselves (McNiff and Neill, 1998). In more recent work in community relations the same mindset is evident. Community relations is assumed to be something that happens in external social contexts, not something in which we are already engaged in classrooms and workplaces. Critique that is life-enhancing and promotes human freedom can happen only from within a situation. We need first to investigate and expose our own prejudices and see them for what they are before we require others to do the same.

Do I do this in my work? Do I live out my own theory? Am I guilty of doublespeak?

> I have learnt to think for myself.

> You never present your knowledge as better than mine. I create my own knowledge.

> I used to feel anxious about challenging you. I don't now.

> The thing I really like is you don't use your title.

I try consistently to encourage people I teach not to take everything I say at face value. I have borrowed an idea of Stephen Brookfield's (1987) and invite course participants to critique my own work and ideas. This is very hard for some but I think essential. I am aware that my own commitment to personal freedom itself constitutes an ideology, and I could be taken to task for not recognising that my own ideas about freedom stem from that ideology. I do, and I try to guard against my own prejudices.

This for me is the strength of critical approaches: they teach us that questions are more important than answers, and questions raised about our own understandings are more important than questions raised about others'. The generative power of critique is to critique itself – provided it makes the courageous leap from abstraction and plays out the theory in real life. That, as they say, is the question.

Eileen Ross learned to critique. She did this by herself, and her academic study then gave her a theoretical framework in which to locate her critique and understand its process. Eileen's story shows in a narrative way the ideas of critical reflection which I have presented in a conceptual way. By showing how ideas are lived out in reality, as Eileen does, and Paul Murphy and Breda Long previously, these colleagues are showing the development of a new form of theory which shows how conceptual ideas may be embodied and take on real-world meaning in real lives. They are also showing the creation of new epistemologies of practice which have significant value for helping us develop insights into how to improve our understanding and take action towards personal and social improvement.

Courage to risk, courage to be free

Eileen Ross

Many people, I suspect, are trapped in lives not of their own making or choosing. Some do not appreciate that they are trapped. Of those who do, many choose to do nothing about it. Traps are thought to be threatening; they can in fact be comfortable places. Although we might rail against where we are, where we are is familiar, and familiarity, perhaps, is the greatest entrapment of them all.

I entered religious life at the age of seventeen. I did so because of my own idealistic expectations about what the life would hold – I would obey my calling to be a Bride of Christ and live a life of bringing my special gifts to others to enrich their lives. I was supported in my chosen vocation by my parents, deeply religious people who were proud of their daughter's wish to dedicate her life to religious service.

While I entirely embraced the values of my religious calling, institutional life and I rapidly came into conflict. There were expectations about how members of religious communities should be, the kinds of behaviours they should adopt. My lively sense of fun was frowned upon; my habit of questioning attitudes and practices got me into deep trouble with my superiors. Had I had any lesser sense of self, or commitment to issues of justice, I would have given in to the coercion that I should come into line with stereotypical norms, not question, blindly obey, and live my life in the spirit of quietude and peace that submissive acceptance brings. While I was prepared to put up with it all through love of Jesus, that love did not stop me being critical of the circumstances of my life or the systems of knowledge that kept them in place.

Perhaps the main source of irritation (which eventually became outrage and anger) was the hierarchical nature of the institutional structures of religious life. These were similar to the patriarchal and hierarchical practices of the institutional Church. To my way of thinking, a theory was emerging relating to the letting go of these defunct and irrelevant structures. However, there appeared to be a strong resistance to putting the theory into practice, and a deliberate ignoring of the lacuna. Voicing such opinions, however, brought me into conflict with those whose dominance and security I was challenging, and I experienced severe retaliation in the form of personal marginalisation and institutional control. I felt diminished and worthless.

Towards enlightenment

In conversation once with Jean I used the word 'conversion'. We were both struck by the irony of the word. In everyday currency it tends to be used when speaking about how people are converted to a religious worldview. In my case, it was a conversion against institutionalised religious life, towards the freedom to think for myself and be the kind of person I wanted to be, to live out my values of love and justice, honesty and autonomous living. The journey towards living out those values was painful and slow.

It is difficult to identify an exact time as the beginning of my enlightenment. I can however name several key episodes that helped me to become critical. One was my entrance to the world of teaching. I loved teaching, and quickly came to develop caring relationships with my students. These relationships were very important, somehow making up for the lack of closeness with the other sisters. I always had deep respect and admiration for those women, strong, caring women who obeyed and lived their lives of sacrifice. I came to understand how much of a sacrifice it was. In taking my vows of poverty, chastity and obedience, I failed to understand how those vows would be interpreted by the wider patriarchal order. Poverty I could deal with. Chastity was interpreted narrowly in the sense that one should not have a caring relationship with anyone, let alone a real man; consequently the warmth and support I hoped for in community life was lacking. Obedience implied blind acceptance of what one was told. This was entirely against my natural curiosity and questioning spirit, and also against my value of care for the other which manifested in respectful dialogue and an attitude of listening. Dialogue was not a feature of religious life. I later came to see how fear lies at the heart of the institutional structures of the Church; once you open the gates to hearing what others have to say, you are in danger of losing control of the entire system. My teaching was an opportunity to invite young people to think for themselves, and in doing so, I began to strengthen my own conviction that it was right for people to think for themselves, including me.

Other episodes in my conversion were a stay in America where I studied the ideas of liberation theology, and later, courses with the Tavistock Institute which helped me to understand more about the systems I was in. Increasingly I came to see that the preservation of the system is the highest priority, and that traditional hierarchical mindsets simply cannot entertain the idea of change. This understanding was deeply poignant for me, since at the time the rhetoric of the Church and of religious life was one of embracing change and being open to all possibilities. The contradiction struck at the heart of my identity as a sister. My vision for religious life was joyous; I saw constant potential in all its systems, but the potential was consistently stifled because of the permeating fear and refusal to engage at a personal level. In my earlier life as a religious I had encountered the idea of an all-powerful punitive God, but I had worked out for myself that this was a myth and I had created my own truth about my own God. Now, however, the coercive nature of the system began to exercise its full potential for oppression, and I constantly received messages that I was to conform and not question.

Such dissonance cannot last. One or the other has to submit. Over a long period of self-questioning and agonising, I finally came to the decision, at fifty, to leave religious life.

Popular images of Audrey Hepburn jumping over the wall are naive and trite. The most difficult wall I had to negotiate was the wall in my own mind. While the relationship with my community members might have been less than perfect, at least it was a relationship. My mother died, and my only family was one sister who lived a distance away. If I left the community I would be on my own. The idea was devastating, a hollow tunnel of emptiness stretching ahead for all time. I would be alone. I would have little support to navigate through an unknown outside world, without the comfort of constraining but familiar structures. Choices are seldom easy.

I chose to go. The nature of my going was as painful as had been the nature of my staying. It was humiliating as I tried to negotiate some kind of financial settlement for broken teaching service, as I tried to explain to people who I had thought respected me the reasons for my decisions, and the importance of a realistic and just financial settlement. I had to accept their refusal to listen or understand. Perhaps they could do neither. I will never know.

Into freedom

Freedom of a sort. My understanding of studies of freedom were that one is free from something, or free to do something. For me it was at first neither. I had not yet reached an understanding that freedom is in attitudes towards relationships. I was empty. I cannot adequately express how empty life was. I had no family close by, and few supports. I was alone. For the first time in my life I had to make my own decisions – what to eat, how to manage my money, when to go to sleep. These are major decisions.

Before I had left the convent, the order had introduced a process of discernment for all members of the community, similar to the process of action research. We were advised to reflect on our actions, to imagine alternative ways of being. I had enjoyed that process; it seemed to legitimise imagining future scenarios of the kind I believed could help establish a good social order. Now I was free to do just that, but how could I find direction in external and internal worlds suddenly alien and empty? I felt bereft, hapless, abandoned to my own devices, if only I could find out what those devices were.

I took a job, many jobs because I had to make money to support myself. I worked as a teacher of children by day, and a teacher of adults during the evenings. I came seriously under pressure of work. The accumulation of pressure and the emotional turmoil of guilt, anger, insecurity and fear generated through leaving the convent contributed to my becoming a hard teacher, not caring in the way that I wanted to be, concentrating on surviving at a surface level and trying to come to terms with the sense of loss that burned away at me continually. Yet I remained convinced that the loss was better than the pain of false belonging.

One of the greatest gifts of life is the capacity of the body to heal itself. I began to heal, mentally and physically. It was long, slow, laborious. I attended therapy and decided to do something for myself that would offer new perspectives in an attempt to make meaning of it all. I had always had a great love of learning; I would undertake a professional development course that would help me to become the kind of teacher I wanted to be. I embarked upon my MA studies.

Becoming consciously critical

We studied forms of enquiry, one of which was critical theory. Immediately I saw the theoretical framework that would help me give meaning to the trauma. I began to appreciate that I was not at fault so much as a casualty of an authoritarian system that did not know, or did not want to know, how to handle issues of freedom and individual autonomy. I began to understand that it is not sufficient to engage in impressive rhetoric around issues of freedom, as had been my experience of working in institutional structures; it is also vital to engage in the practice of freedom. I began to understand how systems oppress personal lifeworlds, and obliterate all critique through the exercise of powerful strategies of control. The most important aspect was my process of understanding itself. I came to question how I was with the people I was teaching: was I exerting the same kind of control over them that had been my normal experience of institutional life? While I could now critique from a legitimate standpoint, could I begin to critique my own practice as a teacher and as a human being?

I am at this point today. I am engaged in research work leading to the writing of my MA dissertation, to try to understand how I can come to a deeper appreciation of personal freedom, how I need to communicate my understanding in my work with others, and how I need to ensure that I am not depriving my students of their chance to explore their autonomy and create their own identities. I am revisiting the literature of liberation theology, and I am also becoming caught up in other literatures, around personal development, the need to understand oneself as having a right to one's place on earth along with others; and I am growing into consciousness as I continue on my journey of conversion.

I imagine my story is similar in principle to many people's stories not in religious life, but in contexts that are similarly oppressive and constraining. In my case, it became an issue of whether I was to submerge my identity entirely into the culture in order to survive with any modicum of self-respect, or whether to break out and create a new identity for myself. For me, it was the proverbial rock and a hard place. I chose, rightly for me, I think. I often wonder what my congregation think of me now, and I find thoughts of compassion filtering through where once there was only anger and disillusionment.

I wonder how many of us are fortunate enough to find the strength to break free. My strength came from despair and desperation. In a way I had no choice. Giving in was never an option. For many people it is, whether it is giving in to the comfort of the traps of financial or domestic security, or the trap of familiar ways of thinking. Change for many people is threatening and destabilising. For me, it has now become a way of life, still frightening but increasingly familiar and reassuring. I no longer know what to expect. Only a few years ago my life was mapped out, not within my control, taken and shaped by others. Now it is mine, entirely and unequivocally. I have come to realise that I can make that life into something quite special if I so choose.

Through my study I have learnt a good deal. I have learnt about Foucault's 'gaze', about how systems of thought control ensure that we do not get too big for the boots our masters decide we should wear. I have also learnt that I can resist. I can sing a different song, a better song, one that I can write for myself. There is no denying the pain which continues, but pain becomes a familiar thing, as familiar as previous lives, to be embraced and lived with rather than avoided. I am learning not to be afraid. I can question the thoughts of my own mind as much as I questioned the thoughts of others. I have become critical of myself, and that is comforting, for I am now not content to stay with unsatisfactory situations, but see where I have the opportunity to change them. I began with my own mind. I now intend to start on the rest of my world.

Critique is being open to new possibilities. Although I have left religious life, I have not left God, nor has God left me. We have a new relationship, one that is based on mutual care and respect, as it manifests in the relationships with others in all the moments of my life. I have come to cherish my inner child, and see that inner child in the children I teach, but the self that cherishes is now fully grown and responsible for this life of a new kind of service. It is a service not to a narrow and distant idea, but a real and present commitment to people, wherever we meet. I do not know where I am going, but I do know what I think, and, wonderfully, am beginning to encounter the person I want to be. The sadness remains, now somewhat tempered by the distance of time and reflection, and is also part of a new joy as I come to know myself for the first time, in relation with others.

8 Action research

Background

The second scientific revolution

The nature of science continues to evolve. The second scientific revolution is now here and, like the first, is associated with the development of sophisticated technology, this time computers. The clockwork of the first scientific revolution has now changed to dynamic adaptive systems.

A parallel change has occurred in how we look at the universe and our place in it. These changing cosmologies have amounted to cognitive revolutions. The first cognitive revolution signalled a shift from (a) an unquestioning faith in an invisible God as the prime mover of the universe, to (b) deliberate rational enquiry into the physical workings of the universe and the processes of human lives. The task of man [*sic*] was how to become more like God and control the natural environment (see Chapter 5). While the new science may be with us, old science epistemologies still tend to dominate, though the playing field is beginning to level out.

The new science operates in multiple worlds, in outer space and inner space (Barrow, 1988). 'The new physics is a physics that presupposes an observer situated within the observed world. Our dialogue with nature will be successful only if it is carried out from within nature' (Prigogine and Stengers, 1984: 218). The nature of the new science is well documented, particularly in explanations of chaos and complexity theory (e.g. Lewin, 1993; Waldrop, 1992), and the new dynamic metaphors fit with the turbulent images of contemporary life and its philosophical and cultural trends. The transient nature of quantum physics is mirrored in the indefinable nature of postmodernism; the dissipative nature of process structures matches the collapsible character of markets and marriages. Ontologies have moved from fixed structures to flow (Csikszentmihalyi, 1990), from being to becoming.

This all finds expression in action research.

The origins of action research

Action research is sometimes associated with the work of John Collier (see

Noffke, 1997b), but more commonly with the seminal ideas of Kurt Lewin. Working in social scientific settings, Lewin caught the increasingly individualistic spirit of the time. The social component of social science had long been recognised: for example, the Hawthorne studies had demonstrated that work practices were likely to be enhanced if people became directly involved with their own work. Lewin showed how individuals' involvement in changing work processes influenced outcomes (1946). His work was initially highly influential in the United States and later found a welcome in the Tavistock Institute in the UK, which in turn inspired a good deal of work in Scandinavia (see Eden and Huxham, 1999: 273–7 for a useful overview of early action research in organisation settings).

The relevance of action research for social change was quickly perceived by workers in education studies, and several seminal texts (e.g. Corey, 1953) showed its potential for changing education processes at a systemic level. However, after enjoying a period of popularity in the USA, action research went into decline, one of the reasons being a resurgence of interest in technological competitiveness after the successful flight of Sputnik (see Carr and Kemmis, 1986). Again attention focused on dominance and control, both of earthly matter and of outer space. Paradigms travelled side by side: the technical rational aim was to control the earth and skies, while the liberal humanitarian aim was to encourage greater understanding of the inner self and relationships with others.

Action research became prominent in education in the UK, particularly through the work of Lawrence Stenhouse and others working in the Humanities Curriculum Project. While not actively using the term 'action research', Stenhouse promoted the idea of teacher as researcher. Teachers, said Stenhouse (1975), were the best judges of their own practice and should be encouraged to develop ways actively to reflect on their practice and improve any aspects they felt needed attention. A strong group of researchers gathered around Stenhouse, and these later were to become some of the key movers and shapers of action research – John Elliott, Clem Adelman, Stephen Kemmis and others. Some developmental work also drew on the social scientific work of Kolb (1984) and systems theorists in organisation studies (Argyris and Schön, 1974; Schön, 1983); but while elements of organisation studies were imported into education studies, the reverse did not happen so readily.

Living educational theories

At the same time, during the 1970s, Jack Whitehead, working in education at the University of Bath, was developing a different approach. In these early days some general frameworks were agreed worldwide by the then quite small group of action researchers. It was held to be a form of enquiry that placed people at the heart of the matter. There was broad agreement that action research was undertaken by individuals in work contexts to improve their understanding of the situation they were working in, in order to improve the situation itself; it built on a collaborative and participatory ethos; it was democratic (see the working definition of action research drawn up collaboratively at the International Symposium on Action Research, Brisbane, March 1989, in Zuber-Skerritt, 1992: 14).

Whitehead's work however diverged quite sharply in other respects. Focusing on the key point that research aims to generate a claim to knowledge, he raised political questions about what kind of knowledge this might be, whose knowledge it was, and what kind of evidence might be produced in support of the claim. For action research to realise its potential for personal-social renewal, it should not be seen as a theoretical discipline but as a lived practice, not something only to be spoken about but also something to be done. Whitehead came to insist on the production of research-based evidence to support practitioners' claims to knowledge that they had improved their practice. The 'living "I"' was at the centre of the enquiry. 'The researcher' was not the abstracted third person of the traditional disciplines but a real-life, flesh-and-blood first person who was telling a story of life itself. Here Whitehead broke with received social scientific knowledge. He began to develop a new kind of theory that was not only in the words that people spoke but in the way they lived their lives. Action research for him became a way of doing research that generated a theory for living; it involved asking questions of the kind, 'How do I improve my practice?' (1989). Because the methodology could be misused by people asking questions such as 'How do I get my own way?', Whitehead emphasised that action enquiries needed to show the ethical dimension of improving practice for others' benefit, a commitment that underpins the concept of education (Dewey, 1916). He developed the idea of living educational theories, stories generated by practitioners to show the process of their own efforts to improve their personal practice for social good.

Whitehead's work is today highly influential but contested, one of the reasons being the challenge it presents to academic theory and the implications it carries for those who position themselves in traditional management roles in education and other disciplines. Traditional approaches suppose that it is enough to produce propositional theories about action research, in the same way that traditional organisation and management texts produce propositional theories about organisation and management. This however does not make better educators or managers, nor improve the quality of life for people in organisational contexts. A living theory approach means that people produce accounts to show how and why they are claiming to have become better practitioners. This involves explanations of what they mean by 'better'. Live evidence is gathered from the testimonies of others on whom the work impacts that the quality of their life really has improved.

Generative transformational theories

I like these ideas, and I have built on them in developing my own. Like Whitehead, I do not see action research as a 'thing'. I prefer to think of people, action researchers, working together to understand their own lives and help one another each to understand theirs. Action research, for me, refers to a way they can do this. When I speak about action research I am speaking about people, in the same way that when I speak about organisations I am speaking about people. I prefer to contextualise explanations of action research in the stories of people's lives.

I see the process of thinking in action, and reflection on thinking in action, as a generative transformational process. As soon as we reach an answer it generates another question. We are never static. Learning, as Weick and Westley (1999) point out, is a process of disorganising stable positions and encouraging variety. This does not mean that our thinking is deficient: on the contrary, each moment represents our present best thinking, yet that is open to change as we refine and improve our ideas. The whole process of being is towards becoming: 'I can become more than I am,' says Data in *Star Trek*. The aim of action researchers is to try to make all our new moments more life-enhancing than the previous ones.

I shall continue with these ideas shortly, particularly as they draw on the influences of the new science.

Action research paradigms

Today a multiplicity of approaches to action research has developed (Dickens and Watkins, 1999).

It is possible to identify three general approaches to action research, which differ in their ontological assumptions and political aims. These constitute three action research paradigms, which reflect the influence of wider paradigms (Figure 8.1):

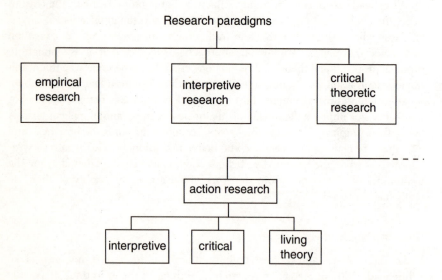

Figure 8.1

The interpretive approach

This approach encourages practitioners to undertake their action enquiries into their workplace practice, supported by researchers, acting perhaps as coaches, who are often positioned as field tutors, managers, consultants or academic supervisors. The aim of these supporters is to observe, describe and explain the research of those whom they are supporting or otherwise monitoring. There are degrees of involvement in the research by the 'external' researcher, and degrees of involvement in the relationship between external researcher and research participants. Sometimes the 'external' researcher monitors their own relationship with the other(s); sometimes not. This approach often appears as a form of process management.

This form of action research is used throughout the world. Some texts in this tradition are Elliott (1991), Hollingsworth (1997), O'Hanlon (1996), Zuber-Skerritt (1996).

The critical theoretic approach

This approach encourages participants to become aware of, and work to over-come, the forces of domination and control that influence and potentially distort their work practices. The focus is on emancipatory issues where participants in all contexts are encouraged to see themselves engaged in collective struggle against the forces of colonisation and oppression. As in interpretive approaches, the relationship between the 'external' researcher and other research participants is negotiated.

The perspective is adopted worldwide and is especially visible throughout Australia and New Zealand, and also in Latin America. Some key texts are Carr and Kemmis (1986), Gore (1993), Kemmis and McTaggart (1988), Smyth (1995), Zeichner (1993, 1999),

Living educational theories

This approach encourages individuals to clarify the values base of their work, and to try to live their values in their practice, recognising that this inevitably gives rise to contradictions. The focus of action research is to try at least to understand, and aim to resolve the contradictions, so that the researcher may work more productively and enable others to do the same. All researchers are in the same research plane; all are researching their practice regardless of their position vis-à-vis one another.

The approach is used worldwide and especially in the UK, USA, Canada and Ireland. Published work includes the writings of Jack Whitehead (1993; and see also http://www.bath.ac.uk/~edsajw for a comprehensive selection of writings), my own texts (McNiff, 1988, 1993; McNiff *et al.*, 1992; McNiff *et al.*, 1996), and those of Lomax (1996), Ghaye and Ghaye (1998), Hamilton (1998), Loughran (1996), Russell and Munby (1992) and Russell and Korthagen (1995).

There is much solidarity of opinion around the potential use value of action research. It challenges positivist views that aim only for observational and descriptive adequacy, and aims for personal-social change at the level of explanatory adequacy. I worry however that some people regard action research as a technology, and there are efforts to codify action research to the extent that it is developing its own 'disciplines', a move that entirely contradicts the democratic principles that started the movement in the first place.

At the moment, action research is best theorised in professional development contexts, usually on higher education courses, and most work has been done in the field of teacher professional education. Those contexts need to be widened to show the relevance of action research for all human developmental practices, whether formal or informal; and to emphasise that it can be done by anyone who is able to be aware of their own process of learning (see Mc Cormack, in McNiff, in preparation). There is also need for people in non-higher education community settings to tell their stories and show the potential for communitarian renewal, to continue traditions developed by people like Freire (1972, 1985) and Fals-Borda and Rahman (1991).

Debates rage in contemporary work about the nature and purpose of action research. At the heart of the debates is the issue of whose knowledge is at stake and what kind of theory is generated. I believe that action research in a living theory key allows all people to make claims that they have improved the quality of their own learning, and to show how that learning potentially influences the lives of others for good. This is the position I adopt now.

1 What is the nature of action research knowledge?

An action researcher begins an enquiry by asking questions of the kind, 'How do I improve my work?' (Whitehead, 1989). They then follow through a fairly systematic research process which may be expressed in the following terms:

> I reach a critical point in my practice;
> I feel the need to act;
> I act in a chosen direction;
> I monitor and evaluate my actions;
> I change the direction of my actions in the light of my evaluations.
>
> (see also Whitehead, 1993; McNiff, 1988)

This is a broad plan only. Sometimes things do not work out neatly and require a good deal of creative zig-zagging to get back on course. Sometimes they do not get back on course. Understanding how to deal with the complexities of the situation is at the heart of the process.

The sequence constitutes an emergent system of values-into-practice. An initial awareness for action develops when values are not lived fully in practice, or when new developments introduce tensions into otherwise stable processes. The instability prompts a felt need to act in a new direction. This can mean new learning; we learn in action and through action. To show whether learning has taken place and to support the claim to knowledge, data needs to be gathered to show the reality of the practice and its potential impact on others. That claim needs to be agreed by others. The new learning then goes forward to inform new practice.

The metaphors of the new science help to communicate the process. An initial point of criticality brings a system to the edge of chaos (Lewin, 1993; Waldrop, 1992) where it needs to change form or direction. Small fluctuations in initial conditions generate potentially infinite changes in the wider system, whose influence may be felt over sometimes extended time and space. The process by which values are transformed into practice demonstrates the principle of emergence in which a system realises its potential in increasingly sophisticated forms at more mature levels of its being. While the process has direction it is inherently volatile because of the unpredictability of the episodes and experiences that may emerge. Any 'outcome' needs to be seen as part of the ongoing process of emergence, and is a new beginning for the development of new forms rather than closure of an old form.

Key elements of action research are:

1   I, the researcher, am central to the process;
2   I am learning first about myself in order, possibly, to change a social situation;
3   I am not aiming for closure but ongoing development;
4   the process is participative;
5   the process is educational.

1 The living 'I' as a living contradiction

Drawing on the work of Ilyenkov (1977), Whitehead developed the idea of 'the living "I"'. In much social scientific enquiry, 'I' am regarded as a hypothetical construct. 'I' however am not a hypothetical construct, a personal pronoun or an abstraction; 'I' am a real-life, flesh-and-blood person, existing in time and space, in company with others. My research becomes a site for my own learning as I attempt to change my situation, and as I struggle to turn my values into practice. Because I am in relation with others, I need to negotiate my own processes with others. This can be difficult, because my values are often denied in my practice and I experience myself as a living contradiction.

2 Developing understanding or changing a situation?

Richard Winter (1989) rightly says that action researchers need to develop their understanding rather than aim to change a particular situation. No one should make judgements about other people's situations until they have shown how they have worked to improve their own; and even then they need to proceed with caution. These are moral-political issues. People acting as agents of social change always need to be honest about their own motives and intentions.

3 Aiming for a happy ending?

Action researchers should not assume that social situations can or should be 'resolved' in neat closure. Janice Huber (1995) tells the story of how a social situation was disimproved through insensitive approaches to a particular issue. Janice's own understanding (and probably that of others) was however considerably enhanced through the process. Action research, as any life process, seldom results in a happy ending (isn't it good when it does). We need to show how we deal with the turmoil, and this is a core value of action research. This means telling the stories of struggles and how we tried to work through them.

4 Participative collaborative practice

While action research, like all learning processes (Chapter 1) begins in the individual mind-brain, it is always socially embedded. When we practise we need to consider the potential implications of that practice. David Peat tells in *Blackfoot Physics* (1996), how American native councils never make decisions without considering their potential implications for the next seven generations. Perhaps we would all do well to remember this. Action research is always work with others. Those others' situations must be catered for, their opinions sought, and their sensitivities respected.

5 For education

Pam Lomax (1999) points out that educational research is not the same as social scientific research, although action research is seen by some as social scientific research. Social scientific research aims to study social situations and find out how they work; it does not suggest ways in which they can be improved. Education is a relational process between people that enhances their understanding of their practice with a view to improving it.

Lomax, Whitehead, I and others link the idea of action research with the idea of educational processes; action researchers show the process of the growth of their own understanding, and how that then has a potential beneficial influence in the lives of others.

2 How is action research undertaken?

Action research can take this form:

1 We review our current practice,
2 identify an aspect we want to improve,
3 imagine a way forward,
4 try it out, and
5 take stock of what happens.
6 We modify our plan in the light of what we have found and continue with the 'action',

7   monitor what we do,
8   evaluate the modified action,
9   and so on until we are satisfied with that aspect of our work.

(McNiff *et al.*, 1996: 47)

Action plans like this are useful but they can be misleading. It is tempting to see them as routines to be followed rather than prompts to encourage people to be creative about their practice. This is not the only way to do action research, but it is a helpful beginning, one possible way. Another inherent danger is that action research appears as neat, following a linear format. It is not. Doing action research requires creative response to unexpected situations, the tacking and retacking that Bateson (1994) speaks about. While action research, as a systemic totality, may be seen as a unified pattern, episodes may fly off at an unexpected tangent and develop as enquiries which, while related to the wider whole, appear to exist as free-standing enquiries. They never are, though, because action research is embodied in the researcher, the integrating focus of the enquiry.

My own visual metaphor is one that shows the creative process of multiple possibilities. It is possible to follow a main focus while allowing for other divergent practices to emerge and be followed through (see Figure 8.2).

The metaphor was influenced by my reading of the new science. Complex adaptive systems are characterised by autopoiesis, a process in which a system self-replicates in an iterative and exponential fashion. Like the snowflake (see below), the pattern emerges at all levels of the system, and the pattern of the overall whole embodies the same pattern that is manifested in its parts. The same happens in action reflection processes. What may be seen as one 'cycle' is the transformation of what went before and contains the potential of what is yet to come, a generative transformational process. One cycle is part of a wider system of cycles; they are connected by and embodied in the self-replicating pattern. Action research is a system of systems, a network of interconnecting networks, in both its form and its practice. The pattern shows the interconnectedness of people, intrapersonal and interpersonal processes, where practice at a

Figure 8.2

personal-social level is integrated by the same pattern of holistic connectedness, the same commitment to find ways of living that accommodate pluralistic and divergent manifestations within the same integrated movement towards continuing life.

Action planning

This section provides a mini-guide to doing action research. This guide appears in published form (McNiff, 1997), and has travelled the world, appearing, among other places, as part of the pack *Action Research: School Improvement through Research-Based Professionalism*, published by the Ontario Public School Teachers' Federation (1998).

Action planning can take as its organising principles this set of questions:

What is my research interest?
Why am I interested?
What kind of evidence will I gather to show why I am interested?
What can I do about it?
What will I do about it?
What kind of evidence will I gather to show that what I am doing is having an influence?
How will I explain that influence?
How will I ensure that any judgements I might make are reasonably fair and accurate?
What will I do then?

(see Whitehead, 1993; see also McNiff, 1988, 1993, 1997)

What is my research interest?

Ask yourself, 'What is particularly high in my mind at the moment in regard to my work? What is claiming a lot of my attention?' Your answer could vary substantially in range and scope, from the state of the economy and provision for your work to a very focused issue concerning one aspect of your work.

The idea of research interest can also be communicated in the question, 'What is my concern?' Often what you might wish to investigate is a concern, or even a problem, but this is not necessarily so. The main thing is to identify an area that you want to investigate because you are at a critical point in thinking and dealing with it.

At this stage it is important to keep your area of interest focused. You need to be practical and ask, 'Can I actually do something about this issue? Can I hope to influence the situation, or is it outside my scope?' If it really is outside your scope, you should be realistic and leave it. Having said that, however, you should not give up altogether. While it might be true that you cannot change the world, you can certainly change your bit of it; and if everyone changed a small bit at a time, starting with themselves, a lot of renewal would happen very quickly.

A research question can be stated in terms of 'How do I ...?' For example,

How do I improve the quality of my relationships with Department A?
How do I help B overcome his anxieties about interviews?
How do I organise my work schedule more efficiently?

The main ideas are:

- you are asking a real question about an issue, and you are hoping to move towards a possible solution;
- you are the real person identifying the issues and asking the questions;
- you are trying to deepen your understanding of a situation in order to improve it.

Remember that any improvement is still improvement, no matter how small.

It is not always important, nor possible, to show how you have influenced a situation; but it is important to show how you have developed your own understanding of the situation through engaging with the problematics, and can show how your improved understanding might now be put to use, possibly within this current situation or another.

Why am I interested?

You need to be reasonably clear why you want to get involved in this issue. The reasons for your actions are in your values base, the things you believe in. If you believe that all people have equal rights, you will try to ensure that your workplace is a place in which everyone does have equal rights, and you will organise your own work so that everyone can exercise their rights. People unfortunately are often in working situations where it is not possible to live in a way that is in line with what they believe in. The workplace could well be a place where the rights of some people are denied. Also, and for a variety of reasons, although a person might believe in equal rights, that person might be the one who is denying equal rights to others.

Action research is a way of working that helps us to identify the things we believe in, to check that we are justified in holding these beliefs, and then work systematically towards making them come true. It might not be possible to realise them completely, but we can go some way towards it.

What kind of evidence will I gather to show why I am interested?

How can you show your situation so that other people can relate to what you are feeling? In doing your action research, you are hoping to find ways to improve things. How can you show things as they are, in this 'now' scenario, so that you can then show how they change?

There are many different data-gathering methods available – journals, diaries, note-taking, audio and videotape recordings, questionnaires, surveys and attitudes scales, and so on.

Data is not evidence. Data is the initial information which shows the situation as it is. It is important to identify criteria which will act as clear indicators about how the situation might be judged to have improved through action. Examples of such criteria might be whether people felt more involved in their work because of your influence; or whether production was improved because people felt more involved. It is then possible, by identifying particular pieces of the data which match the proposed criteria, to show evidence of improvement. The evidence can be used to support claims to knowledge. When you say that you believe you have improved the quality of relationships in the workplace so that production is enhanced, you can support this claim to knowledge with instances in which people say that they feel better about themselves and consequently undertake their work in a more committed manner.

What will I do about it?

You need to imagine how you might tackle the issue in a particular way. You might at this stage wish to consult with other people. They might propose several courses of action. You need to choose one you think is most appropriate at this point. This will involve imagining what might be the outcomes of any decisions you take. The proposed solutions always need to be your choices, though. You are investigating your work and situation, and you need to show how you are aware of your responsibility in making your choices. You need to consider your options and decide what you can reasonably expect to achieve, given the time, energy and other resources available. You also need to recognise the potential constraints to your work, such as how others might react to you or whether your ideas will be met with welcoming or hostile reactions, and how you will deal with this.

Having decided on a possible strategy, you now need to try it out. It might work and it might not. If it does, you will probably want to continue developing it. If it doesn't, you may well decide to abandon it, or modify it, or try something else altogether.

What kind of evidence will I gather to show that what I am doing is having an influence?

You are monitoring your practice as you go, gathering data about what you are doing, and how it seems to be influencing others. You need to turn the data into evidence as an ongoing process. You need to show how an earlier scenario transforms into a later one, and how the later scenario then changes again, and so on; it is an ongoing transformative process. Hopefully later scenarios might show that things are moving in the direction of what you believe in.

How you gather data might be consistent or vary throughout the project. You might use a questionnaire for the initial and later episodes of data-gathering, or you might use tape-recorded open-ended interviews for the initial data-gathering, and analyse your transcripts, and then use field notes for later data-gathering, and analyse those perhaps for behavioural changes. These are your decisions. You may be as creative as you wish or are allowed to be.

How will I explain that influence?

It is important to remember that the focus of your enquiry is you. You are aiming to change yourself, primarily your understanding and how that might influence your behaviour and attitudes, in turn to influence the situation that you are part of. To gauge the potential impact of this change in yourself on other people, you need to check their responses and reactions to you. This is not a cause-and-effect relationship. You are not saying, 'These changes are happening because I did such and such.' You are saying, 'I can show that certain changes took place as I changed my practice, particularly in myself, and different relationships evolved.' You can show the unfolding of new understandings that grow out of people working together in new and different ways, and their influence on one another.

To show this development, it is useful to focus on only a few aspects of the total scene. If I wanted to show that I was a competent driver, for instance, I might identify just one aspect of my driving as representative of the whole. The same principles hold in showing the potential impact of your changed practice. Identify one or two aspects of your practice and its potential impact, and show these aspects clearly.

How will I ensure that any judgements I might make are reasonably fair and accurate?

If you say, 'I think that such and such happened in my workplace situation,' you can expect someone to say, 'Prove it.' The answer to that is that you can't. It is unlikely that anyone can prove anything, ever. You can however produce reasonable evidence to suggest that what you feel happened really did happen, and you are not just making it up.

This is a vital aspect of your work. In saying that you believe you have influenced your work situation for the better, you are making a claim to knowledge. You are producing clear evidence to support that claim. Now you need other people to agree with you that it is not an empty claim, but that you have good reason for saying these things. Other people need to validate your claim to knowledge: they need to agree that things really have developed in the way you think. You can then say in all honesty, 'I am claiming that I have influenced this situation because I investigated how I could improve my work; what's more, I have the backing of other people to endorse that what I am saying is fair and accurate.'

What will I do then?

You will probably carry on working in this new way because it seems to be more effective than the way you were working before, in the sense that you are closer to realising your values through your work.

However, the situation may not yet be right. Although you might have addressed one issue, and you can reasonably say that it is better, other issues now demand your attention. Perhaps in addressing that one issue you have unearthed others. There seems to be no end; and that is the way it is. As long as we live, life is going to be interesting and problematic, always in a process of unfolding. We will probably never get to a situation in which everything is perfect and everything we believe in actually does happen. The good order does not exist 'out there'; but it does exist in the living. As long as we are alive we are always going to find new challenges, provided we are open to them.

An action research approach is a path to potential personal and social renewal. We are thinking and searching all the time, never complacent or content to let less than satisfactory situations go unattended. Complacency and inertia are neither generative nor transformative; they are stultifying to the life process itself. Action researchers grasp the moment, for it is all that we have.

3 How is action research put to use?

Stay with me, please, while I tell you a story.

I first became caught up in the magic of chaos and complexity when, at the age of five, I watched a snowflake settle on the outside window pane. It was perfectly formed. I stared at it, intuitively recognising that each part was a manifestation of the whole, while the whole contained an implicate pattern that was reflected throughout the parts and interwove each part with the others. It was a tiny dynamic world enfolded in itself, the centredness unfolding again into the whole. I had no language then to describe my experience, nor did I acquire the language until almost fifty years later when I began to make connections between my reading and my experience; but I was aware that I had fallen in love with an idea, with the beautiful world of self-organising and self-replicating systems, and I was to follow this idea for the rest of my life.

I still had not the language when, at the age of twenty, I encountered the ideas of Goethe in my undergraduate studies of German literature. Goethe, I learned, was intensely interested in the generative transformational nature of natural phenomena and, through extension, human experience, and brought this into his writing.

Ten years later, now studying for a Masters degree in Applied Linguistics, I engaged with the ideas of Noam Chomsky. I struggled to understand the workings of formal grammar at a conceptual level; and I again recognised, almost kinaesthetically, the familiar thrill of being close to a self-replicating, self-organising pattern, this time with the added dimension of emergent property. One of the themes of Chomsky's work is that a finite number of grammatical rules can generate an infinite number of novel utterances (Chomksy, 1957, 1965). This idea was almost overwhelming. A very small finite number of components can generate an infinite number of new forms. This meant that millions upon count-less millions of sentences were being spoken at every moment around the world, yet each had never been formed or uttered before. By extension, each human being had never said the same thing before; and by extension again, each human being had never existed before. The shifting kaleidoscopic symmetry that these ideas inspired reflected the patterns of the snowflake: each piece of the whole was different and yet identical at the same time, each piece capable of gener-ating an infinity of transformed patterns. I was captivated and in complete awe of the entire system.

Yet the significance of this wonder did not impact on me fully until another ten years had passed and I took up my doctoral studies. I had explored, at a conceptual level, the different research paradigms in education, and I applied, at an experiential level, the principles of action research in the implementation and evaluation of my work.

I fell ill during my final year of part-time study, which was a blessing in disguise in enabling me to write up at a more sensible pace. As I wrote the chapter in my thesis about propositional and dialectical forms an amazing thing happened. I began to see, actually to experience, what propositional and dialec-tical forms were. I was aware of my own thought processes changing, transforming into different ways and developing new connections and relation-ships. I began actually to experience the phenomenon that I was writing about. I remember being elated and excited by the awareness of what was happening. I was engaging in a new way of thinking through writing about a new way of thinking (McNiff, 1990). It was another lovely example of emergent property, of autopoiesis, the ability of a system to transform itself into a latent version of itself, the dynamic of a system when it reaches the point of criticality and becomes unstable. Per Bak shows this in his demonstration of the volatile nature of piles of sand (see Lewin, 1993; Waldrop, 1992). A sandpile will stay together until it reaches a particular point in its growth when grains will begin to slip. Add more sand to the pile and you cause mini-avalanches. This is the point of criti-cality in dynamic systems when something has to give, the system has to transform into a new state. Prigogine and Stenger's work shows us this phenomenon in their discussion of dissipative structures (Prigogine and Stengers, 1984). My thinking had reached this stage. By writing about dialectical forms, I actually began to perceive and experience reality dialectically. I became part of the reality I was describing, rather than an objective outside observer. I began to recognise myself as existing in a dialectical relationship with my environment and to see that I, my own whole, was an inseparable part of a larger whole, both mutually influencing and supporting the other.

I wrote a second thesis, this time about the experience of moving from propo-sitional to dialectical forms; and I used the first thesis as data of my earlier ways of being and thinking. I will never forget the epiphany of that golden time when I became aware of self as thinker in relation to self as the object of thinking.

I was still chasing the pattern, trying to see where all the pieces came together.

Because of my interest in action research I began to develop my political commitments to democracy and social justice, and connected again with the work of Chomsky, this time his political writings. The pattern grew more complex and more hidden. I was sensing more and more that there were deep connections here. Chomsky's work was exerting an enormous influence in my life and I couldn't fathom why. Then I read Salkie's (1990) commentary, and things began to fall into place.

Salkie writes that Chomsky's linguistic and political writings are informed by the same human values and principles: a determination to challenge the reification of axiomatic systems and to engage in open-ended forms of being and thinking. This struck deep resonances within me, and I began to understand that these were the same values that informed my own work. At that time, however, I still felt that the pattern was the key, and I felt impelled to follow my star and connect with the person. Somehow, I sensed, if I could meet directly with the person, I would find the pattern. However, while I felt that Chomsky's work was my key to understanding the pattern, I as yet only dimly saw that the pattern included me. I was still objectifying it, in a propositional sense, rather than living it in an experiential sense.

In 1993 I met with Noam Chomsky, and that meeting had a profound effect on me. I did not find the pattern, and in that sense I was disappointed; but I gained far more in other terms.

At the time I was working in teacher education, and I had sent some of my writing to Noam, in preparation for our meeting. One of the first questions he asked me was, 'Where are the children?' At the time I was quite thrown off balance. What kind of question was that? My work was with teachers, not with children. Wrong. He was absolutely right to ask the question. I had not considered the children, or how teacher education must be related to those they are teaching (Huberman, 1992), how teaching must always be seen in relation to learning. My work *is* with children, and with parents, and with all other members of the community. If I do not understand this, I see my work as a separate fragment, a 'thing' that notionally exists 'out there'.

I did not find the key to the pattern, and I came later to see that one of the reasons I was drawn to the work of Chomsky is that it is itself a wonderful example of the pattern – self-generating systems in which a finite number of properties give rise to an infinite number of new forms (I have adopted the idea of generative transformational forms from Chomsky's work in linguistics). I also gained from that meeting a clear idea of the social and political imperative that informs educational work; while ideas about education might be the property of an individual, how those ideas are used has implications for the development of good social orders.

Living the pattern

The story that strings together the different themes of this book is how I have worked with others to develop an educational organisation in Ireland. The years this has taken have constituted the most profound and difficult learning experiences of my life, and I am now able to draw together the invisible threads that previously eluded me. I can not only offer descriptions of the patterns, and how they operate in a conceptual sense; I can relate this to my real life experience and show how the patterns really do connect what I and others are doing, and how our practices interweave and mutually influence.

The enormity of difficulty of recent years has been staggering at a personal and professional level: separation from my life partner; withdrawal of institutional support for the work that colleagues and I had been doing; a motor accident with long-term effects; systematic loss of hearing; voluntary exile to a strange land, and the desperate yearning for home; loss of all stable reference points which threatened sense of identity and self-worth. The experience of struggling to support people against the power of political and institutional forces to close down their access to learning, while coping with the pain of disillusionment, abandonment and withdrawal of personal and professional supports has led to enervation and despair. Yet I have learnt that despair carries its own challenge, and its own triumph: you either give in or you don't; you either have faith that it will turn out well, or you fall apart. And if you fall apart, you are not much use to anyone, including yourself. Paul Tillich says it well:

> He [*sic*] who is in the grip of doubt and meaninglessness cannot liberate himself from this grip, but he asks for an answer which is valid within and not outside the situation of his despair. He asks for the ultimate foundation of what we have called the 'courage of despair'. There is only one possible answer, if one does not try to escape the question; namely that the acceptance of despair is in itself faith and on the boundary line of the courage to be. In this situation the meaning of life is reduced to despair about the meaning of life. But as long as this despair is an act of life it is positive in its negativity.
>
> (Tillich, 1977: 170)

I have also grown aware of how my faith in an inexorable emergent life process, which some people call universal order and I call God, continues to sustain me, knowing that the natural order is towards life-giving forms, knowing that it will come right. While I can choose to give in or carry on, I have no choice in whether the wider system of which I am a part will grow; I have no choice in whether I continue to grow. The life force is within me and beyond me. Order emerges; the universe, and my own universe, continues to develop into new forms.

Perhaps the most profound learning has been that we are connected, interdependent and mutually influential. Before, I had seen myself mainly in relation to me, Kipling's cat, a self-sustaining entity who had not need of others for personal fulfilment. Other people were not necessary for self-growth. The bad times eroded much of that confidence, ate away at the sense of self, undermined the ability to act with decision and direction. I felt I had lost everything, and was simply surviving by doing the job that I was still passionately committed to, but which had brought such catastrophe with it.

This was when I understood that I needed other people. I didn't just like being with them; I needed them. I discovered friends in the people I had known for a long time. I learned the meaning of sharing and learning together, through the experience of need. The people who officially were my students became my teachers; I learned with them the meaning of what I was doing as their teacher and how I could help them as they in turn were helping me. My experience of despair resulted in transformational learning, as well described by Capra (1989: 216): 'the organism may also undergo a process of self-transformation and self-transcendence, involving stages of crisis and transition and resulting in an entirely new state of balance'. The theory became real.

The patterns in my mind changed. I reconceptualised myself not as an entity independent of others, but as a person who had been fragmented and was now growing back into wholeness; and this wholeness was part of the wider whole-ness of those who had helped me, with whom I was now in meaningful relation. The patterns were connected. The fragmented objects that had been self and others melded and I saw the relationships, the ties that bind (Bateson, 1972, 1979). I began to see a new kind of spirituality in the relationships that connected us, and this had profound implications for future work.

Now I also connected with the theory behind the patterns. I began to under-stand the insights of Jantsch, Bateson, Capra, Bohm and others: that whereas our education and cultural systems, the very systems and categories of thought that we use in the western intellectual tradition, encourage us to see reality in terms of objects and outcomes, those objects are in fact manifestations of the underlying connections of relationships; and I drew again on the idea of the generative transformational nature of systems (McNiff *et al.*, 1992) that the very relationships are dynamic processes, not structures. What I had previously seen as a scaffolding supporting a wall of individual bricks now became a vibrant, dynamic web, with nodes at strategic points, and even those nodes were webs of relation, dynamic and continually transforming. My visual and kinaesthetic metaphors changed from structure (Figure 8.3) to process (Figure 8.4); my atti-tudes changed; and so did my life. I began to see myself not as coming out of a past and working towards closure, but standing on the brink and launching forth into the void, which chaos and complexity theory tells us is the nature of reality, the past and future integrated into the present. Everything is in process of coming into being; reality is full of surprise, the future is unknown and always out of reach. This is 'the edge of chaos'. This is where I found myself, accepting the unknown as a way of life, accepting the danger of an insecure future, but now secure in the faith that the nature of reality is that it emerges into an inte-grated wholeness. The patterns of relationship were the same patterns that connected the wider reality of which I was a part. My lifeworld was inextricably linked with the lifeworld of others.

This is where I am today. In this book I describe the patterns that connect, and show how they act as metaphors for interrelated human practices. I want to

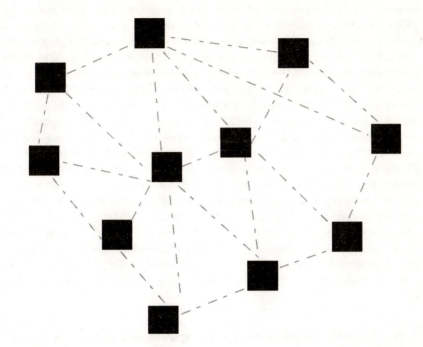

Figure 8.3

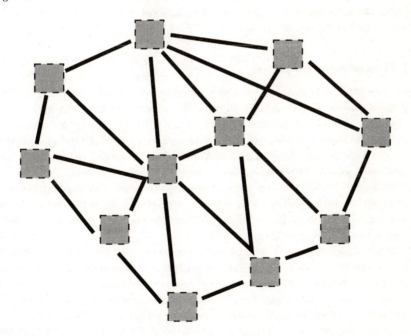

Figure 8.4

show the need to go beyond metaphor. David Steindl-Rast says (in Capra *et al.*, 1992: 157),'Science is concerned with the working of the cosmos. Religion is concerned with the meaning behind it.' I prefer to talk about faith in connectedness rather than religion (which is something different). While the patterns of the new science help us to develop metaphors for understanding our realities, our social and educational intent helps us to give our reality meaning. It is through the nature of our relationships that we give meaning to our own and one another's lives; each moment is an act of creation, each word the beginning. If we can come to see that we are systematically conditioned by our current cultural and intellectual traditions to objectify reality, which leads us to 'see life as a problem rather than a mystery to be experienced' (Steindl-Rast, in Capra *et al.*, 1992: 102); and if we can develop a view of ourselves as in dynamic relation with one another rather than discrete objects existing in our own time and space, and come to understand the nature of those relationships; then, I think, we will move towards developing the kind of theory that will help us to develop good social orders for world sustainability. The theory moves beyond its metaphorical base. It becomes live. We keep the vision and we work to turn it into reality.

My learning has emerged through the struggle; it would not have happened else.

4 What are the implications for organisation theory as a process of social renewal?

Doing action research in organisational settings encourages us to see practice in new ways. Let me here focus on three.

1 Principle-centred praxis

Practice is not only activity. It is work guided by values which we try to live out. When we work in this morally committed way, practice becomes praxis. Our values are those which honour people. We have first to care for ourselves (Lee, 1997) and ensure that, as a resource, ourselves are in good mental and physical mettle. This involves self-evaluation. We then use ourselves as resources, and show our professional accountability in working for others' benefit.

Practising in this way requires considerable courage in demonstrating one's authenticity and preparedness to commit to others. Doing action research, like all learning, may begin in an individual's mind-brain, but it is not isolationist. It is always conducted with others.

Praxis means having the courage to acknowledge that the future is unknown, and we are creating the future every moment. Action generates reflection, and reflection influences new action, a developing cyclical process of new learning. Closure is not possible: any answer is temporary and immediately becomes a new starting point. All endings are potential new beginnings. This is difficult for some people, who like to cling to the secure idea of established facts. Trigger, a character in the British comedy *Only Fools and Horses*, claimed that he had had the same broom for twenty years. It had had four new heads and three new handles, but it was still the same broom.

We have to let go of the need for certainty in order to learn (Wheatley, 1992). The new science shows that self-generating order is everywhere. Dynamic systems are self-organising, self-correcting. Human organisations are self-organising. They don't need external steering or guidance, but they do need collective faith in the ability to learn from experience. Learning often happens in letting go and having faith that things will turn out right if we act with integrity and with best effort.

We also have to let go of the need for formal training programmes as the only vehicles for organisational learning. Most of what is learnt in organisations is learnt without teachers. Learning happens in moment-to-moment interchanges; it is learning in the gaps. To ensure that all learning is valuable and valued, people need to feel that they matter; they need to be encouraged to see practice as creative, responsible, flexible, that their learning matters to the organisation. It is a task for managers to encourage people to nurture an attitude of curiosity and engagement, to know that mistakes will happen and be accepted as part of personal professional learning, and to provide supports to inspire people to engage.

2 Collaborative praxis

I do not know why some writers refer to 'participatory action research' as a special kind of action research. Action research has to be participative. It is however another issue whether it is collaborative.

Higgins (2000) rightly takes some writers to task for not being frank about how difficult aspects of action research can be, such as negotiating access and direction for the research. It is easy to talk about collaboration; doing it is something else.

Collaboration is intimately related with caring praxis. While we aim to develop our own and others' autonomy in organisational life, this is always done with respect for others. In this sense, collaboration becomes an effort to develop mutually respectful autonomy, a practice in which people work together as equals, engage in the give and take of negotiating positions, and agree settlements which are then subjected to critical processes of evaluation and modification. Collaboration is in attitudes and how these manifest in relationships, how willing we are to listen to each other and move in the direction of commonly agreed practices.

Collaborative practice means developing a certain attitude, a capacity to be present to the other (Glavey, 2000), to recognise mutual interdependence and connectedness (see Chapter 9). Action research encourages self-sufficient autonomy and accepting the responsibility for one's own life; and seeing one's life as always in relation with others. Collaboration, life, care and love, are aspects of mutually caring practice enacted reciprocally.

3 Management as educative leadership

The barriers to peace, says John Hume, leader of the SDLP in Northern Ireland, are in the mind. These barriers are constructed through fear, selfishness and greed. The barriers to organisational learning are the same. Decommissioning of the weapons of political and organisational power happens first in the mind.

Initiatives towards changed practices are begun by leaders. Leaders are not only managers, but managers can be leaders. When a person develops new ideas which they wish to share with others, they automatically position themselves as leaders. Leadership, like so many issues, is in the relationships. Leadership is not leading out, leading to, leading from – like power, it does not exist as a 'thing'. Leadership is what people do in relation with one another. We can develop theories of leadership by offering explanations of how we influence the quality of learning for others. This is most effectively done by sharing our own learning and inviting a creative response. All people are potential leaders in the sense that all people can share their learning to influence the learning of others.

This is also the process of education, the kind of relationship that encourages people to develop mutually respectful autonomy. Managers encourage this process of learning as a main managerial responsibility. Management in this sense is educative. Managers model the kind of practice they wish to encourage in others.

None of the foregoing is easy, nor is it impossible, as Chomsky says (1996; see also Chapter 9 of this book). To create sustainable organisations, we need to begin work on our own minds. There is no other way.

Part III

How is organisational knowledge put to use?

This part locates action research in organisational life. It makes connections between the methodology of action research and the organisational contexts where action research might have an influence for wider social change.

It is not possible, nor desirable, to try to study organisational life as an abstract phenomenon. Organisations are part of, and embedded within, wider economic and political movements; all are part of the same evolutionary process. What happens at local level in organisations impacts on wider forces; and the reverse is also true. There are forces at work which are influenced by, and in turn influence, the lives of individual people in community. Those forces, I believe, are the interactions of people as they live in dialectical relationship. The nature of those interactions influences wider social systems and their processes of legitimation, acceptance and institutionalisation as valid social orders.

To appreciate the interconnectedness of individual lives and wider social processes is to focus on how people interact at a personal level. Social processes do not just happen. They are manifestations of people working and living together. Wider social processes are influenced by the quality of relationships at local level. It is the nature of the interactions that moves the social order in a particular direction.

I am hoping in this part to make the case that people need to understand their own potential for social change by focusing on what they do in their moment to moment real lives and ensuring that those moments are the best they can be. Chaos and complexity theory tells us that the smallest perturbation at local level has the potential for influence at a universal level. An implication is that each one of us has the potential to influence world systems.

Whether we believe this, and whether we are prepared to act on our belief, is a matter of personal decision. Action research is not a 'thing' that can be applied to help in making those decisions. Action research refers to the process of people making decisions about what their lives are about, and how to make those lives worthwhile in terms of what they hold to be of value.

Therefore, in Chapter 9 I draw connections between conversational communities and rampaging free markets, and show how, when people become critically aware of their own personal and social development, they can bring that awareness to the business of containing processes which threaten human and ecological environments, and developing new ones which nurture living orders as forces for human and planetary development. In Chapter 10 I explain how theories of organisational change are not theories applied to organisational processes but are embedded within, and arise out of, the processes they are describing and explaining.

Organisation theory on this view is a form of practical theory which people generate as they try to understand how they can use their own power to renew the social orders they live in. The theory is embodied in the lives of people as they work consistently to realising and sharing their humanity for mutual benefit.

9 Action research in organisations

Although I share my time between England and Ireland, for the last three years I have lived more in Ireland. I have become part of communities, a professional one with the action research network, and a personal one with the people in the locality where I live. I have become aware of the importance of community, and how communities nurture relationships through listening and conversation. In Ireland the culture is one of talk and *craic* (fun). Talk in Ireland often has less to do with exchanging opinion on substantive issues than with recognition and relationship.

In my professional education work I have come to see the importance of conversations, not only in matters of professional concern, but also to connect at a human level. My own part in any conversation is that I listen intently because of my hearing loss, and this is important. I have learnt that listening is far more than physiological. It involves inspired guesswork, trying to read the message behind the words, and empathic response (see Corker, 1994; Corradi Fiumara, 1990). Listening and talking, I have also come to see, are the major qualitative characteristics of local communities, and also what distinguishes educative communities. My work is to encourage learning and education in an organisation, so I listen, and I encourage others to listen. Listening in itself is a creative response that can enable another person to reach new levels of understanding of themselves.

Because of my politically charged exchanges with others in institutional contexts, I have also come to understand how different the relationships tend to be in institutions, where conversation is systematically discouraged and eliminated from 'official' discourses. I have become aware of how elites in professional contexts aim to control individuals' mental freedom and factor out interpersonal relationships. By extension, and through my study of organisation theory, I have learnt how business elites also do this, reducing popular involvement in economic debates in order to copperfasten their own ideological messages in the culture. They are adept at controlling public opinion, disseminating an image of the 'good life' and encouraging intensive forms of consumerism in their own interests. People are encouraged to purchase goods without questioning what human costs are involved in the production of those goods. I have also become aware of how professional intelligentsias condone and support this view, by filtering out public participation in decision-making and protecting the sanctity of abstract systems of knowledge.

Chomsky says this well (1988: 42–3):

> In fact, power is very highly concentrated, decision-making is highly concentrated in small interpenetrating elites, ultimately based on ownership of the private economy in large measure, but also in related ideological and political and managerial elites. Since that's the way the society effectively functions, it has to have political theology that explains that that's the way it ought to function, which means that you have to establish the pretense that the participants of that elite know what they are doing, in our interest, and have the kind of understanding and access to information that is denied the rest of us, so that we poor slobs ought to just watch, not interfere.

I recognise myself as having been persuaded to watch and not interfere, until, that is, I had to make decisions in recent times about whether I was going to collude in my own subjugation and that of the people I support, or whether I would resist. Was I going to engage with the official discourse and talk about course participants with the elites, or was I going to support the development of community by relating and talking with course participants, and encourage them to decide their own futures? What values was I going to embrace and try to live out?

This threw into high relief an emergent understanding from my reading of organisation theory of how a desire for profit by corporations systematically eliminates conversation and closes down the potential of people at local level to have a say in their own lives. This is in direct contradiction to my own values of the right of people to speak for themselves and to determine their own lives.

I began to draw strong links between dominant economic theories of corporate profit, and the elimination of popular voice by those who create and promote the theories. I also began to see the potential of initiatives such as action research to restore personal involvement by people in their own lives, probably one of the reasons why action research is systematically marginalised by elitist intelligentsias. This emergent understanding led me to begin reading in the political sciences, and get to grips with the concept of free markets and how this begins to eradicate the idea of local community. It also made me more determined to support the development of local educative communities, and encourage people to develop their own understanding of how they can resist the effects of free markets, have faith in their own relationships with one another, and use that faith to restore a widespread understanding of the need for community living. Out of this commitment I travel the island of Ireland to bring the university to the people, rather than require them to come to me, as a university-appointed worker, at a central point.

I want here to explain why I make the links between personal learning and societal welfare. I want to show how I understand free markets, and how I believe that a commitment to their underpinning ideologies undermines the development of local community in which people engage in lively conversations with one another about themselves; and how the development of free markets encourages a culture of alienation in which people learn not to say anything very significant at all. I want to make a case for public awareness that caring conversations underpin efforts to develop good social orders, and the need for a popular reinstitution of conversational communities as the core unit of organisational life.

The Enlightenment project

At the dawn of the third millennium we are in the wake of the Enlightenment (Gray, 1995), emerging into a postmodern period. The values of the Enlightenment were rational understanding, freedom of mind and the fulfilment of human rights. It is questionable whether those values remain the spirit of contemporary world affairs.

The Enlightenment emerged as part of the continuing development of the western intellectual tradition, but also became politicised (as intellectual traditions tend to do), particularly in terms of nationalistic and cultural ambition. The politicisation of the Englightenment became known as the Enlightenment project. The Enlightenment project has now come to be understood as a politically engineered movement to create a universal civilisation in terms of western ideologies and institutions (MacIntyre, 1988; Gray, 1999).

The Enlightenment project has a long history of colonisation, in which the norms of western intellectual and social traditions have been systematically transplanted into other cultures. The aim has been to colonise not only territory, but also ways of thinking and cultural traditions. This has often happened through the use of coercive power and the violent suppression of dissident voices. These methodologies of power are sometimes gross, as in overt terrorism, and sometimes more insidious and far-reaching. I am thinking of the Irish context as an example; as well as torture and killing, there was also the stamping out of the indigenous language, and the Anglicisation of Irish names, practices whose influence is still apparent in contemporary Irish culture.

One of the most obvious outcomes of the Englightenment project has been the development of free markets.

Global free markets

The free market, say Gray (1999) and others, is a political construction, not a response to cultural or historical world trends. The free market aims to create a new kind of economy, not rooted in social institutions, and freed from social and political control, so prices can be fixed without regard to their effects on society.

Gray points out that markets are normally embedded in social life, and are 'circumscribed in their workings by intermediary institutions' (p. 26). Among these institutions, 'trade unions and professional associations have long been central in standing between individuals and market forces' (p. 26). The construction of a free market, however, means that individuals interact directly with market forces, weakening or altogether eradicating the intermediate institutions. Individuals are placed in direct competition with one another, with serious implications for social stability. In the western world of portfolio and contract work and corporate downsizing, the situation is one in which highly skilled workers are accepting low wages and disruption to their social lives through job mobility. The disappearance of entire workforces is not uncommon.

Gray explains (1999: 2) how the great thinkers of the Enlightenment, such as Thomas Jefferson, Tom Paine, John Stuart Mill and Karl Marx, unquestioningly took western traditions and values as the model for the rest of the world. They envisaged a world order as a cohesive civilisation in which past and present cultures would relinquish their own traditions and values and become osmosed into the new westernised civilisation. Recent interpretations (such as Fukuyama, 1999) have expanded this philosophy, suggesting that the free market would be modelled on the United States, its values and institutions, and would become a single free market which would serve the single universal community.

This might be an attractive theory (at least for the USA); reality diverges considerably. While nation states might espouse the business values of the west, they still retain their own cultural traditions. The global market is not an amalgamation of worldwide cultures, held together by nomadic conglomerates. The idea of a universal civilisation and a global free market has already resulted in massive social upheaval and dislocation, and untold human misery, most visibly in the United States and in Britain, who are the major champions of the new order, but also elsewhere, as in New Zealand during recent decades. The irony becomes increasingly evident, says Gray, that the learning from experiments with the free market is already known, yet the lessons about human degradation are disregarded.

The upshot, observes Chomsky (1996), is that a small opulent corporate minority maintains its privilege by controlling government and policies, as well as state apparatuses such as education, the church, and mass media. Social services such as the welfare state are systematically eroded and eradicated, and the process is wrapped in publicly acceptable terms by a carefully chosen language in which the victims such as the poor and the unemployed become the villains who get no more than they deserve. However, the direct social consequences of the free market and its *laissez-faire* philosophies have not weakened but rather strengthened support for it, particularly in the language of corporate business, where market forces are equated with profit, and social and economic inequality is put down to tough luck. These discourses are contemptuous of human suffering and dismissive of the values of social cohesion and the human need for community. The writing is on the wall: 'Within the view of the world that is dominant in our time economic efficiency has been disconnected from human well-being' (Gray, 1999: 234).

What to do?

Gray is sceptical about future prospects of social amelioration or the rolling back of the effects of increasing trends towards cultural imperialism. He raises questions about the human capacity to mobilise and take action. He is, however, clear about what needs to be done, and whose responsibility it is: 'A basic shift in philosophy is needed ... The task of transnational organisations should be to fashion a framework of regulation within which diverse markets can flourish' (1999: 234–5). Economic life needs again to reconnect with human values and social bonding, to develop companies as social institutions, contexts for meeting the enduring human needs for attachment and affirmation of personal worth. Technologies need to be developed that are more respectful of the environment and are mindful of the need to replace as well as extract resources for future planetary stability (see also Gray, 1993).

This is entirely in the spirit of the 'humanistic conception' of Bertrand Russell (as cited by Chomsky, 1996), who agreed with Dewey that the aim of production was not the production of material goods but the production of free human beings in relationship with one another on terms of equality. Chomsky reiterates that these ideas are relevant for schools, workplaces and all other spheres of life. It is a matter of personal decision whether to subscribe to the monopolies of power and dominant discourses or whether to challenge and aim to change the situation.

> To stem or reverse this course and restore a modicum of respect for the values of the Enlightenment, for freedom and human rights, will be no simple matter. The first step is to penetrate the clouds of deceit and distortion and learn the truth about the world, then to organise and act to change it. That's never been impossible, and never been easy. It's not impossible now, and not easy either. There has rarely been a time in history when that choice carried such dramatic human consequences.
>
> (p. 131)

I want to make a case for organisations to accept responsibility for taking the lead in working towards social and environmental regeneration. I am not alone in this (see for example Robinson Hickman, 1998). Organisations, especially for-profit organisations (for they have the strongest financial resources), are potentially the main means of world economic sustainability. To realise this potential, however, organisations need to move beyond a narrow technicist focus on material productivity and profit, and reconceptualise themselves as forces for social good. Doing so means rethinking the form of theory used to theorise organisation. A narrow technicist theory will reinforce narrow technicist practices. A generative transformational theory will encourage generative transformational practices. How we think about things influences what they become.

Future action? Action research?

Alasdair MacIntyre (1988) responds to the crisis by suggesting that we return to pre-Enlightenment traditions and agree universal values to judge human practices. He proposes a revival of the Aristotelian ethico-political view that the good life stems from a virtuous character, and that virtuous action is what a rational practical person would choose. He also suggests that it is possible to develop forms of communication in which constrained disagreement can flourish (1990), and suggests that universities can model such practices for society. While I agree with these ideas, I also take the view that it is impossible to roll back history. What is done is done; we now need to find new ways of dealing with what is yet to do.

What is yet to do is actively to find and experiment with new ways of living that value individual forms of life, pluralistic points of view and rival philosophies, as MacIntyre suggests. What is yet to do is find a methodology of reconciliation which moves beyond the established Habermasian technical, practical and emancipatory interests, and try to synthesise them in a new focus which emphasises human relatedness and the deep human need for connectedness and community. This means developing new ways of thinking. In terms of realising the potential impact of organisations for world sustainability it means developing new theories of organisation.

The new theories of discourse of Laclau and Mouffe show the need for engagement with ideas of radical pluralism. The political views of theorists such as Gray and Chomsky show the need for social action by committed individuals to withstand the worst excesses of globalising trends and to initiate political action to reverse their effects. The educational theories of Dewey show the need to conceptualise organisations as societies in which people may develop independence of mind and action, free associations on terms of equality. The living theories of Whitehead show the need to develop new forms of theory which are embodied in the real lives of people as they struggle to live out their values, including those of radical pluralistic democracy. These theories, operating on a range of fronts, are synthesised in the idea of action research, a methodology aiming to generate a form of theory that shows the reality of people working together in an honest, committed manner, to improve the quality of their own learning in the service of others.

I am not making grand claims for action research as a force to change the world, nor am I saying that action research is the only, or necessarily the most appropriate way towards social renewal. As well as educational research methodologies we need also to look to other sources, for example to religious communities, artists and social and cultural workers to provide contexts for the realisation of diverse forms of spiritual and cultural communities. I am however speaking from my own experience and conviction that once people decide personally to become involved in understanding the influences that shape their lives, and resolve to position themselves where possible as strategically thinking agents in relation with others, this can then lead to significant personal growth. I am also speaking from experience and conviction that the personal growth of one individual has the potential to influence the personal growth of others with whom the individual is in relation; and that such collective commitment to shared growth has an exponential quality that can strengthen a sense of community to meet cooperatively agreed social goals.

Social regeneration never happens because governments mandate it. Social regeneration happens through people talking with one another and acting purposefully. In this chapter therefore I am setting out how individual learning has the potential for organisational renewal, which has the potential for social renewal on a wider scale. I hope I am making the case for organisations as conversational communities who can collectively generate the power for social change. I believe we have to imagine realistic solutions to our present dilemmas and seriously consider how we can create new, better futures. I am drawing clear links between local conversations and global sustainability, and I hope to continue to show this through both the content and the form of what follows.

1 What is the nature of action research in organisations?

The new epistemology requires a new logic of practice (see also Whitehead, 2000).

Traditional epistemologies use propositional logic which aims to show a cause-and-effect relationship – if x then y; if I do this, that will happen. The logic is conceptual. Models are formed in the mind-brain and applied to practice. In the relationship between conceptual theory and practice, theory is dominant. The theory presupposes an answer; it is a theory of closure. Propositional theory is located on the high ground landscape of technical rationality.

New action-oriented epistemologies use a dialectical form of logic. Dialectics (which has a centuries-old genealogy) resists closure. It is a logic of question and answer, to-and-fro. A solution always contains a new problematic, an end state is always a new beginning. Dialectical logic takes the form 'What if … ?', an imaginative creation of new possibilities.

Action research is essentially practical. People investigate their practice in action. It is however more than activity. The research element of action research requires people to observe and monitor their actions and reflect on them. Monitoring and reflecting on practice generates a theory. Because the theory is the property of an individual practitioner it constitutes a personal theory of practice. When a practitioner considers the knowledge base of their work, and how they came to that knowledge, they are generating their own epistemology of practice.

The research element of action research provides a disciplined framework for helping people make sense of their own learning. We monitor our actions, we reflect on them (and learn), and we use our new learning to inform future action. Imagine how powerful this would be if it were institutionalised, if everyone in an organisation were to regard themselves as always learning from and within their practice, always regarding present best answers as temporary, and finding new ones as situations change. The reality is that people *are* always learning, though they might not be learning about their own process of learning, or developing insights into how they can use their learning productively.

The first step in developing a learning organisation is for people to regard themselves as learning about their practice, to be aware of what they are doing and why they are doing it, what Hoyle (1974) calls extended professionalism. Stenhouse's (1975) idea of teacher as researcher would travel across the professions and all practitioners would see themselves as researchers. A next step is to see how personal learning, itself a transformational process, transforms into collective learning. Clearly managers can exert significant influence here, by arranging the conditions for learning, and modelling collaborative learning practices themselves.

Fields of influence

Doing action research begins with asking, 'How do I improve my work?' Although it is an individual undertaking, it is always undertaken in company with others who might be influenced by the research. Action research is always a collaborative effort in that researchers will call on others in the same social or work grouping to support their claims to new knowledge (or not, as the case may be). Communities of action researchers can in this way constitute groups of learners acting as fields of influence in an organisational context.

Wheatley (1992) explains how shared social intent in organisations constitutes fields of influence. The field theory of quantum physics says that space is not an empty vacuum, as Newtonian physics teaches, but teeming with energy, filled to the brim with 'potentials for action everywhere' (p. 51), particularly when fields meet and merge. While fields, such as magnetism and gravity, are invisible and intangible, they nevertheless represent powerful potentials for influence. People are not alienated from one another as things existing separately from other things; people exist as sets of potential in relation with others who are also sets of potential, in a dynamic interactive universe.

Capra *et al.* (1992) talk about the human need for relation, a sense of belonging. We have a common human heritage. We belong to one another and, because we are made from the same material which makes up the whole of the natural order, we belong ultimately to the universe. Webs of influence permeate creation; the interconnections themselves are fields of influence. Connections form new connections, as when structures dissipate into new process structures; the neural networks of the brain operate most powerfully at their points of intersection where fields of energy connect and explode into new potentials for future energy. When people voluntarily form communities, they generate the potential for unleashing boundless energy, both for themselves and for one another.

Organisations in which people come together by choice (see p. 237) potentially constitute fields of energy. It is a collective responsibility to become aware of potentials for knowing. 'Field creation is not just the task for senior managers. Every employee has energy to contribute; in a field-filled space, there are no unimportant players' (Wheatley, 1992: 56). In organisational terms, participants construct themselves as a collective identity with specific tasks. In action research communities, participants regard themselves as learners who are finding out how to improve the quality of their work for mutual benefit.

A new logic of practice

A traditional logic of practice assumes a pattern of fixed steps in predetermined sequences. If I do this, that will happen. Every event presupposes a cause, and nothing happens to surprise.

A new logic of practice is guided by a vision of life as spontaneous, creative, quite unpredictable. It is a logic of playfulness in which all things are new and every moment full of infinite potential. This logic is the kind used for imaginative practical theorising, when we ask questions of the kind, 'I wonder what would happen if … ?' It is a way of thinking about practice that regards traditional logic as useful for reaching a fixed answer where necessary, but also regards the logician as someone who will use fixed answers as temporary platforms to find more interesting questions. Logic does not exist by itself; it is a form of thinking used by thinkers. Dialectical logic contains propositional logic within itself as part of the transformative process of a knower.

The new scholarship requires a new epistemology of practice, a new logic of practice. It invites us to free ourselves of stereotypical behaviours and mental models, and really see ourselves as beings full of amazing potentials. Who are we not to be brilliant, gorgeous, talented and fabulous? (Mandela, Inaugural Address, cited in Handy, 1997: 210). We are in this together, participants who create new lives out of all their moments, the dancers and the dance, ever-renewing.

2 How is action research supported in organisations?

I have been involved in supporting action research in Irish organisational settings for nearly ten years, and for ten years before that in UK settings. I have learnt that developing and institutionalising action research is very much a strategic and politically negotiated management activity, and involves the creation of appropriate conditions to enable learning to take place throughout an organisation. My greatest resource in developing these initiatives has been the capacity to relate to people and have easy conversations with them. In my consultancy role I never position myself as one-who-knows, so much as one who wishes to learn how she can help others to know. I am a teacher. My aim in consultancy work is to help people feel good about their own knowledge, and to use it to transform their situations for good. I would like to share here my own learning from experience about how it can be done.

1 Developing personal management skills

When I moved into management I realised that I was acting largely in an intuitive way. My management work was driven by the same values that inform my work as a teacher. I realised that I needed to refine my management practice; hence this study. I learned that the most important elements of good management are attitudes which demand certain behaviours from me.

My hopes were to encourage people to think for themselves, to develop their knowledge further, to form communities of reflective practitioners, to work together for educational goals. To encourage them to do this meant putting their needs first. It meant being available to people, recognising myself as a resource for their learning, acting as a friend and confidante when necessary but also insisting that they manage for themselves as soon as possible.

I spoke about this with Derek Hobbs, the senior partner of a medical practice in Dorset.

JM: You help people so far and then you make them stand on their own feet.

DH: Yes, it is important that you try and help people to be responsible for their own well-being, improve their lifestyles in any way for their own benefit, but that's a two-way process. More and more people come to us demanding to be well, sometimes unrealistically. You have to look at the whole individual in context and where they are coming from. Often guidelines don't allow for that. You have to use your own judgement.

JM: I'm interested that you say it's a two-way process. I like the idea of management being educative in the sense that it's a relationship in which both parties learn all the time.

DH: Definitely.

JM: What do you do to encourage this?

DH: In this particular practice we talk to one another a good deal. We've always had team meetings whereby all problems are shared, so if the district nurse is having a problem, then problems are discussed. In that way we develop a collective responsibility and we can all learn from each other's experiences. Everyone feels involved, and they don't feel they are on their own in dealing with issues.

Being a good manager, I believe, involves this kind of educative leadership, the capacity always to nurture relationships that will help people to learn. It means being fully present to the other in a way that they feel you are entirely theirs for the duration of the encounter.

2 Develop an invitational ethic

I made big mistakes in professional education initiatives in earlier contexts. I used to encourage groups of action researchers to see themselves as something very special. Of course they are, but not in an elitist sense. Organisational politics are such that 'in-groups' are quickly identified and run the risk of being excluded by the established community (Fullan, 1993).

This learning informed the work in Ireland. In every case I have emphasised the invitational and inclusive nature of the work. This is particularly relevant in Irish cultures, where people will absolutely not promote their own professional excellence. I emphasise that action research is about learning, and encourage people to share their learning rather than tell of their achievements. I invite people to undertake their enquiries but never force them to. It is important to respect people's wishes and work with them from where they want to be rather than where I want them to be; but I do encourage them to move on to more exciting (but potentially risky) spaces, and I try to provide the support they need to do so.

In institutional contexts the whole staff are invited to take part. Some don't want to, but they know they are welcome and the opportunities will always be available should they change their minds. Good communication is essential for organisational well-being, so when working with staffs I try to find the most effective ways of keeping everyone informed – newsletters, notes on bulletin boards, a few minutes' update at staff meetings. In turn, participants in institutional contexts keep others informed of their own work, for example by producing progress reports. Even if they don't get read, no one can say they were not kept informed.

With my own network I take special care to keep everyone fully up to date. Newsletters are sent out regularly, both by me and by participants. People have their own networks. We use e-mail systems, and we convene meetings of local groups and the whole network. Everyone makes big efforts to stay connected.

It is important to remember the invitational ethic. I remember another professional development initiative where the managers became so enthusiastic about action research that they mandated it across the board. This killed the initiative, and it took years to build up new goodwill to risk its re-introduction. Enthusiasm can be as coercive as negative pressure.

3 Be strategic

It is important to be opportunistic and find ways to move things in specific directions. This means identifying people who are open to new ideas, and finding allies to support. Change is threatening to many people, so finding influential people to support is essential.

David Steeves, who works in government in Alberta, talked about this:

DS: In terms of moving things, you have to find someone within the hierarchy of the organisation who will support what you do, and if you can't, you would probably just leave. You couldn't tolerate it otherwise. You choose your counsel well, and you don't spread yourself too broadly. You find a small band of kindred spirits. And then you talk a lot. You have wonderful conversations and learn about one another, and that gives the whole initiative strength.

This has certainly been my experience. I have found strong allies in a variety of contexts, and am an ally also to them. David is right to say that trying to implement systemic change on your own can be discouraging, and it is important to draw strength from others when times get rough, and celebrate when things go well.

4 Aiming for systemic development

Another big mistake was to concentrate only on one aspect of the system. I have now learnt how important it is to address all levels at the same time. It is important to show managers and policy-makers the potential use value of any initiative, so that they can assess it for themselves. Ultimately, one hopes, they will make it their own, so they have to be there at the beginning.

David Steeves continues:

> DS: From my perspective I work as many ways as humanly possible, so if I can work at the community level, if I can work at the level where there is a receiver of our care or our services, and if I can work at a political level, at a bureaucratic level, if I can work the volunteer side, and I do that too; so I think it's a matter of participating at as many different levels as possible to move an agenda forward. And I never know what kind of impact I'm going to have on people at the grass roots, or at the political level, and that's why I say it's very high risk. But then that is the joy of it.

Originally I concentrated on the practitioners and the success of their learning programmes. In those early days I had no clear vision of systemic development; the strategic learning happened because the wider vision began to develop. The vision refined into one of a coherent in-service provision which would constitute practitioner-generated whole organisational development. It would also provide what the Ontario Public School Teachers' Federation (1998) call a career-long professional pathway for people who wished to study their practice. As the vision became reality I began to understand the need to embed action research systemically. As well as teaching the programmes it was necessary to tap into existing structures and sources of energy. This meant developing working relationships with senior managers across a range of contexts, persuading them of the relevance of the work to organisational development, and finding ways to work collaboratively. This has now developed into a variety of activities: in-house in-service provision, meeting with individual groups of practitioners, supporting professional tutors, producing resources, and so on.

5 Involving senior management

For any organisational initiative to be successful it ultimately needs support and approval from senior management. I have supported colleagues (including managers) whose own managers have been hostile or indifferent to their work.

This has made life difficult, particularly for the colleague, but also for me in providing extra emotional and practical support.

I have learnt the importance of not rushing things. People need time to assimilate ideas and make them their own, particularly people in senior management positions. I have learnt to say enough and then leave. I realise that my enthusiasm to persuade people to listen could have been coercive. I have learnt to be discreet and tread gently. 'We all have corns,' says Dan Condren, a manager in Templemore.

Getting managerial backing for professional development initiatives means meeting with people on their territory, reassuring them that change will not cause undue disruption, that we always start small and proceed step by step. It also means showing the practical relevance of action research to wider policy issues and current research. This means ensuring that I am up to date, so I take pains to inform myself about issues, staying alert in conversations, attending conferences, reading informative material.

Working with senior management at systemic levels means presentations of a high calibre, provision of sufficient and appropriate literature, communicating the importance of the work. It means producing evidence to justify potential investment in the work. I write a good deal, finding every opportunity to promote practitioners' work. In this way high quality validated case study evidence is produced to show managers the quality of the work, and how practitioners are influencing their own workplaces.

Efforts have not always been successful. The work can be arduous, so it is important to have good faith and good allies who keep you going in time of need. Over time one builds up a track record of integrity; and that, combined with quality work from participants who show that they really are making a difference for good in their work settings, constitutes a strong reason for senior managers to listen.

The most powerful form of senior management support is when senior managers undertake their own action enquiries. This does not happen too often (though of course it sometimes does: see for example the 'Heads You Win Project' (James and Vince, 2000)); usually I consider myself fortunate if managers agree to support the work of participants. When it does happen, however, the benefits to organisational learning can be quite spectacular (see Chapter 11 of this book; see also Whitehead, 1994; Lomax, 1996).

6 Embedding action research within organisational development processes

Probably the most successful way of embedding action research in organisations is to locate it within already existing institutional structures and processes. Most organisations have development plans and appraisal processes. These tend to be seen as discrete structures into which people fit rather than processes which people do themselves (see Chapter 10). If action research implies personal professional development, self-evaluation and systematic peer validation, it constitutes an organising process structure and methodology for the implementation and evaluation of organisational development plans.

I work with several agencies in reframing existing organisational structures as action research processes. Managers help practitioners to identify their own needs and priorities, to develop personal and group action plans about how to meet them, and evaluate their outcomes (see also Oldroyd and Hall, 1997). This in turn can lead to the identification and solution of organisational needs through agreed action plans and evaluation strategies.

We develop specific strategies for this. We aim to provide in-house support systems for informal learning in the workplace. This takes the form, for example, of day-to-day guidance by peers acting as coaches or professional tutors; and also the setting up of formal and semi-formal gatherings such as at coffee times or scheduled meetings for practitioners to share best practice and seek advice from one another about problematic issues. It also takes the form of celebrations (for any reason that seems appropriate), in-house newsletters, social gatherings. An atmosphere of fun and good collegiality prevails. We aim consistently to develop conversational communities in a light-hearted (but consciously serious) way. We also develop formal in-service provision. Accreditation is available through our university contacts. At present I do all the teaching and administration myself; conversations are taking place with university-based partners to authorise work-based colleagues to deliver the programmes, but this is very slow work because of the ethos of market accountability in western education contexts and the anxious climates it generates. We believe it is possible however, and we keep trying.

7 Developing systemic in-service provision

It is important that people feel that their learning matters and is valued. Formal learning is valued through the accredited courses. Informal learning is also valued (see p. 249).

Courses take place around the island in different venues. On this model, the university is located in a variety of contexts, usually workplaces, but also in hotels and, in one instance, an inn. People are encouraged to work independently of me, but interdependently with one another. They develop telephone links, learning sets, friendship groupings. They regularly exchange letters, they read one another's work. Each person identifies a learning partner or two, and they telephone each other at agreed times, even if they have nothing to report. Participants work out their own network systems; home-grown strategies are always the best.

It is also important that informal learning is valued. The courses are based on the universities' own commitments to democracy and pluralistic practice, and are so structured that informal learning is valued. Professional portfolio work is encouraged and accredited, to promote reflection on experience, and to show how understanding can travel to other professional contexts (see Chapter 10). Teaching methodologies emphasise the responsibility of practitioners to engage in their own learning, and learn how to critique it, as well as the development of trust so that people do not feel intimidated by one another while they try out new kinds of thinking.

I have to pay tribute to colleagues working in institutionalised university settings who have developed these practitioner-based programmes, and who also support their implementation. In current market climates it is not easy for academics to retain strong educational values in the face of pressures to turn profits. The success of university programmes these days is judged increasingly in terms of profit. Colleagues working in formal contexts fight serious battles of their own, and also battles to support the work; and I have the deepest admiration for them that they withstand the grossest forms of market pressure and find ways collaboratively to support professional learning programmes which are based on the values of educational development for social benefit rather than institutional imperialism.

8 Developing the research base of professional knowledge

A powerful way to overcome cynicism is to produce work of such high calibre that critique is met with confidence and credibility. This means the production of objective evidence to show that practitioner research can have influence in organisational settings.

Professionalism is judged in terms of specific criteria such as care and best interest of clients and capacity to self-evaluate and correct (Carr and Kemmis, 1986; Hoyle and John, 1995). In claiming their professionalism, practitioners need to demonstrate that they achieve these criteria. If they cannot produce concrete evidence to support their claims to professional practice, they risk discredit.

Action research has today refined itself into a rigorous methodology with internally negotiated criteria and standards of judgement which are open to public critique (see Lomax, 1996; McNiff *et al.*, 1996). The production of action research accounts means that practitioners can produce validated evidence to show their own process of learning, and how that learning supports the educational development of those for whom they are responsible.

A good deal of research evidence exists in the action research literature to show professional practice in these terms (for example, Atweh *et al.*, 1998; Collins and McNiff, 1999; Hamilton, 1998; Lomax, 1996; McNiff and Collins, 1994; McNiff *et al.*, 2000; Russell and Korthagen, 1995; Whitehead, 1993). Also collections of case study material exist in the dissertations and theses that practitioners have submitted for their Masters and doctoral awards. Some of these are to be found in the Universities of Bath, Kingston, and the West of England. Much of this literature is still located in mainstream education contexts. Organisation studies and management learning need to build up strong bodies of validated accounts, to show how professionalism might be judged in terms of educational practices that lead to organisational development. Particularly in the field of organisation study, where business values are often in conflict with educational and social values, there is need for an emphasis on the educational research base of professionalism. Indeed, business development needs to be rethought in terms of organisational growth through professional education, rather than through control of production and its outcomes; and business competence needs to be rethought in terms of the degree to which companies can support education rather than make big profits.

9 *The courage to care*

I say throughout that management is rooted in human relationships. If we get the relationships right the outcomes will look after themselves.

I am learning about management. I care passionately about what I am doing, because I care about the people I am supporting, and I care about my own visions and values. My position as a manager is strengthened, I believe, because I see myself as a learner, in company with others whose learning I am supporting.

A colleague in Cork, Máire Áine Uí Aodha (2000), writes of the loneliness of the expert. When we position ourselves as those-who-know we place ourselves in intolerable spaces; the positioning moves us onto the high ground, which can be very cold and windy, not much warmth for the heart.

Caring however is a risky practice. It is risky for one's own personal security, because your care can be abused and you are sometimes left feeling rather foolish. It is a personal decision whether to commit, and we always need to be aware of the risks involved; but this is so of all relationships; no one comes with guarantees. It is also risky because care is not valued in dominant epistemologies or organisation theory. There the language is of abstraction, stripped of emotion and vulnerability, plain talk about objectivised practices and functional strategies, not about people and their pain.

In its weak version care manifests as getting along together, cooperative living for mutual survival (Axelrod, 1990). In its strong version care manifests as the development of mutually responsible relationships, reciprocally enacted through community, whose realisation can lead to social renewal through the generative transformational power of those caring relationships. The research community needs to address these issues much more so than at present – but that takes the energy to care in the first place, and is a personal commitment by theorists to change their own ways of thinking and the forms of theory they generate to understand the educative processes of personal-social renewal.

3 How is action research put to use in organisations?

Action research is a form of personal learning for social benefit, and is a practice undertaken collaboratively. It follows that if all participants were to do action research, an organisation would be a learning society driven by educational values. The vision of all participants doing action research can become a reality, as this book shows, but getting there can be difficult. Developing and sustaining communities of learners means recognising the problematics of how communities come into being, and the trade-offs involved to sustain them.

Constructing our identities in chosen communities

I said in Chapter 2 that people working together in community is a social practice which is politically constructed and potentially conflictual. I want to think about the idea of community here. The work of Hilde Lindemann Nelson (1995) provides a really nice framework.[1]

Writing from a feminist perspective in a nursing context, and also adopting a narrative approach to issues of ethics, she develops the most useful idea of found and chosen communities. A found community, she says, is one in which we find ourselves without choosing to be there, such as beginning a new job. In found communities the stories told set the paradigm; no one questions the right of dominant people to tell their dominant stories. Newcomers may accept these stories and adjust accordingly, or they can resist and develop counterstories.

Telling counterstories potentially generates a chosen community, a community in which people share the experience of living within the found community. These are communities which people form by choice. The stories they tell one another qualify as legitimate stories and enable them to imagine what it would be like to be members of a found community.

There is a constant dialectic between found and chosen communities. The dissident voices of chosen communities challenge the orthodoxies of found communities; yet there is an inherent danger that the chosen community will itself transform into a found community with elitist norms and prejudices, and exclude outsiders.

Nelson comments that communities of choice function 'as a moral space in which its members can examine what they do in the wider community'. Because nursing (and management) is a social practice 'the question, What is it to be a good nurse [or manager] has intimate connection with the question, What is it to be a good human being? For this reason, the moral space created is also a space for reflecting on one's personal identity and one's place in society' (p. 27).

Action research always has to be undertaken by choice. Action researchers come together as chosen communities in which they share their stories of learning. The sharing of stories promotes respectful listening, an attitude of care. The practice of sharing stories of experience manifests as educative relationships.

How do we understand ourselves in relation with others?

Within chosen communities we try hard to understand one another. This means trying to understand our relationships. Buber (1937) says we do this in terms of

---

1   I am grateful to Janice Huber for bringing this work to my attention.

how we see one another. Is another person 'you' or 'Thou' or 'it'? 'I' exist in relation to 'you'; the nature of our relationship is defined by the quality of our response to each other. 'You' may remain 'you', or 'you' may become 'Thou' (the German *Du*); and reciprocally 'I' may remain as your 'you', or 'I' might become 'Thou' to you. (That we are in relation does not in any way deny that there is something special and unrepeatable in my or your 'I'; each of us is and remains unique.)

How we respond to one another and so enable one another to construct our desired identities and decide the quality of our relationships is shaped by whether we see people as faceless figures, all of a type, or whether we see them as individuals. Nelson cites Andrea Dworkin's antinovel, *Mercy* (1991):

> The protagonist, Andrea, who has been raped, abused, and betrayed by men most of her life, takes karate lessons and becomes very good at kicking drunken homeless men to death. She refuses to perceive males as particular individuals, and rights the imbalance without any regard for the identity of those she kicks. As she puts it, 'I can't tell him from him from him.'

How are we in our organisations? Do we accept the need to tell him from him from him, or her from him from her? Do we accept that all people are different and this difference manifests not as a sameness but as individual uniqueness? A woman is not only a woman but also a partner, a manager, a nurse, black, underprivileged. A man is not only a man but also a worker, a father, white, marginalised. As soon as we put a face on others we bring us both into a potential relationship of 'I–Thou', where we are prepared to share our humanity and learn from each other in an educative relationship. Chosen communities are inevitably educative ones, communities in which we help one another to learn.

What kind of theories are appropriate to describe and explain the formation of community? Not traditional ones with technical rational epistemologies. We need new dialectical ways of thinking which see relationships and convergences, which mirror the coming together of people. We need to explore new forms of expression to test our theories, and to have interesting conversations about how we come to understand what we are doing. We need to talk with one another. Communities of action researchers are inevitably conversational communities, and have considerable potential as fields of organisational influence for good.

4 What are the implications for new theories of organisation as theories of conversational communities?

Jean Clandinin is Director of the Centre for Research for Teacher Education and Development at the University of Alberta. We talked about what she does to create success for the Centre.

JM: You create spaces for people.

JC: Yes. It's pushing back borders that sometimes constrain us, allowing people to do the work that they want to do.

JM: How do you create success? How do you understand success?

JC: In some contradictory ways, the work is successful when there are tensions. We should be worried when there is no tension. If we are not making other people nervous, then I know we are not being very successful, because that means we are buying into the dominant university story and language – 'This is what universities should do, the production of knowledge, living life on the high ground.' But that's a hard way to live, Jean.

JM: Yes, you are constantly on the brink.

JC: Well, I suppose we move, hopefully in an educative way.

JM: So what do you do in practice to nurture success?

JC: You know, the year goes in cycles, both natural years and institutional years. One of the things I notice about this time of the year (late November) is that people start to grumble about one another. For me, it is successful if I can remind people, or they can remind each other, that what is important is trying to listen to the other's story and really hear it, if they can engage in a conversation. The acid test is whether people are able to talk with one another.

JM: You spend a lot of time simply being with people. In an earlier time of my life I would have thought, Jean is wasting an awful lot of time. She should be at her desk, writing reports, answering the telephone, running around doing jobs, but she's actually spending time with people in an unhurried, very relaxed, very welcoming way.

JC: That's how people see me, you know. Sometimes inside I'm thinking, How can anyone see this person, who is feeling like this with forty-two deadlines to meet, as relaxed? I think I must have a very good cover story going!

JM: That's the image you do project, and you must work very hard at it.

JC: Yes. I have to tell you a story. Some time ago I worked with a group of principals. They wanted me to help them think about their administrative practices. At first I told them I wouldn't do it. They wanted me to come out and talk at them, and I said, No, I don't do that. One shot things are not for me. You can't pay me enough money. But if you will work with me for three years, and get your district to make that commitment, and if you will make that commitment to getting together and really talking about your practice in thoughtful ways, and meeting in between times and writing about what you are doing, then I'll work with you. Now these were experienced administrators. One of them was a woman called B. who is just amazing. She's a very experienced principal. She told a story that unfolded over the course of a year. At the beginning of the year she said, 'I'm so frustrated. There is a visitors' counter in the school office and I seem to spend all my time at it. How do I get my work done?' By the end of the year she was saying, 'Now I see that my work *is* the conversation. That is what is important in my work.' That was really powerful for me, because in some ways, that's my work, too. If my work at the Centre is about making spaces, then my work has to be about those conversations, because it shows people how to engage with one another, it keeps people engaged in doing their own work. It does so many things, and that is my work. It's also why I have a little hiding office where I write and think, because I don't think my whole academic life is about that. But for some managers it is. Some people could say, 'What I did was talk to people today,' and they would be telling a story of a professional life well lived.

JM: It's the living engagement. That's what I'm trying to show in this book. Management as a lived process of being in relationship. Organisation theory is about people in relationship.

JC: If I think about the Centre, it's all about people in relationship, and that ethic of care and a sense of responsibility to the other, and to ourselves. It's all about how we have a conversation. For me, that is what organisation theory should be about, how we make those kinds of spaces, how we have those conversations.

It might seem a far cry from caring conversations in a professional education centre to rolling back the worst effects of free markets, yet the distance is minimal; in fact, it is no distance at all. The methodology for successful living in community is a methodology of care, as it manifests in conversations and responsible relationships. The value that underpins successful living in community is respect for other people, respect for their right to be the person they want to be, to think their own thoughts.

It is unlikely that societies will ever be anything but agonistic. It is, however, part of the potential of new theories of organisation that they will show the way to social renewal, and provide explanations of best practice, to enable us to live with greater tolerance and kindness than in the past. This will not happen if we are content to stay with abstract theory as a dominant epistemology of practice.

Changing one's theory is much more than changing one's clothes or buying a new car. It actually means changing the way one looks at oneself and the world. To what extent are we prepared to endorse cruel practices by remaining silent? To what extent will we reinforce the belief that we are not capable of speaking for ourselves by dodging the issue and not challenging?

I said above that business organisations have a social responsibility to use their financial resources to restore the communities and earth resources that have so far stood the cost of corporations' success. It is perfectly possible to reverse the trends of the free market and to work consistently to regenerate a sense of local community. There is a huge literature on how corporations and governments need to develop social and environmental awareness, to resist further trends towards globalisation and regenerate local business to avoid further disruption, and work consistently towards community cohesion; as well as develop new technologies to nurture the earth and attempt to reverse the trends towards planetary disintegration. The grand narratives however need to be enacted at local level. We need to return to our roots and recognise ourselves as individuals living and talking with others, trying to get through as best we can. We might not always get it right, but the struggle enables us to stay aware of our humanity and our need for one another.

All the talk on earth will not have any effect unless people at local level recognise that they do have the power and potential to make a difference for good, to change systems and the attitudes and practices that sustain them. It is perfectly possible for people in community, acting with social intent, to generate new local and world orders. It needs confidence and the will to do it. Accepting responsibility for one's own learning and resolving to improve practice for the benefit of others are straightforward starting points.

It also needs academics to endorse the legitimacy of new theories of organisation as communities in conversation. Academics, whose work it is to generate theory, need to uncover and challenge unjust practices that lead to social disintegration and the destruction of community. They need to generate theories about how new forms of thinking and living will lead to better, more sustainable futures. They need to show the importance of practitioners' theories of practice; and to see themselves as practitioners, finding new creative ways to resolve problems of living. They need to have good conversations with one another, recognising all ideological positioning as worthy of respect and critique.

In terms of how organisation is theorised, they need to create and legitimate theories which show people in caring relationships with one another. They need to develop those relationships themselves. Unless the form of theory changes, the practices the theory endorses will stay the same. Unless the practices change, they will not generate new theories and epistemologies of practice.

Academics in university settings are potentially our best teachers. We can learn much from them. At the moment dominant theories are teaching us how to work destructively against the basic human needs for attachment and peaceful living. The real battle for living begins with the battle for ideas, with systems of knowledge and how they are kept in place. Perhaps, through the battles, we will find new integrated forms of knowing and living, but we are not there yet.

10 New theories of organisation

In *Blackfoot Physics* (1996), physicist David Peat tells the story of how he was invited to visit with the Blackfoot tribe to be part of a special celebration ceremony. He arrived at the pre-arranged time, only to find that nothing was happening. Some people were filtering into the meeting grounds, but no special activity seemed to be taking place. He waited. A few days later still nothing was happening. People continued to arrive, chat, connect with one another, enjoy themselves, but no ceremony was taking place. In growing irritation he began to question people: 'Am I in the right place? Did I get the date right? Is something going to happen?' He was greeted with equanimity and the polite advice to be patient.

Peat analyses his own behaviour and response. Coming as he did from an education in the western intellectual tradition, he expected a special event to be organised, a clearly structured event with a beginning and end. Instead he encountered a long loose process of people engaging with one another, no beginning, no end, just the process. He began slowly to realise that people arriving, connecting and departing *was* the event. People in relationship *were* the ceremony. The joy of connecting was both what was celebrated and how it was celebrated.

Peat comments on how different epistemologies and intellectual traditions underpin both his own expectations, and also the character of the celebration. He was expecting a 'thing'; instead he received an invitation to engage in a lived process.

I wonder what expectations were in your mind when you picked up this book. Did you expect to find a theory, neatly set out, to offer advice on how organisation and management should be understood? If so, like David Peat, you are probably still wondering when the main event is going to happen. What you have encountered and become part of is a process of learning, including your own. If you have stayed with me until now, you are aware of how this book constitutes a story of stories, and how those stories are stories of learning. As you read this, you are learning.

Where is the theory? The theory is in the stories, as they tell lives. The theory is in the process. People create their own theories through their lives, and they explain (theorise) their lives through story. All processes are fluid, non-static, and changing, and that is the form of the theory, too. The theory develops as the story unfolds. These stories tell of how people worked out answers to their own questions of practice, checked these answers with one another, modified their opinion, and went on in new ways. They tell of how people learned about what they were doing, and used this learning to help others. This, I hope, has been my story, and I hope I have encouraged other people to tell their stories of how they do the same. The individual stories tell of the development of personal epistemologies of practice. The wider framework story shows the development of a new body of work, as people have mutually influenced one another's thinking so that their work practice is a constant process of gradual improvement. This constitutes a new theory of people in conversational relationship with one another.

This chapter still does not set out a theory as an artefact. It sets out an explanation for how theory itself needs to be theorised as a process if it is to help people understand their own living realities. David Peat had to change his mindset in order to understand the experience he was engaging in, and also to understand how he was to make sense of it all. So do we, in getting to grips with the idea of new theories of organisation, and how they can influence organisational practice. Our theories are not set out in any one document; they are contained in our lives. When we tell the stories that we live by (Connelly and Clandinin, 1999), we are setting out our theories in a narratively contextualised way.

1 What is the nature of new theories of organisation?

The most important thing to remember about organisations is that they are not structures; they are people. Take away the structures and you still have organisations. Take away the people and you have none. Theories of organisation are theories of people's lives. Traditional theories of organisation are theories about places. New theories of organisation are story-theories by people for people.

As I have said throughout, people in community constitute a powerful force for social renewal. They can renew the society which is their organisation by taking care with their own practice in relation with others, and they can renew wider society by influencing other contexts. Making sense of their lives in organisational contexts and showing their potential for social good constitutes people's living theories of organisation. The theories have explanatory power both to conceptualise organisation as people in developmental and collaborative relation with one other, as well as evolutionary potential to explain the process of their organisational development. Organisation theory constitutes the descriptions and explanations that people offer for how they understand and improve their lives in the service of others in organisational contexts. Organisation theory has the potential to transform into a social theory with far-reaching implications for world orders. Chomksy has written (see Chomsky, 1988) that it would be possible to create a science of what aspects of human nature can lead to a better society. I like to think we are on that track here.

New theories of organisation are living theories. They show the process of people working together. The theory is not an abstract concept which is applied to practice. It is contained within the practice, as people ask, 'How do I understand and develop my work?' The theory is embodied in people's lives as they reflect on action in action, and attempt to make sense of what they are doing. The theory is generated in and through practice, evaluated within the new practice, and modified in the light of the evaluation to generate new practice. The content of the theory is potentially always changing, congruent with its transformational form. The content of a manager's theory may develop, for example, as she realises that she needs to develop new strategies in a particular area. The evolutionary form of her theory accommodates the shifting nature of the practice.

Living theories are always generative and transformational. They enable people to change their minds and practices as they attempt to live out their values more fully. The stories honour the values base of human living, and encourage people to develop high levels of personal-social awareness. These are theories of personal and social living, which address Plato's questions of 'How should we be?' and 'How should we live together?'

A good example of this is found in the work of James Finnegan (2000) as he investigates how he can facilitate more democratic actions in his classroom. In addressing issues of how he can work at improving his teaching and helping his sixth-form (17–18-year-old students) to improve their learning, he contends that he is creating his own educational theory (Whitehead, 1993). Critically reflecting on his own work, on how effective he is as a teacher in encouraging democratic practices, and why he can justifiably claim to be effective, he comments:

> Claiming to know my own educational theory, as a teacher, is clearly a political issue, or to say it differently, an issue of power. My own argument, I maintain, emanates from a position of reasonable and responsible self-advocacy where I account for my own changing practices and for my own growing understanding of those changing practices.
>
> (Hopkins, 1993: 4; Carr and Kemmis, 1986: 180)

The value of this kind of work is recognised by the Editor of *Irish Educational Studies*, the journal in which Finnegan's work appears. He writes:

> Finnegan ... has the courage to take the considerable risk of holding his own practice of teaching ... up to critical scrutiny and of involving colleagues and students as critical friends in the process. This action research study advocates the paper's substantive focus and method as means of improving the quality of teaching and learning as well as advancing democracy in schools.
>
> (Sugrue, 2000: ix)

How should we be and how should we live together? James Finnegan is one person who helps us find answers.

The development of organisation theory

I have said throughout that organisations should provide opportunities for people to come together on an equal footing to pursue commonly agreed goals. From a narrow perspective of corporatist profit or imperialism, those goals would be the continuation of policies and practices which ensure the security that corporations need to continue their pursuit of profit and colonisation. From a more humanitarian and educational perspective, the goals would be the creation of democratic forms of engagement which would encourage popular participation in decision-making at local and systemic levels. The nature and purpose of organisation theory on this view assumes an educational mandate. If people are to participate in decision-making, if organisations are to be sites of learning, what needs to be learnt to turn the values into realities? How does the high-sounding rhetoric become a reality of organisational life?

I reflect on my own experience, of how I have resisted efforts, of both a persuasive and a coercive nature, to bring me into line with institutional thinking. In retrospect I remember occasions when it would have been much easier to give in to the pressure to be obedient. I could have not spoken out at conferences and challenged dominant jurassic perspectives. I could have not challenged decisions about the organisation of my teaching. I could have not insisted on remaining independent, and so secured the necessary freedom to maintain the educational ethic of my practice. So many things I could have not done, but how well do we live with ourselves in the light of the decisions we make about what is worth living for.

What have I done? I have lived with dignity, staying true to my own rhetoric. I have encouraged others to do the same. I am, and always will be, a teacher. I have encouraged participation in decision-making at local and systemic levels. I have protected the educational ethic of the organisation which I have helped to create. I have presented my own educational theory of organisation in a variety of contexts and using a range of forms of expression: in my daily lived practice; in this book; in presentations and conversations; and, most importantly, in the conversations with people with whom I am in caring relationship. It is up to them now to show how the theory lives in their own lives as they aim to improve the quality of their own understanding for the benefit of others (see Part IV).

2 How are new theories of organisation generated?

In setting out his agenda for the new scholarship, Boyer (1990) identifies four forms of scholarship appropriate to the task: the scholarship of discovery (the commitment to knowledge for its own sake, to freedom of enquiry and following, in a disciplined fashion, an investigation wherever it may lead); the scholarship of integration (giving meaning to isolated facts, putting them in perspective, making connections across the disciplines); the scholarship of application (theory and practice interact and one renews the other); and the scholarship of teaching (teaching both educates and entices future scholars) (pp. 17–25).

Any theory that claims to be informed by the values of the new scholarship therefore needs to demonstrate the elements of discovery, integration, application and teaching. To what extent might a new theory of organisation fulfil these requirements? Further, how might the theory be validated, and what kinds of criteria and standards of judgement will be used to do so?

Theories of organisation are the stories people tell of their work in organisational contexts, using a variety of forms of representation to present the stories. The form of theory is therefore narrative. The theory is communicated in a contextualised way (as in this book). As the new scholarship suggests, the stories show the development of personal epistemologies of practice. These epistemologies of practice constitute narratives of practitioners' experience and accountability, as people ask one another reciprocally, 'How can I help you?' These new theories contribute to a new professionalism. On this view, professionalism is no longer an abstract concept that can be judged by checklists and indicators, but a caring practice that can be judged in terms of whether or not a practitioner made a difference for good in other people's lives. Professionalism becomes a morally committed praxis which demonstrates the scholarships of discovery, integration, application and teaching.

New theories of management exist as part of new organisational theory. They show management as an educative practice which aims to help people develop the kinds of relationships which will help them learn and grow. The theories appear as narrative self-studies as managers tell their stories of how they helped people to develop educative relationships, and they contain the evidence of other people's stories which confirm that the stories are authentic. There is clear evidence of the development of learning. Such collections of educational narratives can contribute to a body of new educational organisational knowledge which will have significant influence in wider contexts of enquiry. The literature of new era organisations is already moving in this direction. Narrative action research needs now to develop a strong theoretical framework to lend academic credibility to its commitment to social renewal and show the solid research base of professionalism.

Accounting for our professionalism

How will these stories be judged? What criteria and standards of judgement do we need to develop to determine their validity and legitimacy? This is a sticking point in current debates about the legitimacy of personal theories. Personal theories are manifestations of the new scholarship in practice. Difficulties arise when they are judged by traditionalists who use the criteria and standards of judgement of old theories of scholarship. Thus Clarke (1992) among others raises questions around the theoretical basis of action research because the stories do not meet the normative criteria of replicability and generalisability. Of course they do not. The criteria are not appropriate for judging the quality of action research accounts. One does not judge the legitimacy of metric measurements using imperial gauges, nor the quality of digital technology using the criteria of analogue technology. These are different realms of discourse, judged in terms of their own internal criteria and in terms of the purposes for which they were created. We do not invite bricklayers to judge the quality of steel by its potential to act as brick. Different areas of enquiry have their own internal criteria and their quality is assessed using standards of judgement which set out the expectations of different communities.

The development of criteria and standards of judgement are social and cultural practices which evolve over time. They are also inevitably political as people negotiate which ones they think are most appropriate. Richard Winter among others has done significant work here. In 1989 he suggested six principles for conducting action research. He says that accounts should demonstrate reflexivity and dialectical critique; action research should act as a collaborative resource and demonstrate risk; the process should show a pluralist commitment and the transformation of theory and practice. The world of action research is caught up in this developmental process of negotiating acceptable criteria right now, and debates are likely to continue for some time. The irony is of course that by the time criteria are agreed, the concepts and practices of action research will probably have moved on.

I want to suggest that the new scholarship requires new kinds of criteria and new standards of judgement. The criteria themselves need to be transformational. The criteria would focus on the integration of theory and practice and its evolutionary potential for transforming personal-social lives for good. In their practice, do practitioners live their values in a way that those with whom they are in relation can say that their lives are improved? Are practitioners able to theorise their practice to show a developmental process for themselves and others? Do they show the reality of their knowing in action, and their reflection on knowing in action, and how they used this reflection to modify their practice? Do they show how their own living constitutes a theory of personal-social improvement? Are they able to produce evidence for their theories as told in the stories of others with whom they are in relation? Can they validate these claims against the best critique of others who might or might not be in sympathy with the work? Can they show the evolutionary potential within their theories which allows for revisiting and rethinking practice and reflection? Can they show the potential for influence within their theories for wider social renewal? Whitehead (2000: 99) explains the nature of these kinds of criteria:

> What makes the educational standards of reflective practitioners differ from traditional, 'linguistic' standards is that the living standards are embodied in the lives of practitioners and require ostensive definition to communicate their meanings. I am indebted to Moira Laidlaw for the insight that the meanings of the values I use as my educational standards are themselves living and developmental in the course of their emergence in practice (Laidlaw, 1996).

Perhaps a major criterion is whether practitioners can set their own criteria, and justify their choice by showing how the criteria act as legitimation points in their narratives of practice (see Lomax, 1994). People who develop the confidence to stand over their work and show its use value in other people's lives are, I think, demonstrating their accountability for practice. This for me is the nature of professionalism.

Such criteria set new standards for what counts as professional practice, and are a long way from the normative checklists of the Management Charter Initiative (MCI) (1991) or Teacher Training Agency (TTA) (1998). They are much harder to achieve, because they call for real engagement by all; they are not a functional activity of ticking boxes. The assessment process itself should be educational, one which holds the potential for growth for all participants. The standards of judgement used are not the technical rational ones of whether or not people perform to a certain level – behaviourist standards which simply expect people to perform in a required way, and prioritise skills over people. In the old scholarship, professionalism is judged in terms of technical excellence, 'can do'. In the new scholarship, new standards of judgement are based on the values and life commitments that people bring to their practice and whether they have contributed to another's well-being.

It has to be acknowledged that anyone undertaking formal or semi-formal action enquiries these days is therefore faced with a daunting task. Because technical rational knowledge is still the dominant university epistemology, and universities are still the major accrediting bodies, traditional criteria still apply (see Chapter 4). There is still an expectation that people will produce reports that demonstrate conventional academic rigour, as well as fulfil the kinds of criteria outlined here, not easy in anyone's terms. Yet this is what happens in the networks associated with colleagues who are pioneering work in the new scholarship. For example, Chapter 12 by Jackie Delong is drawn from her doctoral work undertaken at the University of Bath. Jackie meets both conventional and newer forms of criteria, as she accounts for her own practice as a manager and educational leader. Carmel Lillis does the same in Chapter 13, as she sets out her explanations for practice as constituted in her doctoral work. More of the same are needed.

Assessing professionalism

On this view, assessing professionalism means assessing learning of a kind that shows how personal understanding has deepened through reflection, and how that understanding now works for other people's interests. This cannot be done via a competences approach that tests for skills and behaviours, and which ignores the values base of practice and its purposes. It can be done through the production and critical scrutiny of practice, which shows in a narrative way how people managed to improve their work.

Considerable pressure is brought to bear these days to test professionalism within the technical rational frameworks of behavioural capacity (MCI, 1991; TTA, 1998). Some organisations have never known any other way. Such forms of assessment perpetuate the theory–practice gap, the reification of abstract knowledge, and the hierarchical nature of assessment procedures.

More equitable and educational ways exist. I would like to discuss two of them here, and show how they demonstrate the values of the new scholarship.

Professional portfolios

The accredited programmes in Ireland accept the production of professional portfolios as part of a Masters award. These portfolios are not an accumulation only of descriptions of activities. They are personal narratives that constitute descriptions and explanations of practice, activities and reflections on those activities. It is straightforward enough to say what one has done. It is more difficult to reflect on the activity and show the learning that has arisen from it. It is also difficult to produce an account that shows how the learning impacts on current professional practice so that practice changes in educational directions. To date seventy Masters awards have been granted for study undertaken through taught programmes which also recognise and value personal professional learning in a variety of contexts.

The same approach is evident in the guided doctorate programmes. All participants are encouraged to observe and reflect on their work, and produce reflective accounts to show the development of educative practices. These are not only personal narratives. They show the development of personal theories of practice which are critically tested against existing theory.

Checking the authenticity and rigour of the original claims to knowledge as embodied in the work is a stringent process. An expectation exists that all participants will present their work as formative evaluative accounts of practice to their peers, as an ongoing part of courses. The group acts as a critical validation group, to agree that the claims to knowledge are legitimate, or to suggest possible new courses of action. The group always acts in a supportive way, but its function is also to critique and advise. We value one another, and we value the authenticity and internal validity of claims to knowledge. We tell truth with kindness. Our practical ethic of care ensures that we protect one another's emergent thinking while urging one another to reframe questions or rethink conclusions (see Lomax, 1999). By the time the accounts are submitted for final approval through the formal university accrediting procedures, they have already been through a rigorous process of reworking through the peer evaluation process.

Educational values inform the whole process.

1   In valuing previous learning, and also experiential learning, it is recognised that learning is not only a feature of formal taught courses, or happens only in official contexts. Learning is learning in all life contexts. The purpose of learning is not to pass an examination; it is to improve the quality of life for someone somewhere.

2   It is recognised that assessment practices are not hierarchical or abstract. They should be educational for all parties. In the process described all

participants learn, both about validating the contents of accounts, and about educative practices with one another. How we are counts as much as what we produce. This understanding carries over to workplaces.

3   The assessment practice therefore becomes a feature of ongoing personal and collective learning. The individual learns about their work by offering it for validation by their peers. Peers learn about their work, both by listening to the account and also by monitoring their own response to the account. The whole process can be a powerful collaborative learning experience.

4   When professionals prepare their portfolios of learning, they readily see the relevance to those whom they are supporting. A number of participants whom I support have already implemented the same practices in their workplaces. Teachers, for example, encourage their students to present their portfolios (for example, C. Buckley, 2000; M. Buckley, 2000; Ní Murchú, 2000; Ó Muimhneacháin, 2000); managers work with staffs to do the same (O'Brien, 2000; Ryan, 2000). This, I think, shows the generative transformational capacity of educational enquiry.

Whether or not portfolio work continues to be accepted as part of degree-bearing professional development programmes is a matter of the politics of knowledge. The dominant epistemology does not recognise personal accounts of practice; the new epistemology does. In the battle for educational ideas we need not only to produce conceptual arguments to show the use value of professional accounts (as I am doing at this point). We also need to build up bodies of case study work to show their use value and educational potential (as shown throughout the book).

Appraisal systems

Traditional approaches regard appraisal from a technical-functional perspective of hierarchically organised inspection processes which are initiated by managers. Appraisal is something that A does to B. Organisational change is assumed to reside in organisational systems rather than in people, and capacity to judge its effectiveness is assumed to be a managerial property rather than the responsibility of practitioners themselves. This approach assumes that practitioners are not able to think for themselves (James, 1991) and not capable of accepting the responsibility for their own work.

Staff appraisal is another area which is largely theorised in a conceptual way (see for example Poster and Poster, 1997). Models abound to show the uses of appraisal and strategies for its implementation. Some of these unfortunately communicate messages that appraisal is a concept to be applied to practice, rather than an integral aspect of reflective practice itself.

In asking the question, 'How do I improve my work?', a practitioner is deliberately making practice problematic and consciously looking for ways in which the work can be a living-out of values. Appraisal is not an add-on; it is at the heart of any practice that counts as professional, in that a practitioner evaluates what they are doing and its potential benefit in the lives of others. Appraisal is not something done unto others, but a practice undertaken by practitioners themselves in their efforts to improve their work. This is particularly powerful when it is enacted by managers and other educational leaders.

Two initiatives with which I am involved illustrate this. The first is from Ireland. In 1999, Beneavin De La Salle College in Dublin appointed a new principal, Joe Twomey, and a new deputy principal, Derek O'Donoghue. Having completed a year in their posts, Derek and Joe intend to begin a process of school-based evaluation, starting with an evaluation of their own work. They intend systematically to evaluate their practice since their appointments to see where they have come from, where they are now, and where they feel they ought to be going. They want to establish whether or not they are living their educational values in their practice. The second example is from the 'Heads You Win' Project in Wales, where a group of ten principals, supported by the University of Glamorgan and the Education Support and Inspection Service that serves the local education authorities neighbouring the university, have all undertaken to investigate their practice as headteachers. They are monitoring their practice in terms of whether they are exercising educational leadership in a way that will positively influence the quality of education for teachers and their pupils in classrooms with particular relevance to the quality of literacy, numeracy and the use of Information and Communication Technology (see James and Vince, 2000). Participants' reports of their experience of being involved in the project indicate that they would have been doing the work in any case, but their involvement in the project offered additional support, and also the opportunity critically to reflect on and theorise their practice in a focused way. Their experience suggests that their own focus on evaluating their practice is encouraging staffs to do the same.

Initiatives such as this, which are rooted in the commitment of individual practitioners to accept the responsibility for the quality of their work, are what lead to educational progress at local and wider levels. Appraisal and evaluation are not additional to day-to-day working; they are the patina of quality which emerges as participants concentrate on showing how they are consciously reflecting on what they are doing to maintain standards of educational excellence.

3 How are new theories of organisation put to use?

The accounts that people produce do not appear out of thin air. They are rooted in practice. Practice is located in developmental organisational processes, and this is where new theories of organisation can have a significant impact, because they constitute not only personal but also organisational development plans and evaluative reports.

There is considerable emphasis these days on producing organisational development plans. Senior managers are urged to produce development plans which will identify targets, show anticipated organisational growth, and set out action plans for the implementation of strategies to accomplish this. They are also urged to identify ways in which they will evaluate successful progress. A recent Government of Ireland (1999a) plan shows this process. It asks questions such as

> Where are we now?
> Where do we want to be?
> How will we get there?
> How will we check whether we are getting there?
> How will we know if we have got there?

The document in question is specifically for educational settings: it is however an example that is appropriate to all organisation contexts.

Organisational development plans sometimes consolidate as mission statements or (say) three-year action plans. I have been present at corporate discussions about mission statements, often characterised by the expenditure of a good deal of energy in finding the correct form of words to communicate what the organisation hopes to do. The agreed form of words can often signal action's end. Once statements of intent are produced and agreed, people tend to think that there is no more to be done. The mission statement and the glossy brochure are there; things will happen now.

This is often not the case. Rhetoric needs to be accompanied by action, and action by evaluation. Rhetoric without action, and action without evaluation are irresponsible. Many organisations, however, become paralysed simply because they do not know what to do next. A main course of action then is to call in an outside evaluator to do the job.

Paralysis happens because of the inert nature of technical rational epistemologies. The technical rational tendency to see organisations as fixed structures, and development plans as enshrined in the words of brochures and mission statements, demonstrates the same mindset that sees organisations as abstract entities. Everything is 'out there' – the organisation, the brochure, the development plan. They all exist as external objects. The idea that a development plan needs to be produced often brings to mind words on paper. The plan exists on the paper; it is not alive. This kind of thinking is well borne out in the same Government of Ireland document (1999a: 34), where I read:

> Format of the … Plan
>   The … plan can be formulated as:
> • A single cohesive document, or
> • A series of related documents, or
> • A central comprehensive document and a range of booklets for various
>   constituent groups
> • A central document dealing with the relatively permanent features of
>   the [organisation] and a separate document on the developmental aspects
>   of the plan.

This kind of statement, I suspect, appears in business and civil service documents too.

Where are the people? Where are the lived processes? An organisation is not a place; it is people. A organisational plan is not a piece of paper; it is people's plans for their lives.

Organisations are people. Organisations are us. When we speak about development plans we are speaking about us, and how we hope to develop our work. Development plans are how people make sense of their work to improve it. Organisational development plans are how we real people aim to live, and what we hope to do, in organisational contexts. When we speak about organisational goals, these are what we hope to achieve in collaboration with others. Evaluation of development plans means checking to see whether we are living in the direction of our values, whether our practice is influencing others for good, or whether we need to rethink. Development plans are not words on paper; they are living processes.

In Schön's language of the topology of professional practice (1995), brochures and mission statements are produced on the high ground. An organisation's visions and goals are set out in the clean sanitised air. Sometimes organisations pay researchers good sums of money to produce their mission statements or write an impressive brochure. The researchers who do this are regarded as 'real' researchers. Prestige hangs on the quality of the statement or publication. Practice however goes on in the swampy lowlands. Practice is not called research but regarded simply as getting through the day. Yet organisational development happens only in practice. Where else can it happen? Organisational development happens as real people carefully observe themselves and one another in action, imagine how they might do things better, collaboratively work to create better futures. Organisational evaluation happens when people reflect on practice, imagine alternative ways, try them out, and check to see whether they are having the desired effect. This is also called learning. Organisational evaluation is learning from experience and doing things in different, better ways.

This is of course action research. Organisational development and evaluation, when organisation is seen as people, cannot be anything else.

When people reflect on practice they generate their own theories. These can be theories of management, of education, of practice, of organisation. We are generating theories all the time; it is part of the process of learning. The theories we generate about our lives in organisational contexts are our theories of organisation. People's theories are the real development plans. When managers are called on to produce development plans, the obvious thing to do is talk with other people, remembering though Schön's aphorism that organisational learning means learning for *all*, managers included.

Possibly the hardest thing for corporations to do is acknowledge that this is the case. To acknowledge that practice is real research, that practitioners are legitimate researchers, that organisational development is people imagining ways to create their own futures, and that evaluation is people reflecting on their emergent practice, means acknowledging the validity of personal knowledge as the basis of organisational success. This means adopting a form of epistemology that is not currently favoured in institutional life. Board room occupants still tend to move towards the high ground and its technical rational epistemologies; there is still a tendency to see a corporate plan as words and diagrams on glossy paper. Such published statements do not serve organisations well. Paper tears and print fades. Brochures get lost or used as notepads. Words are forgotten. Visions and values, however, live on in real practices.

If we are serious about investing in people we need to invest. It is easy enough to invest money; it is much harder to invest faith. This is what needs to be done. Managers need to have faith in themselves and in the people they support that the answers are already in the practice. Organisations as abstract structures do not develop; people do. All people in organisations need encouragement to produce their own developmental theories of practice. Planning for organisational development means planning how to encourage maximum participation of people undertaking action research collaboratively.

4 What are the potential implications for organisation theory as a theory of research-based professionalism?

Theories of organisation are not only for local organisations. I believe that organisations have potential for wider social influence; consequently theories of organisation potentially go beyond local boundaries into global arenas. New theories of organisation have the generative capacity not only for the development of individual organisations but also for social renewal – that is, of course, assuming that organisations wish both to develop the whole organisation and to exercise their potential to contribute to wider social development. The social capacity depends on political will. Whether or not we wish to change situations however depends on the epistemology we use and how it represents our political intent.

The dominant organisation epistemology is technical rationality; but organisations can get stuck in the mud of their own epistemology. Once a system becomes set in its ways and no longer seeks out new opportunities, it begins to die. This is the kind of heat death explained by the Second Law of Thermodynamics. This Law states that a closed system deliberately works towards closure, a state of equilibrium. As the system wears down it gives off energy that can never be retrieved. When it reaches its desired end state of equilibrium it has used up its productive energy and no longer has the capacity to change. The image is of a slow decline towards a stable, non-productive state of inertia. This is the image many people have of work (and indeed of life), that it is a long slow process towards retirement or death.

Some people have no choice in these matters. The works of Toni Morrison and Franz Fanon well describe experiences of people for whom the only release from a miserable life is death; and the theme of despair also appears in organisation studies (for example, Morgan, 1997a: ch. 7). For many young people, school is a time of great pain and disillusionment, a place to escape from (see for example, Goodson and Dowbiggin, 1990; and McLaren, 1995: ch. 2, for discussions on the creation of 'docile bodies'). Many of us however do have choices. It is what we do with those choices that counts.

The image of moving towards closure, whether voluntarily or not, is also the image of technical rationality. The purpose of this kind of research is to control reality as a stable state, to predict potential turbulence which may introduce disequilibrium and control for it. This may also involve factoring it out entirely. Such philosophies provide the staple diet for traditional corporations, who instruct their managers to identify potential sources of disequilibrium and initiate correctives to maintain stability. The same practice travels to social and political practices: so-called dissidents and anarchists are identified as threatening the social order and subjected to corrective measures. History is peopled by those who have been weeded out, scapegoated and eliminated to preserve an established status quo.

There is significant evidence on a range of scientific and social fronts that disequilibrium is a feature of open living systems. The scientific evidence exists in the work of scientists such as Plank, Jantsch, Bohr and Heisenberg, who demonstrated that dynamic systems move towards increasing instability, or chaos, not towards closure. The social evidence exists in the disintegration of social orders that attempt to impose autocratic forms of control, manifested perhaps most spectacularly in the collapse of the Berlin Wall. The spontaneously self-generating patterns of Julia Set fractal images shows the inexorable movement towards self-generating creativity, and these metaphors serve well to describe the capacity of the human spirit for self-renewal. In early systems theory, systems were seen and studied as structures; in more recent approaches, systems are seen as processes. Structures are static; processes are mobile. Organisations on the move show their commitment to the free movement and growth of people.

Technical rational forms actively work towards the presentation of stasis, not only to support a view of organisations as structures, but also to support the dominant technicist business worldview which is concerned with preserving the hegemony of a privileged elite and ensuring the means of their survival, often at the expense of the survival of others. A narrow view of economics as monetarism, and organisational purpose as income generation, serves to secure the tenure of the elites for whom technical rationality becomes a powerful resource, not to be ceded gracefully.

It is very difficult to change the way one thinks. It calls first for an awareness of one's own way of thinking, an evaluation of that thinking in light of one's own values system, and an openness to personal renewal to change the thinking. Changing one's way of thinking is I suspect impossible for those who are not aware of the need to change, or are possibly aware but who don't want to change. Many of us are secure in our own situated contexts and do not want to think in different ways. Even if we are aware that we could change, new untried forms are potentially risky, so it is much easier to stay as we are.

What can I say to those who do not see the need for living theories of organisation, and stay with safe propositional forms; who do not link the idea of organisational development with social renewal? I say that they are living in a fantasy world which perhaps they deliberately create themselves. The world of real organisation practice actually is moving in new directions; the world of abstract theory is lagging behind. Those who stay with abstract theory are creating themselves as a new generation of dinosaurs, hoping to dominate the planet but nurturing their own demise.

Managers can lend direction to social trends by enabling people to discover the truth about the world and mobilise to change it (Chomsky, 1996). Managers can create their own educational theories of organisation, theories which describe practices in which they encourage others to generate their theories of organisation, and they can contribute significantly to the development of good orders and social betterment.

If we wait for the celebration of the good social order as something that will happen only in the future, as David Peat discovered, we will wait for ever. In waiting and watching for something to happen we will miss the most obvious point: in celebrating the good order we create it. It is a personal choice whether we wait for someone else to show us the way, or whether we decide to make our own way ourselves, together.

Part IV

What are the implications of living theories of organisation for social living?

Living theories of organisation contain the generative transformational capacity to show how processes evolve and continue to develop themselves. The patterns demonstrate the iterative quality of relationships of influence: one aspect influences another to develop in a new way from what went before. The current form is enfolded within the new form, which itself unfolds in new directions with the potential of influencing yet other new forms. The whole is an unfolding system of new forms, each with its own generative transformational capacity for further influence, a never-ending process of coming into being.

If I am to stay true to this idea, I have to show how it is embodied within my own life. In the current discussion, I have to make the process visible within this book. The book is about organisation theory as it is embedded in people's personal-social lives, and I now need to show how I am influencing others to show how they can influence wider change. This is the nature of my own theory of educative management for organisational development.

This part contains three chapters. Chapter 11 is 'What should be the focus of management education?' I contacted colleagues around the world and invited them to write 1,000 words on the questions, 'What should be the focus of management education? What should business schools and schools of management education teach?', and also with an eye to how action research might play a part. Some of the answers appear here, not representative of all opinion by any means, but showing some interesting perspectives, and all implying that personal action enquiry has significant potential for the kind of organisational knowledge base that is required for wider and sustainable systemic change. It is noticeable that not many women's voices appear. That does not mean I didn't contact women. I did, but it also possibly says something about where women are in management in organisations.

Can the ideas expressed in Chapter 11 be realised in new living educational theories of organisation, as embodied in the lives of educative managers? Clearly they can be; the following two stories show the process in action. The stories are written by two women, continents apart, yet who have developed the same kind of educative management and leadership that has the capacity to change systems on a potentially unbounded scale.

Chapter 12 is written by Jackie Delong, a superintendent of schools in Brant County, Ontario. It needs emphasising that although Jackie's work is located in education contexts, the functional purpose of her work is administration. She is responsible for a multi-million dollar business. At the same time, Jackie holds strong educational values that lead her to transform her own business work into educational work, and her purpose here is to show how she is developing her living theory of educational leadership as an administrator and superintendent of schools.

Chapter 13 is written by Carmel Lillis, the principal of a primary school in Dublin. Carmel's story shows the generative transformational quality of systemic development through an action research approach. Although Carmel's work is in mainstream education, the processes that she describes have the potential to travel to all organisational contexts, and her descriptions of the kind of relationships she is nurturing show the potential for organisational change that is informed by personal-social commitments of the highest order.

Where am I in this? Throughout the book I hope I have shown how the ideas expressed here have been drawn from the work of others. My learning is learning from others. I have made those ideas my own, and I now express them in a variety of ways, and hope that they will influence people for social benefit.

In Jackie's story I appear as an influence through texts, and through intermittent personal contact, as does my colleague Jack Whitehead. Jackie has developed her own educational theories, which she now communicates to others, who in turn will make them their own, if they wish, and hopefully use them for social benefit. This is the process of generative transformational learning. The same is so of Carmel. Carmel studied on the Masters courses in Dublin, and she has made the ideas her own. In turn the teachers, parents, children, administrators and wider community she is influencing will take the ideas and make them their own, and use them for wider social purposes.

We live in ever-widening circles within circles of influence. It is unlikely that anyone can say that they knew something they did not learn from someone else. Perhaps what is new is how we make connections, how we reconfigure and reconstruct, how we put our own stamp of individuality on that which we learn so that we can use our learning in new, untried and exciting ways.

Recently there were sad reports of the death of Jonathan Philbin Bowman, a journalist in Ireland. Many tributes poured in, and as I listened to the car radio one day, I heard a newscaster say how Jonathan had always asked his son on their way home, 'Shall we go home or shall we have an adventure?' Jonathan's son would always reply, 'Let's have an adventure.'

I have learned that it is always possible to have an adventure. Life and learning are adventures. We might think we are on our own, but we need always to be aware of the countless millions who are the potential beneficiaries of our own legacies of learning. It is the responsibility of each of us to make sure that our potentialities for educative influence are realised, and that our influence is the best it can be for other people's benefit.

11 What should be the focus of management education?

In response to the questions:

> What should be the focus of management education?
> What should management and business schools teach?

colleagues said the following.

Action research and the production of working knowledge

John Garrick, University of Technology, Sydney

Donald Schön (1983) convincingly demonstrated in *The Reflective Practitioner* how knowledge of an action-oriented character is embedded in professional activity. Schön pointed out that professional knowledge can be not only open, but subject to real-time critical reflection by the professional practitioner and to public demonstration and examination in teaching situations. In Schön's sense of practice then, professional knowledge is potentially open-ended even in its action elements and indeed we have come increasingly to recognise professional knowledge as being valid in its own right. It is knowledge that does not rely on validation established by scientific research, nor is it beholden to the legitimising practices of the academy. Working knowledge emanates from actually doing the work. In this working knowledge, good professional practice involves making the best judgements in specific contexts and for ethical as well as commercial considerations. Work is both site and instrument of evaluating working knowledge. Working knowledge then is in work and it is what works.

The business world and the corporate sector in particular now encourage new ideas and even critical ideas (Drucker, 1995), although thorough-going critique, I would argue, continues to be largely discouraged. If working knowledge is to be a coherent construction and not just a fashionable description of particular elements of technological-age work, or a disguise for technical and financial interests, it should follow that adequate avenues for reflexivity need to be built into its production. This is a key challenge for the action oriented research approaches now favoured by many organisations. Transparency, openness, critical self-reflection, highly developed systems that promote peer assessment and review, and the development of professional associations that have contact with the academic world, would be among possible components of a new epistemological infrastructure for working knowledge. And there are signs that such components are beginning to take shape. Government higher education policies across European Union member nations, the USA, Canada and Australia are actively encouraging new university–industry partnering arrangements emphasising collaborative research between faculties and particular companies and flexible and work-based (as distinct from classroom-based) approaches to learning. Much more is at stake in the emerging discourses of working knowledge than mere terminology. What is at stake is both the character of what we take knowledge to be and, even more seriously, the extent to which we are moving towards or away from a more open society. In a global world saturated by information available through the Internet, openness may turn out to be one pragmatic option.

In the knowledge society, the issue arises as to where an organisation is positioned: in terms of knowledge, with which knowledge networks is it connected (Castells, 1997)? Furthermore, as Barnett (2000: 20) points out:

> We are seeing the rise of corporate universities such as that in the UK spawned by British Aerospace but they are not noted for their sponsorship among their employees of a receptivity to Greek philosophy or the nineteenth century novel. A knowledge audit would reveal that they focus on technical and managerial knowledge; and, even there, will want to develop among their employees certain usable knowledges and their associated skills with likely productive value for the organisation.

Indeed, in her study of a large manufacturing multi-national in the USA, Casey (1996: 320), for instance, argues that:

> the archetypical new Hephaestus employee is one who enthusiastically manifests the values of dedication, loyalty, self-sacrifice and passion for the product and customer, and who is willing to go the extra mile for his or her team.

Edwards and Tait (2000) argue that this entails an active subjectivity aligned to organisational goals, producing what Casey terms 'designer employees'. Here the alienation of industrialisation is displaced by an enthusiasm for work. This has been particularly marked in those organisations involved in human resource practices such as employee development schemes, action learning sets, quality circles and the like. For many, the down-side of this is an intensification of work (p. 133).

Against this complex backdrop of post-industrial work conditions, where do we epistemologically locate working knowledge and how might we evaluate this form of knowledge? As I have argued elsewhere (see Garrick and Rhodes, 2000), the emerging discourse of working knowledge is indicative of a pragmatic turn in our orientation towards what counts as knowledge. Epistemologically, working knowledge is not only in work; it is what works. The question of what works is invariably a matter of judgement made by those in power, with outcomes shaped by criteria such as economic growth, organisational projections and company research into areas such as consumer satisfaction. Working knowledge can, as a consequence, easily become a vehicle for forging particular policies or projects that represent dominant perspectives. Working knowledge then, whilst heralding a welcome alternative definition of knowledge, faces its own problematic: it is deficient where academics' propositional knowledge was strong. As Barnett (2000) puts it, this raises questions such as: What are the tests for knowledge that are independent of the aphorism that it is what works? So far as propositional knowledge comes to the fore, it will often be kept secret because company researchers will be limited in what they can say for fear of reducing their company's competitive advantage. Further, although modern information and communications technologies (and the call from shareholders for greater accountability) are helping to generate a climate of openness and mutual evaluation, commercial discourses remain dominant. As such, Lyotard's (1984: 9) questions: Who decides what knowledge is, and who knows what needs to be decided? remain very pertinent to those involved in action oriented research practices.

The strategies of action research in contemporary work conditions are contributing to a challenge to traditional modes of knowledge production and legitimisation by creating new ones. There is a vitality that comes with such opportunity and, at the same time, the possibility of contributing to new forms of epistemological closure. The challenge at this point is to develop new and credible ways of evaluating working knowledge beyond heavily circumscribed observations of what appears to work in specific organisational contexts.

Dialogue, learning and management education

Carl Rhodes, University of Technology, Sydney

At the end of a postgraduate course I taught on organisational communication, I conducted an evaluation that, in one section, asked participants to write free form comments on what new aspects should be incorporated to improve the course the next time that it was conducted. Below is an excerpt from the comments of one student.

> Challenge more the superficial comments from some participants. Examine the sacred cow theorists. Some participants too easily accepted some

concepts; [these] should be challenged not necessarily by you but other participants [should be] encouraged to challenge.

On reading this comment, I started to think of my own teaching practice and how it set up the relationship between me, the students and the content of the course. In particular it made me think about the nature of how students, such as this one, reacted to the subject matter and the role that the teacher and students play in the classroom. The evaluation comments suggest that this student approached the subject matter with a critical eye, not to understand and apply theory, but rather critically to engage with it. Further, this person suggests that the role of the student should be to challenge, rather than accept, the knowledge presented in the ideas and theories that they are exposed to through the class. With this in mind, my purpose here is briefly to discuss how the sorts of interactions suggested by the evaluation comments above might be incorporated into the practice of management educators.

My own professional practice has encompassed both management training in organisations and teaching organisational communication and change management to postgraduate students at universities. In reflecting on this practice in both of these settings what seems apparent is that what is on the teacher's agenda does not necessarily correspond to what is learned. A way to examine this is through the notion of learning as occurring through the interaction between what is taught and the existing knowledge of the learner. This relationship is one of dialogue and, as the evaluation comments suggest, it involves a critical interaction with the knowledge embedded in management theory. As I have argued elsewhere (Rhodes, 2000), dialogue is a way that knowledge is done. This approach stresses the active nature of knowledge. Here knowledge is not an object but rather it is a practice. This perspective, which derives much of its influence from Mikhail Bakhtin (1981), proposes that any understanding of the social world is dialogic; it is made up of the interaction of different voices that come into contact with each other. This dialogue, however, is not to be confused with conversation; the dialogic character of knowledge is such that as human beings we interact with a variety of discourses in order to make sense out of the world. These discourses, however, exist prior to us. They are not our private property, but rather we adopt and react to them. In doing so, we also define ourselves and who we are in relation to the world we live in. For example, when a person becomes a manager, the nature of what it means to be such a subject is not something that the individual invents. Instead, it is a position that a person adopts and, in so doing, takes on the expectations of what being a manager is supposed to be. In other words, the person comes into dialogue with a discourse of management and as a result, they generate new knowledge of management through the interaction of their new position and their existing knowledge. Learning to be a manager is, in this way, produced dialogically.

This learning however is not necessarily straightforward or harmonious. As managers forge their identities from the discourses available to them, there will be times where these discourses can be a site of struggle; including, potentially, struggle with their educators. Bakhtin discusses this through the twin concepts of the centripetal and centrifugal forces of language. He sees language as being stratified into different ways of seeing the world; for example, the language used in trade union meetings would inevitably be very different from that used in a board meeting, even if the explicit topic being discussed were the same in both. The issue for Bakhtin, however, is that power is embedded in different uses of language. To this end, he sees that there are centripetal forces that aim at centralisation through the production of shared meaning by dominant social groups (such as management educators and people who write about management education!). This use of language seeks to impose a single truth about the world on others by centralising all knowledge around one particular way of using language. Working against such centripetal forces are centrifugal forces; this suggests that claims to centralise meaning and truth can only be made in the face of alternatives. Difference in language exists because of the presence of alternative ways of seeing. The dialogue in this way is not so much a conversation between people as an interaction of different ways of using language to understand the world.

Turning back to management education, the curriculum is a way of trying to impose a particular way of understanding business and management on the students. A naive view would suggest that the best outcome from management education would be that the students learn that which is taught. Many forms of management education promote such a view. The use of competency-based training and behavioural objectives models for example works to predefine the reaction of students to the material and judges success to be a result of the students' ability to match these predefined outcomes (Rhodes, 1996). This is an example of Bakhtin's centripetal power – an attempt to centralise knowledge by promoting a single way of understanding and behaving in the world. In other words, it presents a strong monologue that tries to drown out alternatives and ignore the dialogic character of learning.

Faced with such monologue, as they so often are, what reactions might students have? Dominant ways of understanding organisations have significant power through their widespread use and acceptance as being canonical. Human resource management, strategic management, quality management are but a few examples of what has come, in the contemporary scene, to be viewed as standard knowledge. These, like other forms of management knowledge, are powerful in the way that they become the common sense of managing. Faced with such knowledge, I suggest that students can react in three possible ways.

- *Didactic Learning:* Where students accept and fully internalise what is taught. Here what is taught replaces what is already known. Although never fully realised, this form of learning is one where centripetal power dominates the learning.
- *Non-Learning:* Where students reject what is taught (although they may go through the motions of pretending that they have internalised it). Here what the students already know remains intact and little or no learning occurs.

- *Dialogic Learning:* Where the result of education is that knowledge is generated through the dialogic interaction between the taught and the known. Here, no pre-set outcomes are achieved in terms of what is learned; the disciplinary knowledge of the institution comes into a dialogic interaction, and potential struggle, with the student's own experiences and ways of seeing the world, to produce a new knowledge.

Dialogic learning becomes an approach where learning is the questioning of homogenous, totalising accounts of organisations. It is here that participation and dialogue amongst diverse points of view allow people to develop knowledge that accounts for differences and actively avoids the creation and maintenance of rigidly defined social truths, conformity, consensus fabrication, minimum resistance and the domination of glossy pre-packaged knowledge (Rhodes, 1997). Such a practice, however, is dramatically in conflict with dominant approaches to management education that have focused on the discovery and dissemination of the 'truth' about business and, instead, abandons 'practices that reinforce hierarchy in favour of strategies that diffuse and decenter power' (Boje, 1996: 235). Such approaches work both to understand and critique dominant approaches to management as well as to encourage people critically to reflect on their own management practice and the discourses on which it is based. The teaching here is reflexive in the sense that it applies 'critical perspectives to understanding one's own position in relation to the educational process, and to understanding and managing the learning milieu jointly with participants' (Reynolds, 1997: 320). Dialogue will always be a feature of how people respond to education. The challenge for management education, however, is to seek ways to enhance rather than to stymie the dialogue.

Enquiry in action in business education?

John H. M. Ellis and Julia A. Kiely, Business School, University of Bournemouth, United Kingdom

Organisations are confronted with a fast-paced and turbulent environment. External challenges abound in the domains of technology, internationalisation and business ethics, while internal challenges have prompted a raft of initiatives to bring about people changes and organisational capacity-building (Ellis and Kiely, 2000; Fisher and Torbert, 1995; Hurst, 1995; Stacey, 1996; Torbert, 1999; Weick, 1995; Weil, 1999). In this time of rapid change, instant answers provide at best transient solutions. There is no doubting the usefulness and value of accumulated academic knowledge, but, given the rate of change, is it enough?

For many years, business schools have been aware of two key considerations. First, general solutions sit uneasily with the diverse range of business organisations and business cultures within which they work. Second, while traditional subject disciplines frequently appear in the early stages of Masters programmes, managerial issues and concerns are eclectic and a far cry from discrete subject specialties. Intuitively, educators in business schools are conscious of the wealth of knowledge and experience of those on their Masters and Doctoral programmes.

Capitalising on such knowledge and expertise has long been a prominent feature of education in business schools. The rich learning experience of working with other participants is frequently acknowledged. However, business schools are becoming increasingly conscious of the need to help managers and organisations tackle their own problems and issues themselves by drawing on a range of resources. Action enquiry strategies provide a means of accomplishing this. It enables issues and concerns to be addressed in a manner which is truly 'fit for purpose' in the sense of being appropriate to the business context and those who are working within it.

Action enquiry strategies are a way of bridging the gap between theory and practice and addressing the pressing problems of a quickly changing world. For many years, business schools have been aware of the power of action enquiry strategies. However, only in comparatively recent years have business educators embraced it to help managers and organisations tackle their own problems and issues. Here, we are only able to touch on some of the key features in the approach being adopted in some business schools (Eden and Huxham, 1996; Godfrey, 1999; Park, 1999; Putnam, 1999; Tranfield and Starkey, 1999).

The action enquiry process resembles a spiral in which emergent action is reviewed in a systematic manner. Four interwoven strands – construct reality; enabling change; co-enquiry; cycles of action and reflection – are common to all action enquiry strategies.

Construct reality

The relationship between people, events and activities is not context free. It can only be understood fully by an appreciation of the context and way in which people interpret their world. Starting by questioning how we make sense of our world in terms of our values, attitudes, actions and interpretations is an essential first step.

Theories about what should be done and ways of acting are themselves the product of previously 'taken for granted' action. Questioning assumptions and unravelling taken for granted views and perspectives helps to set new coordinates and thereby redefines problems and issues. In this sense-making process, managers draw on both accumulated wisdom and academic knowledge and their own personal experience and reflection.

Business organisations tend to assume the dominant logic is correct and fail to question whether or not the values on which they are based remain appropriate or desirable. Are the right issues being tackled? Are the right questions being asked? Questioning taken for granted assumptions helps managers break away from preconceived ideas and solutions. It makes clear the organisational values and beliefs on which actions are based. Instead of asking 'What is the solution to a particular problem?' there is often a need to reformulate understanding of the problem to ask, 'Is this the correct issue for us to be attempting to solve?'

Enabling change

What makes action enquiry strategies particularly appealing to managers is the focus on real problems that are happening here and now. The strategies make it possible for businesses to take appropriate intervention and change. Any change accomplished by action enquiry strategies involves the full commitment and participation of those in the joint enquiry process. Employees themselves set the boundaries, reflect and take action.

The importance of reflection cannot be over-estimated. Reflection enhances awareness of actions, interpretations and 'theories in use'. Learning from action leads to a deeper understanding of context-based issues. Some of the change facilitated by action enquiry strategies will be simple incremental change or single-loop learning. In such cases, strategies or action change while the underlying values and assumptions on which they are based remain the same.

Transformational change or double-loop learning (Argyris, 1999; Flood and Romm, 1996) occurs when both strategies and the assumptions on which they are based change, at the same time or perhaps because of a change in values. This is not simply a case of finding new alternative ways of resolving a short-term operational challenge more effectively. Additional insights envisaging a preferred future and organising effectively to achieve such an outcome must be present. For example, a business may change both their mission and values to reflect and respond to fundamental societal demands for a more ethical product/service offering. Given our rapidly changing environment, transformational change is essential for long-run business survival.

Co-enquiry process

The joint enquiry process means all levels of employees create their own knowledge and theory relevant to their own specific situation. Businesses become the creators of knowledge and theory embedded in their own work settings. Instead of frameworks being developed – perhaps in the academic domain – and then applied by business practitioners, a new paradigm is enacted. Solutions do not arise from existing knowledge, although elements of existing knowledge will be integrated within the solution. Knowledge and solutions emerge incrementally in the trans-disciplinary world of business. Diffusion of knowledge occurs initially to those participating in the knowledge production process. Diffusion to practice occurs at the point of discovery.

Managers and those with whom they are interacting are thus creating their own knowledge and theories in practice. This is not to deny the importance of traditional methods of knowledge production through academic agendas. Knowledge and theories produced by action enquiry strategies are pluralistic rather than elitist and exist alongside the more traditional separation of knowledge producers and users. Knowledge produced in this way is more socially and politically responsive as it reflects and is grounded in real-world practice.

Cycles of action and reflection

Through a cyclical process of action and reflection with regard to a meaningful problematic situation, theory and practice are interlinked and build on each other. Evaluation leads to diagnosing the problem situation anew based on learning that has occurred from our previous activity. Fresh insights and understandings are developed through continuing spirals of action and reflection on action. The relationship between improved knowledge through action and improved action through reflection is the main idea behind action enquiry.

The cyclical process helps individual personal development and enhancement of professional managerial practice. Theory is no longer something which is taught outside the workplace or read about in management texts. Individuals develop theory themselves in real time in their workplace. Knowledge without action is of little value. Professional practice informs theory and vice versa. Real problems are being tackled and solved in real time. Businesses develop and move forward simultaneously with individual employees. The process creates a true learning environment.

Adoption and rejection of action enquiry strategies

Business schools know they are not the gatekeepers of knowledge and learning. Business education is increasingly becoming the facilitation of managers' learning, so professional practice informs theory and vice versa. However, there is a caveat. In some businesses the general climate is not conducive to work being undertaken by action enquiry. For others the business climate and culture is such that action enquiry approaches will be of tremendous value to the professional development of managers, all levels of employees and business practices. Aspects working for and against success with this approach are shown in the accompanying figures.

As Figure 11.1 shows, the overall business climate needs to be right for action enquiry interventions to be a meaningful way of solving real business problems and developing professional practice. Aspect profiles at or towards the 'F' end of the scale indicate the climate is right for action enquiry interventions. The wholehearted commitment of senior management is vital. Senior managers, who have experienced the power of action enquiry, perhaps through the facilitation of a business school, will be converted. Others may not. Action enquiry takes a path over virgin territory. As such, both the process and outcomes may lead to surprises. People are working on real tasks with unknown results. Employees need to know that management has faith in them and is receptive to constructive criticism. The power to learn, influence and direct actions and reflections is shared by all. Inevitably, there must be truthful communication by all partners. A playful curiosity and healthy openness to future possibilities is ideal.

Figure 11.2 reveals that action enquiry is stifled in secretive cultures, where fear dominates and mistakes are penalised. Aspect profiles at or towards the 'A' end of the scale indicate a climate where action enquiry interventions are not

A	B	C	D	E	F

Accept assumptions and governing values	○	○	○	○	○	⊘	Challenge assumptions and governing values
Focus on formal rules and communication	○	○	○	○	⊘	○	Focus on group empowerment
Hierarchical organisation and authority	○	○	○	○	⊘	○	Participative orientation and autonomy
Individuals highly risk averse	○	○	○	○	○	⊘	Individuals encouraged to be risk takers
Taking action, little or no reflection	○	○	○	○	○	⊘	Taking action, together with active group learning

Figure 11.1 A typical 'adoption' profile

A	B	C	D	E	F

Accept assumptions and governing values	⊘	○	○	○	○	○	Challenge assumptions and governing values
Focus on formal rules and communication	○	⊘	○	○	○	○	Focus on group empowerment
Hierarchical organisation and authority	⊘	○	○	○	○	○	Participative orientation and autonomy
Individuals highly risk averse	○	⊘	○	○	○	○	Individuals encouraged to be risk takers
Taking action, little or no reflection	⊘	○	○	○	○	○	Taking action, together with active group learning

Figure 11.2 A typical 'rejection' profile

likely to be successful. If senior management merely pay lip service to this change process, employees will not be immersed in and excited by new-found possibilities of adding to professional practice. They will sense that not everything is being disclosed. Quite correctly, they will be sceptical regarding senior managers' willingness to proceed with outcomes not of their choosing. Action enquiry strategies concern both process and outcomes. People learn from the process itself. If concern is just for the outcome only single-loop learning will result. If the work climate is such that mistakes are penalised, learning will be stifled and mistakes will be hidden rather than openly discussed. People will not seek feedback for fear of exposing their vulnerability.

Conclusion

In short, the relationship between improved knowledge through action and improved action through reflection is the main thrust of action enquiry strategies (Kiely and Ellis, 1999). Facilitating this relationship is the direction in which we believe business schools should be moving. The dichotomy between knowledge production and knowledge use is nonsense. The days when business schools considered it sufficient for managers attending their programmes to be taught theory and its application to business are long gone. Theory does not 'trickle down' to practice or practice 'trickle up' to academic theory. Instead, managers are creating their own knowledge embedded in their professional practice. In so doing they are drawing on existing knowledge in the wider domain and their own personal knowledge. The process itself equips managers and businesses for dealing with future challenges (Schön, 1995). Actions do speak louder than words, as we build critical reflection in managers as an integral part of business education, and through them, in the culture of their organisation. They learn to act and reflect so as to learn, and then reflect on learning in order to act more effectively.

What should be the focus of management education?

Liam Nagle, Nortel Networks, Republic of Ireland

[I met with Liam Nagle, Vice President of World Wide Operations, Enterprise Solutions, Nortel Networks, and our conversation covered a range of issues, some of which we focus on here.]

JM: What do you see are the links between business and business schools, and management and schools of management?

LN: For business schools to have any useful impact they need to be aware of contemporary issues in business. That should go without saying. In that case it is important to take stock of what are the big issues in business, and what are the trends that will help us anticipate where we will be in a year's time. In terms of schools of management, they should teach managers how to manage in a practical way. At the moment there is too much concentration on abstract theory and not enough emphasis on learning through practice.

One of the most important aspects that people need to be educated in is implementation. I come across people who are highly qualified, and they are not successful in business because they do not understand what it takes to get things done. I also come across people who are not highly qualified, yet they are successful because they have the ability to get things done. Getting things done means an appreciation of what the problem is you are trying to solve, an ability to understand the problem in depth, and the ability to discriminate between aspects of the problem in order to get to the heart of the matter quickly and accurately. The speed at which that is done is very important. It cannot be learnt from a book. Wherever it comes from, whether it is an inherited tendency, or the wisdom of experience, what matters in today's business is the speed at which we change and move.

What then is important for the future? The Internet is significantly changing the way we work and I believe the Internet itself, and its use, will change. This I think will fall into four phases. Phase 1 is now almost a thing of the past and is very basic: you log on and you learn something. It was fun and novel. Phase 2 (which to some degree we are in today) is the transactional base: you buy your books from Amazon.com. Phase 3 will be much more complex, the customer relationship management, the process of managing customer relationships at close quarters. This will probably be a threat to education institutions. Colleges today are beginning to offer supported study at home via the Internet. This has to have substantial implications for traditional university management courses. It is closely followed by Phase 4, freedom of information. It is possible to disseminate information to thousands of people at the same time with very simple procedures and distribution lists. This is quite recent; even two or three years ago it would not have been possible.

The speed at which the Internet is changing and also changing our views of business is quite awesome and is bound to change the nature of business and management education. A key consideration is how people are going to learn how to access, use and disseminate information. To some degree it will eliminate the need for layers of management. Communications will be faster, problem-solving will be quicker, managers' ability to access all levels of the organisation will be almost instantaneous. If the Internet is ubiquitous today, imagine what it is going to be in two years' time.

To stay in business themselves, business schools need to address these and related issues. They need to provide courses to enable people to learn the very practical skills of accessing, using and disseminating information, as well as the more theoretical capacities of understanding the nature of the information they are using. At the moment many business schools are not doing this, probably because the issue has not existed until now. The sheer amount of data currently coming any business person's way is unprecedented – the push versus pull concept of communication. Business schools need to help people to educate themselves in this direction and prepare them for future use of the Internet.

JM: You said earlier that leadership was a key issue.

LN: Leadership is key. Organisations will survive because of the people who lead them. How leadership is learnt is at issue. Leadership tends to be taught in a conceptual way; the theory is presented and people are invited to apply the theory to their practice. This does not work. Leadership is learnt within practice. It follows that more outplacement work should be arranged so that managers will learn the skills of the job in practice situations, and develop a more refined concept of how to handle their own real situations.

JM: We spoke earlier about how traditional education courses require people to write quite lengthy reports, yet this is contrary to contemporary business practices.

LN: Given the reality of today's world, reports of 5,000 words simply will not get read. Unless a report sits on one page in three or four points, it is not going to get air time. Business is looking for a short, concise report or recommendation. An interesting issue to be addressed by academics is how to find a balance between traditional expectations and today's needs for concise information. For that matter, why must a course be assessed through a written report? Why isn't it possible to assess managerial capacity in real ways, such as a manager demonstrating that she or he can actually manage?

JM: I said that I believe business should develop a sense of societal responsibility.

LN: If you look at business today, particularly the multinationals, the biggest drivers are growth and profitability. Those two things, along with technology and product offer that has a sustainable future, drive the capital value of the company. Most senior managers of a multinational are tied up in those things in some way. Are we growing, are we growing faster than anybody else, are we competitive for the future, do we get a value associated with that? What is becoming increasingly evident, certainly in Ireland, and in my experience, the rest of the world, is the difficulty of finding good people to drive those four parameters. If you don't have the people to do that, you haven't got an awful lot. Ultimately people have to design and deliver the four parameters. Companies have to pay a great deal of attention to how they treat people. This means accommodating individual needs, being creative with structures such as using flexi-time or job-sharing, as well as the way they recruit and reward people. Large steps have been taken, particularly for older multinationals, in how we treat our workforce and reward them. Many people are getting wealthy today with things like stock options or stock participation plans, which used to be the prerogative of senior executives and now, rightly I think, are available throughout all levels of the organisation. Consequently more and more wealth is being generated and shared throughout all levels. Companies have to be more creative and flexible in accommodating people's needs in order to attract and retain the right people.

JM: We spoke about how organisations are constituted of people, and organisation theory needs to recognise the people base.

LN: I agree that organisation is people. But there are two other important elements. One is the culture and the other is the values, and they are both interlinked. Different companies working out of different cultures and values systems are going to get different results. I've got a varied company background, and I've seen companies for example that are process oriented and others that are results oriented, and they are very different places to be. Companies need to decide for themselves what they want their culture to be, and this is decided by the values they hold. The interesting thing is that working people are much more knowledgeable about these things today, and will ask questions, and make decisions on what the company has to offer them. To go back to the issue of what should business and management schools teach, they need to understand how organisations work in terms of their cultures and values systems, and how these impact on people; and they need to build these understandings into courses. If schools themselves are to survive as credible services, they need to encourage people to understand their real-world situations, and find out for themselves how to identify and solve their own problems. This I think is where your action research comes in. To teach about business or management in an abstract way is not very helpful. It needs to be rooted in practice. A real understanding of practice and its implications is where good business management lies. But business schools are faced with the real problematic of how to keep up with the changing pace. If they are to provide a service to business, they have to be ahead of business in terms of current issues, and this is just not possible. So perhaps business schools need to change their attitudes and self-perceptions, and regard themselves as learning alongside businesses how to cope with current change in the same way as the businesses they are supporting. Now, that would be something.

What should be the focus of management education?

Chris James, University of Glamorgan

The simple answer to the question 'What should be the focus of management education?' is 'What managers do'. The rational response to constructing curriculum based on that answer is to do an analysis of managers' work of the kind carried out by Stewart and Mintzberg and to employ an 'expert' in conveying that information to the learners. That approach has taken the management education curriculum down a content-based path where the focus is on the 'delivery' of the various different elements of management practice, such as managing people, strategy, and finance. This has become what one might call the 'traditional approach' to management education. There are a number of problems with that approach, some of which are set out below. In essence, the problems can be solved by focusing the process and content of management education on individual managers' experience of what they do and what they need to learn.

The first problem is that each participant brings her/his own history and experience to a management development programme. This problem can be solved by recognising that every participant's learning will start from a different 'place', and starting the learning from 'where each participant is' and addressing their learning needs. This approach means that the learner's needs should drive the learning, that is, move it forward and steer its direction, and that the formal content of the programme should support the participant's learning rather than lead it.

Second, it is likely that the participants will manage in a very wide range of contexts. Even within one specific setting, the context is continually changing. So every participant in a traditional management course, a lecture-based programme for example, is faced first with the problem of reconfiguring the content to match their own particular context and then adapting their learning to fresh situations as they arise. This problem can be overcome by locating the learning in the learner's own context from the outset and encouraging the learner to explore and analyse the features of the context which impact on their practice and learning.

The third problem with traditional approaches is that the management learning is typically an individual event with individual participants returning to their workplace with the task of applying what they have learnt. This individual focus gives the learner an uphill task because there is no such thing as individual learning in organisations. Any change in an individual and in the way in which they organise (and create what we come to experience as an organisation) must be accompanied by a change in the other members of the organisation and the way they as members organise. This interpretation means that learning must be a group process at some level, otherwise it is likely that any learning will stay at the cognitive level and will not be brought to life in practice.

Fourth, there is the danger that participants unknowingly see a management development course as a defence against the emotional experience, which is typically one of anxiety, of taking up a management role. The course is a protection against the emotional experience of managing ('I can face the uncertain and taxing task of managing because my course has prepared me for all eventualities'). This view means that learning must embrace the emotional dimension of organising, so that participants come to appreciate that management learning is not part of the process of controlling emotions, but is part of the process of embracing the emotional dimension of organising, and containing it.

So, in summary, management education should:

- focus from the outset and continually on the learner's needs;
- develop expertise in how fully to experience the context so that the participant's management actions are the most appropriate ones;
- involve the participant's working group so that the learning may be organisational;
- and explore the emotional dimension of organising lest the process of management development simply colludes with the participant's social defences against managing.

12 My epistemology of practice of the superintendency

Jacqueline Delong

Introduction

In this chapter I would like to describe and explain the nature of my influence as an educational leader in a school district of over 32,000 students. The chapter is set in the context of paradigm proliferation (Lather, 2000) and new epistemologies of scholarship and practice (Boyer, 1990; Schön, 1995) at the beginning of the new millennium. There is much evidence that the written word cannot capture the nature of that influence and therefore much of the real message is lost without the visual images that can be captured on video and multi-media. For that reason, I am supporting professional educators to use those media to develop and share their knowledge. In the visual images we can see the generative and transformative quality of the discourse which enables the creation of the knowledge that is the life and learning of teachers and administrators.

Nevertheless, this chapter contains a linguistic representation of my life as a superintendent over a span of five and a half years in terms of my learning and growth. Much of that growth has come about through a self-discovery of freedom which I found through breaking out of the controls exerted in family and professional relationships. This freedom has been expressed in my subsequent desire to enable others to free themselves from constraints on their creativity and life-affirming energy (Bataille, 1987).

My current situation

I have worked since 1995 as a superintendent of schools in a school board in Southern Ontario, Canada. These years in the post have seen significant changes in administrative and organisational structures throughout the education system. An issue which has had particular significance for my work has been the amalgamation of boards to ensure the effective implementation of rationalist economic policies, a move which has resulted in substantial chaos for teachers, administrators and other personnel. Living through the chaos has been a difficult but valuable learning experience.

During those same years I have also been conducting action research into my own practice as a superintendent, collecting and analysing data, writing about what I was learning, and encouraging others to do the same. The work and research have rolled in and out and have often mixed together in the formation of waves, sometimes creating images of great strength and beauty, and sometimes of trauma and pain.

I want here to tell the story of how I have developed my own epistemology of practice of the superintendency. I hope to show how my epistemology is rooted in strong and caring relationships, and how I have enabled people to learn, and value their own learning. I believe I have enabled people to develop their own epistemologies of practice, so that they are able to reflect on their action and show how they have improved the quality of education for themselves and others.

To show that and how I have done this is of particular importance for me. I recall an episode at the 1996 American Educational Research Association (AERA) annual meeting. Key members of the newly formed Special Interest Group on Self-Study were gathered in the lobby. I joined the conversation, and in response to a question about what I intended to research, said that I hoped to research my practice and demonstrate improved educational leadership. I hoped to demonstrate this in terms of how the quality of my influence impacted on principals, teachers and student learning. A colleague wished me luck because, evidently, to date no one has been able to do that satisfactorily. I took from the comment that the distance from my position as superintendent to the classroom was perceived as too great to demonstrate any line of influence. Showing the connection wouldn't be a simple matter, I thought, but it would be worth the effort.

The reservations of this colleague are well borne out in the invited paper to Division A (Administration) by David Clark, a professor at the University of North Carolina, at the 1997 AERA conference, when he talked about his terrible disappointment in his and the academy's inability to capture the essence of educational leadership:

> The honest fact is that the total contribution of Division A of AERA to the development of the empirical and theoretical knowledge base of administration and policy development is so miniscule that if all of us had devoted our professional careers to teaching and service, we would hardly have been missed.
>
> (Clark, 1997)

He went on to challenge the academic community to create a new field, 'the sociology of the interesting', and to focus more on practitioner-leaders and less on publishing research papers; for it is in practice that real social change takes place, and practitioner-leaders are key agents in the process.

I took from this comment that Clark felt that there was ample propositional advice about what educational leadership might look like, but little research-based evidence to show its realisation in practice. This helped me to firm up my own resolve to theorise my own practice as an educational leader; part of my research would be to produce validated evidence that I had beneficially influenced the quality of learning for people at all levels of the educational system.

This, then, became my research project for my doctoral studies, beginning in 1996, and about to conclude, I hope, in 2000.

What does a superintendent of schools do?

There are two facets to the position of the superintendent in my board: one is the responsibility for a family of schools, and the other is a number of system portfolios. System portfolios refer to broad frameworks of educational activity, and include the implementation of policies and procedures. The portfolios for which I had responsibility on my appointment in 1995 were School–Work–Community, Staff Development, Safe Schools, Compensatory Education and Career Education; today they are Assessment, Evaluation and Reporting, Staff Development and Leadership, Community Relations and Career Education. My family of schools in 1995 in the former Brant County area was the Pauline Johnson Family of Schools – fourteen elementary and secondary schools, and about 5,000 students. Today it is the former Norfolk area: Delhi, Simcoe, Valley Heights and GELA (Grand Erie Learning Alternatives) and the supervision of the Simcoe School Support Office and its principal-leader. The work is demanding, and over the years I have come to realise that the driving force that sustains me throughout is my vision of a school system whose purpose it is to improve student learning.

This vision of improving student learning places my own understanding of my work in a different plane from the traditional literature on educational leadership, which emphasises the functional and task-oriented nature of the work. I do not subscribe to this view. I engage more readily with the writings of authors such as Stephen Covey, who challenges the dominant theme in the success literature as 'one filled with social image consciousness, techniques and quick fixes', and proposes a return to the 'Character Ethic as the foundation of success – things like integrity, humility, fidelity, temperance, courage, justice, patience, industry, simplicity, modesty and the Golden Rule' (Covey, 1989: 18). These values are the ones that inform my work, and I systematically find ways to let them transform into educative practices throughout aspects of the system where I am able to have an influence.

What was the nature of my research?

At the same time as I was beginning my new job, I was also learning about and supporting action research processes through a pilot project that I had initiated with Linda Grant, the then Executive Assistant with the Ontario Public School Teachers' Federation. By 1996 I was coming to the conclusion that I was supporting teachers in doing their action research, but not doing it myself. Here was I, one who took pride in saying that she never asked anyone to do anything that she wasn't willing to do herself, experiencing myself as a living contradiction (Whitehead, 1989) in that I was saying one thing and doing another. The situation changed when I lunched with Tom Russell, Professor at Queen's University, Ontario, and Jack Whitehead at the first 'Act, Reflect, Revise' Conference (convened by the Ontario Public Schools Teachers Federation in February). Tom and Jack convinced me that I actually had something worthy of researching and writing about in my life as a senior woman manager (which still comes as a surprise to me). Tom talked about my capacity to speak with the authority of experience (Russell, 1995), and Jack was interested in taking me on as a student. I was excited about doing advanced research that was practical in nature and gaining accreditation for the work of improving myself and trying to become a better leader for my school system.

What I think my research has come to demonstrate is how I hold together many different activities, relationships and influences, and continue to address powerful politically driven influences in the education system in directions which enable me to continue to exert my educational leadership in ways that I value. These ways primarily involve understanding the quality of my relationships with other people, and how I can influence those relationships so that they lead to learning. Understanding the nature of my educative relationships has become the focus of my research. Throughout my practice I concentrate on ensuring that the quality of relationships is educative in the sense that I support people to make their own decisions, become autonomous and act in ways that will ensure student learning.

Given the diverse nature of my job, my relationships are also many and varied. My work involves me with senior administrators and trustees at Board level, principals, vice-principals, teachers, teacher unions, parents, students, and business, industry and university personnel. I believe that being an effective leader involves creating, developing and sustaining positive relationships built on trust and respect. A relationship of this kind is earned and requires time together. Whitehead (1993) speaks about extending educational enquiry from a personal to a social orientation so that 'educational theory is a form of dialogue which has profound implications for the future of humanity' (Kilpatrick, 1951). McNiff *et al.* (1992) see action research as a means to improve the social order. How could I do this? How could I show that my work did exist as a form of dialogue with profound implications for the future of humanity, and did contribute to a good social order? While I recognise that improving the social order is not a small task, I firmly believe that it is attainable in small ways by each one of us, and is certainly one of my purposes in my sphere of influence (Covey, 1990). How could I show that I was attaining my vision? This became a driving factor as my research began to develop.

More changes

In 1996–97 it became apparent that the new Progressive Conservative government was going to shake up the school system. As the new minister of education said early in his tenure, it was time to 'create a crisis' in order to bring about change in education. In addition to reducing the power of the teacher unions and trustees, the government intended to create a new curriculum, test students provincially, change the funding policy, reduce the power of school boards, and increase the size of school boards. This caused unprecedented upheaval among the workforce, and I found myself wondering how I could continue to support practitioners to maintain their morale and commitment to education. While what was happening in Ontario was part of the wider economic rationalist policies evident in the UK, USA and New Zealand, my concern still was how to support people at the local level. I saw the development of personal relationships as the key to challenging wider global trends through a personal commitment to practice; but those relationships were in danger of erosion because of the enormous significance that external political and economic factors were exerting on people's lives.

With this in mind, I began to concentrate on supporting communities of practitioner researchers, and systematically to build up networks of support. I began to work with the principals in my family of schools to create a 'collaborative community of learners and to move them from dependence to independence to interdependence' (Covey, 1990). I began to work with curriculum support members of staff; and also to work systematically to enhance relationships with community, business and industry groups to create partnerships. I aimed to involve staff and community in creating the new board. In the former Brant Board I had seen the potential of building partnerships for the purpose of 'enhancing programs and services for students' (Delong and Moffatt, 1996b). I wanted, through my efforts to develop educational communities, to provide a counterbalance to the worst effects of technical rationalist policies which were driven by anything but educational values.

I concentrated on developing programmes of staff development. This included the planning and implementation of professional development programmes for teaching and non-teaching staff, and programme implementation. Action research was part of the staff development model that I created, and during this time I initiated an action research pilot project with Linda Grant and four other boards with five teachers and two school administrators. This initiative in turn led to publications (Delong and Wideman, 1996, 1998b), presentations at the Ontario Education Research Council, and presentations on a wider front, including the American Educational Research Association annual meetings.

Developing the research

As I was learning the job of school superintendent I was consistently documenting my actions and reflections through taping and transcription of meetings and workshops, daily journal keeping, photos, evaluations of my practice by my family of schools' principals and the director and submitting my writing to public scrutiny for response. This was hard work, for I never perceived myself as an academic, and have felt somewhat intimidated by the academic community. This however did not deter me. I spent time during the summers of 1996–98 working with Jack, my supervisor, in Bath, UK, and I developed my range and understanding of issues in educational research. As time progressed, the focus of my research began to emerge as being an investigation of my life as a superintendent for the purpose of contributing to the knowledge base on educational leadership. I also developed my understanding that it was not sufficient to produce only abstract accounts about leadership, as Clark says (see p. 275). To stay true to the exciting ideas of the new scholarship (Schön, 1995), I would have to show how I was generating my own theory from within my practice, and also explain how I was generating circles of influence that would show leadership as a lived practice that had profound implications for other people's lives.

The political backdrop continued unfolding into new stories of disaffection and dismay. During the fall of 1998 there was persistent conflict between the teacher federations and the government culminating in a two-week strike of all teachers and most school administrators. A six-month term was lost to coping with the unrest and anger. The economic rationalist policies were implemented in all their realities in Ontario. Funding was slashed from anything that didn't produce and make a profit.

September 1997 saw the beginning of the preparation for the amalgamation process, with widespread structural change and re-allocation of administrative responsibilities. The government had mandated the merging of boards, none of which wanted the merger, and some put up considerable resistance. It was my job to help steer the whole process through, in spite of my own opposition to the changes that were taking place. I tend to embrace change where I see an opportunity for improvement, but I could discern none such here. However, I was still driven by my concern to maintain the quality of educational experience for students, teachers and other partners in the education system, so I directed increased efforts to trying to make the best of what I saw as a potentially disastrous situation.

The process of amalgamation was disruptive for all and characterised by an atmosphere of anger, fear and imminent disruption. Because one of the government's intentions in amalgamating boards was cost-cutting by downsizing senior administration, my own job came under threat, as well as those of many of my colleagues. The crisis had been well and truly created. Early retirement was offered to both teachers and administrators close to retirement but the drain on leadership ranks, particularly principals, grew into a crisis situation as the numbers leaving increased. It was my task to solve the problem within my Leadership portfolio.

So how did I maintain my enthusiasm for my research in light of these massive structural changes with their implications of personal instability and closure? My response to the crisis was to maintain my commitment to providing a quality educational experience for students. I saw opportunities to use my influence to combat the external disruption by concentrating on building up confidence in action research approaches to professional development, and disseminating work to show its usefulness. We renewed a partnership with the now amalgamated Elementary Teachers' Federation of Ontario, Nipissing University and the new Grand Erie District School Board. Colleagues and I developed the *Ontario Action Researcher*, an electronic journal, of which Ron Wideman, Assistant Professor at Nipissing, and I became the editors. Our first issue was in December 1998. In the *International Electronic Journal for Leadership in Learning*, we describe how the quality of our relationship and trust of each other has supported us in finding opportunities for new development.

I was interested at the 1998 AERA meeting in San Diego to listen to a presentation at the Special Interest Group on the Superintendency which suggested that superintendents were interested only in power and money and not at all interested in children and learning. The presentations at this symposium were given by academics who spoke about the role of the superintendent, in a predominantly negative way. I was angered by the distortion of my reality, and suggested that the presenters might want to reconsider their conclusions. My comments were endorsed by other superintendents at the session.

The experience brought home to me the importance of generating public theories of the superintendency. Contemporary influential research is noting consistently the need for the creation of insider, practitioner, design enquiry research and the need for new policies and legitimisation from the universities for this approach (Anderson and Herr, 1999; Boyer, 1990; Clark, 1997; Donmoyer, 1996; Schön, 1995; Zeichner, 1995). It became evident to me that I was fortunately positioned in that I was able to show how I was influencing the quality of education for students through my practice as a superintendent. The generation of my own theory became a moral imperative of essential import in the development of new theories of leadership which would have implications for good social orders.

Moving on in the research

I successfully transferred to PhD study in 1998, and now focused on generating evidence to support my claim that I have positively influenced the quality of education for people at all levels of the education system. The evidence I produce comes from a variety of sources. I can show for example how I have worked with Diane Morgan, Program Coordinator, in the Pauline Johnson Family of Schools, such that she and I have increased our knowledge about testing and ways to use the process and data in the tests themselves and in the results to improve student learning (Delong and Morgan, 1998). I can show that my involvement with the Principals' group inspired them to monitor their practice such that they influenced positively the quality of educational experience for the teachers and students in their schools (Delong and Wideman, 1998b). Evidence exists of how I have supported other administrators to help those for whom they are responsible, so that the same circles of influence are evident in their dealings with people at grass roots level (Black and Rasokas, 2000; Knill-Griesser, 2000; Mills, 1999).

If I had to choose one episode that captures how I believe I have influenced the quality of educational experience for others on a wide range of fronts, I would cite my work with Cheryl Black. We tell of our work in our papers for the International Conference on Teacher Research (Black and Delong, 1999, 2000). In the papers we deal with the concept of influence, and I will explain shortly what is of particular significance in our work for the idea of developing communities of reflective practitioners through action research.

My epistemology of educational leadership

During the summer of 1999 I began synthesising my research as my thesis. This would be the public presentation of my theory of leadership, as I understand it in relation to the people I support. I think it is worth spelling out here what that entails.

When I read traditional texts on educational leadership, I encounter a domain of propositional ideas. I read about what leaders should do, and how they might possibly achieve the recommendations. This is the situation which Clark lamented (see p. 275).

Now let me tell you of the reality of my own practice.

In the 1998–99 school year, I accomplished the following:

- visited all 21 schools in my family of schools at least three times and some many more times;
- created a new family of schools meeting structure with a Professional Development planning committee responsible for the staff development part of the agenda and reviewed it twice;
- set expectations in place for the school support centre;
- developed and implemented an 8-facet Leadership programme;
- developed a partnership with Brock University to pilot an on-site MEd course;
- trained new support staff;
- developed and implemented processes for the provincial assessments, new report cards and enhanced assessment strategies;
- expanded the Career Education Centres and other partnerships into the new areas of the board;
- developed new leaders and expanded the action research networks across the board;
- reviewed and implemented elementary and secondary curriculum;
- extended the corporate side of staff development;
- conducted a secondary school accommodation (school closing) study.

On the face of it, I am of course busy, creating new opportunities, sustaining initiatives, conducting my work in an efficient and effective manner. Describing my work in this objective way, however, does not communicate what makes my work successful, or why I believe I am justified in calling it educative. In order to communicate the value of my work in terms of how I understand my educative influence, I need to theorise my practice as a leader in a way that shows how the work is educationally influential. For this, I have to explain the criteria and standards of judgement I use to judge the quality of my work.

The criteria I choose for my work

I identify as a major criterion for judging the quality of my work the issue that I need to show how the work is having an impact in all the contexts of education where I am active. In the list above, can I be reasonably sure that all these contexts are educative? Can I be sure that the quality of education is as active in the formal contexts of developing an MEd programme as it is in my informal interactions with colleagues in the family of schools? This overarching criterion embeds a set of other criteria. How can I be sure that my own commitment to educative relationships is apparent in the practices of other people? Have they learnt from me? Have I communicated to all persons with whom I am in contact what I have learnt to be necessary in educational leadership? Given the diversity and wide range of my own activity, how can I be sure that my influence is felt in all the contexts of my professional life?

At a practical level, the criteria I have identified manifest as issues of care and support. Do the people with whom I come into contact feel that their lives are enriched because of our interaction? Do we feel sufficiently confident within our own relationships that we can take responsibility for our own learning and encourage others to do the same?

My standards of judgement

I judge the quality of my work and influence in terms of the values which drive my life.

At the heart of my seemingly multitudinous tasks remains intact the sanctity of personal relationship. I believe that it is in nurturing people, in caring about them in a way that they feel valued and honoured, that I can help them to become autonomous and strive to realise the educative potential within themselves. In all my dealings with people, regardless of their rank, context or position, I approach them with respect, regarding them as my equals and capable of generating their own creative responses. I have learnt the importance of not speaking on behalf of others; I encourage and support them to speak for themselves. I judge the quality of my work in terms of whether I live these values in my encounters with all people in all my contexts – am I the same person in an encounter with a vulnerable person such as a student as I am in an encounter with a powerful person such as a senior administrator? Do I bring the same values of respect and honour to all my encounters?

Further, by consistently living my values in my work and never accepting any slippage between my values and my practice, am I able to influence other people to do the same? Do I live out what I say I believe? Can I show the integrated nature of my theory and practice so that the way I live manifests as a personal educational theory that potentially has influence in the lives of others for personal-social development?

Evidence

I have identified a baseline for myself in this regard. I believe that if I can show that one child benefited from one teacher, and that I can trace the quality of the relationship between the child and teacher to my influence, I can begin to think that, yes, I am having an influence. Such an opportunity presented itself.

In December 1999 a delegation of three Japanese professors visited with me to learn from my experience in implementing action research in a school system. I wanted to give them a complete view of the work I am doing, and I provided a number of opportunities for them to hear the voices of the teachers and students working together. It was at a session with Cheryl's students that the evidence emerged which my colleague had challenged me to find four years ago.

Cheryl's students talked with her about their involvement in her research on her teaching practice, and their growing capacities to enquire about and reflect on their learning. Several of the students commented that they felt they were learning better because Cheryl was giving them opportunities to think critically, to speak on their own behalf, to create and voice their own ideas without anxiety, to feel valued, to believe that their contributions were worthwhile. The conversation was tape-recorded, and the evidence exists in publicly available form.

This I think is a key episode to show how the students felt that the quality of their educational experience had been enhanced because of Cheryl's teaching. Cheryl relates how the quality of her educational experience has been enhanced because of my influence (Black and Delong, 1999). At the heart of the relationships within all our contexts is the quality of relationship, the capacity to live out our commitment to education.

I like to think, following McNiff's idea of the iterative nature of generative transformational systems, that the same qualities that characterise this episode as educative are visible throughout all my work and relationships. Perhaps they are not yet there in fully realised form in all contexts, but it is clear that the influence is becoming visible as demonstrated in this episode. I like to think that I will continue to exercise my influence in all the contexts of my professional life such that, eventually, anyone visiting any context within the system for which I am responsible will encounter the same kinds of relationships and hear the same kinds of stories of educative influence.

This, then, is my educational epistemology of the superintendency. It is an educational story of educational stories, circles within circles of influence. I intend to continue trying to show how I aim to influence people in all contexts, so that the quality of education for teachers, students, union representatives, administrators, and all other participants, will demonstrate their own commitment to the kinds of relationships that will ensure that the work is a living-out of educational values.

Summary

These are interesting times in which to be an educational leader. I have matured personally and professionally, and am now able more to understand the importance of the research in which I am engaged. My research has helped me improve, be accountable for my actions, and 'shape a professional identity' (Connelly and Clandinin, 1999). I am fortunate to work with many talented and caring people – staff, students, parents and community members. The growing strength of the action research movement in my board and in the province and its capacity to improve student learning sustains my commitment to its potential. I believe that my research is contributing to the development of insider educational theory. I intend to encourage others to produce their accounts of practice to show how my influence has inspired them to exercise their influence in the lives of others for personal-social benefit. If our aim as educators is to create a world better than the one we currently live in through education, and if we feel we are in positions of influence to do so, we need to support the development of the kind of practical theory in action that will show our practices and also explain the justifications we give for what we are doing. For me, educational administration and leadership are educative, and I hope that I am contributing to a theory of education that will show that educational reality.

End note

Iterative patterns of influence are evident throughout my story. I am showing how I was influenced by Jack, and how he encouraged me to discover and develop my potential for influence in the lives of those in my care. In turn, I have encouraged the people for whom I am responsible to do the same. In turn, we hope, the children who are the focus of the educational system will find the capacity themselves to become reflective and consider their responsibility in developing a social order in which their children will be happy to live.

Thank you, Jack, for your leadership in inspiring me to develop my own epistemology, and thank you, colleagues, for listening to me while I encourage you to become leaders in your own right.

13 How one school is fulfilling the vision of Peter Senge's 'learning organisation'

Carmel Lillis

Introduction

In *The Fifth Discipline*, Peter Senge says: 'The organizations that will truly excel in the future will be the organizations that discover how to tap people's commitment and capacity to learn at *all* levels in an organization' (1990: 4; emphasis in original). I believe that the school of which I am privileged to be principal is such an organisation. If you were to visit our school you would encounter people at all levels who are engaged in learning, not only learning about subject matters, but also learning about themselves and their own process of thinking, and how to work cooperatively with others. You would be invited to talk with them in the spirit of learning: to see what they are learning, and to engage in a learning experience yourself. I like to think that the school can claim that it is a learning organisation, and that all its members will be well prepared to contribute to the educational practices of any future learning organisations of which they might become a part.

I believe the situation is a living-out of the recommendations of the new revised Primary School Curriculum (Government of Ireland, 1999b), which echoes Senge's sentiments and suggests ways for achieving them through education (p. 10):

> The curriculum seeks to satisfy the developmental and educational needs of the children it serves in the context of the contemporary society in which they live. It provides for children's immediate needs and interests, and at the same time prepares them to benefit from further education. It enables children to function effectively in a changing society and to cope successfully with the demands of modern life.

For 'children' one could substitute 'manager' or 'participant' as the context requires.

How this situation came about is recounted in the story which follows.

On becoming a principal

In 1993 I was appointed principal of a mixed infants school in Dublin. On my appointment I was anxious to learn how to do this new job, for I now perceived myself in a position of management and educational leadership, and wanted to find ways to use my influence to fulfil, as I saw it, my responsibility to make the experience of being in school educative for all members of the community and enable them to understand how to live life to the full as members of a learning community. At that time there was no formal training available for newly appointed principals. It was normal practice for them to join support groups in their local education centres, and learn about the work from more experienced colleagues.

With some misgivings, I went along with established practice and attended three meetings of the group in my nearest centre. My unspoken lack of ease was compounded by the kind of advice I was then given. I was evidently expected to keep rules and regulations, and to control colleagues and others for the educational good of the children. This advice however was quite contrary to my understanding of my work and aims as a principal, aspects which I had articulated in the selection process that had led to my appointment. Although I did not use this form of words at the time, I can see that I was already beginning to generate my own theory of educational leadership, and this emergent theory took as a central tenet the idea that I was a teacher and administrator who has a responsibility to continue to pursue development and perfectibility, as Tolstoy says, both for myself and also for others.

Development and perfectibility, however, do not simply happen. They are nurtured through reflecting on experience, and through developing the confidence to act on the new learning that is generated through the reflection. I intuitively knew what kind of principal I wanted to be. I knew the kind of leadership I wanted to offer. I already had experience of other people's leadership. I was convinced that, if I could reflect and draw on my own life history in education and continue to learn about my work, I would be in a stronger position to lead the school community in my own way which would fulfil the values of education that informed my practice. From subsequent study I can now articulate this vision as a wish to generate my own living educational theory for my professional practice (Whitehead, 1993: 119). In telling my story of the creation of my own epistemology of educative leadership I am engaging with questions of the kind, 'How do I live my values more fully in my practice?' (Whitehead, 1989), and producing the evidence to show that I am doing so.

I did not continue as a member of the support group. Although well-intentioned, the members of the group were content to stay at the level of propositional theory, in which they offered ideas about best practice, but did little to support me in my desire to explore my own practice and test my ideas about education against the reality of working with other people to achieve educational goals. If I had stayed with the group, and subscribed to their dominant propositional epistemology, I think I might have become the living contradiction that Whitehead speaks about (1993), in that I would have stayed with unsatisfactory practices while also holding a vision of alternative solutions which could lead to improved practices. So I broke free and decided to forge my own way in company with those in school whose lives I might be able to influence positively.

The school experience – early days

When I was first appointed I felt quite isolated by virtue of the fact that I had come from another school, and I felt myself a stranger. I reasoned that colleagues would need time to get to know me, and develop confidence in me and my way of working. Isolation, I soon discovered, was the norm. Teachers were isolated in their own classrooms (see Fullan, 1992; Hargreaves, 1994). In spite of the efforts of the Home–School Co-ordinator to involve parents in the education of their children, parents did not feature in the school life. It seemed that our school was closed to the public. Attitudes and practices that isolated were everywhere: teachers were content to teach in a fairly hierarchical manner, and they insisted on stereotyping me as a traditional principal, probably basing their perceptions on a model of other principals with whom they had worked in the past. I could understand this, of course, having just recently left the ranks of teachers myself, and I was acutely aware of the kind of anger that builds up from hierarchical relationships. I often took part in informal conversations where I heard stories of teachers' lives in school, and how organisational arrangements withheld time, encouragement and responsibility from committed staff, and so inhibited their development as educators (Johnson and Johnson, 1989). I recognised myself here, and I was determined that things would be different for the teachers I had the responsibility to support.

With this value in mind, and in spite of the difficulties of my new position, I resolved to work with an attitude of generosity and respect towards my colleagues (McNiff *et al.*, 1992). I began to address the problems we faced one by one. All the time my main concern was, 'How do I improve my practice such that colleagues, students and parents will find professional and personal satisfaction in their work?' My first challenge was to combat hostility and try to generate an atmosphere of trust. I reasoned that if colleagues currently saw me as a traditional hierarchical principal, I had to change the perception and offer an alternative image of how a principal could act as a servant-leader. This would not be easy, but it had to be done, in order to persuade people to revise what they saw as established reality and accept the existence of other forms of leadership. I decided to act in very practical ways which would show my respect for every member of staff. If resources were required, I personally saw that they were available. I collaborated with teachers when they taught music and art, always adopting a supportive role to themselves. I cooked treats for special days. I accepted criticism without defensiveness or retreat into aggression. I began the spiralling journey of action research which has allowed me to work towards the transformation of practice in school.

My deepest values commit me to honouring the other as a manifestation of the sacred. I recognise that each individual in the organisational setting has their own set of values on which they base their practice. My task as principal would be to support teachers, parents and students such that their work was a lived manifestation of these values, in cooperative negotiation with other workplace colleagues.

So what was new in my scholarship?

Researching one's own practice and becoming a practitioner-researcher in the practice context (Whitehead, 1993: 121) was, at this time, an entirely new concept in Irish education. In traditional research methodologies, research was something done on others, not on oneself. To accept that practitioners were entitled to do research on their own work would legitimise practitioners as competent judges of their own practice, and that was contrary to the dominant epistemology of the time. In my own developing awareness of my principalship, accompanied by a growing critical understanding of the form of theory used to understand the principalship, I began to question how an analysis of the work of others could guarantee improved practice for the researcher. I began to become increasingly convinced that an educative form of leadership can be nurtured only by a resolve to reflect on action in action, and free oneself from the dependency on the categories of established theory and technique, and be free to construct a new theory of the unique case (see Schön, 1983, 1995). This implies that any principal, if they are living up to their own high standards of human and professional competency, can construct their own theory of what it means to be a principal. They aim to live this theory, in the sense that they act so that their ideals can be seen to be lived in practice. Their vision for practice and the practice itself are synthesised. There is no contradiction between what they believe to be a possibility and the lived reality (Whitehead, 1993). They ask colleagues if the refined practice is more conducive to learning for students and teachers. They produce empirical evidence from the recorded responses from colleagues that what they say has happened actually has happened. Obviously some colleagues may disagree, and may suggest other ways of facilitating learning. All critique is welcomed in the search for improvement.

The validation by colleagues that events happened as reported has to be authentic, but this places the researcher in a vulnerable position. When I asked teachers in my school to suggest ways in which I could improve my practice as principal I came to them with open hands, willing to accept criticism, and hoping that through working and reflecting collaboratively we might journey together in our search for the ideal learning conditions in our school.

Authentic research

Jean McNiff supported me as I undertook my research into the question, 'How do I improve my effectiveness as principal of an infant school?' (C. Lillis, 1998). The study, based on my work in school and validated by colleagues, led to the award of Master of Education from the University of the West of England. To gain the award, I presented evidence to the university of the positive effects of my self-study during the period of my research. Zeichner (1999) speaks about the tremendous impact of self-study, suggesting that it has probably been the single most significant development in the field of teacher education. This comment is particularly relevant in the Irish context. In studying my practice and narrowing my research focus on my attempts to introduce improvements in the areas of staff development, communications and cultivating a climate of care in the school, and producing validated evidence to show the outcomes of my work, I was, I believe, generating a form of theory that could have significant implications for the future of Irish education (C. Lillis, 2000).

The kinds of practices my study generated in school have, I believe, transformed the professional lives of teachers and the lives of the parents and children we serve. Possibly most significantly, we appear to have evolved into a community of care. We actively try to care for one another, doing our best to enable one another to live in a way that is authentic for ourselves in company with others. Caring on this view goes beyond sentimentality and embraces all persons, whatever their social grouping, ethnicity or position. Caring for others, nurturing their growth and development as I nurture my own, has paradoxically enabled me to experience real maximal moral development (Noddings, 1984). When I began my research I focused on practices that could make our school a more effective institution. A solid communications structure would ensure that information was disseminated quickly and efficiently. Staff development would mean that colleagues would begin to reflect on how they might improve their work. Nurturing a climate of care could help all of us to feel valued so that we could do our educational work more effectively. I learned through my research that caring for others was the most important aspect of my work (C. Lillis, 2000). Having spent time thinking about these issues, I now appreciate that caring involves open and trusting dialogue (the research aspect of communication) that flourishes easily when people can speak together about what they consider worthwhile in their work and how they see themselves as caring human beings. Caring as an integral part of a principal's practice also implies a responsibility to encourage and nurture colleagues as they make choices about their own professional development and identities (the research aspect of staff development). I began to see how my range of influence and responsibility was spreading in ever-increasing circles. I sensed that my ability to respond to others' needs would be in direct relation to my capacity to develop as an educational leader within my context.

In order to make this a reality, I resolved that our school should become a centre for educational enquiry, and I systematically set about developing structures and processes to enable this to happen. I convened a formal research group in September 1998, so that colleagues could explore for themselves the potential of personal action enquiry to improve practice. The members of this group include the supervisor of a community employment scheme situated in the school, a visiting teacher for traveller children, a home/school/community co-ordinator, resource and class teachers. The group has now attracted members from other schools. We meet each month to discuss ways in which we can improve our work for our own professional development and for the educational benefit of the children. Jean facilitates the group. I can trace the impact of my own educational influence here. By accepting the moral imperative of improving my own practice, I believe I have inspired others to do the same. There are five participants from our staff in the group. They have acted as a leaven for the development of other colleagues. By this I mean that they have envisioned and acted out an improved way of being educators in our school. They have managed to bring the attitudes of the action researcher into their conversations and dealings with other members of staff so that we are now able to engage in productive analysis of a student's difficulties without individual teachers feeling criticised. Colleagues work cooperatively to focus on the needs of the children. The acceptance by the teachers of the freedom to work together has enabled me to enlist the expertise of other professionals, psychologists, counsellors and family therapists, in an effort to improve the situations of our most vulnerable children.

I resolved to make spaces for colleagues to have creative conversations with one another (see Jean Clandinin's comments in Chapter 9). I had come to appreciate the value of this from my previous research. At that time, by being creative with my own work and taking on some of the responsibilities of their teaching duties (I regularly took the whole school for singing at one point), I had enabled colleagues to come together to discuss their work during the school day. Their conversations allowed them to share with one another the values that inspired their work and how they tried to live them in practice. Nixon (1995; in Ghaye and Ghaye, 1998: 37) contends that articulating their values is the prime task of teachers. He insists moreover that these values should not be worked out in isolation and abstraction, but in collaboration with colleagues and amid the complexities of school life. I believe it is not enough only to articulate our values; it is also necessary to take action and find ways to live them out in practice. This moves us beyond propositional theories and into action theories. Colleagues in school worked out their values while debating issues such as discipline, parental involvement in school, and staff development. They also decided for themselves how they would achieve the realisation of those values. I was not present for these discussions (again in my attempt to create spaces for others), although I always received a written report on the deliberations. Over time it has been possible to see the results of the initiative in the lived practices of teachers. There is general agreement among the staff that staff meetings became more positive, and there was greater exchange of views in an enhanced atmosphere of supportive critique. In simple terms the air was cleared so that we were able to make progress on evaluating our performance in school.

I have continued with the practice of creating conversational spaces for colleagues. One striking feature of the change that has happened, they say, as a result, is the difference in teachers' language as they talk about their teaching or about children. Their language has become more concise, more informed, more dialogical, as I understand it. They have adopted a reflective attitude to their work that is evident in their conversations with personnel from other contexts who visit the school to help our children with special educational needs. There is also substantial evidence in our formal records, and also in informal encounters, that teachers speak more with children, particularly as they are now undertaking collaborative research enquiries (see p. 293).

We have together made efforts to upgrade our school in terms of the curriculum that is offered to the children, in collaborative practices among colleagues and in together finding time to reflect continually on what we are doing. Our work together has helped us to create caring and committed relationships (Johnson and Johnson, 1989; in Beck, 1994: 65).

I have heard teachers and parents say that their interactions are grounded in the belief that the integrity of human relationship should be held sacred, echoing Starratt's idea that the school as an organisation 'holds the good of human beings within it as sacred' (1993: 53). In reality this means that parents are free to talk to their children's teacher at any time during the day. Such ease of access and welcoming attitudes have enabled parents to unburden themselves of concerns for their children at critical moments without feeling further disadvantaged by the kinds of power games that characterise many parent–teacher interactions in conventional school scenarios. Parents and teachers share significant life events. Teachers listen to stories of illness, loss and bereavement. Parents are generous in their support of teachers who may be experiencing a hard time in their own personal lives. This kind of communication is not gossip. It is based on a genuine care for others and empathy for real-life situations.

Parents have come to see the school as a centre for learning, not only for their children but also for themselves. Courses and classes for parents are organised by the Home/School/Community coordinator at their request. In this way we are hopeful that the children, embraced by this example of continuing learning, will stay longer in the education system.

Parents as action researchers

I want to return to my aim of living my values in my practice. If I value all persons, and if I hold the good of all persons as sacred, then I must share the benefits of whatever I find good in the life of the school with parents in the school. I have therefore embarked, with Jean's help, on the process of convening a group of parent action researchers in school.

The group (all mothers) came together as Mothers for Education (their choice of title, though I wonder what will happen when fathers join us) to prepare an Easter fair of dough-craft designs. The proceeds of the sale would buy a computer. I thought that I could work two strands together, supporting the practical work of the mothers while encouraging them to keep diaries of their learning. This was more difficult than I had foreseen.

Participants were initially distrustful of the language I used. I had to find a way of communicating that spoke to parents' experiences. The initiative was planned partly to help them gain confidence in their capacity for learning. Over time we developed a professional language about our work, and one day, during a conversation with Jean about their own process of learning, people began to articulate what form their learning was taking and speak about themselves as researchers. A picture emerged of their being comfortable with their tutor, Geraldine, and acknowledging the collaboration that had developed in the group and pride in the beautiful objects being made. What we were describing was in fact an optimum learning situation. All agreed that this could be transferred to a home situation. We discussed how we need to have high expectations for our children and to accept them and all their efforts with what Rogers (1967) calls unconditional positive regard. Geraldine Smyth, the group tutor, has written about her experience of working with the parents, and the learning this has generated in herself (Smyth, 2000).

The Minister for Education and Science opened the Easter fair. Members of the group were presented with certificates, a source of great pride in their achievements. My work now is to record and disseminate this process, with the parents' help, so that the learning that has taken place can be acknowledged and disseminated, and will hopefully also inspire new learning for others. I believe that this phase of the project will be complete when each participant can claim ownership of their own learning, and can speak confidently to others about this.

Children as action researchers

In the same way as there is a temptation to speak about marginalised groups such as parents, the poor, or travellers (Lynch, 1999), there is also a temptation to speak about children as data, and not to speak directly with them. As our different research groups developed, so a public professional awareness grew that we were not involving the children in choosing the form or content of their own education. We had grown accustomed to the traditional model of teaching, as something done to children, rather than a model of learning, as a creative conversation in which children and adults engage about their learning (see also Elliott, 1998). Our image of children had been one of fairly passive recipients rather than active choosers. Our encounters with our own learning made us critical of our own practice, and we began to see how we were marginalising the children by not inviting their opinions about their own learning. We were speaking on behalf of our children instead of helping them to speak for themselves with us.

Coincidentally, this awareness was growing at the same time as the consultation process which led to the publication of the revised Primary School Curriculum (Government of Ireland, 1999b). This relates to the set of policy recommendations that children themselves should become researchers of their own practice who are responsible for identifying their own learning needs and monitoring their progress as they learn how to access information and develop the kind of knowledge that will enable them to become responsible citizens for the twenty-first century.

I have recently focused on how I can generate evidence to show that these recommendations are lived out in the daily practices of our school. The evidence exists in the stories that teachers tell of how they can show the nature of their educative influence with their children. In our school, through the confidence-building of the action research group, several teachers had begun to plan developmental portfolios for the children. During our conversations they were able to validate their new methodology by giving examples of the responses of the children to their own learning. They showed how children were invited to maintain records of their work, and, over time, were able to comment on why they felt one piece of work was to be preferred to another. The children helped one another, and engaged in animated conversations about how they could make judgements about their own work. Teachers recount stories from their class-rooms in which children share the excitement of their learning with the teacher. In this way, we believe, we are encouraging children to become reflective researchers (Steinberg and Kincheloe, 1998) who are able to make critical judge-ments on the quality of their work and their own learning, as well as live out the recommendations of the new Primary Curriculum.

As a group, the teachers and I have found opportunities to present our work to a variety of audiences, such as at the Action Research Conference held at Dublin City University, 10 June 2000. We explain how we can theorise our indi-vidual and collective practice in terms of how we can show the nature of our educative influence in the lives of others – parents, children, colleagues and administrators (C. Lillis *et al.*, 2000).

This work is still at an initial phase, but we are progressing. I like to think that our school is becoming the centre of educational enquiry which I had envi-sioned, a place where lively and creative conversations of learning go on among all participants in all contexts. We are developing into a community of enquiring practitioners.

Validation

In making original claims to educational knowledge, it is important to produce validated evidence to show the reality of the situations one is claiming to have improved. As part of my own research I have done this consistently (C. Lillis, 2000) and encouraged others to do the same. I can produce documentation from children, parents, teachers, advisors, other principals, inspectors, to show that the quality of education throughout the school remains at a consistently high level. I also claim that the quality of education can be directly linked to my own efforts to raise children's and teachers' expectations of their potential for personal and collaborative learning. In this way, I hope, I am demonstrating how my own theory of educational leadership has contributed to the development of a learning organisation that has significant potential for future societal benefit.

Reflection

I recognise the development that has taken place in my own professional response, parallel to the development in the school community, as a result of my research on my practice as a principal. I have tried to deepen my understanding of my practice as an educational leader, as someone who has the potential to transform the lives of others. I see my leadership not in the sense of bringing people to places, but of encouraging them to find their own way to the places of their choice, in negotiation with others. I lead by encouragement and the invitation to become autonomous, to develop a capacity for free thinking and action.

I have tried to overcome my reluctance to believe that my work as principal of an infant school is any less important or serious than the work of practitioners in secondary schools or university settings. Throughout the research I have made an honest effort to make a case for practitioners to create their own epistemologies of practice from the accounts they give of their lives as they engage with everyday experience. I understand that my own theory of principalship will shift and develop in a variety of ways as I try to respond to the multitude of situations that will come my way. In all of them I will be guided by reflection on the values that underpin my life: values such as reflection, care, support, democracy and justice. These have always been the cornerstones of my life in education and are the living standards by which I judge my practice (Whitehead, 2000).

The action research methodology has enabled me to find practical ways of positively influencing myriad areas of educational life. I am attracted by its ethical stance and the rationality of its approach. I know from my own experience the positive benefits that have accrued to our school and to the individuals who have engaged with action research as a way of personal and professional development. I have now begun my doctoral studies with Jean through action research. I do not know where these studies may lead, but I do recognise that I am more self-assured, more confident in my capacity to generate legitimate educational theory than when I began my studies four years ago.

I can trace patterns of influence in the story of my development. At first I relied on seminars and conferences at which I accepted propositional forms of knowledge about what others insisted was my role. The same propositional framework was evident in the support group I joined when I was first appointed as principal. I was already intuitively assessing ways and means of furthering my understanding when I met with Jean and enrolled on a Masters programme. I can honestly say that this has had the most influential impact on my personal and professional development. I came away altogether from the idea of role, and saw that I created my work as I lived it. I became consciously reflective and critical, consciously aware that I was generating my own theory of principalship which was embodied in my practice. In turn, I have encouraged colleagues to study their practice, using the same methodology and developing the same educative practices. The influence is becoming felt at wider levels. During the past two years I have been invited to speak to the wider educational community on the benefits of personal action research for professional development. In this way, I believe, the circles of influence will continue to grow and expand, and solitary action researchers will soon find themselves taken up within communities of supportive reflective practitioners, all of whom are committed to learning how to improve their own work for the benefit of others.

Development and perfectibility, says Tolstoy, are endless. I agree. I accept the exciting challenge always to be in the process of creating my own life, and encouraging others to do the same. As parents, teachers, students and citizens, it is entirely within our grasp to create the kinds of futures we wish for our children. In our school, we know that our future is already in our present, and we consciously work together to achieve the educational goals we envision.

Epilogue

Reconciliations

I came off the ferry early tonight to the familiar and strangely welcoming lights of Rosslare. Strange; they have never welcomed me before. Until now they have glared down at me as I drove up the long hill from the harbour, What nationality are you, where are you going, please? I have not known for a long time.

For a while I lost my sense of identity. Who am I, tossing around on the sea in an effort to reclaim myself? I fled to Ireland to escape the pain at home, to find a new self in a new land. I never quite did. The home at home claimed me still. I settled in, though, and planted fuchsias in the garden and came to share the joys and sorrows of my neighbours, not hard to do in Ireland. For a while I had two homes and did not know which one to choose; whenever I was in one I felt homesick for the other.

I came to see myself as a person living in the margins, as Giroux (1992) describes those who occupy the spaces of border crossings. I belonged neither here nor there. Of Scottish parentage, I had never regarded myself as English though I lived in England; here in Ireland they say I speak with an English accent, and in England they call me Irish.

Who am I, working here but with British universities; part-timer, non-salaried (my choice), neither within nor without. Do I stand on the high ground or splash around in the swampy lowlands? Am I an academic or a practitioner? Do I become a juggler, speaking the right form of words in the right accent as the place dictates? Is my identity in an institution, and if not, where is it?

I began to doubt whether I was a person in my own right, turned into a wife when I married, turned into a displaced person when I divorced. Within two weeks of my marriage, the institutions – bank, solicitor, insurers, church – all changed my name. I became a property of an Other; I no longer had my own identity. Because I was divorced I had significant difficulty negotiating a mortgage in Ireland; divorced women are newly arrived strangers in the Irish establishment. Who are you, female, foreign, wilfully disobeyed your master, not quite right; who are you, wanting to live here, to teach ideas that we in the Establishment don't like; you who don't hear us properly, we who try to make you invisible because we don't quite understand what you are about.

Western intellectual traditions love categorisations and binary opposites. Still dominant technical rational epistemologies teach us to analyse, dissect, allocate to categories. Things have to be black or white, no intermediate shades of grey. We are taught from the cradle that we have to fit into a category. To belong we must identify with a structure, be a structure, and the structure is always fixed. To belong, we have to fit into mental boxes: step outside and you are outlawed (hooks, 1994). We learn, as the song says, to paint flowers with green leaves only.

The love of categorisation and binary opposites leads us to believe that This is Truth and That is Not. It has to be either–or, this or that, not both at the same time, or neither, or a mix. The empiricist colonisation of mind rejects the heart, extends its empire across inner and outer worlds, a domination of identity which manifests as the hegemony of nationalism. Was there ever an island so divided against itself – North or South, Catholic or Protestant, Irish or British, settled or traveller, rich or poor, democrat or aristocrat, struggling with the contradiction of the entrenched positioning of a patriarchal religious society caught up in a wild economic boom and its seduction of ready money. What of those in the gaps, Jews and people of colour, we who are working out who we are? Was there ever such a torrent of blame as the peace process totters and teeters, winners and losers, bullies and victims, it's your fault, no it's yours. A good place for a fragmented soul to learn to make its peace.

As I studied the literature of organisation theory I came to see how it was deeply rooted in the technical rational metaphors of fragmentation. I came to see how it engaged in a safe language of its own; as they say in Northern Ireland, you can talk a lot without saying anything important. Traditional organisation study says a lot about the safe issues of structures and processes, from a safe place of abstracted observation, up there on the high ground of Stormont or university administration towers. The words are not heard on streets or shop floors, where risky words are spoken, real people with real emotions, who are ready to transcend their difference in an effort to share their humanity.

They do not serve us well, these binary opposites, nor their metaphors of violent conflict. They do not help us see that we are more than our socially created categories; that the categories of skin colour, gender, physical capacity, intellectual ability, nationality are as hubristic and destructive as the manufactured categories of original sin and purgatory, categories which keep us under control and relegate countless millions to heartbreak. They do not come clean and say they are imaginary fantasies, not reality. They do not move us away from the metaphors of violence and domination, of imperialism and colonisation. The metaphors of categorisation and violence permeate the safe abstractions, ensure that they remain safe, out of reach of the peacemakers who rejoice in the language of real people and real lives, talking a lot and saying plenty.

Perhaps it takes extreme dislocation to re-group. Perhaps it takes the threat of personal disintegration to become humble and see the need for others. The struggle is the site for peace, the site for letting go one's prejudices, and learning to be present to the other. Perhaps it is within the struggle of coping with fragmentation that wholeness emerges, part of the evolutionary process towards ongoing life.

Might this be so of mental models as well as lived experience? As we come to appreciate that wholeness is an emergent property of human systems and win through the potentially destructive episodes of living, so also we come to appreciate the need to change the metaphors we live by in describing the process. The dominant metaphors of fragmentation intensify the dislocation of experience; there is no breaking free of the experience until we break free of the mental model.

I am not an identity created by someone else. I am not a displaced person. My identity is in my self, not in an institution or place; it is in relation with other people for whom I care. My care for them embeds my concern for self. They are my greater vision, not part of an Otherness which by definition renders all things the same. They are part of me. We share a common heritage and our one planet. How we care for one another determines our future. That we care gives us hope.

Let me be free to understand who I am, more than in opposition, more than in isolation. Let me see myself as a person first and a woman second; as a thinker rather than a category called an academic. Let me see myself as a person of integrity who cares for her mental world within her physical world within the social world, who is at home in the present as much as in a geographical place. What does it matter that the accent might seem strange? What matters is the quality of listening, the quality of relation.

New theories of organisation reflect the attributes of new organisations: collaborative, compassionate, holistic, emergent. The pictures are those of integration, and the patterns those of community. What metaphors might we develop for these new theories? Perhaps they are the metaphors within our stories as we tell the narratives of our lives, as journeys, as wanderings and homecomings. Perhaps, when we describe educative encounters and show how these nurtured our own learning, we can find new forms of expression to communicate the richness of the experience in which nothing is hidden and trust is a constant. These are metaphors of wholeness.

The lights are welcoming, and above them the stars which shine over my home in England and point the way to Dublin. What nationality are you, where are you going? I am more than my passport. I am a free citizen of the universe. Wherever I am, I am coming home.

References

Adlam, R. (1999) '"We need a night shift": notes on the failure of an educational design for police managers', *Educational Action Research* 7(1): 51–62.

Adorno, T. W., Frenkel-Brunswick, G., Levinson, D. J. and Sanford, R. N. (1950) *The Authoritarian Personality*. New York: Harper.

Ahier, J. and Esland, G. (eds) (1999) *Education, Training and the Future of Work*, vol. 1: *Social, Political and Economic Contexts of Policy Development*. London: Routledge and the Open University.

Alderfer, C. P. (1972) *Existence, Relatedness and Growth: Human Needs in Organisational Settings*. New York: Free Press.

Alvesson, M. and Deetz, S. (1999) 'Critical theory and postmodernism: approaches to organization studies', in S. Clegg and C. Hardy (eds), *Studying Organization: Theory and Method*. London: Sage.

Alvesson, M. and Willmott, H. (1996) *Making Sense of Management*. London: Sage.

American Psychological Association (1987) *Casebook on Ethical Principles of Psychologists*, rev. edn. Hyattsville, Md.: APA.

Anderson, G. L. and Herr, K. (1999) 'The new paradigm wars: is there room for rigorous practitioner knowledge in schools and universities?', *Educational Researcher* 28(5): 12–21.

Appignanesi, L. and Maitland, S. (eds) (1989) *The Rushdie File*. London: Fourth Estate.

Apple, M. (1993) *Official Knowledge: Democratic Education in a Conservative Age*. New York: Routledge.

Argyris, C. (1960) *Understanding Organizational Behaviour*. Homewood, Ill.: Dorsey.

Argyris, C. (1990) *Overcoming Organizational Defences*. Boston, Mass.: Allyn and Bacon.

Argyris, C. (1999) *On Organizational Learning*. Oxford: Blackwell.

Argyris, C. and Schön, D. (1974) *Theory in Practice: Increasing Professional Effectiveness*. San Francisco: Jossey-Bass.

Aronowitz, S. and DiFazio, W. (1999) 'The new knowledge work', in J. Ahier and G. Esland (eds), *Education, Training and the Future of Work*, vol. 1: *Social, Political and Economic Contexts of Policy Development*. London: Routledge.

ASTI (Association of Secondary Teachers, Ireland) (2000) 'Making sense of learning', *ASTIR* (Dublin: ASTI, April): 13.

Atkinson, M. (1971) *Orthodox Consensus and Radical Alternative: A Study in Sociological Theory*. London: Heinemann.

Atweh, B., Kemmis, S. and Weeks, P. (1998) *Action Research in Practice: Partnerships for Social Justice in Education*. London: Routledge.

Axelrod, R. (1990) *The Evolution of Co-operation*. London: Penguin.

Bachrach, P. and Baratz, M. (1962) 'Two Faces of Power', *American Political Science Review* 56: 948.

Bakhtin, M. M. (1981) *The Dialogic Imagination: Four Essays*, trans. C. Emerson and M. Holquist (eds). Austin: University of Texas Press.

Ballyantyne, M. and Teale, M. (1990) *Learn to Learn*. Lothian Regional Council: ABE.

Barnett, R. (2000) 'Working knowledge', in J. Garrick and C. Rhodes (eds), *Research and Knowledge at Work: Perspectives, Case Studies and Innovative Strategies*. London: Routledge.

Barrow, J. D. (1988) *The World within the World*. Oxford: Oxford University Press.

Bassey, M. (1999) *Case Study Research in Educational Settings*. Buckingham: Open University Press.

Bataille, G. (1987) *Eroticism*. London: Marion Boyers.

Bateson, G. (1972) *Steps to an Ecology of Mind*. New York: Ballantine.

Bateson, G. (1979) *Mind and Nature*. New York: Dutton.

Bateson, M. C. (1994) *Peripheral Visions: Learning Along the Way*. New York: HarperCollins.

Baum, J. (1999) 'Organizational Ecology', in S. Clegg and C. Hardy (eds), *Studying Organization: Theory and Method*. London: Sage.

Beck, A. T. (1989) *Cognitive Therapy and the Emotional Disorders*. New York: Penguin.

Beck, L. (1994) *Reclaiming Educational Administration as a Caring Profession*. New York: Teachers College Press.

Bell, B., Gaventa, J. and Peters, J. (1990) *We Make the Road by Walking: Myles Horton and Paulo Freire, Conversations on Education and Social Change*. Philadelphia: Temple University Press.

Benedict, R. (1934) *Patterns of Culture*. Boston, Mass.: Houghton-Mifflin.

Bennis, W. (1989a) *Why Leaders Can't Lead*. San Francisco: Jossey-Bass.

Bennis, W. (1989b) *On Becoming a Leader*. Reading: Addison Wesley.

Bergquist, W. (1998) 'From the pendulum to the fire: coming to terms with irreversible change', in G. Robinson Hickman (ed.), *Leading Organizations: Perspectives for a New Era*. Thousand Oaks, Calif.: Sage.

Bernstein, R. J. (1991) *The New Constellation: The Ethical-Political Horizons of Modernity/Postmodernity*. Cambridge: Polity Press.

Bertanlanffy, L. von (1950) 'The theory of open systems in physics and biology', *Science* 3: 23–9

Bertanlanffy, L. von (1968) *General System Theory*. New York: Braziller.

Best, R. (1999) 'Pastoral care and the millennium', in Ú. M. Collins and J. McNiff (eds), *Rethinking Pastoral Care*. London: Routledge.

Billington, R., Hockey, J. and Strawbridge, S. (1998) *Exploring Self and Society*. Basingstoke: Macmillan.

Black, C. and Delong, J. (1999) 'How can we, as teacher and superintendent, improve our practice by assessing our influence on each other in our roles as educational leaders and critical friends?' A paper presented at the International Conference on Teacher Research, Magog, Quebec.

Black, C. and Delong, J. (2000) 'Improving the quality of student learning by valuing the voices of others'. A paper presented at the International Conference of Teacher Research, Baton Rouge, Louisiana.

Black, C. and Rasokas, P. (2000) 'Supporting the process', *Ontario Action Researcher* 3(11E) (Editorial), available from http:www.unipissing.ca/oar.

Blanchard, G. T. (1995) *The Difficult Connection: The Therapeutic Relationship in Sex Offender Treatment*. Brandon, Vt.: The Safer Society Press.

Boas, M. and Chain, S. (1976) *Big Mac: The Unauthorized Story*. New York: Dutton.

Boff, L. (1985) *Church, Charism and Power: Liberation Theology and the Institutional Church*. London: SCM Press.

Bohm, D. (1983) *Wholeness and the Implicate Order*. London: Ark Paperbacks.

Bohm, D. (1987) *Unfolding Meaning*. London: Ark Paperbacks.

Bohm, D. (1996) *On Dialogue*, ed. L. Nichol. London: Routledge.

Boje, D. M. (1996) 'Pedagogy for the postmodern management classroom: Greenback Company', in D. M. Boje, R. P. Gephart Jr and T. J. Thatchenkery (eds), *Postmodern Management and Organization Theory*. Thousand Oaks, Calif.: Sage.

Bourdieu, P. and Passeron, J.-C. (1977) *Reproduction in Education, Society and Culture*. London: Sage.

Boyatzis, R. E. (1982) *The Competent Manager: A Model for Effectiveness Performance*. New York: Wiley.

Boyce, D. G. and O'Day, A. (eds) (1996) *Modern Irish History: Revisionism and the Revisionist Controversy*. London: Routledge.

Boyer, E. (1990) *Scholarship Reconsidered: Priorities of the Professoriate*. New Jersey: The Carnegie Foundation for the Advancement of Teaching.

Braverman, H. (1974) *Labor and Monopoly Capital*. New York: Monthly Review Press.

British Psychological Society (1991) *Code of Conduct, Ethical Principles and Guidelines*. Leicester: BPS (mimeo).

British Sociological Association (1989) *BSA Guidelines on Anti-Sexist Language*. London: BSA (mimeo).

Brookfield, S. (1987) *Developing Critical Thinkers: Challenging Adults to Explore Alternative Ways of Thinking and Acting*. Buckingham: Open University Press.

Brooks, J. and Brooks, M. (1993) *In Search of Understanding: The Case for Constructivist Classrooms*. Alexandria, Va.: Association for Supervision and Curriculum Development.

Brown, J. (1992) 'Corporation as community: a new image for a new era', in J. Rensch (ed.), *New Traditions in Business*. San Fransico: Berrett-Koehler.

Bruce Ferguson, P. (1999) 'Developing a research culture in a polytechnic: an action research case study'. Unpublished PhD thesis, the University of Waikato, Hamilton: available from http://www.twp.ac.nz/research.

Buber, M. (1937) *I and Thou*, trans. R. G. Smith. Edinburgh: T. & T. Clark.

Buckley, C. (2000) 'How can I use drama in my Irish lesson to improve my practice?' Unpublished MA dissertation, Cork, University of the West of England, Bristol.

Buckley, M. J. (2000) 'How can I improve my practice by using creative writing?' Unpublished MA dissertation, Cork, University of the West of England, Bristol.

Burawoy, M. (1979) *Manufacturing Consent*. Chicago: University of Chicago Press.

Burgoyne, J. (1993) 'The competence movement: issues, stakeholders and prospects', *Personnel Review* 22: 6–13.

Burgoyne, J. and Reynolds, M. (eds) (1997) *Management Learning: Integrating Perspectives in Theory and Practice*. London: Sage.

Burke, A. (1992) *Oideas: Teaching: Retrospect and Prospect*. Dublin: Stationery Office.

Burrell, G. (1999) 'Normal science, paradigms and metaphors, discourses and genealogies of anlaysis', in S. Clegg and C. Hardy (eds), *Studying Organizations: Theory and Method*. London: Sage.

Burrell, G. and Morgan, G. (1979) *Sociological Paradigms and Organizational Analysis: Elements of the Sociology of Corporate Life*. London: Heinemann.

Calás, M. and Smircich, L. (1991) 'Voicing seduction to silence leadership', *Organization Studies* 12(4): 567–602.

Capra, F. (1983) *The Turning Point: Science, Society and the Rising Culture*. London: Flamingo.

Capra, F. (1989) *Uncommon Wisdom: Conversations with Remarkable People*. London: Flamingo.

Capra, F. and Steindl-Rast, D. with T. Matus (1992) *Belonging to the Universe: New Thinking About God and Nature*. London: Penguin.

Carr, W. and Hartnett, A. (1996) *Education and the Struggle for Democracy: The Politics of Educational Ideas*. Buckingham: Open University Press.

Carr, W. and Kemmis, S. (1986) *Becoming Critical: Education, Knowledge and Action Research*. London: Falmer.

Casey, C. (1996) *Work, Self and Society: After Industrialism*. London: Routledge.

Castells, M. (1997) *The Rise of the Network Society*, vol. 1. Oxford: Blackwell.

Casti, J. L. (1990) *Paradigms Lost: Images of Man in the Mirror of Science*. London: Scribners.

Champy, J. and Hammer, M. (1993) *Reengineering the Corporation*. London: Nicholas Brealey.

Chandler, A. D. and Deams, H. (eds) (1980) *Managerial Hierarchies*. Cambridge, Mass.: Harvard University Press.

Chen, J., Krecheveshy, M. and Viens, J. with E. Isberg (1998) *Building on Children's Strengths: The Experience of Project Spectrum*. New York: Teachers College Press.

Chia, R. (1997) 'Process philosophy and management learning: cultivating "foresight" in management', in J. Burgoyne and M. Reynolds (eds), *Management Learning: Integrating Perspectives in Theory and Practice*. London: Sage.

Chomsky, N. (1957) *Syntactic Structures*. The Hague: Mouton & Co.

Chomsky, N. (1965) *Aspects of the Theory of Syntax*. Massachusetts: Massachusetts Institute of Technology.

Chomsky, N. (1966) 'The Responsibility of Intellectuals', reprinted in N. Chomsky (1988) *The Chomsky Reader*, ed. J. Peck. London: Serpent's Tail.

Chomsky, N. (1982) 'Punishing Vietnam', reprinted in N. Chomsky (1988) *The Chomsky Reader*, ed. J. Peck. London: Serpent's Tail.

Chomsky, N. (1985) 'East Timor', reprinted in N. Chomsky (1988) *The Chomsky Reader*, ed. J. Peck. London: Serpent's Tail.

Chomsky, N. (1986) *Knowledge of Language: Its Nature, Origin and Use*. New York: Praeger.

Chomsky, N. (1988) *The Chomsky Reader*, ed. J. Peck. London: Serpent's Tail.

Chomsky, N. (1989) *Necessary Illusions: Thought Control in Democratic Societies*. London: Pluto.

Chomsky, N. (1996) *Powers and Prospects: Reflections on Human Nature and the Social Order*. London: Pluto.

Chomsky, N. (1997) *Class Warfare*. Vancouver, BC: New Star Books.

Clandinin, D. J. and Connelly, F. M (1995) *Teachers' Professional Knowledge Landscapes*. New York: Teachers College Press.

Clandinin, D. J. and Connelly, F. M. (2000) *Narrative Inquiry: Experience and Story in Qualitative Research*. San Francisco: Jossey-Bass.

Clark, D. (1997) 'The search for authentic educational leadership: in the universities and in the schools'. Invited presentation to Division A at the American Educational Research Association Annual Meeting, Chicago, April.

Clarke, L. (1992) 'Qualitative research: meaning and language', *Journal of Advanced Nursing* 17(2): 243–52.

Clegg, S. and Dunkerley, D. (1977) *Critical Issues in Organizations*. London: Routledge & Kegan Paul.

Clegg, S. and Dunkerley, D. (1980) *Organization, Class and Control*. London: Routledge & Kegan Paul.

Clegg, S. and Hardy, C. (1999) *Studying Organization: Theory and Method*. London: Sage.

Cluskey, M. (1997) 'How can I facilitate learning amongst my Leaving Certificate Applied students?' Unpublished MEd dissertation, Dublin, University of the West of England, Bristol.

Codling, A. (1997) 'Developing the right research environment' Paper presented at the 'Research and the New Tomorrow' Conference, UNITEC Institute of Technology, Auckland.

Collins, Ú. M. and McNiff, J. (eds) (1999) *Rethinking Pastoral Care*. London: Routledge.

Commission of the European Communities (1988) *The Future of Rural Society*. Brussels.

Condren, D. (1998) 'To design, test and develop a model of Action Planning which will stimulate large schools to improve the school experience for potential early school leavers, and to improve my own support role for the process'. Unpublished MEd dissertation, Dublin, University of the West of England, Bristol.

Condren, D. (2000) 'The Mol an Óige Project', in J. McNiff, G. McNamara and D. Leonard (eds), *Action Research in Ireland*. Dorset: September Books.

Conger, J. A. (1998) 'The dark side of leadership', in G. Robinson Hickman (ed.), *Leading Organizations: Perspectives for a New Era*. Thousand Oaks, Calif.: Sage.

Connelly, F. M. and Clandinin, D. J. (1990) 'Stories of experience and narrative inquiry', *Educational Researcher* 19(5): 2–14.

Connelly, F. M. and Clandinin, D. J. (1999) *Shaping a Professional Identity: Stories of Educational Practice*. New York: Teachers College Press.

Corey, S. M. (1953) *Action Research to Improve School Practices*. New York: Teachers College Press.

Corey, M. S. and Corey, G. (1997) *Group Process and Practices*, 5th edn. San Francisco, Calif.: Brooks Cole.

Corker, M. (1994) *Counselling: The Deaf Challenge*. London: Jessica Kingsley.

Corradi Fiumara, G. (1990) *The Other Side of Language: A Philosophy of Listening*. London: Routledge.

Couture, M., Delong, J. and Wideman, R. (1999) 'A school board, university, teacher federation partnership', *International Electronic Journal for Leadership in Learning*, available from www.acs.ucalgary.ca/~iejll/.

Covey, S. (1989) *The Seven Habits of Highly Effective People: Restoring the Character Ethic*; New York: Simon & Schuster.

Covey, S. (1990) *Principle-Centred Leadership*. London: Simon & Schuster.

Covey, S., Merrill, A. R. and Merrill, R. R. (1994) *First Things First*. New York: Simon & Schuster.

Crainer, S. (1996) *Key Management Ideas: Thinkers that Changed the Management World*. London: Financial Times Management.

Crites, S. (1971) 'The narrative quality of experience', *Journal of the American Academy of Religion*, 39(3): 191–311.

Csikszentmihalyi, M. (1990) *Flow: The Psychology of Optimal Experience*. New York: Harper-Collins.

Cunningham, B. (1999) 'How do I come to know my spirituality as I create my own living educational theory?' Unpublished PhD thesis, University of Bath.

Cunningham, I. and Dawes, G. (1997) 'Problematic premises, presumptions, presuppositions and practices in management education and training', in J. Burgoyne and M. Reynolds (eds), *Management Learning: Integrating Perspectives in Theory and Practice*. London: Sage.

Dahl, R. A. (1986) 'Power as the control of behaviour', in S. Lukes (ed.), *Power*. Oxford: Blackwell.

Daubner, E. (1982) 'Deified, denied or deprived: moral nature and counselling', *Counselling and Values* 26 (April).

Davies, P. (1984) *Superforce*. London: Unwin Paperbacks.

Deetz, S. and Kersten, S. (1983) 'Critical models of interpretive research', in L. Putnam and M. Pocanowsky (eds), *Communication and Organizations*. Beverly Hills, Calif.: Sage.

Delong, J. and Moffatt, P. (1996) 'Building a culture of involvement', *ORBIT* 27(4). Toronto: OISE/UT.

Delong, J. and Morgan, D. (1998) 'What we learned from grade three testing', Ontario Association for Supervision and Curriculum, *Curriculum Connections* 3(2).

Delong, J. and Wideman, R. (1996) 'Action research: school improvement that honours teacher professionalism', in N. D. Halsall and L. A. Hossack (eds), *Act, Reflect, Revise: Revitalize: Moving beyond Problem-solving to Renewal*. Toronto: Ontario Public School Teachers' Federation.

Delong, J. and Wideman, R. (1998) *Action Research: Improving Schools through Action Research* (video). Toronto: Ontario Public School Teachers' Federation.

Delong, J. and Wideman, R. (eds) (1998) 'Celebrating the Research of Teachers', *Ontario Action Researcher* 1(1E) (Editorial), http:www.unipissing.ca/oar.

de Porter, B. (1993) 'Discovering your personal learning style', in *Quantum Learning: Unleash the Genius Within You*, London: Paitkus Press.

de Saint-Exupéry, A. (1991) *The Little Prince*. London: Mammoth.

Dewey, J. (1916) *Democracy and Education*. New York: Free Press.

Dickens, L. and Watkins, K. (1999) 'Action research: rethinking Lewin', *Management Learning* 30(2): 127–40.

Dieks, D. (1994) 'The scientific view of the world: introduction', in J. Hilgevoord (ed.), *Physics and Our View of the World*. Cambridge: Cambridge University Press.

Ditton, J. (1979) 'Baking time', *Sociological Review* 27: 157–67.

Donaldson, L. (1985) *In Defence of Organization Theory: A Reply to the Critics*. London: Cambridge University Press.

Donaldson, L. (1995) *American Anti-Management Theories of Organization*. Cambridge: Cambridge University Press.

Donaldson, L. (1999) 'The normal science of structural contingency theory', in S. Clegg and C. Hardy (eds), *Studying Organization: Theory and Method*. London: Sage.

Donmoyer, R. (1996) 'Educational research in an era of paradigm proliferation: what's a journal editor to do?', *Educational Researcher* 25(2): 19–25.

Donovan, V. (1978) *Christianity Rediscovered: An Epistle from the Masai*. Indiana: Fides/Clarentian.

Douglas, M. (1996) *Purity and Danger*. London: Routledge & Kegan Paul.

Dreyfus, J. L. and Rabinow, P. (1983) *Beyond Structuralism and Hermeneutics*, 2nd edn. Chicago: University of Chicago Press.

Drucker, P. (1974) *Management: Tasks, Responsibilities, Practices*. London: Heinemann.

Drucker, P. (1989) *The New Realities*. New York: Harper & Row.

Drucker, P. (1993) *Post Capitalist Society*. Oxford: Butterworth Heinemann.

Drucker, P. (1995) 'The information executives truly need', *Harvard Business Review* (January–February).

Drudy, S. (2000) 'Preface', in J. McNiff, G. McNamara and D. Leonard (eds), *Action Research in Ireland*. Dorset: September Books.

Dworkin, A. (1991) *Mercy*. New York: Four Walls, Eight Windows.

Dyrberg, T. B. (1997) *The Circular Structure of Power: Politics, Identity, Community*. London: Verso.

Easterby-Smith, M. and Thorpe, R. (1997) 'Research traditions in management learning', in J. Burgoyne and M. Reynolds (eds), *Management Learning: Integrating Perspectives in Theory and Practice*. London: Sage.

Eden, C. and Huxham, C. (1996) 'Action research for management research', *British Journal of Management* 7(1): 75–86.

Eden, C. and Huxham, C. (1999) 'Action research for the study of organizations', in S. Clegg and C. Hardy (eds), *Studying Organization: Theory and Method*. London: Sage.

Edwards, D. (1998) *The Compassionate Revolution: Radical Politics and Buddhism*. Totnes, Green Books.

Edwards, R. and Tait, A. (2000) 'Forging policies in flexible learning', in V. Jakupec and J. Garrick (eds), *Flexible Learning, Human Resource and Organisational Development: Putting Theory to Work*. London: Routledge.

Egri, C. P. and Pinfield, L. T. (1999) 'Organizations and the Biosphere: Ecologies and Environments', in S. Clegg, C. Hardy and W. Nord (eds), *Managing Organizations: Current Issues*. London: Sage.

Elliott, J. (1991) *Action Research for Educational Change*. Buckingham: Open University Press.

Elliott, J. (1993) *Reconstructing Teacher Education: Teacher Development*. London: Falmer.

Elliott, J. (1998) *The Curriculum Experiment: Meeting the Social Challenge*. Buckingham: Open University Press.

Ellis, J. H. M. and Kiely, J. A. (2000) 'Action inquiry strategies: taking stock and moving forward', *Journal of Applied Management Studies* (June).

Esland, G., Esland, K., Murphy, M. and Yarrow, K. (1999) 'Managerializing organizational culture: refashioning the human resource in educational institutions', in J. Ahier and G. Esland (eds), *Education, Training and the Future of Work*, vol. 1: *Social, Political and Economic Contexts of Policy Development*. London: Routledge and the Open University.

Fals-Borda, O. and Rahman, M. A. (1991) *Action and Knowledge: Breaking the Monopoly with Participatory Action Research*. New York: Apex.

Fanon, F. (1967) *The Wretched of the Earth*. London: Penguin.

Farrell, S. (2000) 'Education for mutual understanding', in J. McNiff, G. McNamara and D. Leonard (eds), *Action Research in Ireland*. Dorset: September Books.

Ferguson, K. (1994) 'On bringing more theory, more voices, more politics to the study of organization', *Organization* 1(1): 81–100.

Ferguson, P. (1991) 'Liberation theology and its relevance to the Kiwi Christian'. Unpublished MSocSci thesis, University of Waikato, Hamilton.

Feynman, R. (1992) *The Character of Physical Law*. London: Penguin.

Fineman, S. (1999) 'Emotion and organizing', in S. Clegg and C. Hardy (eds), *Studying Organization: Theory and Method*. London: Sage.

Finnegan, J. (2000) 'Utilising an educational action research approach: facilitating more democratic actions in the classroom', *Irish Educational Studies* 19: 120–38.

Fisher, D. and Torbert, W. R. (1995) *Personal and Organizational Transformations*. London: McGraw-Hill.

Fitzgerald, M. (1998) *Learning for Life for CSPE*. Dublin: Gill & Macmillan.

Flood, R. L. and Romm, N. R. A. (1996) *Diversity Management: Triple Loop Learning*. Chichester: Wiley.

Foucault, M. (1977) *Discipline and Punish*. Harmondsworth, Penguin.

Foucault, M. (1980) 'Truth and power', in C. Gordon (ed.), *Power/Knowledge: Selected Interviews and Other Writings, 1972–1977*. Brighton: Harvester.

Foucault, M. (1991) *Remarks on Marx*, trans. R. J. Goldstein and J. Cascaito. New York: Columbia University Press.

Fox, S. (1997) 'From management education and development to the study of management learning', in J. Burgoyne and M. Reynolds (eds), *Management Learning: Integrating Perspectives in Theory and Practice*. London: Sage.

Freire, P. (1970) *Pedagogy of the Oppressed*. New York: Seabury.

Freire, P. (1972) *Cultural Action for Freedom*. New York: Penguin.

Freire, P. (1985) *The Politics of Education*. South Hadley, Mass.: Bergin & Garvey.

Frost, P. (1980) 'Towards a radical framework for practising organization science', *Academy of Management Review* 5(4): 501–7.

Fukuyama, F. (1995) *Trust: The Social Virtues and the Creation of Prosperity*. New York: Free Press.

Fukuyama, F. (1999) *The Great Disruption*. London: Profile Books.

Fullan, M. (1992) *What's Worth Fighting For in Headship?*. Buckingham: Open University Press.

Fullan, M. (1993) *Change Forces: Probing the Depths of Educational Reform*. London: Falmer.

Gadamer, H. G. (1975) *Truth and Method*. London: Sheed & Ward.

Gagliardi, P. (1999) 'Exploring the aesthetic side of organization life', in S. Clegg and C. Hardy (eds), *Studying Organization: Theory and Method*. London: Sage.

Gallagher, K. (1998) 'How can I monitor and support computer based training efficiently and effectively?' Unpublished MEd dissertation, Dublin, University of the West of England, Bristol.

Gardner, H. (1983) *Frames of Mind: The Theory of Multiple Intelligences*. New York: Basic Books.

Garfinkel, H. (1967) *Studies in Ethnomethodology*. Englewood Cliffs, N.J.: Prentice-Hall.

Garrick, J. (1998) *Informal Learning in the Workplace: Unmasking Human Resource Development*. London: Routledge.

Garrick, J. and Rhodes, C. (eds) (2000) *Research and Knowledge at Work: Perspectives, Case Studies and Innovative Strategies*. London: Routledge.

Gaughran, L. (1998) 'Developing business processes through collaborative staff development'. Unpublished MEd dissertation, Dublin, University of the West of England, Bristol.

Geertz, C. (1973) *The Interpretation of Culture*. New York: Basic Books.

George, W. H. and Marlatt, A. G. (1989) 'Foreword', in R. D. Laws (ed.), *Relapse Prevention with Sex Offenders*. New York: Guilford Press.

Ghaye, A. and Ghaye, K. (1998) *Teaching and Learning through Critical Reflective Practice*. London: David Fulton.

Gibb, J. R. and Gibb, L. M. (1955) *Learning to Work in Groups*. New York: Columbia University Press.

Gibson, R. (1986) *Critical Theory and Education*. London: Hodder & Stoughton.

Giddens, A. (1998) *The Third Way: The Renewal of Social Democracy*. Cambridge: Polity Press.

Gilligan, C. (1982) *In a Different Voice*. Cambridge, Mass.: Harvard University Press.

Giroux, H. (1988) *Teachers as Intellectuals: Towards a Critical Pedagogy of Learning*. South Hadley, Mass.: Bergin & Garvey.

Giroux, H. (1992) *Border Crossings*. New York: Routledge.

Giroux, H. and McLaren, P. (eds) (1989) *Critical Pedagogy, the State, and Cultural Struggle*. New York: SUNY Press.

Giroux, H. and Shannon, P. (eds) (1997) *Education and Cultural Studies*. New York, London: Routledge.

Glasersfeld, E. von (1995) *Radical Constructivism: A Way of Knowing and Learning*. London: Falmer.

Glavey, C. (2000) Dublin, personal correspondence.

Glavin, T. (2000) 'Where are we today in Irish education?' Unpublished working paper, Cork.

Godfrey, P. C. (1999) 'Service-learning and management education: a call to action', *Journal of Management Inquiry* 8(4): 363–78.

Goleman, D. (1996) *Emotional Intelligence: Why It Matters More Than IQ*. London: Bloomsbury.

Goodlad, J. I., Soder, R. and Sirotnik, K. (eds) (1990) *The Moral Dimensions of Teaching*. San Francisco: Jossey-Bass.

Goodson, I. and Dowbiggin, I. (1990) 'Docile bodies: commonalities in the history of psychiatry and schooling', in S. Ball (ed.), *Foucault and Education: Disciplines and Knowledge*. London: Routledge.

Gore, J. M. (1993) *The Struggle for Pedagogies: Critical and Feminist Discourses as Regimes of Truth*. New York: Routledge.

Gorinsky, R. and Ferguson, P. (1997) '(Ex)changing experiences of insider research'. Paper presented at the New Zealand Association for Research in Education Conference, Auckland, December.

Gould, S. J. (1990) *Wonderful Life: The Burgess Shale and the Nature of History*. London: Hutchinson.

Government of Ireland (1992) *Green Paper: Education for a Changing World*. Dublin: Stationery Office.

Government of Ireland (1995) *White Paper: Charting Our Educational Future*. Dublin: Stationery Office.

Government of Ireland (1998) *School Development Planning*. Dublin: Stationery Office.

Government of Ireland (1999a) *Whole School Evaluation: Report on the 1998/1999 Pilot Project*. Dublin: Stationery Office.

Government of Ireland (1999b) *Primary School Curriculum: Introduction*. Dublin: Stationery Office.

Gramsci, A. (1971) *Selections from the Prison Notebooks*, ed. Q. Hoare and G. Nowell-Smith. New York: International Publishers.

Grant, D. and Oswick, C. (eds) (1996) *Metaphor and Organization*. London: Sage.

Gray, J. (1993) *Beyond the New Right: Markets, Government and the Common Environment*. London: Routledge.

Gray, J. (1995) *Enlightment's Wake: Politics and Culture at the Close of the Modern Age*. London and New York: Routledge.

Gray, J. (1997) *Endgames: Questions in Late Modern Political Thought*. Cambridge: Polity Press.

Gray, J. (1999) *False Dawn: The Delusions of Global Capitalism*. London: Granta.

Grundy, S. (1996) 'Towards empowering leadership: the importance of imagining', in O. Zuber-Skerritt (ed.), *New Directions in Action Research*. London: Falmer.

Habermas, J. (1970) 'Towards a theory of communicative competence', *Inquiry* 13.

Habermas, J. (1972) *Knowledge and Human Interests*, trans. J. J. Shapiro. London: Heinemann.

Habermas, J. (1973) *Legitimation Crisis*, trans. T. McCarthy. Boston: Beacon Press.

Habermas, J. (1974) *Theory and Practice*, trans. J. Viertel. London: Heinemann.

Habermas, J. (1979) *Communication and the Evolution of Society*, trans. T. McCarthy. Boston: Beacon Press.

Halsey, A. H., Lauder, H., Brown, P. and Wells, A. S. (1997) *Education: Culture, Economy, Society*. New York: Oxford University Press.

Hamilton, M. L. (ed.) (1998) *Reconceptualizing Teaching Practice: Self-Study in Teacher Education*. London: Falmer.

Hanafin, J. and Leonard, D. (1996) 'Conceptualising and implementing quality: assessment and the Junior Certificate', *Irish Educational Studies* 15: 26–39.

Handy, C. (1990) *Inside Organisations: 21 Ideas for Managers*. London: BBC Books.

Handy, C. (1994) *The Empty Raincoat*. London: Hutchinson.

Handy, C. (1995a) *The Age of Unreason*. London: Arrow (original work 1989).

Handy, C. (1995b) *Beyond Certainty*. London: Century.

Handy, C. (1997) *The Hungry Spirit*. London: Hutchinson.

Haralambos, M. C. and Holborn, M. (1991) *Sociology: Themes and Perspectives*. London: Collins Educational.

Hargreaves, A. (1994) *Changing Teachers, Changing Times: Teachers' Work and Research Interaction*. London: Cassell.

Hargreaves, D. (1996) 'Teaching as a research-based profession: possibilities and prospects'. The Teacher Training Agency Annual Lecture. London: TTA.

Harré, R. and van Langenhove, L. (1999) *Positioning Theory*. Oxford: Blackwell.

Hassard, J. (1999) 'Images of time in work and organization', in S. Clegg and C. Hardy (eds), *Studying Organization: Theory and Method*. London: Sage.

Hayek, F. K. (1960) *The Constitution of Liberty*. Chicago: University of Chicago Press.

Heaney, S. (1999) *Beowulf: A New Translation*. London: Faber & Faber.

Heisenberg, W. (1989) *Physics and Philosophy*. New York: Penguin.

Held, D. (1987) *Models of Democracy*. Cambridge: Polity Press.

Henderson, C. (1998) 'How can I become a more effective adult educator and teach information technology appropriately?' Unpublished MEd dissertation, Dublin, University of the West of England, Bristol.

Henderson, H. (1996) *Building a Win-Win World: Life Beyond Global Economic Warfare*. San Francisco: Berrett-Koehler.

Herman, E. S. and Chomsky, N. (1988) *Manufacturing Consent: The Political Economy of the Mass Media*. London: Pantheon.

Heron, J. (1981) 'Experiential research methodology', in P. Reason and J. Rowan (eds), *Human Inquiry*. Chichester: Wiley.

Heron, J. (1992) *Feeling and Personhood: Psychology in Another Key*. London: Sage.

Hertzberg, F. (1966) *Work and the Nature of Man*. Cleveland, Ohio: World Publishing.

Higgins, A. (2000) 'Action Research: a means of changing and improving the clinical learning environment', in J. McNiff, G. McNamara and D. Leonard (eds), *Action Research in Ireland*. Dorset: September Books.

Hitchcock, G. and Hughes, D. (1995) *Research and the Teacher: A Qualitative Introduction to School-based Research*, 2nd edn. London: Routledge.

Hochschild, A. R. (1983) *The Managed Heart: Commercialization of Human Feeling*. Berkeley: University of California Press.

Hodgson, V. (1997) 'New technology and learning: accepting the challenge', in J. Burgoyne and M. Reynolds (eds), *Management Learning: Integrating Perspectives on Theory and Practice*. London: Sage.

Holley, E. (1995) 'What is good quality educational research?', *Action Researcher* 4 (Autumn).

Hollingsworth, S. (ed.) (1997) *International Action Research: A Casebook for Educational Reform*. London: Falmer.

Holt, J. (1982) *How Children Fail*. London: Penguin.

hooks, b. (1994) *Outlaw Culture; Revisiting Representations*. New York: Routledge.

Hopkins, D. (1993) *A Teacher's Guide to Classroom Research*, 2nd edn. Buckingham: Open University Press.

Hoyle, E. (1974) 'Professionality, professionalism and control in teaching', *London Educational Review* 3(2).

Hoyle, E. and John, P. (1995) *Professional Knowledge and Professional Practice*. London: Cassell.

Huber, J. (1995) 'A story of failed professional development', in D. J. Clandinin and M. F. Connelly (eds), *Teachers' Professional Knowledge Landscapes*. New York: Teachers College Press.

Huberman, M. (1992) 'Critical introduction', in M. Fullan, *Successful School Improvement*. Buckingham: Open University Press.

Hurst, D. (1995) *Crisis and Renewal: Meeting the Challenge of Organisational Change*. Boston: Harvard Business School Press.

Hutchinson, F. (1996) *Educating Beyond Violent Futures*. London: Routledge.

Hyland, Á. and Hanafin, J. (1997) 'Models of incareer development in the Republic of Ireland: an analysis', *Irish Educational Studies* 16: 144–72.

Ilyenkov, E. (1977) *Dialectical Logic*. Moscow: Progress.

James, C. and Vince, R. (2000) 'Developing the leadership capacity of headteachers'. Working paper, Treforest, University of Glamorgan.

James, G. (1991) *Quality of Working Life and Total Quality Management*, Work Research Unit Occasional Paper No. 50. London: ACAS, WRU.

Jarvis, P. (1987) *Adult Learning in the Social Context*. London: Croom Helm.

Johnson, D. W. and Johnson, R. T. (1989) *Cooperation and Competition: Theory and Research*. Edina, Minn.: Interaction.

Juran, J. (1988) *Juran on Planning for Quality*. New York: Free Press.

Kanter, E. Moss (1989) *When Giants Learn to Dance*. London: Simon & Schuster.

Kauffman, S. (1995) *At Home in the Universe: The Search for Laws of Complexity*. London: Viking.

Kearney, R. (1997) *Postnationalist Ireland*. London: Routledge.

Keep, E. and Mayhew, K. (1999) 'Evaluating the assumptions that underlie training policy', in J. Ahier and G. Esland (eds), *Education, Training and the Future of Work*, vol. 1: *Social, Political and Economic Contexts of Policy Development*. London: Routledge and the Open University.

Kemmis, S. and McTaggart, R. (eds) (1988) *The Action Research Planner*, 3rd edn. Geelong: Deakin University Press.

Kiely, J. A. and Ellis, J. H. M. (1999) 'Actions speak louder than words', *Management Services* 43(10): 32–4.

Kilpatrick, W. (1951) 'Critical issues in current educational theory', *Educational Theory* 1(1): 1–8.

Kingsley, C. (1995) *The Water Babies*. London: Penguin (original work 1863).

Knill-Griesser, H. (2000) 'Improving math attitudes through action research: attitude is the key to success', *Ontario Action Researcher*, http://www.unipissing.ca/oar.

Knowles, M. (1984) *The Modern Practice of Adult Education*. New York: Association Press.

Kolb, D. (1984) *Experiential Learning: Experience as the Source of Learning and Development*. Englewood Cliffs, N.J.: Prentice Hall.

Kotter, J. P. (1973) 'The psychological contract', *California Management Review* 15: 91–9.

Kuhn, T. S. (1970) *The Structure of Scientific Revolutions*, 2nd edn. Chicago: University of Chicago Press.

Kydd, L., Crawford, M. and Riches, C. (1997) *Professional Development for Educational Management*. Buckingham: Open University Press.

Laclau, E. (1977) *Politics and Ideology in Marxist Theory*. London: Verso.

Laclau, E. (1990) *New Reflections on the Revolution of Our Time*. London: Verso.

Laidlaw, M. (1996) 'How can I create my own living educational theory as I offer you an account of my educational development?' PhD thesis, University of Bath, available from the Living Theory Section of http:www.actionresearch.net.

Lakatos, I. and Musgrave, A. (1970) *Criticism and the Growth of Knowledge*. Cambridge: Cambridge University Press.

Lather, P. (2000) 'The Possibilities of Paradigm Proliferation'. A paper presented at the American Educational Research Annual Meeting, New Orleans, April.

Laurillard, D. (1993) *Rethinking University Teaching: A Framework for the Effective Use of Educational Technology*. London: Routledge.

Lee, B. (1997) *The Power Principle: Influence with Honor*. New York: Simon & Schuster.

Leonard, D. (1996) 'Quality in education and teacher development', *Irish Educational Studies* 15: 56–67.

Lévi-Strauss, C. (1963) *Structural Anthropology*. New York: Basic Books.

Levinson, D. J., Darrow, D. N., Klein, E. B., Levinson, M. H. and McKee, B. (1978) *The Seasons of a Man's Life*. New York: Knopf.

Levinson, M. (1962) *Men, Management and Mental Health*. Cambridge, Mass.: Harvard University Press.

Lewin, K. (1946) 'Action research and minority problems', *Journal of Social Issues* 2(4): 34–46.

Lewin, R. (1993) *Complexity: Life at the Edge of Chaos*. London: Phoenix.

Lillis, C. (1998) 'How can I improve my effectiveness as principal of an infant school?' Unpublished MEd dissertation, Dublin, University of the West of England, Bristol.

Lillis, C. (2000) 'Reclaiming school as a caring place', in J. McNiff, G. McNamara and D. Leonard (eds), *Action Research in Ireland*. Dorset: September Books.

Lillis, C. and Associates (2000) 'How do we show the nature of our educative influence in creating our school as a learning organisation?' A paper presented at the 'Action Research, Reflective Practice and Organisational Development' Conference, Dublin City University, Dublin, June.

Lillis, S. (1984) 'Rural development: the challenge for learning organisations', *Studies* no. 336 (Winter): 384–91.

Lomax, P. (1994) 'Standards, criteria and the problematic of action research', *Educational Action Research* 2(1): 113–26.

Lomax, P. (ed.) (1996) *Quality Management in Education*. London: Routledge.

Lomax, P. (1999) 'Working together for educative community through research', Presidential Address, *British Educational Research Journal* 25(1): 5–21.

Lorenz, C. (1994) 'Time has come for a revolution in style', *Financial Times*, 22 April.

Loughran, J. J. (1996) *Developing Reflective Practice: Learning About Teaching and Learning through Modelling*. London: Falmer.

Lovelock, J. (1991) *Gaia*. London: Gaia Books.

Lukes, S. (1974) *Power: A Radical View*. London: Macmillan Education.

Lynch, K. (1993) *The Hidden Curriculum*. London: Falmer.

Lynch, K. (1999) 'Equality studies, the academy and the role of research in emancipatory social change', *The Economic and Social Review* 30(1): 41–69; reprinted in J. McNiff, G. McNamara and D. Leonard (eds), *Action Research in Ireland*. Dorset: September Books.

Lyons, J. (1970) *Chomsky*. London: Fontana.

Lyotard, J.-F. (1984) *The Postmodern Condition: A Report on Knowledge*. Manchester: Manchester University Press.

Macdonald, B. J. (ed.) (1995) *Theory as a Prayerful Act: The Collected Essays of James B. Macdonald*. New York: Peter Lang.

MacIntyre, A. (1981) *After Virtue*. London: Duckworth.

MacIntyre, A. (1988) *Whose Justice? Which Rationality?*. Notre Dame, Ind.: University of Notre Dame Press.

MacIntyre, A. (1990) *Three Rival Versions of Moral Enquiry: Encyclopaedia, Genealogy, Tradition*. Guildford: Duckworth.

MacLure, M. (1996) 'Telling transitions: boundary work in narratives of becoming an action researcher', *British Educational Research Journal* 22(3): 273–86.

Macmurray, J. (1950) *Conditions of Freedom*. London: Faber & Faber.

Management Charter Initiative (1990) *Occupational Standards for Management*. London: MCI.

Management Charter Initiative (1991) *Management Standards*. London: MCI.

Management Learning (1999) 30(2), June.

Marcuse, H. (1964) *One Dimensional Man*. Boston: Beacon.

Marino Institute of Education (1992) *School Communities and Change*. Dublin: MIE.

Marsden, R. and Townley, B. (1999) 'The owl of Minerva: reflections on theory in practice', in S. Clegg and C. Hardy (eds), *Studying Organization: Theory and Method*. London: Sage.

Marshall, J. (1984) *Women Managers: Travellers in a Male World*. Chichester: Wiley.

Marshall, J. (1995) *Women Managers Moving On*. London: Routledge.

Marshall, J. and Reason, P. (1997) 'Collaborative and self-reflective forms of inquiry in management research', in J. Burgoyne and M. Reynolds (eds), *Management Learning: Integrating Perspectives in Theory and Practice*. London: Sage.

Martin, J. and Frost, P. (1999) 'The organizational culture war games: a struggle for intellectual dominance', in S. Clegg and C. Hardy (eds), *Studying Organization: Theory and Method*. London: Sage.

Marx, K. (1967) *Writings of the Young Marx on Philosophy and Society*, ed. L. D. Easton and K. H. Guddat. New York: Anchor.

Maslow, A. (1954) *Motivation and Personality*. New York: Harper & Row.

Matzinger, P. (1994) 'Tolerance, danger and the extended family', *Annual Reviews in Immunology* 12: 991–1045.

McAllister, J. (1996) *Beauty and Revolution in Science*. New York: Cornell University Press.

McClelland, D. (1961) *The Achieving Society*. Princeton, N.J.: Van Nostrand.

McClelland, D. and Burnham, D. H. (1976) 'Power is the great motivator', *Harvard Business Review*, March–April: 100–10.

Mc Cormack, C. (in press) 'Action research at home' in J. McNiff, *Action Research: Principles and Practice*, 2nd edn. London: RoutledgeFalmer.

McDermott, K. (1999) 'Reading practice: essays in dialogue and pedagogical conversation'. Unpublished working paper, Treforest, University of Glamorgan.

McGregor, D. (1960) *The Human Side of Enterprise*. New York: McGraw Hill.

McLaren, P. (1995) *Critical Pedagogy and Predatory Culture: Oppositional Politics in a Postmodern Age*. London: Routledge.

McLaren, P. (1997) *Revolutionary Multiculturalism: Pedagogies of Dissent for the New Millennium*. Boulder, Co.: Westview.

McLaughlin, H. and Thorpe, R. (1993) 'Action learning – a paradigm in emergence: the problems facing a challenge to traditional management education and development', *British Journal of Management* 1: 19–27.

McNiff, J. (1988) *Action Research: Principles and Practice*. London: Routledge.

McNiff, J. (1989) 'An individual's claim to know her own personal and social development through the dialectic of action research'. University of Bath, unpublished PhD thesis.

McNiff, J. (1990) 'Writing and the creation of educational knowledge', in P. Lomax (ed.), *Managing Staff Development in Schools: An Action Research Approach*. Clevedon: Multilingual Matters.

McNiff, J. (1993) *Teaching as Learning: An Action Research Approach*. London: Routledge.

McNiff, J. (1995) 'A generative transformational approach to educational theory'. A paper presented at the American Educational Research Association Annual Meeting, San Francisco, April.

McNiff, J. (1996) 'How can I promote an understanding of the generative transformational nature of lifelong learning?' A paper presented at the American Educational Research Association Annual Meeting, New York, April.

McNiff, J. (1997) *Action Research for Professional Development*, 2nd edn. Dorset: September Books.

McNiff, J. (in press) *Action Research: Principles and Practice*, 2nd edn. London: RoutledgeFalmer.

McNiff, J. and Collins, Ú. (eds) (1994) *A New Approach to InCareer Development for Teachers in Ireland*. Bournemouth: Hyde.

McNiff, J. and Neill, J. (1998) 'Education for mutual understanding through action research'. A summary document presented at the British Educational Research Association Annual Conference, Belfast, August.

McNiff, J., Whitehead, J. and Laidlaw, M. (1992) *Creating a Good Social Order Through Action Research*. Bournemouth: Hyde (available only direct from authors).

McNiff, J., Lomax, P. and Whitehead, J. (1996) *You and Your Action Research Project*. London: Routledge.

McNiff, J., McNamara, G. and Leonard, D. (eds) (2000) *Action Research in Ireland*. Dorset: September Books.

Mc Wey, J. A. (1999) *An Evaluation of Cross-Border Community Development Conference*. Dublin: Commission for Peace and Reconciliation.

Mead, M. (1970) *Coming of Age in Samoa*. Harmondsworth, Penguin (original work 1928).

Mead, M. (1973) 'Our open-ended future', in *The Next Billion Years*. Lecture Series at the University of California, Los Angeles.

Medawar, P. (1996) *The Strange Case of the Spotted Mice and Other Classic Essays on Science*. Oxford: Oxford University Press.

Mezirow, J. (1991) *Transformative Dimensions of Adult Learning*. San Francisco: Jossey-Bass.

Mezirow, J. and associates (1990) *Fostering Critical Reflection in Adulthood*. San Francisco: Jossey-Bass.

Middleton, S. (1998) *Disciplining Sexuality*. New York: Teachers College Press.

Middlewood, D., Coleman, M. and Lumby, J. (eds) (1999) *Practitioner Research in Education: Making a Difference*. London: Paul Chapman Publishing.

Midgley, M. (1981) *Heart and Mind: The Varieties of Moral Experience*. London: Methuen.

Midgley, M. (1989) *Wisdom, Information and Wonder: What Is Knowledge For?* London and New York: Routledge.

Midgley, M. (1992) *Science as Salvation: A Modern Myth and its Meaning*. London: Routledge.

Milgram, S. (1973) *Obedience to Authority*. London: Tavistock.

Miller, J. (1990) *Seductions: Studies in Reading and Culture*. London: Virago.

Mills, R. (1999) 'Improving early literacy through action research', *The Ontario Action Researcher* 2(13), http:www.unipissing.ca/oar.

Mintzberg, H. (1973) *The Nature of Managerial Work*. New York: Harper & Row.

Mintzberg, H. (1989) *Mintzberg on Management: Inside Our Strange World of Organization*. New York: Free Press.

Mitchell, C. and Reid-Walsh, J. (1997) 'And I want to thank you, Barbie', in H. Giroux and P. Shannon (eds), *Education and Cultural Studies*. New York: Routledge.

Mitroff, I. and Linstone, H. (1993) *The Unbounded Mind: Breaking the Chains of Traditional Business Thinking*. New York: Oxford University Press.

Mol an Óige (1999) 'Developing and testing a model for applying action research to promote a better education system at systems, institutional and classroom levels: Interim Report'. Nenagh: Mol an Óige.

Morgan, G. (1997a) *Images of Organization*, 2nd edn. Thousand Oaks, Calif.: Sage.

Morgan, G. (1997b) *Imaginization*. San Francisco: Berrett-Koehler and Sage (original work 1993).

Munsch, R. (1980) *The Paperbag Princess*. Toronto, Annick.

Murdoch, I. (1985) *The Sovereignty of Good*. London: Ark Paperbacks.

Musgrave, J. (1997) *An Investigation into the Mismatch between Student and Tutor Perceptions of the Value of Group Speaking Tasks in the ESOL Classroom*. Hamilton: Waikato Polytechnic.

Musgrave, J., Cleary, D., de Lisle, J., Ferguson, P., Matheson, R., Oliver, J., Spencer, M., Stewart, C. and Thwaite, D. (1996) 'Research for the classroom teacher: finding a way'. A paper presented at the Fifth National Conference on Community Languages and English for Speakers of Other Languages, Hamilton.

Nelson, H. Lindemann (1995) 'Resistance and insubordination', *Hypatia* 10(2): 23–40.

New Zealand Qualifications Authority (1993) *The Approval and Accreditation of Degrees and Related Qualifications*. Wellington: NZQA.

Newman, Cardinal J. H. (1915) *On the Scope and Nature of University Education*. London: Dent.

Ní Murchú, S. (2000) 'How can I improve my practice as a teacher in the area of assessment through the use of portfolios?' Unpublished MA dissertation, Cork, University of the West of England, Bristol.

Nichol, L. (ed.) (1996) 'Introduction', in D. Bohm, *On Dialogue*. London: Routledge.

Nixon, J. (1995) 'Teaching as a profession of values', in J. Smyth (ed.), *Critical Discourses on Teacher Development*. London: Cassell.

Noddings, N. (1984) *Caring: A Feminist Approach to Ethics and Moral Education*. Berkeley: University of California Press.

Noddings, N. (1992) *The Challenge to Care in Schools*. New York: Teachers College Press.

Noffke, S. (1997a) *Professional, Personal, and Political Dimensions of Action Research. The 1997 Review of Educational Research*, vol. 22. Washington: American Educational Research Association.

Noffke, S. (1997b) 'Themes and tensions in US action research: towards historical analysis', in S. Hollingsworth (ed.), *International Action Research: A Casebook for Educational Reform*. London: Falmer.

Nonaka, I. and Takeuchi, H. (1995) *The Knowledge Creating Company: How Japanese Companies Create the Dynamics of Innovation*. New York: Oxford University Press.

Noon, M. and Blyton, P. (1997) *The Realities of Work*. Basingstoke: Macmillan.

Nord, W. and Fox, S. (1999) 'The individual in organizational studies: the great disappearing act?', in S. Clegg and C. Hardy (eds), *Studying Organization: Theory and Method*. London: Sage.

O'Brien, O. (2000) 'Planning for the future', in CORI Pastoral Commission (eds), *Religious in Parish: Reflecting on the Experience, Directions for the Future*. Dublin: CORI Publications.

O'Hanlon, C. (ed.) (1996) *Professional Development through Action Research in Educational Settings*. London: Falmer.

Oldroyd, D. and Hall, V. (1997) 'Identifying needs and priorities in professional development', in L. Kydd, M. Crawford and C. Riches (eds), *Professional Development for Educational Management*. Buckingham: Open University Press.

Ó Muimhneacháin, C. (2000) 'How can I support student personal and social development through my assessment practice?' Unpublished MA dissertation, Cork, University of the West of England, Bristol.

Ó Murchú, D. (1997a) *Reclaiming Spirituality: A New Spiritual Framework for Today's World*. Dublin: Gill & Macmillan.

Ó Murchú, D. (1997b) *Quantum Theology: Spiritual Implications of the New Physics*. New York: Crossroad.

O'Neill, R. (1997) 'How can I contribute to an understanding of administrative systems of accreditation as educational practices, in line with the espoused educational aims of the programmes that are being offered for accreditation?' Unpublished MEd dissertation, Dublin, University of the West of England, Bristol.

Ontario Public School Teachers' Federation (1998) *Action Research: School Improvement through Research-Based Professionalism;*. Ontario: OPSFT.

Ornstein, R. and Ehrlich, P. (1989) *New World, New Mind: Moving Toward Conscious Evolution*. New York: Simon & Schuster.

Outhwaite, W. (1975) *Understanding Social Life: The Method Called Verstehen*. London: Routledge & Kegan Paul.

Pareto, V. (1935) *The Mind and Society*. New York: Harcourt Brace.

Park, P. (1999) 'People, knowledge, and change in participatory research', *Management Learning* 30(2): 141–57.

Parker, B. (1999) 'Evolution and revolution: from international business to globalization', in S. Clegg, C. Hardy and W. Nord (eds), *Managing Organizations: Current Issues*. London: Sage.

Parlett, M. and Hamilton, D. (eds) (1977) *Beyond the Numbers Game*. Basingstoke: Macmillan.

Peat, D. (1996) *Blackfoot Physics: A Journey into the Native American Universe*. London: Fourth Estate (original work 1994).

Pedler, M. J. (1996) *Action Learning for Managers*. London: Lemos & Crane.

Pedler, M. (1997) 'Interpreting action learning', in J. Burgoyne and M. Reynolds (eds), *Management Learning: Integrating Perspectives in Theory and Practice*. London: Sage.

Peters, T. (1992) *Liberation Management*. New York: Knopf.

Peters, T. and Waterman, R. (1982) *In Search of Excellence*. New York: Harper & Row.

Pfeffer, J. (1982) *Organizations and Organization Theory*. Boston: Pitman.

Polanyi, M. (1958) *Personal Knowledge*. London: Routledge.

Polanyi, M. (1967) *The Tacit Dimension*. New York: Doubleday.

Polkinghorne, J. (1988) *Science and Creation: The Search for Understanding*. London: SPCK.

Popper, K. R. (1962) *The Open Society and its Enemies*, vol. 2: *Hegel and Marx*. London: Routledge (original work 1945).

Poster, C. and Poster, D. (1997) 'The nature of appraisal', in L. Kydd, M. Crawford and C. Riches (eds), *Professional Development for Educational Management*. Buckingham: Open University Press.

Postle, D. (1989) *The Mind Gymnasium*. London: Macmillan.

Prigogine, I. and Stengers, I. (1984) *Order out of Chaos: Man's New Dialogue with Nature*. London: Heinemann.

Pring, R. (1984) *Personal and Social Education in the Curriculum*. London: Hodder & Stoughton.

Pugh, D. S. and Payne, R. (eds) (1977) *Organizational Behaviour in Its Context: The Aston Programme III*. London: Gower.

Putnam, R. W. (1999) 'Transforming social practice: an action science perspective', *Management Learning* 30(2): 177–87.

Raphael Reed, L. (1998) 'Power, pedagogy and persuasion: schooling masculinities in the secondary school classroom', *Journal of Education Policy* 13(4): 501–17.

Raphael Reed, L. (1999) 'Troubling boys and disturbing discourses on masculinity and schooling: a feminist exploration of current debates and interventions concerning boys in school', *Gender and Education* 11(1): 93–110.

Rawls, J. (1972) *A Theory of Justice*. Oxford: Oxford University Press.

Reason, P. and Rowan, J. (eds) (1981) *Human Inquiry*. Chichester: Wiley.

Reflective Practice. London: Carfax.

Revans, R. (1982) *The Origins and Growth of Action Learning*. Bromley: Chartwell-Bratt.

Reynolds, M. (1997) 'Towards a critical management pedagogy', in J. Burgoyne and M. Reynolds (eds), *Management Learning: Integrating Perspectives in Theory and Practice*. London: Sage.

Rhadhakrishnan, S. (1978) *True Knowledge*. New Delhi, Orient Paperbacks.

Rhodes, Carl (1996) 'Postmodernism and the practice of human resource development in organisations', *Australian and New Zealand Journal of Vocational Education Research* 4(2): 70–88.

Rhodes, Carl (1997) 'The legitimation of learning in organizational change' *Journal of Organizational Change Management* 10(1): 10–20.

Rhodes, Carl (2000) 'Doing knowledge at work: dialogue, monologue and power in organisational learning', in J. Garrick and C. Rhodes (eds), *Research and Knowledge at Work: Perspectives, Case Studies and Innovative Strategies*. London: Routledge.

Rifkin, J. (1995) *The End of Work*. New York: Putnam.

Robertson, R. (1992) *Globalization: Social Theory and Global Culture*. London: Sage.

Robinson Hickman, G. (ed.) (1998) *Leading Organizations: Perspectives for a New Era*. Thousand Oaks, Calif.: Sage.

Robson, C. (1993) *Real World Research: A Resource for Social Scientists and Practitioner-Researchers*. Oxford: Blackwell.

Rogers, C. R. (1967) *On Becoming a Person: A Therapist's View of Psychotherapy*. London: Constable.

Rose, N. (1990) *Governing the Soul: The Shaping of the Private Self*. London: Routledge.

Roy, D. F. (1960) 'Banana time: job satisfaction and informal interaction', *Human Organization* 18: 156–68.

Russell, T. (1995) 'Returning to the physics classroom to re-think how one learns to teach physics', in T. Russell and F. Korthagen, *Teachers Who Teach Teachers*. London: Falmer.

Russell, T. and Korthagen, F. (1995) *Teachers Who Teach Teachers*. London: Falmer.

Russell, T. and Munby, H. (eds) (1992) *Teachers and Teaching: From Classrooms to Reflection*. London: Falmer.

Ryan, J. (1999) 'My increased understanding of multiple intelligence, preferred learning styles and accelerated learning and its potential for improving our practice as managers/facilitators of learning'. Assignment on MA in Education course, Thurles, University of the West of England, Bristol.

Ryan, J. (2000) 'Researching practitioners' understanding of management learning in order to improve my practice.' Unpublished MA dissertation, Thurles, University of the West of England, Bristol.

Ryle, G. (1949) *The Concept of Mind*. London: Hutchinson.

Said, E. (1991) *The World, the Text and the Critic*. London: Vintage (original work 1983).

Said, E. (1994a) *Culture and Imperialism*. London: Vintage (original work 1993).

Said, E. (1994b) *Representations of the Intellectual: The 1993 Reith Lectures*. London: Vintage.

Salkie, R. (1990) *The Chomsky Update: Linguistics and Politics*. London: Unwin Hyman.

Schein, E. (1995) *Learning Consortia: How to Create Parallel Learning Systems for Organization Sets: Working Paper*. Cambridge, Mass.: Centre for Organizational Learning, Massachusetts Institute of Technology.

Schön, D. (1983) *The Reflective Practitioner: How Professionals Think in Action*. New York: Basic Books.

Schön, D. (1995) 'Knowing-in-action: the new scholarship requires a new epistemology', *Change*, November–December.

Schrage, M. (1989) *No More Teams! Mastering the Dynamics of Creative Collaboration*. New York: Doubleday.

Schüssler-Fiorenza, E. (1983) *In Memory of Her: A Feminist Theological Reconstruction of Christian Origins*. London: SCM Press.

Schwab, J. J. (1970) *The Practical: A Language for Curriculum*. Washington DC: National Education Association, Centre for the Study of Instruction.

Scott, D. and Usher, R. (1996) *Understanding Educational Research*. London: Routledge.

Searle, J. (1995) *The Construction of Social Reality*. London: Penguin.

Senge, P. (1990) *The Fifth Discipline: The Art and Practice of the Learning Organization*. New York: Doubleday.

Sergiovanni, T. J. (1996) *Leadership for the Schoolhouse: How is it Different? Why is it Important?* San Francisco: Jossey-Bass.

Sidgwick, H. (1907) *The Methods of Ethics*. London: Macmillan.

Silverman, D. (1970) *The Theory of Organization: A Sociological Framework*. London: Heinemann.

Skinner, B. F. (1954) 'The science of learning and the art of teaching', *Harvard Educational Review* 24: 86–97.

Skolimowski, H. (1994) *The Participatory Mind: A New Theory of Knowledge and of the Universe*. London: Arkana.

Smith, A. (1976) *The Theory of Moral Sentiments*; Indianapolis: Liberty Classics (original work 1759).

Smith, A. (1996) *Accelerated Learning in the Classroom*. New York: Network Educational Press.

Smyth, G. (2000) 'Self confidence in the making'. Unpublished working paper, Dublin.

Smyth, J. (ed.) (1995) *Critical Discourses on Teacher Development*. London: Cassell.

Sowell, T. (1987) *A Conflict of Visions: Ideological Origins of Political Struggles*. New York: Morrow.

Stacey, R. D. (1996) *Complexity and Creativity in Organisations*. London: Berrett-Koehler.

Stannard, R. (1996) *Science and Wonders: Conversations about Science and Belief*. London: Faber & Faber.

Starratt, R. J. (1993) *The Drama of Leadership*. London: Falmer.

Steinberg, S. and Kincheloe, J. (1998) *Students as Researchers*. London: Falmer.

Stenhouse, L. (1975) *An Introduction to Curriculum Research and Development*. London: Heinemann.

Sugrue, C. (2000) 'Editor's preface', *Irish Educational Studies* 19: vii–xviii.

Tarnas, R. (1991) *The Passion of the Western Mind: Understanding the Ideas that have Shaped Our World View*. New York: Ballantine.

Tavris, C. (1993) *The Mismeasure of Woman*. New York: Simon & Schuster.

Taylor, F. (1911) *The Principles of Scientific Management*. New York: Norton.

Teacher Training Agency (1998) *National Standards for Qualified Teacher Status; Subject Leaders; Special Educational Needs Co-ordinators; Headteachers*. London: Teacher Training Agency.

The PHOENIX COREspondent – Therapeutic Update (1996) at http://www.pheonixre search.com/spr96/thera.htm.

Tillich, P. (1977) *The Courage to Be*. London: Fount Paperbacks (original work 1952).

Time (2000) Special Edition: *How to Save the Earth*, April–May.

Toffler, A. (1990) *Powershift: Knowledge, Wealth and Violence at the Edge of the 21st Century*. New York: Bantam.

Torbert, W. R. (1999) 'The distinctive questions developmental action inquiry asks', *Management Learning* 30(2): 189–206.

Torfing, J. (1999) *New Theories of Discourse: Laclau, Mouffe and Žižek*. Oxford: Oxford University Press.

Tranfield, D. and Starkey, K. (1999) 'The nature, social organisation and promotion of management research', *British Journal of Management* 9(4): 341–55.

Twomey, J. (1997) 'How do I improve the motivation and achievement of students in my mixed ability classes?' Unpublished MEd dissertation, Dublin, University of the West of England, Bristol.

Uí Aodha, M. Á. (2000) 'How can I improve the quality of my practice as a principal so that the quality of the educational experience of my colleagues in the school is improved?' Unpublished MA dissertation, Cork, University of the West of England, Bristol.

Veenema, S., Hetland, L. and Chalfen, K. (1997) *The Project Zero Classroom: New Approaches to Thinking and Understanding*. Cambridge, Mass.: Harvard Graduate School of Education.

Vygotsky, L. (1978) *Mind in Society: The Development of Higher Psychological Processes*. Cambridge, Mass.: Harvard University Press.

Waldrop, M. M. (1992) *Complexity: The Emerging Science at the Edge of Order and Chaos*. New York: Simon & Schuster.

Walsh, P. (1998a) 'Getting through: the therapeutic process in sex offender treatment', *Inside Out: A Quarterly Publication for Humanistic and Integrative Psychotherapy* no. 34. Society for Humanistic and Integrative Psychotherapy, Dublin.

Walsh, P. (1998b) 'Child sex offenders: the case for treatment', *Irish Journal of Psychology* 19.

Walsh, P. (1999) 'Prison is not enough: the role of community-based treatment programmes', in *Collected Papers of the Irish Penal Reform Trust Conference 'The Treatement of Sex Offenders'*. Dublin: IPRT.

Waterman, R. (1994) *The Frontiers of Excellence*. London: Brealey.

Weber, M. (1961) *The Theory of Social and Economic Organization*. New York: Free Press.

Weber, M. (1978) *Economy and Society*. Berkeley, Calif.: University of California Press.

Weick, K. E. (1979) *The Social Psychology of Organizing*. Reading, Mass.: Addison-Wesley.

Weick, K. E. (1995) *Sensemaking in Organizations*. London: Sage.

Weick, K. E. and Westley, F. (1999) 'Organizational learning: affirming an oxymoron', in S. Clegg, C. Hardy and W. Nord (eds), *Managing Organizations: Current Issues*. London: Sage.

Weil, S. (1999) 'Rhetorics and realities in public service organizations: systemic practice and organizational learning as Critically Reflexive Action Research (CRAR)', *Systemic Practice and Action Research* 11(1): 37–62.

Welton, M. (1991) *Toward Development Work: The Workplace as a Learning Environment.* Geelong: Deakin University Press.

Wheatley, M. (1992) *Leadership and the New Science: Learning about Organization from an Orderly Universe.* San Francisco: Berrett-Koehler.

Whelan, A. (1997) 'How can I improve the quality of CERT's in-service provision for teachers of the Level 2 programmes?' Unpublished MEd dissertation, Dublin, University of the West of England, Bristol.

Whitaker, P. (1997) 'Changes in professional development: the personal dimension', in L.Kydd, M. Crawford and C. Riches (eds), *Professional Development for Educational Management.* Buckingham: Open University Press.

White, H., Bruce Ferguson, P., Fox, R., Ngata, C., Nikora, E., Paxton, P., Reynolds, P. and Robertson, N. (1998) *The Development of Protocols/Principles for Conducting Research in a Maori Context.* Hamilton: Waikato Polytechnic.

Whitehead, J. (1989) 'Creating a living educational theory from questions of the kind, "How do I improve my practice?"' *Cambridge Journal of Education* 19(1): 41–52.

Whitehead, J. (1993) *The Growth of Educational Knowledge: Creating Your Own Living Educational Theories.* Bournemouth: Hyde.

Whitehead, J. (1994) 'How do I improve the quality of my management? A participatory action research approach', *Management Learning* 25(1): 137–53.

Whitehead, J. (1998) ' Developing research-based professionalism through living educational theories'. Keynote presentation to the 'Action Research and the Politics of Educational Knowledge' Conference, Trinity College, Dublin, 27 November; reprinted in J. McNiff, G. McNamara and D. Leonard (eds) (2000) *Action Research in Ireland,* Dorset: September Books.

Whitehead, J. (2000) 'How do I improve my practice? Creating and legitimating an epistemology of practice', *Reflective Practice* 1(1): 91–104.

Willmott, H. (1987) 'Studying managerial work: a critique and a proposal', *Journal of Management Studies* 24(3): 249–70.

Willmott, H. (1994) 'Management education: provocations to a debate', *Management Learning* 25(1): 105–36.

Willmott, H. (1997) 'Critical management learning', in J. Burgoyne and M. Reynolds. (eds), *Management Learning: Integrating Perspectives in Theory and Practice.* London: Sage.

Winter, R. (1989) *Learning from Experience: Principles and Practice in Action-Research.* London: Falmer.

Winter, R. (1999) 'The University of Life plc: the "industrialization" of higher education?', in J. Ahier and G. Esland (eds), *Education, Training and the Future of Work,* vol. 1: *Social, Political and Economic Contexts of Policy Development.* London: Routledge and the Open University.

Woodhouse, D. (1997) 'Auditing research, and the research/teaching nexus'. A paper presented at the 'Research and the New Tomorrow' Conference, UNITEC Institute of Technology, Auckland, July.

Woodhouse, M. B. (1996) *Paradigm Wars: Worldviews for a New Age.* Berkeley, Calif.: Frog.

Wrightman, L. S. (1964) 'Measurements of philosophies of human nature', *Psychological Reports* 14: 743–51.

Wrightman, L. S. (1974) *Assumptions About Human Nature.* Monterey, Calif.: Brooks-Cole.

Wrightman, L. S. (1977) *Social Psychology.* Monterey, Calif.: Brooks-Cole.

Young, M. F. D. (ed.) (1971) *Knowledge and Control: New Directions for the Sociology of Education.* London: Collier Macmillan.

Zeichner, K. (1993) 'Connecting genuine teacher development to the struggle for social justice', *Journal of Education for Teaching* 19(1): 5–20.

Zeichner, K. (1995) 'Beyond the divide of teacher and academic research', *Teachers and Teaching: Theory and Practice* 1(2): 153–72.

Zeichner, K. (1999) 'The new scholarship in teacher education', *Educational Researcher* 28(9): 4–15.

Zimbardo, P. G. (1969) 'The human choice: individuation, reason and order versus deindividuation, impulse and chaos', in W. J. Arnold and D. Levine (eds), *Nebraska Symposium on Motivation*, no. 17. Lincoln, Nebr.: University of Nebraska Press.

Žižek, S. (1989) *The Sublime Object of Ideology*. London: Verso.

Žižek, S. (1990) 'Beyond discourse analysis', in E. Laclau (ed.), *New Reflections on the Revolution of Our Time*. London: Verso.

Zuber-Skerritt, O. (ed.) (1992) *Action Research in Higher Education: Examples and Reflections*. London: Kogan Page.

Zuber-Skerritt, O. (ed.) (1996) *New Directions in Action Research*. London: Falmer.

Index